RACE-ING FARGO

RACE-ING FARGO

Refugees, Citizenship, and the Transformation of Small Cities

Jennifer Erickson

CORNELL UNIVERSITY PRESS ITHACA AND LONDON

First published 2020 by Cornell University Press

Library of Congress Cataloging-in-Publication Data

Names: Erickson, Jennifer Lynn, 1974– author.
Title: Race-ing fargo : refugees, citizenship, and the transformation of small cities / Jennifer Erickson.
Description: Ithaca [New York] : Cornell University Press, 2020. | Includes bibliographical references and index. |
Identifiers: LCCN 2020000049 (print) | LCCN 2020000050 (ebook) | ISBN 9781501751134 (hardcover) | ISBN 9781501751158 (paperback) | ISBN 9781501751141 (pdf) | ISBN 9781501751196 (epub)
Subjects: LCSH: Race—Social aspects—North Dakota—Fargo. | Refugees—North Dakota—Fargo. | Race awareness—North Dakota—Fargo. | Social integration—North Dakota—Fargo. | Cultural pluralism—North Dakota—Fargo. | Place (Philosophy)—Social aspects—North Dakota—Fargo.
Classification: LCC HN80 .E65 2020 (print) | LCC HN80 (ebook) | DDC 305.8009784/13—dc23
LC record available at https://lccn.loc.gov/2020000049
LC ebook record available at https://lccn.loc.gov/2020000050

In memory of Aida Brasnić (1950–2016) and Sandra Morgen (1950–2016)

For all those seeking a better life, free from violence and discrimination,
and for those who welcome them

Contents

Illustrations

Preface

I arrived in Fargo to conduct this research through a myriad of geographic, intellectual, activist, and atavistic avenues. I grew up in Luverne, Minnesota, a town with a population of about 5,000 people. I am the daughter of a public school teacher turned middle-school counselor and a social worker turned administrative assistant for a human service agency. I am six generations removed from Norwegian Lutheran immigrants in the Midwestern United States. Most of my ancestors were farmers. My nuclear family was comfortably situated in the middle class in a Midwest, white habitus. I obtained my bachelor's degree in 1997 from Luther College, where I studied psychology, German, and English, focusing on African American literature, but I got a healthy dose of Norwegian history and literature as well.

At first, doing fieldwork in my own backyard for my dissertation sounded, well, boring. When I was applying to graduate schools, I planned to conduct a comparative study of Bosnians and Southern Sudanese *in* Bosnia-Herzegovina (BH) *and* South Sudan, to trace the routes that refugees from different places take to get to the United States. After working as a volunteer for a local women's nongovernmental organization (NGO) in BH (1998–2000) and as a case manager with refugees in Sioux Falls, South Dakota (2001–2002), which I describe in more detail below, I arrived at the University of Oregon in the fall of 2002, excited about the prospect of taking classes, writing papers, teaching, and discussing what I was sure would be interesting, important topics, different from the direct service and applied research I had been doing. Because I had not majored in anthropology as an undergraduate student, it wasn't until my graduate studies that I was first confronted with the ways that anthropology complied with European colonialism (Asad 1973), and learned about "salvage ethnography," which sought to record the folklore and practices of Native Americans and other indigenous peoples before they disappeared—or so it was believed. I also learned about the scant attention given to African Americans in early anthropology (Baker 2010; Willis 1972; but see Hurston 1935).

In graduate school, I also learned about anthropology's focus on working with marginalized people in other countries while leaving the powerful understudied and unmarked (Nader 1972). One class period in particular shaped the direction that this study would take. Guided by the work of Linda Tuhiwai Smith (1999), a Maori woman from New Zealand, my social theory class and I discussed what a decolonized anthropology would look like. There were Native American students in the class who were trying to reconcile their place in a discipline that had not exactly treated their ancestors well (Deloria 1969), and these students, along with some of my professors, shaped the way I saw the discipline and my position in it. I began to recognize that "the more closely we engage with power, the closer we come to examining our own reflections in the powerful and even our own complicities as we go about producing knowledge" (Priyadharshini 2003, 434). I decided that, rather than travel abroad for my dissertation research, I would conduct my fieldwork in the United States, near where I grew up. The goal was to study refugee resettlement up, down, and sideways in order to understand refugee resettlement from a variety of actors with various degrees of power and authority in the city. Before embarking on that path, however, I returned to Bosnia-Herzegovina to conduct additional research for my master's paper, based on my previous applied research with Romani women (Erickson 2004).

From 1998 to 2000, between my undergraduate and graduate degrees, I worked for Medica Infoteka, a local women's NGO founded as a response to rape against women during the 1992–1995 war. I mostly worked for Infoteka, the team that established and maintained networks with other NGOs and governmental institutions. Because of my background in psychology, Infoteka asked me to design and coordinate a research project. I proposed a project with Roma after visiting with an African American man, who introduced me to the situation of Roma in BH and who believed that their situation was worse than that of African Americans in the United States. In Medica's research on the prevalence of domestic violence, they recommended that similar research be conducted with Romani women. Their 1999 sample population of approximately five hundred women did not include even one woman who identified herself as Roma (Medica Infoteka 1999).

Over the course of three months in 2000, three colleagues and I completed 112 quantitative interviews and twenty-four oral history interviews with Romani women. Using the data from Medica Infoteka's 1999 study on domestic violence with non-Romani women, we compared the socioeconomic status and prevalence of domestic violence between Romani and non-Romani women. We found that due to racism, classism, sexism, and political indifference toward Roma, Romani women appeared to face greater degrees of domestic and structural forms of violence than non-Romani women. We published our results in the Bosnian, English, and Romani languages (Erickson 2003; Medica Infoteka 2001). My master's paper further explored the prevalence of multiple forms of violence, from individual to state-sponsored, throughout Romani women's lives. I addressed the role of international organizations, the state, and local NGOs in regard to their (lack of) programs with Roma (Erickson 2004, 2006, and 2017a).

My work in BH helped me to better understand some of the challenges facing refugees and migrants in the United States. Before I moved to BH, I did not speak Bosnian (also known as Serbo-Croatian). I learned to speak it fluently, but my first few months were strange, overwhelming, exciting, and challenging. Being a young American volunteer in postwar BH is certainly not akin to being a Bosnian refugee in the United States, but I did learn what it felt like to be a stranger in a strange land, immersed in a new culture, language, and political economy. My time in BH was foundational to my development as a feminist anthropologist.

When I returned to the Midwest from BH in December 2000, I discovered that many refugees and immigrants were living near the place I grew up, in small cities such as Sioux Falls, Fargo, Omaha, Lincoln, and Des Moines—cities that had, since Europeans occupied and colonized the region, been primarily white and Christian. In 2001, I began working as a case manager for Lutheran Social Services Center for New Americans (LSS) in Sioux Falls. I worked with single mothers, families, or individuals who experienced difficulties achieving self-sufficiency in the allotted eight-month period or longer, and with secondary migrants—that is, refugees who were resettled to another city in the United States but migrated to Sioux Falls. I mostly worked with Bosnians and Southern Sudanese. Many of my Bosnian clients were Roma who had originally been resettled to Fargo but migrated in and out of Sioux Falls in search of employment, social services, family support, scrap metal, and other resources. My job consisted of helping refugees navigate the educational and welfare systems, finding housing, childcare, healthcare, assisting with family disputes, and interpreting for Bosnians. Some of the biggest challenges for my clients were transportation, an inability to find a job that matched their skills, childcare, difficulty in learning English, and psychological and physical health problems.

When I arrived at work on September 11, 2001, my colleagues—who were from Ethiopia, Bosnia-Herzegovina, South Sudan, Iraq, Canada, and the United States—were solemnly huddled around a TV in one of the English classrooms. They told me that a plane had hit the South Tower of the World Trade Center, and then we watched the horror unfold as another plane flew into the North Tower, and then both towers collapsed. Many of my colleagues, like our clients, had fled war and come to the United States in search of safety, security, and opportunity. After the towers fell, we began processing what we had watched. My colleagues spoke about their shattered illusions of safety and dreams of a better life in the United States. We feared for our clients and how members of the dominant population—many of whom were already suspicious of foreign-born nationals, people of color, and Muslims—would treat our clients after this wretched day. The next morning, I received an e-mail from a friend in Bosnia asking if I knew anyone in New York, and whether we needed advice from Bosnians, who knew all too much about war.

During my time working in refugee resettlement, I learned more about war, forced migration, cultural diversity, and case management, but I also came to see my home differently, as a place that alternately welcomed and rejected strangers. I found myself asking questions: What causes war? What makes some people more open to diversity than others? Why are organizations so critical of one another's programs? Why do some refugees adjust well to life in the United States while others struggle? How could institutions and cities better serve all or at least most residents? These questions were first planted in me during my time in Bosnia, but they grew as I worked in refugee resettlement. Anthropology had the tools that I needed to answer these questions.

Acknowledgments

I am humbled and inspired by all who have accompanied me on this book's long journey. This project could not have happened without the collaboration of many people and institutions in Fargo. I am grateful to the staff and volunteers at New American Services, Cass County Social Services, the Giving Plus Learning Program, and in city institutions from teachers and police officers to housing workers. Thank you for opening your organizations to me and for taking time to explain refugee resettlement, your jobs, and Fargo culture to me. I am equally grateful to the Bosnians and Southern Sudanese who invited me into their homes and lives. Special thanks to the New Sudanese Community Association for supporting my research and inviting me to be on their board of directors. Thank you to Rachel Mertz-Rodriguez, Michele McRae, Hatidža Asović, Malka Fazlić, Amy Philips, Cristie Jacobsen, Darci Asche, Sabina Abaza, Kevin Brooks, Deb Dawson, Rachel Asleson, Erin Hemme Froslie, Michele Willman, Anita Hoffarth, Ann Arbor Miller, Jane Skunberg, Melissa Tomlinson, and Kirsten Jensen for guidance, kindness and help to a stranger in a not-so-strange land.

Aida Brasnić came to Sioux Falls as a refugee in 1996 after surviving the siege of Sarajevo from 1992 to 1996. She read about my work in Bosnia in the Sioux Falls newspaper and found a way to contact my parents in nearby Luverne. When I briefly visited home in 1999, Aida and I met for the first time, and when I returned from Bosnia in 2000, she encouraged me to apply to work at LSS in Sioux Falls. I am grateful for her encouragement, friendship, and collegiality, along with other great colleagues at LSS. Special thanks to Deb Worth for keeping me in the loop! Aida also assisted me with research in the summer of 2005. I dedicate this book to Aida, who passed away in 2016.

I am indebted to my professors and colleagues at the University of Oregon for their mentorship during my graduate school years. Carol Silverman's unflinching support and guidance were key to my success as a graduate student. Carol demonstrated the best ways to be an advocate and activist for Roma. Sandi Morgen made me a better ethnographer and mentor. For years, she trained me through her research on the politics of taxes in Oregon. Her death from ovarian cancer on September 27, 2016, was a devastating loss. I also dedicate this book to her. Lynn Stephen provided critical points that strengthened my research, especially in encouraging me to explain similarities and differences between refugees and immigrants. I am also honored by the opportunity to have worked with

Susan Hardwick, a human geographer, who worked with refugees and whose support made my dissertation stronger. Thanks also to Lamia Karim, Stephen Wooten, and Diane Baxter for their support and guidance in my teaching and research while at the University of Oregon.

I would not have survived graduate school without the supportive and entertaining friends I met: Nicholas Malone, Patrick Hayden, Shayna Rohwer, Meredith Fisher Malone, Britta Torgrimson-Ojerio, Kathryn Barton, Josh Fisher, Maurice Magaña, Tiffany Brannon, Emily Taylor, Hillary Colter, and Carolyn Travers. Melissa Baird, Tami Hill, Deana Dartt, and Darcy Hannibal provided friendship, support, and guidance through our writing group. Camille Walsh was a brilliant writing partner and helped ease my move from Oregon to Indiana by getting a postdoc at Indiana University the same year I started at Ball State. Many thanks to Elissa Helms, my *cimerka*, friend, and anthropology big sister for her support and guidance. Caroline Faria and I met through our mutual collaboration and board work for the South Sudan Women's Empowerment Network. I wish all collaboration could work as ours did. I credit Medica Infoteka (Duška, Meliha, Belma, Mersiha, Arijana, Sabina, Jaca, and Rada) for inspiring and encouraging me to conduct applied, activist, collaborative, feminist research, and to the women of the South Sudan Women's Empowerment Network, especially Lula and Rosa, for allowing me to accompany them on their inspiring path all the way to South Sudan.

I am grateful to the Ball State Anthropology Department for giving me a job and for their support, especially Homes Hogue and Caílin Murray. Ball State friends Melinda Messineo, David Concepcion, Juli Thorson, Cathy Day, Kathy Denker, and Kristen McCauliff: thank you for teaching me how to teach, for advising me on how to navigate university and parenting structures, and for laughter. My writing group and friendships with Nick Kawa and Amit Bayisha, who provided feedback on early drafts of this manuscript, were helpful for rethinking how to transform a manuscript into a book. Thanks also to John West, Jim Connolly, and Nihal Perera for providing support and useful feedback on later drafts.

I am lucky to have met Shona Jackson and Rob Carley on a playground in Yellow Springs, Ohio. Shona suggested "Race-ing Fargo" as a title for the book and coached me through the publication process. Their family made my sabbatical semester so much more fun and productive.

I am grateful to Ball State graduate students who have assisted me with this manuscript. Felicia Konrad analyzed Change.org comments on an antirefugee resettlement petition (chapter 4). Chelce Carter and Jordan Keck spent hours formatting chapters and the bibliography. Thanks also to Angela Gibson in the Ball State Libraries, who made all of the maps in this book.

Thank you to my parents, Keith and Joan, sister Kim, and extended-family sister-cousins Lisa, Sonya, Curt, and Jean for providing multiple forms of support and encouragement throughout my life, not to mention the best nieces and nephews. Thanks to my partner, Nikos, for editing and coparenting and for patience, humor, listening skills, brunches, and epic family road trips. Our daughter and my three bonus kids give me purpose and inspire me to do good in the world.

A National Science Foundation Dissertation Improvement Grant funded the fieldwork on which this book is based (2007–2008). The Wayne Morse Center for Law and Politics and the Center for the Study of Women in Society at the University of Oregon supported analysis and the writing of my dissertation, respectively. Ball State University funded some of the trips to Fargo to conduct follow-up research.

Parts of chapter 1 were previously published in the article "Intersectionality Theory and Bosnian Roma: Understanding Violence and Displacement" (*Romani Studies* 1 [2017]: 1–28) and appear in the book courtesy of the journal.

Finally, I am grateful to two anonymous reviewers for their insightful feedback on the manuscript and to Jim Lance and the editorial collective at Cornell University Press for believing in this manuscript, for copy editing, and for shepherding me through the process. Thanks, also, to Victoria Springer for her superb proofreading skills. The book is better for their feedback, but all errors and inconsistencies are mine.

I will donate all royalties from this book to organizations serving refugees.

Acronyms

AFDC	Aid to Families with Dependent Children
BH	Bosnia-Herzegovina
CCSS	Cass County Social Services
CDR	Cultural Diversity Resources
CPA	Comprehensive Peace Agreement (between North Sudan and South Sudan)
DAPL	Dakota Access Pipeline
ELL	English Language Learning
ERRC	European Roma Rights Center
F-M	Fargo-Moorhead
INGO	International Nongovernmental Organization
IOM	International Organization on Migration
JOBS	North Dakota Job Service
LIHEAP	Low-Income Home Energy Assistance Program
LSS	Lutheran Social Services
MIRC	Metro Interpreter Resource Center
NAS	New American Services
NATO	North Atlantic Treaty Organization
NGO	Nongovernmental Organization
NSCA	New Sudanese Community Association
ORR	Office of Refugee Resettlement
PRM	Bureau of Population, Refugees, and Migration
PRWORA	Personal Responsibility and Work Opportunity and Reconciliation Act
RCA	Refugee Cash Assistance
RMA	Refugee Medical Assistance
SNAP	Supplemental Nutritional Assistance Program (food stamps)
SPLA	Sudan People's Liberation Army
SPLA-IO	Sudan People's Liberation Army in Opposition
SPLM	Sudan People's Liberation Movement
SPLM-IO	Sudan People's Liberation Movement in Opposition
SSI	Social Security Income
TANF	Temporary Assistance to Needy Families
UN	United Nations

UNHCR   United Nations High Commissioner for Refugees
URM   Unaccompanied Refugee Minors
USCIS   United States Citizenship and Immigration Services
VOLAGS   Voluntary Agencies

Note on Transliteration

I write Bosnian names using the Bosnian alphabet. The following pronunciation key will assist those more familiar with the English language: C "ts" as in *bats*, Ć "ch" as in *change*, which is softer than Č "ch" as in *perch*, Š "sh" as in *shop*, Ž "s" as in *treasure*, Đ "j" as in *judge*, which is softer than Dž "j" as in *Jennifer*.

VALLEY TO THE WORLD

During the winter of 1996–1997, North Dakota experienced more than ten blizzards, the first in November and the last on April 5–6. Fargo recorded 117 inches, about ten feet, of snow. That winter, I went to Fargo-Moorhead, sister cities on the North Dakota–Minnesota border, to visit my cousin, a student at Concordia College. I can still visualize the massive and blinding white piles of snow imprisoning cars and small homes in their massive drifts and recall my astonishment that life went on. Unbeknownst to me at the time, more than two hundred Bosnian refugees were resettled to Fargo that winter. Conditions did not get any easier when the weather warmed that spring. Rain, falling on top of lingering snow, swelled the Red River and caused the worst flooding Fargo had experienced in more than one hundred years. Alma Hubić, a woman from Bosnia-Herzegovina, arrived in Fargo that winter.[1] She recalled:

> It was a very bad winter to come (laughs). If we had money, we would have probably moved. My friend wanted me to come to St. Louis, but we just didn't have money to move. So we decided to stay, and I'm really glad that we did. We decided to stick around and wait it out, and so it was . . . very, very difficult. I was . . . a young mother with a three-month-old baby, didn't speak the language. . . . There was not a lot of Bosnians. . . . We were one of the first groups. . . . I saw my case manager once and that was it. I felt so, you know, disoriented and confused and . . . that's not what I was expecting (laughs). And then our apartment, we lived in the basement, [and it] flooded in the spring and it's just (laughs) scary.

From the mid-1990s until 2001, the increasing number of refugees resettled to Fargo sent reverberating shocks through city institutions, from schools to medical offices, churches to social service organizations. Kathy Hogan, then director of Cass County Social Services, the welfare agency located in Fargo, the seat of Cass County, told me this:

> I remember when the Bosnians came during the flood of '97, and we placed . . . forty new Bosnians that month of flood. . . . It was horrible, just horrible. It . . . was chaos. And of course, the whole community was in chaos. And then . . . at some point I get lines of 250 to 300 people outside my doors getting food stamps. [They were from] all over . . . and then we had these Bosnians (laughs) and they were so terrified. . . . It was one of the most fearful, the time right after 9/11, and this time, during the flood. They came and they thought, "What have we gotten ourselves into?" They were so afraid.

Fast-forward five years to February 2001. An airplane approaches the runway in Fargo, and the pilot tells the passengers to prepare for landing. Looking out the tiny windows, as far as the eye can see, the passengers see that the landscape below is white. On the plane are refugees from South Sudan, coming from the Kakuma refugee camp in Kenya. They have never seen snow. "What *is* that?" asks one young woman. "Milk?" Another wonders, "Ash from an atomic bomb?" "I want to go home" is a common feeling among the passengers, who are queasy with feelings about the known and the unknown and all that happened to bring them to this moment. The plane lands. The passengers disembark. Likely there is someone waiting for them, to welcome them and take them to their new apartment and provide a warm meal. Most refugees in Fargo receive such a greeting, but not all. A local journalist covering the arrival of refugees from South Sudan to Fargo reports:

> Philip Aret arrives after 10 p.m., alone and sick at the Fargo airport. He has been suffering a fungal eye infection for three months so United Nations doctors apparently sent him to the United States for treatment. However, he finds no greeting party and no ride at the airport. Lutheran Social Services, the agency hired by the government to resettle refugees in Fargo, didn't know Philip was coming. Thick liquid dribbling from his eye, he asks a stranger for a ride and spends his first night in America on a pastor's floor in south Fargo. (*Forum of Fargo-Moorhead* 2001)

When Philip Aret arrived in 2001, staff at the resettlement agency in Fargo were scrambling to resettle some six hundred refugees from Sudan, Bosnia, Albania, Somalia, Iraq, Cuba, Haiti, and Burundi—more refugees than had ever been resettled to Fargo in one year. That was before 9/11. Charged with finding refugees apartments, jobs, and community support, resettlement staff members were stretched thin, as they had been for several years.

Race-ing Fargo is a case study for how citizenship is practiced and how diversity is approached in Fargo, North Dakota, and what the consequences of these practices are. *Race-ing Fargo* compares citizenship practices among two social service institutions, the refugee resettlement and county welfare agencies, and two groups of refugees—New Americans—Bosnians and Southern Sudanese.[2] In relating refugee resettlement and welfare practices, I highlight the shared goal of economic self-sufficiency for clients but the divergent programs and practices for executing this goal. In doing so, I draw attention to racialized and gendered differences, cultural backgrounds, and training among staff at the agencies as a way of examining underlying differences between the public and private sectors in Fargo, and how we might analyze and shape these practices and use their differences to build a stronger common good. Cities "no longer exist as bounded spaces, but as sites in global social and economic flows and networks" (Amin 2007, 101), but place still matters.

Fargo has been resettling refugees since 1948, but it was not until the 1990s that resettlement began to noticeably change the city. In the 1980s, nationwide, resettlement shifted from an earlier model of voluntary church-based sponsorship to an institution with paid staff and case management. Refugees also increasingly began staying in the region rather than migrating out, as previous waves had done (Cambodians and Vietnamese), and more refugees were resettled to Fargo than ever before. From 1997 through 2015, Fargo resettled an average of four hundred refugees per year (7,405 total to North Dakota in this eighteen-year period), but this does not include thousands of secondary migrants, who moved in and out of the city, to and from other parts of the United States. As Lutheran Social Services (LSS) placed more refugees, other institutions, such as the police, schools, and welfare agencies, began speaking out about resettlement. The city's white, English-speaking residents became ever more curious and opinionated about the new residents, while businesses embraced the potential for a new workforce in a city with some of the nation's lowest unemployment rates and a labor shortage.

I chose to work with Bosnians and Southern Sudanese because both groups had refugee status and were some of the largest groups of New Americans in Fargo, along with Somalis, Iraqis, and more recently, Bhutanese. They also differed in key ways. Bosnians came from the formerly Socialist Republic of Yugoslavia, a multiethnic state in Southern Europe that experienced a rapid, bloody dissolution with the fall of communism and violently competing nationalisms. The 1992–1995 war in Bosnia-Herzegovina cost more than 200,000 lives and displaced more than a million people, roughly a quarter of the population. Many of them fled to elsewhere in Europe, where they found temporary refuge but sought permanent third-country resettlement with a pathway to legal citizenship. The U.S. government accepted more than 125,000 Bosnian refugees between 1993 and 2004. Of these, about 1,500 were resettled to Fargo in the 1990s, not including secondary migrants. About two-thirds of these Bosnian refugees were Roma (Gypsies), who sometimes (but not always) have darker skin color than other Bosnians and speak Romani in addition to Bosnian. Roma were less than 8 percent of the prewar population in Bosnia. They not only faced discrimination in their Bosnian homeland, but they also had one of the worst reputations among New Americans in Fargo due to their allegedly suspicious scrap metal businesses, early marriage practices, and aversion to formal education.

The 1983–2005 wars between northern and southern Sudan, along with interethnic and regional wars, poverty, and disease, resulted in more than two million deaths and four million displaced people. In 2011, nearly four million southern Sudanese voted in a historic referendum, and 99 percent chose secession from Sudan. On July 9, 2011, the Republic of South Sudan became the world's newest country. Since 2013, it has been racked with civil war and, in 2019, remains politically, socially, and economically fragile, though a peace agreement between Southern political factions was signed in 2018.[3] The U.S. government began resettling Sudanese refugees in the 1980s. By the early 2000s, roughly 60 percent of all African refugees resettled to the United States were Southern Sudanese, but they numbered fewer than 25,000 total (USCIS 2004). From 1997 to 2015, LSS resettled about five hundred Southern Sudanese to Fargo, but those who work with refugees in Fargo believe this number is higher due to secondary migration.

Southern Sudanese distinguished between themselves by ethnicity/tribe, kinship, language, age, gender, and region in South Sudan. They mostly identified as Christian. There were five Southern Sudanese congregations in the Fargo-Moorhead metro region. Their Christian practices bolstered their reputation in Fargo. Many people I spoke with who worked with refugees saw Southern Sudanese as nicer, politer, more grateful, and more civically engaged than, for example, Bosnians. Their faith, politeness, and outspoken activism in regard to improving the living conditions in South Sudan helped mitigate some of the racism and discrimination leveled against Southern Sudanese in Fargo. Nevertheless, Fargo is a predominantly white city, a fact that shapes everyday forms of citizenship and treatment of immigrants and refugees.

Race-ing Fargo has three main aims: The first is to challenge stereotypic perceptions of refugees as mere victims, dependents, or recipients of aid (Besteman 2016; Harrell-Bond 1998; Malkki 1995; Ong 2003) and instead show that New

Americans are change agents. They have power in shaping their own lives and the life of a city. The second aim is to give more visibility to people working on diversity in places that are not considered to be diverse, including those who work toward social justice and inclusivity. The Midwest and Great Plains are saddled with pejorative stereotypes: flyover country, homogenous, provincial, but also "as symbols of America's heartland, the place where the media imagine our most authentic controversies are deeply rooted" (Ginsburg 1998, xviii).[4] Such portraits are also incomplete and can serve to undermine progressive practices of people in those places while elevating the agency, power, and political subjectivity of people living in larger urban centers. In focusing acutely on a city, the third aim of this book is to contribute to the scholarship on urban assemblages by highlighting practices in Fargo that resulted from refugee resettlement and that provide examples of mutual support, negotiation, and experimentation required to live together in a diverse world.

Fargo

Fargo is located in the Red River Valley on the eastern edge of the vast Great Plains of North America, next to the Minnesota border, in one of the most fertile farming regions in the world (see map 1 in chapter 1).[5] As far as the eye can see, there is striking flatness, field after field, dotted by an occasional barn or farmhouse surrounded by groves of nonnative trees and endless sky. Once the bottom of a glacial lake, Fargo's uniquely flat topography has effectively no slope, which creates perpetual problems with even modest rain, spring snowmelt, or flooding from the Red River. The highest points in the region are embankments on highway overpasses. Follow these highways, and they will lead to more fields and small towns. Ninety percent of North Dakota's land is devoted to farming, and a fifth of the population is employed in agriculture. Key agricultural products include wheat, sunflower seeds, flaxseed, barley, and milk, as well as canola seeds, honey, navy and pinto beans, oats, rye, soybeans, sugar beets, and livestock.

North Dakota is the coldest of the forty-eight contiguous states, with January temperatures averaging a low of two degrees Fahrenheit. Until you reach downtown, populated with trees, wide boulevards, older homes, and varied urban architecture, there is little protection from the harsh climate that characterizes the region. Among people I spoke with on an everyday basis, no other topic arose as frequently as the weather, which underlined a momentary point of commonality as well as deeper human differences. During mandated orientation sessions for newly arrived refugees, a local meteorologist showed them how to dress warmly for the winter and keep safe during a tornado. Over the years, I have watched fear rush over the faces of hundreds of refugees as they heard about tornados and blizzards for the first time. Despite the orientation classes, refugees and their advocates told me unsettling stories about newly arrived refugees shivering in their apartments or walking to work in January (an uncommon practice in Fargo in winter due to the frigid temperatures and heavy reliance on cars), or about refugees who were displaced by the epic 1997 Red River flood.

Approaching the metropolitan area, billboards foreshadow a more urban area, then agricultural industries and gas stations appear. Next come blocks of apartment buildings that mostly look the same, and cul-de-sacs of new homes with vinyl siding in dull shades of beige, brown, and green, all miles from the city center, an indication of how quickly the metro region is expanding. When you approach the city from the west or south, the interstate highway and sky dominate the view. When you approach from the east, rolling hills mark the landscape in Minnesota lake country before flattening out near Dilworth and Moorhead, Fargo's sister city in Minnesota. The flatness is palpable; as soon as you leave your vehicle, your body feels exposed to the elements, often a strong wind that drives rain or snow. Under clear skies, the sunshine is bright and unrelenting.

Fargo is a thriving and rapidly growing city. It is not just the largest in the state, but the largest within a 240-mile radius, with a population of 105,549 people in 2015. Including its sister cities of West Fargo and Moorhead, Minnesota, the population of the metropolitan area is 224,000. Over the last fifty years, Fargo has transformed from a city with an economy centered on manufacturing and agriculture to one with a more diversified economy that includes education, healthcare, software, and service-based industries. It has alternately benefited and suffered from the oil boom in the western part of the state. From 2004 to 2014, employment in the region grew 24 percent. During the Great Recession of 2007–2009, as the rest of the nation saw employment contract by more than 6 percent, the Fargo-Moorhead regional economy contracted only 1 percent and had recovered fully by 2010 (GFMEDC 2015).

While many U.S. cities lost nearly one in four manufacturing jobs over the last few decades, Fargo's manufacturing sector grew more than 12 percent from 2004 to 2014 (GFMEDC 2015). Over the past ten years, Fargo-Moorhead's unemployment rate has remained below 4 percent, except at the height of the recession when it reached a peak of 4.3 percent. Underemployment rates have also been some of the nation's lowest (9–11.9 percent in 2011), which is a key reason why the State Department continues to send refugees to this region and thus why Fargo has some of the highest numbers of refugees per capita in the country. In 2015, Fargo resettled more refugees per capita than any other U.S. city (Glass-Moore 2015). States that have welcomed the most refugees relative to their populations are North Dakota, South Dakota, Idaho, Nebraska, and Vermont (Guo 2015). These states share several factors, including low population density, low unemployment rates, and the lowest rates of racial diversity in the country. The increase in racial diversity in Fargo at the turn of the twenty-first century can be largely attributed to refugee resettlement, along with the diversification of the economy and prevalence of high- and low-skill job opportunities, including the oil and natural gas boom in the western part of the state and the technology used for extracting and maintaining it. The region is a successful business and technology destination, ranked by *Forbes* in 2013 as the second-best small place for business and careers in the country.

In 2006, oil companies began drilling in the Bakken formation in western North Dakota. The formation is one of the largest contiguous deposits in the country and was deemed unsuitable for production until hydraulic fracturing ("fracking") was used to extract the oil. Fracking is a process that injects water and chemicals into black shale, siltstone, and sandstone, which holds the oil. More than 90 percent of North Dakota's crude oil and natural gas production comes from the Bakken region, and the drilling instantly transformed once-small, sleepy farm towns into magnets for transient, mostly male, workers from places around the country, places reeling from the effects of the Great Recession. In 2004, just 2 percent of North Dakota's economy relied on oil and natural gas production, but in 2014, it accounted for nearly 16 percent (Silva 2017). Poor farmers turned into millionaires overnight. Employment increased by more than 35 percent, and wages more than doubled between 2007 and 2011 (Ferree and Smith 2013). North Dakota quickly surpassed Alaska to become the second-largest producer of oil in the country, after Texas. Despite production declines in 2016, North Dakota remains the second-largest oil-producing state, accounting for 11 percent of the total U.S. crude oil production (U.S. Energy Information Administration 2018). Oil and gas revenues have produced significant state budget surpluses that Governor Doug Burgum (elected in 2016) argues will be put into infrastructure projects that will help advance private sector industries. North Dakota ranks forty-eight in terms of total state population, but during the early years of the oil boom, it was the fastest-growing state in the union. The *Bismarck Tribune* reports that since the last decennial census in 2010, North Dakota has been one of the nation's fastest-growing states, with an estimated growth rate of nearly 13 percent. Only four states—Colorado, Florida, Texas, and Utah—are estimated to have grown by a higher percentage (Holdman 2018).

Though the impact of the Bakken formation has not been as significant on Fargo and the eastern part of the state as it has in Williston and the western part of the state, local businesses experienced a boost from the oil industry, but at a cost. Unintended consequences of the oil boom include environmental damage; unplanned-for population surges, especially of temporary resident workers who do not pay taxes; increased crime; and lack of social services, education, and infrastructure for booming populations. Nevertheless, in 2018, North Dakota continued to set records for oil and natural gas production.

Fargo holds a unique place in the national imagination. People in Fargo are aware of their cultural image. From 1996 to 2007, the slogan for Fargo-Moorhead's chamber of commerce was "More Than You Expect." In 2007, it was "Always Warm," referring to niceness and hospitality as dominant forms of sociality while also alluding to the notorious climate. In 2015, the slogan became "North of Normal," which attempted to highlight Fargo-West Fargo-Moorhead's creative, "quirky" cosmopolitan characteristics. A promotional video (Fargo-Moorhead-West Fargo 2015) describes Fargo as "different, not like anywhere you've been before." "If normal is a mainstream mindset," the narrator states confidently, "Fargo more than transcends it. In a way, it's a bit of a misfit, a new hub of creativity, unconventional thinking, and innovation planted firmly in the Upper Midwest." The video also stresses Fargo's "adventurous pioneering spirit."

Brothers Ethan Coen and Joel Coen, raised in a suburb of Minneapolis, made Fargo infamous with their Academy Award–winning film *Fargo* (1996). The film—and more recently, the FX television series loosely based on the film—has contributed to the image of Fargo as remote, arctic tundra inhabited by passive-aggressive, violent, if not also "nice" people, with a distinctive accent ("You betcha!"). In his National Public Radio show, *A Prairie Home Companion*, Garrison Keillor popularized this Midwest brand of nice through satire. The program problematized niceness as a form of communication that can discourage and infuriate both locals and newcomers to the region. Keillor called this "Wobegonics" after the fictional town in his program, Lake Wobegon. Wobegonics is designed to exclude outsiders through coded references and gestures; in Keillor's words, "it's basically just your ordinary English except that there are no confrontational verbs or statements of strong personal preference" (Keillor 1997). A 2012 Minnesota Public Radio program on the topic of "Minnesota nice" professed that people in the Upper Midwest are friendly; they just don't want any more friends (Yuen 2012). Niceness was more than a caricature; it was a form of sociality used to maintain order and avoid controversy.

Northern European ancestry, religion, socioeconomic processes, and niceness shaped whiteness in Fargo. Most Fargo residents identify as Christian, especially Lutheran or Catholic. More than 80 percent of Fargo residents claim Scandinavian ancestry. Fargo-Moorhead has a Scandinavian cultural center, an annual Scandinavian festival, Scandinavian stores, and a prevalence of Norwegian and Swedish flags in homes and businesses. Local bookstores offer sections on local or regional authors accompanied by a section of contemporary Scandinavian authors. Throughout the Upper Midwest, one can find signs in Swedish, Finnish,

Norwegian, and German. One of the *Fargo* film's actors, a Swede, noted in an interview on the DVD that he was so surprised by the number of Scandinavians in the region that he cried. He found the region to be "more Sweden than Sweden," because Scandinavian-Americans continued to speak the language and practice customs that their ancestors did when they left Northern Europe in the nineteenth and early twentieth centuries.

An artist introduced me to the term *Janteloven* ("laws of Jante") to describe Fargo culture. In 1933, Aksel Sandemose, a Danish-Norwegian writer, coined the term in his satirical novel *En flyktning krysser sitt spor* (*A Refugee Crosses His Tracks*). The laws are part of a wider critique of Scandinavian society, and specifically of the fictional Danish town of Jante. The laws allude to a long-standing Scandinavian attitude that emphasizes modesty, uniformity, and not drawing attention to oneself.[6] The rules aim to hold everyone to a modest average. The logic behind the rules results in individuals who are rewarded for thinking "It's no big deal, anyone can do it, probably better than me. I'm not special." Based on the biblical Ten Commandments, the laws seek to weaken social hierarchies and encourage individuals in various social circles to interact with one another freely and openly because no one is considered better than anyone else. The laws can be viewed as a mechanism for fostering and maintaining social equity, but also for diminishing individualism, creative thinking, ambition, or challenges to the status quo.

The novel argues that the main character, Espen Arnakke, commits murder in response to the repressive nature of small town, provincial life that placed too many demands on the individual. The book also examines the negative consequences for failing to follow social norms. Though I only heard the term "Janteloven" from one person in Fargo, the ideology behind the laws was present in my interactions with people in Fargo and in my own family. When I explained "Janteloven" to interlocutors or family members and friends, particularly those with Scandinavian and Lutheran heritage, there was a resounding recognition of the laws at play in their lives. During an episode of *The Late Show with Stephen Colbert* on November 10, 2018, Swedish actor Alexander Skarsgård told Colbert that "Jantelagen" (Swedish for "Janteloven") prevented him from boasting about his Emmy and Golden Globe awards. He said, "We have something in Sweden. It basically means 'Don't think you're special. . . . No ostentatious flaunting of your accolades.'" Janteloven do not have as much cultural influence in the United States as in Scandinavian countries—after all, U.S. culture brazenly promotes individualism, which is at odds with the laws of Jante—but they were not inconsequential, and newcomers would certainly encounter diluted versions of them.

Before the 1980s, migration to Fargo mostly came in the form of white people, likely other Scandinavian Americans, from smaller towns in the Great Plains and

Upper Midwest. The "old" new migrants were largely accustomed to the language, political and economic system, cultural norms, and climate. The same could not be said of refugees who came in the latter part of the twentieth century. At the same time that New Americans began coming to the region, young people whose families were established in Fargo were fleeing, moving to larger urban centers like Minneapolis-St. Paul and beyond. According to demographer Richard Rathge, refugees were the only reason that Fargo showed any population growth at all in the 1990s (*Forum of Fargo-Moorhead* 2001).

Throughout the twentieth century, whites in Fargo believed themselves to be especially friendly, hardworking Americans, capable of withstanding their notoriously cold climate. Fargo's status as an economically thriving, if small, city with one of the lowest unemployment rates in the country, a healthy industrial sector, and an increasingly diverse economy bolstered this idea of the productivity of white labor and the forms of sociality that it supported, like "North Dakota nice." As more refugees arrived and stayed in the region, they began to complicate understandings of citizenship in the dominant population. In new ways, race began to shape whites' perceptions about belonging, work, and friendliness, forms of sociality that would serve to categorize and monitor racial minorities, New Americans, and other outsiders. Hard work and friendliness were sometimes code words for unexamined whiteness or nationality in Fargo, a mechanism for maintaining power, privilege, and status.

Due to international migration and globalization, diversity has become a key concern for many cities. At the local level, cities at once welcome and reject the kinds of diversity that migrants bring. In Fargo, diversity usually referred to *racial* diversity. Race is more than interpretation of physical differences between groups of people. "Race" is a broadly encompassing term that refers to skin color and physical variations among people *and* the harmful social judgments based on those differences, and it also references language, behavior, dress, and ethnicity. Race has justified apartheid, genocide, and slavery, and it continues to justify systemic forms of violence, prejudice, and discrimination in education, healthcare, the legal system, and housing. The concept of "race" also draws upon covert forms of racism, for example, in terms of "ideal" beauty standards. Racial thinking has proven to be dangerous for people of color. It invokes irrational fears of people of color in whites and continues to structure the everyday lives of people of all racial groups, deeply influencing the ways we think about cultural differences and ourselves. Construed as commonsense, racist thought has become so powerful, in part, because it draws authority by invoking nature and biology (Lutz and Collins 1993, 156).

The construction of race is linked to other forms of power and privilege, such as gender and socioeconomic class (Crenshaw 1991; Sacks 1989; Stoler 2002).

Whiteness or blackness or brownness is not restricted to skin color alone but can be accrued via gender, socioeconomic status, sexual orientation, and national origin (Anthias and Yuval-Davis 1992; Brodkin 1998 and 2000). For example, in Fargo, large regional hospitals such as Sanford and Essentia, companies such as Microsoft, and higher education institutions such as North Dakota State University bring high-skill labor to the region, including foreign people of color, but these workers are less visible. High-skill workers become racially "lightened" (Ong 1996) and less threatening to many in the dominant white population. Members of the dominant population often view refugees and poor people, especially poor people of color, as undeserving and unworthy of employment or social services. Because race is fluid, if we are to decrease its potency in creating and maintaining inequality, it is vital to understand the variable ways in which race is constructed differently across political, economic, and cultural terrains (Harrison 1998; Hartigan 2005; Ong 1996; Williams 1989).

"Race-ing" in the context of Fargo means analyzing a history of race alongside contemporary approaches to diversity—for example, how refugee resettlement disrupted the discourse and (mis)recognition of race in terms of physical attributes (white/nonwhite), language (English/not English), religion (Christian/not Christian), nation (us/them), and sociality (nice/not nice). Race-ing acknowledges the toxic social construct of race that continues to be a "primary and decisive way of coding difference and social worth in a world after 9/11 accustomed to defining the social in ethno-cultural terms" (Amin 2012, 3–4). Accordingly, and regardless of social or legal status or cultural practices, migrants and minorities are coded as "not white" and therefore "out of place in an otherwise shared commons" (4). Race-ing includes whiteness as a category of racial analysis.

Whiteness is a privileged status granted on the basis of arbitrary, malleable phenotypic traits and has been produced through legal, economic, and cultural institutions from slavery to present-day courts and schools, to medical, religious, and financial institutions, and to different media representations (Brodkin 1998; Buck 2012). Whiteness is all the more powerful because it is so often unmarked and invisible (Frankenberg 1993 and 2001). However, whiteness takes different forms, including the ability to fracture as well as to dominate (Durington 2009). For example, anthropologist John Hartigan (1999 and 2005) shows how poor whites in Detroit were members of an oppressed socioeconomic group while some Blacks were not.[7] Nevertheless, discussions about race in the United States must foreground larger historical and national contexts of racism that shape local understandings and practices (Mullings 2005, 681).

In Setha Low's work on whites in gated communities, she argues that niceness "is about keeping things clean, orderly, homogenous, and controlled so that housing values remain stable, but it is also a way of maintaining whiteness" (2009, 87). The context and history behind the urban gated communities that Low studied and the small, primarily white city of Fargo differed, but I too found that niceness in Fargo was tied to whiteness and to maintaining the status quo. Across the world, in various ways, whiteness is defined by "the ability to have access to and make use of things like higher education and social graces, vocabulary, and demeanor that allow one to prosper or at least compete within the dominant culture" (82). In Fargo, this demeanor was referred as "North Dakota nice."

Put differently, being white in Fargo is different from being white in Detroit, or in the Southern United States, where different categories of race were constructed through plantation slavery, "one-drop rules," and Jim Crow laws, or in Chicago, Baltimore, St. Louis, and other Northern cities, where redlining of Black neighborhoods and extrajudicial violence is more prevalent (Massey and Denton 1993). Nevertheless, race relations in some parts of the country influence how race-ing processes and practices play out in other parts—via national laws and policies, media and popular culture, travel, the Internet, and interactions with people in other parts of the country and the world.

During the 2016 annual Building Bridges conference, which brings together local and national actors in refugee resettlement to learn and share information, the CEO of Lutheran Social Services presented on refugee resettlement to North Dakota since 1997, which included statistics on the increase of racial diversity in four cities across the state. The connection was clear: refugee resettlement brings *racial* diversity, but left out of this discussion were other forms of diversity, such as gendered, political, social, ability, and class-based diversity, and everyday practices. Making diversity *only* about race downplays other forms of diversity and elevates race as the most important marker of difference. Expanding our approach to diversity could help us to better define and understand what constitutes dominant populations, besides whiteness, and help to make dominant populations more inclusive and receptive to other forms of difference and diversity. It's worth mentioning that there is a countertendency to not make diversity about race at all. Along with other scholars, I challenge us to think beyond race when it comes to diversity while at the same time acknowledging the power that racial categories continue to have in people's lives (Clarke and Newman 2012).

Refugees and other immigrants arriving in Fargo carried with them their own forms of diversity. As I mentioned above, Bosnians in Fargo distinguished between one another by ethnoreligious categories (Roma, Muslim), language (Romani/Bosnian) and region (rural/urban, Bosnia/Herzegovina). Southern Sudanese distinguished between one another by language, age, region, gender, and levels of education. These historically contingent, relational identities intersected in Fargo and responded to and transformed one another. What it meant to be Rom in Bosnia was not the same as to be a Bosnian Rom in Fargo. What it meant to be Dinka (the largest ethnic group in South Sudan) in South Sudan was different than what it meant to be Dinka in Fargo, and what it meant to be ethnically Norwegian in Fargo in 1915 was different than what it meant in 2015. Identity and belonging transformed through the city on an everyday basis through interpersonal relationships, practices, and institutions.

Small Cities

Considering Fargo's geopolitical location and its relatively small population of people of color and of people born in other countries, it may seem an exaggeration, absurd even, to think of Fargo as a worldly city. A city poster plays on this idea. It pictures four cities, three of which are unquestionably global and cosmopolitan cities: Moscow, London, and Paris (figure 0.1). The fourth city is Fargo. Fargo *is* global, though, because we are all global. We are all global through our histories of migration, through processes of colonialism, through our contemporary commodity chains, through our social networks, through the media, and through our connections with contemporary forms of immigration and refugee resettlement.

While much scholarly attention has been given to megacities such as Moscow, London, and Paris, more of our urbanizing populations are moving to smaller cities. In 2015, more than half of the world's population lived in cities (UN 2014). By 2050, this number is forecasted to rise to two-thirds. By 2030, the number of cities with more than 10 million residents will grow from twenty-eight to forty-one, but only one-eighth of the world's population will live in them. In 2014, half of all city dwellers lived in cities with less than 500,000 people. Over the last few decades, cities like Fargo (or Sioux Falls, South Dakota, and Omaha, Nebraska) have been transforming from regional centers mostly populated by white Euro-Americans with a minority of Native Americans, to bigger, more diverse cities. More scholarship is necessary to analyze the diversity *of* and *in* small cities (Ehrkamp 2011). In so doing, it will be important to look at the unique attributes of a city, while also paying attention to how the city shapes and is shaped by regional, national, and global circuits and assemblages of people, ideas, goods, services, and practices (Çağlar and Glick Schiller 2018; Glick Schiller and Schmidt 2016; Ong and Collier 2005).

Small cities have benefits and challenges of both small towns and large cities, but their unique characteristic is that they occupy a distinct geographic center that is not suburban, and, as sociologist Jon Norman writes, they "frequently function as centers for vast hinterlands, particularly in the Midwest and West" (2013,

Moscow.

London.

Paris.

Fargo.

FIGURE 0.1.   Fargo 4 Cities poster.

3). While suburbs may have their own distinct neighborhoods, they are more likely to be defined by their proximity to and reliance on the neighboring city in terms of employment, entertainment, and economic development. The identity of small cities is shaped by their distance from and relation to other cities and larger metropolitan regions. Echoing Norman, I believe that small cities are quantitatively and qualitatively different than larger cities and that they present "a different story of urban life" (2013, 2).

My characterization of small cities is wittingly vague, because identity—whether individual, group, or city—is arbitrary and relational. For someone accustomed to living in a major urban center, a city of 250,000 residents may seem small and provincial. For someone from a small town of less than 2,000 people, a city of 50,000 may feel overwhelming. Small cities can feel like "big small towns," which is what some residents told me about Fargo, while others, who worked in the city, told me they preferred to live in smaller towns outside of Fargo because the city was too big. Scholars of urban studies are increasingly arguing that "the town/country divide that once appeared to offer a stable, even self-evident, basis for delineating the specificity of city settlements, today appears increasingly as an ideological remnant of early industrial capitalism that maps . . . problematically onto contemporary urban processes" (Brenner, Madden, and Wachsmuth 2011). Neil Brenner (2011) has gone so far as to critique the privileging of the city as the spatial epicenter of urban studies and instead argues that capitalist urbanization has resulted in planetary urbanism producing "urban theory *without an outside*" (cited in Peake 2016, 222). Feminist geographer Linda Peake is wary of such an approach to urban life because it is a grand theory that fails to take into account feminist ways of looking at the city. Scholars tend to see more connections and fewer differences between urban and rural populations than the people who live there.

Some small cities have features in common with some large cities—for example, in density. In 2010, Minneapolis–St. Paul had the twenty-seventh densest urban population in the country, with 2,594 people per square mile (Cox 2014) across a metro population of more than three million. Fargo's urban density is 2,268, which is higher than that of Birmingham, Alabama, which has 1,414 people per square mile (and more than twice Fargo's population, at more than 212,000 people). The densities of urban areas in the north central Midwest are some of the smallest in the country, especially when compared to cities in the West (Cox 2014), but this varies from city to city. Regardless of size and population density, large cities have more centers of power, and as a result, more forms of diversity in terms of race, ethnicity, language, religion, and international populations.

WalletHub (2017) analyzed 501 of the largest cities in the United States in terms of five forms of diversity: household, religious, cultural, socioeconomic, and economic. Socioeconomic diversity was calculated using household income and educational attainment. Cultural diversity was measured using racial, ethnic, and linguistic diversity as well as birthplace. Economic diversity was calculated based on industries, occupational diversity, and worker-class diversity, and household diversity was measured in terms of marital status, age, household type (male- or female-headed), and size. Fargo's overall rank was 325 of 501. The researchers characterized Fargo as a "midsize city," for which it garnered a ranking of 121 of 144 for diversity. The point is that studying smaller, more racially homogenous cities, such as Fargo, gives us an opportunity to analyze race and migration patterns in ways that are different from large metropolitan areas, where there are more variables and more centers of power. Examining the political, economic, and cultural assemblages or circuits in a given city and comparing them with a wider array of cities allows us to learn more about the relationship between the local and global, rather than take notions of scale for granted (Bell and Jayne 2009; Ehrkamp 2011; Massey 2004; Robinson 2006).

Large cities have dominated most social science research on urban life over the last one hundred years (Sassen 1991), but small cities and towns once occupied a more influential place in the urban studies literature. Robert and Helen Lynd's research on Middletown (1929) served as a seminal study of urban sociology and ethnographic methods. The Lynds chose Muncie, Indiana, as their field site due to its small size, rapid transition from agriculture to industrialism, and the relatively small foreign-born and "Negro" population (8). In reality, Muncie's African American population was proportionally higher in the 1920s than it was in New York, Chicago, or Detroit. It had a relatively small foreign-born population because the local business class imported workers from Tennessee and Kentucky in a concerted effort to keep foreign workers out (Younge 2016). The Lynds believed they could more easily isolate and analyze culture change and socioeconomic class over time if they ignored race and citizenship status. In *The Other Side of Middletown*, Lassiter, Goodall, Campbell, and Johnson (2004) challenged the Lynds' omission of minorities by addressing African Americans' resilience and influence in Muncie over time. Although ethnographic methods have evolved since the Lynds' time, their framework that small cities can provide a valuable lens for studying urban life is still accepted (Connolly 2010). A growing number of scholars are studying immigrants in small cities as a way to better understand ethnic diversity and how immigrant assimilation is similar to and different from that in the past (Glick Schiller and Çağlar 2009; Goździak and Martin 2005; Massey 2008).

More scholarship is necessary to reflect the diversity of refugees *and* resettlement cities and how migrants contribute to contemporary urban (re)structuring (Foner 2005; Glick Schiller and Çağlar 2009, 178). Urban life and diversity symbolize growth, creativity, and cosmopolitanism to some, and fear, danger, and contamination to others (Amin 2012). In small cities, refugee resettlement is viewed both negatively and positively as a key institution bringing sociocultural, linguistic, religious, economic, and racial diversity (Goździak and Martin 2005). There are fewer global networks of power operating in small cities than in large cities, but due to globalization, "we all participate in social fields that extend beyond the local" and that "link in some way to institutions of differential power based in many places" (Çağlar and Glick Schiller 2018, 12).

In large cities, refugees may be viewed negatively, as "terrorists" for example, but people in large urban centers are less able to racially profile people *as refugees* due to the presence of so much racial diversity when compared to small, white cities. Thus, while this book focuses on the relationship between refugee resettlement and the city of Fargo, the characteristics of citizenship, the management of diversity, and everyday relationships observed in this small city are by no means isolated; they have broader implications. In the introduction to her book about abortion in Fargo, Faye Ginsburg writes that Fargo serves as a kind of mirror for the state of abortion in the country as a whole (1998, ix). Fargo can serve as a mirror for the state of refugee resettlement in the country as a whole as well.

Refugees and Immigrants

One approach to thinking about the difference between immigrants and refugees is that "migrants" voluntarily leave their countries of origin in order to find employment and other economic incentives, and possibly permanent residence, in another country, whereas "refugees" are forced to leave their home. A refugee is classified as an individual who is outside his or her home country—if he or she has no home country, then outside of the country in which he or she last habitually resided—and who is unable or unwilling to return to that home country due to persecution or well-founded fear of persecution on the basis of race, religion, nationality, political opinion, or membership in a social organization (UNHCR 1967). Scholars contend that to be considered a refugee, an individual must first be denationalized, considered "homeless" in a world where nationality very much matters (Agamben 1996; Malkki 1995).

Migrants—documented or not—are considered by international bodies such as the United Nations and the media to be individual actors who weigh "push" and "pull" factors in choosing whether or not to migrate. "Push" factors are seen as coming from the sending country and include things like poverty. "Pull" factors are viewed as being located in the receiving community and include economic and social networks and opportunities. Anthropologists who work with immigrants, especially undocumented migrants in the United States who come from Mexico and other places in Latin America, explain that the framing of immigration in terms of push and pull factors is limiting, just as the dichotomy "between voluntary, economic, and migrant on the one hand and forced, political, and refugee on the other" is misleading (Holmes 2013, 17). The main distinction is often attributed to motivations for leaving and degrees of choice (Ferris 1993) and has to do with who should have access to political and social rights in the receiving country. In reality, these dichotomies are not so clear. For many, "migration is anything but 'voluntary'" and is not a clear choice (Holmes 2013, 7; De León 2015; Stuesse 2016).

It is becoming increasingly difficult to make distinctions between refugees, migrants, and immigrants, because the definitions are largely political. There is ambiguity surrounding notions of "choice"; choice too is political (Hein 1993; Zolberg, Suhrke, and Aguagyo 1989). There are several overlapping features of all global migrants: they consciously or unconsciously challenge the sanctity and hegemony of the sovereign state by demonstrating that it is possible, if not easy, to "belong" to more than one country (Glick Schiller, Basch, and Szanton Blanc 1992; Glick Schiller and Fouron 2001). However, immigrants and refugees have different legal statuses in the United States. Unlike undocumented migrants, refugees are provided a social security card and can legally work upon arrival. They also have access to services that undocumented immigrants do not—for example, food stamps and other forms of social welfare. However, despite their "legality," refugees are sometimes treated as "illegal" when it comes to social respect and deservedness of rights, especially in regard to claims made to the state.[8] In his autoethnography on living as an Iranian refugee in Sweden, anthropologist Shahram Khosravi explains, "Migrant illegality is a consequence of the borders, not a cause of them" (2010, 115). Refugees and asylum seekers, he continues, face invisible borders that keep "immigrants strangers for generations" (76).

Refugees comprise about 10 percent of annual immigration to the United States, but they are among the dominant groups of foreign-born residents in small metropolitan areas and consequently have a unique role in influencing the cities where they settle. Sociologist Jeremy Hein worked with Hmong and Khmer refugees in the small cities of Eau Claire, Wisconsin, and Rochester, Minnesota, and compared their experiences to the experiences of Hmong and Khmer refugees in Minneapolis and Chicago. Hein found that ethnic background was more important in shaping adaptation patterns than the place in which they settled. Though I concur with the importance of ethnic background in shaping resettlement experiences, I believe that cities are more important in shaping refugee and immigrant experiences than Hein's study indicated.

Citizenship

Citizenship refers to political, economic, civic, and social rights and duties of individuals in a community or nation-state. Traditional approaches to citizenship imply membership in a sovereign state with clear political borders. According to this conceptualization, citizenship is a legal status that confers certain privileges and protections, such as voting, education, and employment. Underlying this status is a more complicated and controversial understanding of citizenship that involves challenges to straightforward definitions of who belongs to a given community or state. As such, citizenship—like diversity—is a capacious concept and not always coherent in an increasingly globalized, transnational world. I approach citizenship as a set of practices (Lazar 2013) that seek to establish belonging to one or more places and that are relational and always in flux. Such practices are multiscalar (Çağlar and Glick Schiller 2018; Staeheli 2003)—that is, they are shaped by horizontal and vertical dimensions, by people with a lot of power and social standing and by those with little power or status. These practices have as much to do with feelings of belonging and inclusion as they do with legal status.

Citizenship is "lived history" sustained by everyday practices (Holston 2008, 22). Both within countries and internationally, these practices are heterogeneous; they inform struggles for inclusion and equality but also sustain deep desires to exclude and limit. Following Balibar's (2001) metaphor of citizenship as always "unfinished" (*imparfaite*), Clarke, Coll, Dagnino, and Neveu (2014) call for an approach to citizenship that emphasizes practices, points, and processes of connection and mobilization. Such an approach "stresses the importance of understanding the (variable) meanings of citizenship in its different contexts: social, political, cultural, spatial and temporal" (14); to understand them, we must use "thick contextualization" (9). By focusing on what people do, not only on what they say, where they are located, or whether they have legal status or not, we can shift our approach to citizenship to better comprehend and analyze citizenship in an age of migration (Isin 2009). For example, I learned of a strong friendship between two women, one from Bosnia and the other from Somalia, who worked together at the refugee resettlement agency in Fargo. After learning why the Somali woman wore a hijab (head covering), the Bosnian woman too began to cover her head as a show of her faith, a bold move in a city that was predominantly Christian and for which both women faced discrimination and prejudice.

Classic liberal approaches to citizenship lumped rights, states, entitlement, and territories together. In an age of migration, these concepts have become disarticulated and (re)articulated in new terms, more defined by markets, neoliberal values, and global human rights. Aihwa Ong (2006) calls these new versions of citizenship "mutations." She argues that these mutations of older forms of citizenship can be traced to global flows of markets, people, ideas, and things. Social scientists pay attention to how these flows configure in new spaces and entanglements, which come into existence as people move—whether by choice or by force—as a result of geopolitical processes (Puar 2012, 58). According to Isin, "Citizenship is a dynamic (political, legal, social and cultural but perhaps also sexual, aesthetic and ethic) institution of domination *and* empowerment that governs *who* citizens (insiders), subjects (strangers, outsiders) and abjects (aliens) are and how these actors are to govern themselves and each other in a given body politic" (2009, 371).

Cities are especially good sites for investigating modern citizenship because they are the spaces when dense assemblages of capital, industry, migration, communication, and democracy come together in new formulations of citizenship. "City streets," James Holston writes, "combine new identities of territory, contract, and education with ascribed ones of race, religion, culture, and gender" (2008, 23). The chemistry of these assemblages of people, with their unique and overlapping lived histories, means that people in cities "develop new sources of rights and agendas of citizenship concerning the very conditions of city life. This chemistry in turn transforms the meaning and practices of national belonging." Of course, such practices can also be found in rural areas and small towns, but cities provide more and denser articulations of citizenship and power: "In the process, cities become both the site and the substance not only of the uncertainties of modern citizenship but also of its emergent forms" (23). Small cities like Fargo have fewer articulations of citizenship than global cities or large cities, like São Paulo, where Holston works, but they are nevertheless important sites for understanding the relationship between citizenship, diversity, and the characteristics that divide people as well as those that build common ground. New approaches to citizenship have emerged in Fargo as a result of refugee resettlement.

Assemblages and the Commons

Assemblage is a theoretical concept that challenges the idea of nations, cities, or communities as bounded or homogenous spaces and instead focuses on diverse practices and relations that occur in and through the city. Social scientists use the term to describe different actors and practices shaping the life of a city. Some use assemblage to analyze networks, most notably Bruno Latour's Actor-Network Theory (ANT), which seeks to better understand capitalist urban development, commodification of urban space, social networks and inequalities, power, the relationship between humans and technology, and relations of social-material life

(Latour 2007). Urban scholars use ANT to understand the nature of cities and urban life (Farías and Bender 2010). Others build on philosopher Gilles Deleuze's *agencement*, "a term that means design, layout, organization, arrangement, and relations—the focus being not on content but on relations, relations of patterns" (Phillips 2006, 108; cited in Puar 2012, 57). Anna Tsing's work joins this last configuration, where she describes assemblages as "open-ended gatherings [that] allow us to ask about communal effects without assuming them. They show us potential histories in the making. . . . Ways of being are emergent effects of encounters. . . . Patterns of unintentional coordination develop in assemblages. . . . Assemblages cannot hide from capital and the state; they are sites for watching how political economy works" (Tsing 2015, 23).

Feminist theorist Jasbir Puar encourages us to think about what assemblages do, not what they are (2012, 57). Approaching the city in terms of assemblages, *Race-ing Fargo* examines everyday social practices in one city among a variety of individuals and institutions, focusing on the ways in which power is articulated through the city, not simply in the city. The city was more than a backdrop for these transformations; it was an important part of the process (Isin 2002). In examining assemblages at play in Fargo, I also examine the city as commons, a site for envisioning and building futures.

"The commons" are a shared public resource that generates commonalities, "resources that human beings hold in common . . . and which are essential to their biological, cultural, and social reproduction" (Nonini 2006, 1). The commons are usually thought of as a public space that eschews private ownership in favor of "common wealth," in both a material and political sense. As such, it is a space that can promote a more just and equitable society, or alternatively, a space to be plundered because it is to everyone's individual benefit to draw as much as possible from the commons, depleting the resource through the cumulative effect of our individual actions. In the former view, the commons are a social institution that is antithetical to capitalism, which is driven by ownership, profit, and individualism. The latter view is most commonly referred to as "the tragedy of the commons" (Hardin 1968). Under capitalism, the commons have come under attack as states privatize public services and corporations perpetually search for more capital and labor, but, says David Bollier, "as an empirical matter, the commons can work, and work well" (Bollier 2016, 6; see also Ostrom 1990). Like citizenship and assemblage, anthropologists have begun to view the commons as a set of practices that encompass ongoing and contested struggles (Susser 2017, 7) and collective actions whereby citizens attempt to change the political discourse and diminish socioeconomic hierarchies caused by capitalism. Following Bollier, I use the term "commoning" and not only "the commons" because "the commons is an active, living process. It is less a noun than a verb because it is primarily about the social practices of *communing*—acts of mutual support, conflict, nego-tiation, communication, and experimentation that are needed to create systems to manage shared resources" (2016, 1). "Commoning" as a verb highlights how people are fighting to create new and different, more equitable public spaces as the state and market encroach upon them (De Angelis and Stavrides 2010).

Long before capitalism became the dominant mode of economic and politi-cal organization, there "was a world where members of human communities en-joyed access to an array of common resources that were essential for their social survival": land, water, forest, game, and pasture (Kalb 2017, 67). Urban life in the twenty-first century obviously has a different form of the commons than our human ancestors had. Henri Lefebvre (1968) first put forth the idea of the city as a commons. He viewed "right to the city" movements as a way of reclaiming con-trol over decisions about how the city develops and grows, and to promote greater access of urban space and resources for all urban residents. Developed in tandem with a critique of neoliberalism, the commons has become a way to pro-mote a more equitable future outside of the market and state (Bollier 2016, 3).

In cities today, the commons have to do with public space, public transporta-tion, welfare and a social safety net, access to affordable housing and healthcare, clean and safe drinking water, and secure bridges and roads. A more expansive and contemporary understanding of the commons includes knowledge commons, cultural commons, infrastructure commons, and neighborhood commons, among others (Foster and Iaione 2016). As governments privatize their services, wages stagnate, and housing, healthcare, and food costs skyrocket, people must fight harder and more creatively for their right to the commons. Cities and pub-lics have different reasons and paths of approaching the commons, which is why they must take root at the local level, for example, at the level of a city or neigh-borhood, but—in an age of globalization—that is likely to include a variety of assemblages, social movements, cultures, and demands. The commons in cities around the world are melding specific struggles with other alliances, but they must all confront multiple assaults caused by neoliberalism and inequality (Susser 2017, 19). The commons, in other words, can and should highlight connections across urban and rural landscapes and other traditional political borders, rather than iso-late the local from the global.

Research Design and Methodologies

As a feminist anthropologist, I approach my research, teaching, and the world using a set of tools that address relations and inequalities between and among genders and social relations at large. This means examining global pluralities in societal roles in regard to socioeconomic class, race, ethnicity, history, culture, and sexualities. My feminist approach developed in my earlier work with organizations that sought to promote Southern Sudanese women's political subjectivities (Erickson and Faria 2011) and to decrease violence and discrimination against Bosnian Roma (Erickson 2017a), but I do not view women as the sole subjects, authors, or audience of feminist research (Visweswaran 1997, 616). Feminist researchers study power; we look for inequalities and analyze practices and relations across diverse landscapes and new ways of knowing (Peake 2016).

A comparative approach allowed me to develop my argument and explain patterns among and between groups more fully than I found in the existing literature or that I could write about each group individually. This approach allows for rethinking and reevaluating cross-cultural patterns in order to better examine how a city has received and incorporated refugees over time. A comparative analysis can also bring together scholarship that Nancy Foner argues "often flow[s] in separate streams" and can help us to "step back and examine what are often time-bound, culture-bound, and even city-bound assumptions" (2005, 4). Peter Van der Veer believes that anthropologists have the best tools for cross-cultural, comparative studies because we are trained to engage with difference and diversity and to focus on problems of cultural translation (2016, 9). As such, we understand that comparison means being aware "of the conceptual difficulties in entering 'other' life worlds" and the challenges of translating them into "radically new and open ways of understanding reality" (11). Comparison is more than a "juxtaposition and comparison of two or more different societies"; rather, explains Van der Veer, "it is a complex reflection on the network of concepts that underlie our study of society as well as the formation of those societies themselves. It is always a double act of reflection" (29).

At times, using a multi-sited, comparative approach was challenging. The populations and institutions I worked with had different (if not also connected) histories and, sometimes, competing agendas. By studying the everyday practices of organizations, I can better explain how inter- and intra-institutional conflicts, inconsistencies, and convivial strategies were central to refugee resettlement and to the reproduction of and challenge to dominant citizenship practices. Institutional ethnographies of state bureaucracies can also help us to "understand their relation to the public and the (elite or subaltern) that they serve" (Sharma and Gupta 2006, 27).

I conducted hundreds of hours of participant observation among institutions and businesses in Fargo, primarily with Cass County Social Services (the welfare agency), Lutheran Social Services' New American Services, and the Giving Plus Learning Program (an English-language-learning nonprofit organization). I also visited schools, medical clinics, and nonprofit organizations that were stakeholders in refugee resettlement. I attended meetings for the Interagency Network for New Americans that consisted of representatives from the above organizations. At both the welfare and resettlement agencies, I attended staff meetings. I interviewed all of the staff at NAS, which included case managers, employment specialists, the director, assistant director, administrative assistants, the CEO of LSS, the state refugee coordinator for North Dakota, and volunteers. In addition to attending staff meetings, I also interviewed fifteen people at CCSS and JOBS, including the director of CCSS, Kathy Hogan, as well as supervisors and staff from Economic Assistance, Child Protection Services, TANF, and North Dakota Job Service. I interviewed the director and the one full-time staff member of the Giving Plus Learning Program, as well as seven volunteers. Almost all of the volunteers at this program were elderly white women, a representative sample of the volunteers for this program at the time I lived in Fargo.[9]

New American interlocutors had different, sometimes competing goals for working with me as a researcher.[10] During my year in Fargo, there was a fledgling Bosnian folklore group that organized youth dancing festivals and presentations and tried to raise money for costumes, but they met infrequently and did not have deep ties with many other Bosnians. Generally speaking, Bosnians preferred to spend time with their families and small groups of close friends. Without a formal organization to work with, even with my fluency in Bosnian, it was difficult to find Bosnians to speak with me. Once I met Bosnians, I would ask them to pass along my information to others who would be willing to speak, but this rarely happened. One Bosnian woman told me that Bosnians were acting as gatekeepers "because they didn't want to share me." Additionally, some Muslims did not want to work with me because they heard that I was also working with Roma. Others told me that Bosnians did not like researchers, while others asked, understandably, what was in it for them if they participated. I explained that I hoped that the knowledge produced from my research would help organizations and cities to better manage diversity and refugee resettlement and earn more respect for New Americans. For reasons that I outline in chapter 5, Roma are wary of outsiders in general. The interviews and participant observation that I conducted among Bosnians was in both Bosnian and English.

In contrast to Bosnians, generally speaking, Southern Sudanese, men especially, were more open to discussing their lives with me, often in hopes of garnering social and economic capital for themselves, their families, and/or their local and transnational social, religious, and political organizations. This sometimes resulted in feelings of competition, such as asking me to help them start their own NGO or to help with various other causes. For many Southern Sudanese, the goal of speaking with non-Sudanese was to raise awareness about atrocities in Sudan. However, I also met strong Southern Sudanese women who challenged perceptions of women from the global South as being in need of developmentalist intervention (Erickson and Faria 2011).

Using a comparative, multi-sited analysis meant collaborating with research interlocutors on the goals and methods of my research projects, as well as giving and reporting back to them. For LSS, I helped set up apartments for new arrivals, assisted with public event planning, coordinated college student volunteers, and helped with administrative work. I served as a mentor to Southern Sudanese and Roma though the Giving Plus Learning Program. I briefly served on the board of directors for the New Sudanese Community Association, which involved participating in grant-writing workshops, providing feedback on grant proposals, taking meeting notes, and advocating for Southern Sudanese in the city. On an individual level, I assisted Bosnians and Southern Sudanese in filling out job and welfare applications and occasionally drove them to appointments, stores, or meetings.

I maintained a blog about my fieldwork. My blog helped me to formulate initial analyses and gave me a platform to publicly share preliminary thoughts about the project. It presented my analysis in an accessible way and allowed my interlocutors to ask me questions about how I was processing the data and offer feedback. I believed, as Paul Stoller argues, that "any anthropologically informed contribution to public discourse promotes the public good" (2013, 94). On the blog, I shared information about myself, thereby increasing the amount of personal knowledge that interlocutors knew about me and ideally humanizing myself as a researcher. These methods of data collection and dissemination—along with news media and social media such as Twitter and Facebook—have been useful in helping me stay abreast of news surrounding refugee resettlement in the years since I left and to share my work with others. I ultimately discontinued the blog due to the time required to manage it along with my other professional and personal responsibilities.

Finally, in order to call attention to my own identity, and especially my power in mapping the terrain of refugee resettlement and citizenship in Fargo, in 2010, I returned to present my findings at the LSS-sponsored Building Bridges conference, the same conference that brought me to my field site four years earlier. I also met with supervisors at the welfare agency to share my findings. In 2011, I was invited to give a presentation about my research for a retirement community out of which the Giving Plus Learning Program was then based. I revisited Fargo in 2014 and 2016 to trace how the contours of resettlement continued to change over time.

HISTORIES, ASSEMBLAGES, AND THE CITY

The histories of North Dakota, Bosnia-Herzegovina (as well as the rest of the former Yugoslavia), and (South) Sudan are not separate or isolated. They have been interconnected in different ways through histories of colonialism, capitalism, and migration. These global processes and legacies are neither random nor orchestrated or predictable, but we can find patterns among them, and legacies of these histories in contemporary culture and practice. "History is not just background or the stage upon which urban life plays out," explains Thomas Bender. "It is an actant, a participant in the networks" (2010, 310). This chapter provides histories of these regions to highlight connections and commonalities, but it also draws attention to differences, so that they may be read against one another. Through these histories and everyday practices of citizenship that I discuss in future chapters, we see how the city shapes and is shaped by regional, national, and global circuits and assemblages of people, ideas, goods, services, and practices (Çağlar and Glick Schiller 2018; Glick Schiller and Schmidt 2016).

North Dakota

The area we know today as North Dakota has been home to nations and tribes of Native Americans for millennia, including the Dakota, Nakota, and Lakota Sioux nations (and Sisseton, Wahpeton, and Yanktonai tribes) as well as the Assiniboin, Chippewa (or Ojibwa), Cree, Blackfeet, Crow, and Three Affiliated Tribes (Mandan, Hidatsa, and Arikara). When Europeans expanded their search for wealth in North America, their quest for fur, and later land, dramatically altered the lives of Native Americans. With the fur trade came horses and guns. Before 1730, Dakota were pedestrian horticulturalists and hunters in the woodlands and prairies west of Lake Superior, but the Hudson Bay Company supplied the Cree, Assiniboin, and Ojibwa with guns and forced the Dakota west. By 1775, the Dakota were using guns while riding on horses and trading directly with European merchants (Wolf 1982, 177). New trade opportunities, guns, and horses fundamentally changed the livelihoods of the Dakota by enhancing their ability to kill buffalo, which became a new commodity (pemmican) to trade with Europeans, thereby diminishing the power of women in matrilineal horticultural societies, and established new social, political, and economic hierarchies that prefaced assimilation and homogenization over diversity (177–181).

Northern Europeans settled the region in the 1860s, although some had been present since at least the early 1800s. The first recorded birth of a white, European child in North Dakota was in 1807, to Isobel Gunn, a woman posing as a man in order to work for the Hudson Bay Company, which hired only men for its labor force (Eriksmoen 2008). White women were not allowed into the territory. Historical evidence suggests that a member of the same brigade, John Scarth, who shared her cabin, raped her. After the birth of her child, Gunn worked as a washerwoman until returning to the Orkney Islands of Scotland. She died in 1861, the same year the Dakota Territory was formed.

The U.S. Army began building forts in the region in 1819. The Dakota Territory was formed in 1861. In 1862, after decades of forced migration, broken treaties, disease, and promises of things that never came, Dakota in Renville County, which is today near the Canadian border, attacked white settlers. Known as the Dakota War of 1862, or alternatively as the "Shakopee Sioux Rebellion" or "Great Sioux Uprising," fighting between Dakota and whites lasted until the Battle of Wood Lake on September 23, 1862. More than five hundred settlers died, as did high numbers of Dakota. The rebellion led to the largest mass execution in U.S. history, when President Lincoln ordered thirty-eight Dakota to be killed in Mankato, Minnesota. These wars and the subsequent occupation of the Dakota Territory are parts of settler colonialism.

Settlers to the Dakotas came primarily from Northern Europe and established homes in the upper Midwest and Great Plains. Like immigrants today, they fled famine, high unemployment, poverty, and overpopulation in Scandinavia. They were farmers and fishermen, accustomed to a harsh northern climate. The Homestead Act of 1862, through which the U.S. government gave land to settlers for "free" so long as they developed the land for at least five years, provided a tremendous economic incentive to the immigrants. My maternal and paternal ancestors obtained land through the Homestead Act.

Fargo was incorporated as a settlement in 1871 in anticipation of the expansion of the Northern Pacific Railroad over the Red River from Moorhead. It was named after William G. Fargo, one of the Northern Pacific Railroad's directors and cofounder with Henry Wells of Wells Fargo Express Company, today's Wells Fargo financial services company. This industrial expansion would not have been possible without the labor of immigrants. In 1887, Congress passed the Dawes General Allotment Act, which broke up large reservations and facilitated the sale of indigenous tribal land to individual Native Americans and white settlers (Biolsi 1992, 1995; Medicine 2001). The primary objective was to abolish communal landownership and facilitate private property ownership. North Dakota was granted statehood on November 2, 1889, on the same day as South Dakota. Two states were created from the Dakota Territory because the two population centers were far apart and it was a large territory. By 1885, serious resistance to the U.S. Army had come to an end, though other forms of resistance have persisted to this day.

Historian Karen Hansen compares the different means by which Dakota and Norwegians attempted to gain full citizenship in North Dakota, particularly in the region of Spirit Lake. Hansen examined court cases that challenged Dakota citizenship and those that provided Dakota with more rights, such as land allotment, taxes, voting privileges, and other entitlements. Court documents revealed the attitude of settler colonials whose "civilizing" mission and resentment of Native Americans sought to eradicate indigenous beliefs and practices altogether. Settler colonialism is an ongoing process that continues to disenfranchise indigenous citizens of this country. It was not, nor is it now, a complete or uniform process.

Unlike some other indigenous nations, "Dakotas at Spirit Lake participated in electoral politics by exercising their right to vote, asserting their citizenship, contesting its limitations, and indefatigably pressing their cases before the Court of Claims" (Hansen 2013, 199). Settler colonialism forced Dakota to shift their worldview from approaching land as a communal resource to viewing land as property to be owned and passed down to other generations. While some chose assimilation, other Dakota sought to maintain cultural uniqueness and communal land. It was not until 1924 that the U.S. Congress passed the American Indian Citizenship Act, which granted full citizenship to all Indians regardless of their "bloodedness" or allotment status. Lakota anthropologist Beatrice Medicine argued, "Despite superordinate governmental dictates and decision-making that has been external to the Native community, tribes have maintained some aspect of cultural and linguistic integrity. Therefore, in assessing public policy and tribal enactment of the rule and regulations, an ethnographic sophistication and an awareness of the interface between two different modes of social organization is essential" (2001, 36).

According to Hansen (2013, 213), for both Dakota and Norwegians, "land-owning was a similar source of power," but the groups pursued differential access to it. Dakota focused on federal legislation and individual land allotments, whereas "Norwegians saw state government as a tool to counterbalance and restrain the market" (209). Norwegian immigrants came to the United States already embracing the notion of private property. They had a different legal status than Native Americans, as immigrants with the possibility of becoming full naturalized citizens. Like Dakota, however, Norwegians struggled with how much to assimilate and how much to retain of their Norwegian customs (Hansen 2013). In contrast to some other immigrant groups, Norwegians rejected the dominant mentality of assimilation, fought to maintain their language and culture, and sought agrarian reform. Norwegians formed the Nonpartisan League, which rejected standard party politics of both Democrats and Republicans (the latter of which was the more progressive party of the time) and called for state ownership of grain elevators, flour mills, and cold-storage plants (202). Norwegians were a powerful voting bloc that shaped North Dakota politics early on.

Despite their mutual appreciation for both land and citizenship, and their more progressive political leanings, Dakota and Norwegians did not form political alliances; rather, writes Hansen, "the shared geographic space was divided by a gaping social chasm" (Hansen 2013, 240). Though Norwegians did not create allotment, they certainly benefited from it. As such, "in the face of the outrage of dispossession, Scandinavians past and present have eluded the thorny past by misremembering it or by living uncomfortably with their personal or ancestral culpability" (236). Hansen chronicles immigrants' "unbridled resentment" toward Native people due to their perceived reliance on the government for necessities. There was an association between Native people who paid taxes and were therefore "competent" and assimilated citizens, and the "incompetent," who did not pay taxes and relied on government. There was little introspection about the destruction of Native Americans' economic base prior to European colonization, their confinement to reservations, and the ongoing eradication of their culture and ways of being. The perhaps unwitting but nevertheless active participation in the process of settler colonialism can be seen in letters from Norwegian immigrants to their families in Norway.

Ethnohistorian Orm Øverland (2009) analyzed 1,650 immigrant letters by rural settlers in the United States from the 1830s until 1914 and noted the troubling lack of mention of Native Americans, whom the settlers were most certainly encountering. Letters from immigrants to Norway portray the Great Plains as a desolate, fierce, and unkind land (see Rølvaag 1927). When "Indians" were mentioned in letters, they were portrayed only briefly as a hindrance to deal with or part of everyday, reciprocal trade exchanges. The letters that Øverland analyzes chronicle hatred and violence as well as practical and personal relations between Norwegian settlers and indigenous peoples (Øverland 2009, 96).

Øverland (2009, 80) notes that between 1838 and 1904, Norwegian settlers mentioned Native Americans just forty-seven times in 1,429 letters. Numbers were slightly higher between 1858 and 1868, with twenty-three of 184 letters mentioning "Indians" and, of these, ten referring to the Sioux rebellion in 1862. Øverland describes settlers who expressed hatred of Native Americans but also those, notably "liberals" in the East, who supported them. Øverland argues that immigrants learned this fear, hatred, and prejudice not only from violent, personal encounters with Native Americans, but from the culture of a rapidly expanding United States, through media and government discourse of westward expansion, though some immigrants appeared to feel empathy toward Native Americans. Iver Lee, a Norwegian immigrant, wrote the following to his family in 1891:

> The government is responsible for the unrest among the Indians. They are in a way the wards of the government. . . . So as the land has gradually been taken from them, their sources of livelihood have diminished and as compensation the government has agreed to supply them with food and clothes. This is done through government agents, but these have been under so little control that they've made themselves wealthy at the Indians' expense. So, the Indians have often suffered from hunger and this is what has led them on the warpath. It seems quite reasonable that they would rather fight for survival than die of starvation. (Øverland 2009, 95)

Immigration was not monolithic, but there is a troubling lack of critical history about the contested frontier and indigenous histories of the Midwest and Great Plains that has served to wipe away the foundations of settler colonialism (Kiel 2014, 12). Critical histories expose the fact that "actions, events, and choices that once seemed random revealed themselves as the harsh result of global forces that dislocated peasants and dispossessed Native peoples" (Hansen 2013, 238; see also La Flamme 2018 and Ostler 2004).

It is beyond the scope of this book to cover the heterogeneities and everyday practices of accommodation and resistance by Native Americans in North Dakota, historically or in the present. The settler colonial past of North Dakota is nevertheless informative in understanding how current Fargo residents see themselves and why refugee resettlement was both desired and contested. Just as Euro-Americans attempted to assimilate diverse groups of Native Americans into the new nation through violence and education with the mantra "Kill the Indian, save the man," so too did the descendants of European settlers desire the assimi-

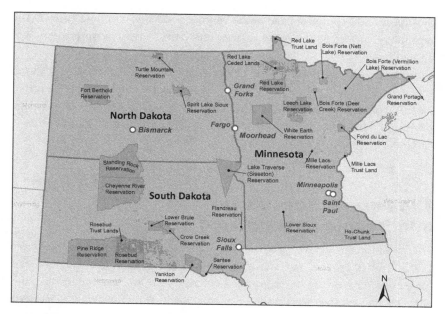

MAP 1.   North Dakota, South Dakota, and Minnesota, including Tribal Nations

(cartography by Angela Gibson, Ball State University, 2018)

lation of diverse groups of refugees—also forced from their homes—into the nation.

In 2017, Native Americans remained the largest group of minorities in the state, with about 5 percent of the total population. According to the North Dakota Indian Affairs Commission, there are five federally recognized tribes and one Native American community located partly in North Dakota, including the Mandan, Hidatsa, and Arikara Nation (Three Affiliated Tribes), the Spirit Lake Nation, the Standing Rock Sioux Tribe, the Turtle Mountain Band of Chippewa Indians, the Sisseton-Wahpeton Oyate Nation, and the Trenton Indian Service Area. About 60 percent of Native Americans in North Dakota live on reservations, and nearly half are under the age of twenty. There are five Indian reservations in North Dakota: Turtle Mountain, Fort Berthold, Spirit Lake, Standing Rock, and Lake Traverse. The latter two are colocated in South Dakota (see map 1). Indigenous nations continue to fight for rights, recognition, and sovereignty, despite ongoing efforts by powerful companies, politicians, and individuals to disenfranchise them, as demonstrated by protests and court cases over the Dakota Access Pipeline (DAPL), which threatens the Standing Rock Sioux's only water source, the Missouri River. Despite years of activism to block the construction of the pipeline, including a federal judge ordering DAPL to revise its environmental analysis, the pipeline was completed and began commercial service on June 1, 2017. The pipeline is part of 250 years of attacks on Native American sovereignty and human rights.

Settler colonialism in the United States is part and parcel of the history of global economic, political, and social expansion of Europeans that connects the rest of the world to the Dakotas in a variety of ways, strands of which can be seen through migration patterns of refugees from Bosnia-Herzegovina and South Sudan to Fargo.

The Former Yugoslavia and Bosnia-Herzegovina

The Balkan Peninsula has long been viewed as a bridge or crossroads between East and West, Europe, and Asia. Empires have attempted to control the region for centuries: the Byzantine, Habsburg, Romanov, and Ottoman Empires all came, changed, and left their legacies in the region. World War One began in Sarajevo, ushering in the modern nation-state, followed by World War Two and then communism. Historian Maria Todorova argues that the metaphor of the bridge not only portrays the region between different so-called distinct geographic regions (East and West) but also "between different stages of growth, and this invokes labels such as semideveloped, semicolonial, semicivilized, semioriental" (1997, 16). This perception is disquieting, because it paints the Balkans, as "abnormal," in a perpetual "state of transition, complexity, mixture, ambiguity . . . considered [by Europeans as] an intolerable state of existence" (58). After all, "one cannot live on a bridge or on a crossroads" (Georgieva 1994, 33; cited in Todorova 1997, 59).

Western Europeans have long portrayed the Balkans as having a so-called frustrating "'handicap of heterogeneity' . . . that has continued to defy easy categorizations and . . . was held responsible for the instability and disorder of the peninsula" (Todorova 1997, 128). Heterogeneity alone was not the problem; the more vexing issue was "ethnic complexity in the framework of the idealized nation-state," which was supposed to lead to ethnic homogeneity, although that did not happen in the Balkan states (175).

Yugoslavia was formed in the wake of World War One and consisted of six republics: Bosnia-Herzegovina, Croatia, Slovenia, Macedonia, Montenegro, and Serbia (including Kosovo and Vojvodina) (map 2). It was a semi-industrialized country with a high standard of living compared to other communist countries. In the communist countries of the Cold War era, Yugoslavs were unique in their familiarity with elements of both communism and capitalism, for example, in

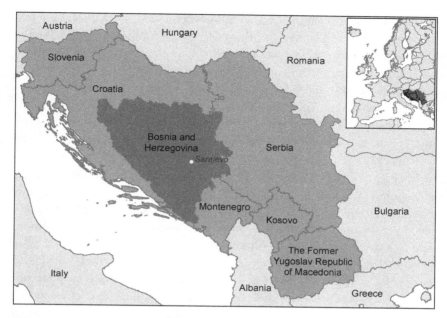

MAP 2.   The former Yugoslavia and Bosnia-Herzegovina

(cartography by Angela Gibson, Ball State University, 2018)

terms of their access to a range of consumer goods and services. Many families were devastatingly poor after World War Two but were able to improve their economic status considerably under communism and with the leadership of Yugoslav president Josip Broz Tito. In the 1980s, as cracks in communist bloc countries began to show, many believed that Yugoslavia would experience a relatively smooth transition from communism to capitalism. However, questions of ethnic origins played a major role in Yugoslavia due to its religious, linguistic, and geographic heterogeneities.

The former Yugoslav state recognized ethnic and religious diversity in the following terms: *Narodi* (nations) applied to constituent peoples, those who were not a majority outside of Yugoslavia; these were Serbs, Croats, Slovenians, Montenegrins, Macedonians, and Bosnian Muslims.[1] *Narodnosti* (nationalities) applied to national minorities that were majority populations elsewhere (Albanians, Hungarians). *Etnički grupi* (ethnic groups) were groups of distinctive people who had a religion other than the three majority religions (Jews) or had no nation-state outside of Yugoslavia (Roma). Religious identity roughly corresponded with ethnonational identity but was not synonymous. In Bosnia-Herzegovina, Croats mostly identified with Catholicism, Serbs with Orthodox Christianity, and ethnic

Muslims with Islam, but there was variation within groups in adherence to religious orthodoxy and secularism (Bringa 1995). In Montenegro's and Bosnia-Herzegovina's constitutions, Roma (Gypsies) were considered *narodnosti*, but in other Yugoslav republics and other Eastern European countries, Roma were categorized as *etnički grupi* (Silverman 2012, 297). Roma in the former Yugoslavia arguably enjoyed more rights than Roma in other communist countries, even during communism, but they rarely competed with others for employment or political clout and occupied the lowest socioeconomic strata (Emigh, Fodor, and Szelényi 2001).

In order to establish a notion of Yugoslav citizenship, the Communist Party of Yugoslavia downplayed social factors such as gender, ethnicity, religion, level of wealth, or age in political identity and participation in favor of a "Yugoslav identity" (Watson 1997, 24). Those men and women who had a good relationship with the League of Communists of Yugoslavia (or simply "the Party"), good social network connections (*veze*), and education and family were considered some of the worthiest citizens. Everyone did not have equal access to social connections or to the Party. From 1945 until his death in 1980, Tito established and, if necessary, enforced ethnic harmony in the multinational state. An example of this top-down form of citizenship was evident in the educational system. From elementary through high school, the state attempted to develop solidarity through lessons emphasizing self-managed socialism and *bratstvo i jedinstvo* (brotherhood and unity) (Höpken 1997, 81–82). The Yugoslav educational system glossed over potential divisionary historical events and wars between the ethno-nations as well as universal civic values based on individual rights. There was no prescription for how to get along in a multiethnic society but rather a focus on how to be Yugoslav. Educational goals sought to develop an ideological identity favoring a collective identity and not a civil society identity, which arguably produced a set of codes for simply conforming to Tito's political system (Höpken 1997). But ethnic identities never entirely disappeared from everyday life (Bringa 1995).

Before Tito died in 1980, the country began to experience economic downturns (Halpern and Kideckel 2000; Hayden 2000). Tito's death marked the beginning of the long slow end of the socialist state and a decade of brutal wars in the former Yugoslavia. After Tito died, the media played a strong role in elevating the role of ethnicity (Žarkov 2007). Some noticed an increase in nationalist rhetoric. By 1991, the country began to violently unravel.

Ethnically homogenous Slovenia declared independence in 1991 with little fanfare, but as ethnically heterogeneous republics declared their own independence, wars broke out: Croatia in 1991, Bosnia-Herzegovina in 1992, and Kosovo/a in 1999.[2] The war in Bosnia-Herzegovina suffered the worst violence in Europe since World War Two. Of a total prewar population of 4.4 million, the war resulted in at least 100,000 civilian and soldier deaths and about 800,000 displaced persons and refugees. Muslims suffered a disproportionate amount of ethnic violence during the war because Bosnian Serbs and Croats targeted Muslims, but there were atrocities committed by all sides. The violence included torture, imprisonment, and death; this was most obvious during the ethnic cleansing of eastern Bosnia by Serb forces at the beginning of the war and the massacre of more than eight thousand Muslim men at the hands of Serb soldiers in Srebrenica in 1995. Bosnian Roma, a majority of whom lived in eastern Bosnia before the war, shared the same fate as Muslims (also referred to as Bosniaks); in other words, they were ethnically cleansed from their homes in eastern Bosnia, imprisoned in camps, and killed, although they are rarely mentioned in accounts of war atrocities (but see ERRC 2004; Latham 1999; Memišević 1999).

Susan Woodward argues that the wars in the former Yugoslavia in the 1990s are "inseparable from international change and interdependence and [are] not confined to the Balkans but [are] part of a more widespread phenomenon of political disintegration" (1995, 4). Western powers, Woodward argues, did not understand the nature of the conflicts and underestimated "the interrelationship that exists between the internal affairs of most countries and the international environment" (3). Until 1994, in North Dakota, the most visible personal connection between the United States and the former Yugoslavia could be seen through soldiers who served as part of the peacekeeping and stabilizing missions in Bosnia-Herzegovina. (General Giselle Wilz of North Dakota was commander of the NATO headquarters in Sarajevo.) The routes of soldiers and refugees uncover historical as well as contemporary global tracks of power. Todorova (1997, 185) puts it this way:

> Understandably reluctant as the West was to involve itself directly in a war in Yugoslavia, it was certainly neither aloof, nor indifferent, nor inactive, nor even unanimous at the time of country's breakdown and throughout its ugly divorce. It is preposterous to refuse to face the responsibility of both internal and external thugs and missionaries who plunged Yugoslavia into disintegration, and explain the ensuing quagmire by "Balkan mentalities" and "ancient enmities." There are equally important practical reasons for the West's final involvement in Yugoslavia. Most of them are prompted by extra-Balkan considerations: the place and future of NATO, the role of the United States as the global military superpower and especially its strategic stake in European affairs, and so forth.

The war in Bosnia ended in 1995 with the signing of the Dayton Accords. The war in Kosovo ended in 2000, but the former Yugoslavia continues to serve as a strategic military site for the United States amid ongoing Russian efforts to exert political influence across the region. The region remains heavily dependent on external economies and continues to struggle politically and economically with high rates of corruption and unemployment.

In a series of articles written by social scientists on the precarious situation of Bosnia-Herzegovina twenty years after Dayton, authors argued that while the Dayton agreement did officially end the war in Bosnia, it also ushered in "a political-economic order of inequality and dispossession, not only of the means of dignified livelihood, but of a future and the agentive capacities to shape that future" (Gilbert and Mujanović 2015). Larisa Kurtović (2015) argues that Dayton-structured reforms produced an unsustainable model of power sharing, while also enabling new forms of structural violence and creating "new (transethnic) surplus populations, that cannot be accommodated within the existing (and largely clientelist) regimes of redistribution" (641). As such, Dayton "bears a strong family resemblance to other forms of neoliberal restructuring, that have over the last twenty years decimated developing economies and welfare states across the world" (641). The precarious postwar years have resulted in a "post-industrial graveyard," run by a small, wealthy elite, a large pool of unemployed and increasingly impoverished citizens, and an insecure middle class largely employed in the public sector. The official unemployment rate in Bosnia-Herzegovina is 44 percent, which does not include temporary or undocumented employment.

More than twenty years after the war ended, dozens of schools in Bosnia-Herzegovina remain ethnically segregated (Surk 2018). In the divided city of Mostar, there are two fire departments, one for Muslims, one for Bosnian Croats (Higgins 2018). However, there is more to Bosnia-Herzegovina than ethno-national affiliation. In 2014, Bosnian youth in cities and towns across the country rose up to challenge the political and economic elite and promote social justice. Because some of them used violence, they were seen by many as "hooligans"; others saw them as a new generation of Bosnians (Kurtović 2015). Anthropologists are looking beyond ethnonationalism to understand post-Dayton Bosnia-Herzegovina, for example, through a variety of social practices (Jansen, Brković, and Čelebičić 2017). Some show how gender and ethnonationalism are mutually constituted (Cockburn 1998; Helms 2007 and 2013) or how ethnonational categories intersect with urban identities (Hromadžić 2015; Maček 2009; Sorabji 2006), while others approach the post-Dayton period of Bosnia-Herzegovina as part and parcel of postsocialism (Gilbert 2006; Jansen 2014).

Bosnia-Herzegovina applied to join the European Union in 2016, but the stability of the European Union itself is in jeopardy with, for example, the financial crisis in Greece, the Brexit vote in Great Britain, worker-led protests in France, and the unsettling and dramatic specter of populist nationalism in Hungary. Igor

Štiks, a Bosnian-born journalist, said of the 2014 protests, "Bosnia is an image of Europe's future: ungovernable populations, exhausted by austerity measures and left to their own devices after the collapse of remnants of the welfare state—a state with no prospect for growth, run by elites of dubious, if any legitimacy who deploy heavily armed police to protect themselves against ordinary citizens." As we witness the rise of populism around the world and austerity measures that demonstrate the ubiquity and false promises of neoliberalism, we can see that "the East is not the only political space of postsocialism," as Kurtović (2015) argues. She continues: "The entire world is still working through the consequences of the demise of a rival political modernity that revolutionary socialism embodied—one associated with greater fairness, equality and substantive redistribution" (655).

Sudan/South Sudan

Like the former Yugoslavia, Sudan has been viewed as a geographic and ideological crossroads between diverse cultural traditions—in this case, linking the Mediterranean, sub-Saharan Africa, and Egypt. Sudan and South Sudan have rich and extensive premodern histories that long predate European contact (Breidlid, Said, and Breidlid 2014; Davies 2014; Edwards 2007). Northern and Southern Sudan had contact and conflicts well before the modern era, especially through the enslavement of Southerners by Northerners (Sharkey 2003). The Turco-Egyptian Empire (1820–81) brought Sudan into the monetized global economy. During this time, Egyptian armies under the wider Ottoman Empire invaded Sudan. South Sudan became a source for slaves, gold, ivory, and timber (Sharkey 2003). Members of the Turco-Egyptian Empire, Europeans, and Northern Sudanese collaborated in raids against the South; millions of Southerners were forced into slavery in the Arab world and beyond.

From 1898 to 1956, the Anglo-Egyptian Condominium controlled Sudan (Collins 1983; Collins and Deng 1984; Daly 1991; Deng 1995; Powell 2003). Emphasizing Sudan's distinction from other Colonial Office territories, the British placed Sudan under the "Foreign Office" rather than the "Colonial Office" and controlled Sudan indirectly by using Egypt as a proxy colonizer (Sharkey 2003). In addition to antagonizing well-established differences between Northern and Southern peoples, the British fostered economic development and education in the North but not in the South. Under British colonialism, the overall socioeconomic transformation of Sudanese society, including new forms of waged labor, created a gendered, occupational, and ethnic labor force and reinforced economic hierarchies that situated Southerners at the bottom (Bascom 1998; Sikainga 1996).

In 1930, to minimize the spread of Islam and anticolonial sentiments by North-erners, the British initiated the "Southern Policy." This policy sought to adminis-tratively and culturally isolate the South from the North, and it contributed to ongoing violence in Sudan throughout the twentieth and into the twenty-first century. The British did not allow Southerners to go to school or take govern-ment positions. They did encourage Christian missionaries to enter southern Su-dan but barred northern Sudanese from entering it (Daly 1991). The British used religion, including religious education, and other mission-based activities to foster the civilizing mission (Shandy 2007; Wheeler 2002). The history of mis-sionary work in South Sudan is significant here because it would, in part, shape not only the conflicts between North and South Sudan, but relationships between Southern Sudanese refugees and Americans in the twenty-first century.

Early missionary work in Khartoum, the capital of Sudan, centered on the re-demption and education of slaves, especially children (Wheeler 2002, 285). The year 1848 marked the first contact in the modern era between Christian mission-aries (Roman Catholics) and Southerners. However, ongoing Catholic attempts at missionization at the end of the nineteenth century were largely unsuccessful due to ongoing disturbances from the slave and ivory trades and attempts from the North to Islamize the South. Nevertheless, Catholic missionaries, joined by Presbyterians and Anglicans, continued their evangelizing efforts into the twen-tieth century (Pitya 1996, 165, cited in Shandy 2007, 41). While colonial govern-ments and missions were often at odds, missionization became increasingly successful during the twentieth century because "both government and mis-sion . . . had an interest in isolating southern Sudan from the disturbing influences—political, religious, educational, and commercial—that came from the North" (Wheeler 2002, 286).

By the 1950s and 1960s, the role of missionaries and churches in building a resistance to the Northern Arab Muslim elite began to take root. Many mission-aries were forced to abandon church activities and focused instead on education. In 1964, the Northern government expelled at least 272 Catholic and sixty-two Protestant missionaries (Wheeler 2002, 294). Despite the work of missionaries during the nineteenth and twentieth centuries, it was the second bout of wars (1983–2005), including violent attempts to Islamize the South, that aided mis-sionaries the most in converting southern Sudanese to Christianity in the 1990s (Johnson 2003, xvi).[3]

Sudan gained independence from its British colonizers on January 1, 1956 (map 3). Violence between Northern government troops and Southern rebels be-gan in 1955 in anticipation of independence. By 1962, full war broke out. The war lasted until March 3, 1972, when the Sudanese government and the South-

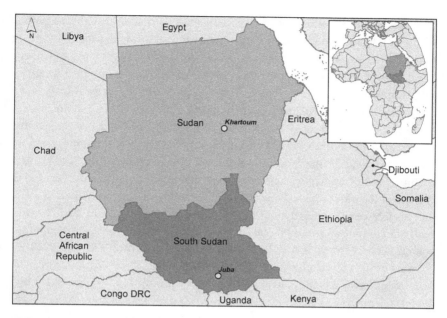

MAP 3.   Sudan and South Sudan

(cartography by Angela Gibson, Ball State University, 2018)

ern leadership of Anyanya reached a peace agreement in Addis Ababa, Ethiopia. The South technically became a self-governing region, but remained isolated, underdeveloped, and dominated by the North (Deng 1978 and 1995). In 1973, following the oil crisis in the West, President Nimeiri invited George H. W. Bush, who was Richard Nixon's ambassador to the UN, to Khartoum. An oilman from Texas who would become vice president under Reagan in 1980 and president in 1988, Bush told Nimeiri about remote-sensing technology that had found that oil might be present in the southeastern part of the country. He added that U.S. oil companies could assist Sudan in finding that oil (Scroggins 2002). In 1974, Chevron was granted the license to drill for oil in southern Sudan. According to Scroggins, Chevron also signed a secret agreement to explore a region in northern Bahr el-Ghazal, where uranium deposits could be refined for use in nuclear weapons (128). In 1978, the South's relative autonomy began to erode further.

In 1983, President Nimeiri declared Islamic *sharia* law. Southerners, the Sudanese Communist Party, and other political dissidents opposed the law. Though sharia was not applied in the South, it was imposed on millions of Southerners who had migrated to the North in search of economic opportunities and to flee violence in the South (Bascom 1993 and 1998; Karadawi 1987 and 1999). While there are Muslim Southerners, more identify as Christian or with indigenous forms of religion and spirituality, or some combination of all three. That same year, after eleven years of relative peace, war broke out between the government of Sudan and the newly formed Sudan People's Liberation Army (SPLA) led by John Garang, who held a doctorate in agricultural economics from Iowa State. "In the early 1980s," explains Scroggins, "foreign aid had paid for almost three-fourths of Sudan's annual budget" (2002, 88–89). As the Cold War waned, the United States and other wealthy countries began to loose interest in the region. U.S. aid to Sudan shrunk from $350 million in 1985 to about $72 million. In 1985, a coup against President Nimeiri succeeded, and the National Islamic Front took control of the government. Omar el-Bashir became president of Sudan in 1993, and his tenure was defined by internal political strife and war. In 2010, he won reelection despite an International Criminal Court arrest warrant against him for war crimes and crimes against humanity. He was overthrown in a coup in 2019.[4]

Wars in Sudan, including the violence that engulfed Darfur beginning in 2003, were fought over religion, oil, gold, and water (Shandy 2007, 31; see also Deng 1995 and James 2007). According to anthropologist Dianna Shandy, "Religion was an ideological force coalescing with economic forces to make the plight of southern Sudanese noticeable to US policy makers" (2007, 31). Oil is located in the Upper Nile and Bahr al-Ghazal provinces. There is gold in Equatoria and a geopolitical importance in the region of the headwaters of the White Nile. Water has long been a source of tension between groups living along what is now the North/South border (Jok 2001; Simonse 1992). In addition to natural resources and religion, Southern military leaders have been fighting over their political differences, attempting to establish their own economic power along ethnic or tribal lines.[5] Civilian populations continued to suffer from unchecked violence, including brutal murders and rape (Hutchinson 2001; Jok 2001). Peace was not brokered in Sudan until 2005. Journalists, activists, and scholars accused the international community of literally and figuratively feeding the wars (Beswick 2004; Deng 1995; Harrigan 2004; Hutchinson 1996; Johnson 2003; Jok 2001; Macklin 2004).

The 1983–2005 wars between North and South Sudan, in addition to inter-ethnic and regional wars, poverty, and disease, resulted in more than four million displaced people and two million deaths, more than Bosnia and Rwanda combined. On January 9, 2005, John Garang signed the Comprehensive Peace Agreement (CPA) with the government of Sudan. Southern Sudanese around the world rejoiced, ecstatic that after a brutal twenty-two-year war, peace was finally in sight. One of the CPA's stipulations was that Garang would become vice president of Sudan, a position the Northern ruling elite had never before granted to a

Southerner. On July 14, 2005, in Khartoum, the capital of Sudan, Garang was sworn in as first vice president. Southern Sudanese flocked to the capital to witness the historic event, and Southern Sudanese across the globe watched enraptured as he took his oath. Three weeks later, on August 1, 2005, Garang's helicopter crashed in the mountains of Uganda, killing everyone on board.

That summer, I was in Sioux Falls, South Dakota, conducting research on the relationship between Southern Sudanese and the city of Sioux Falls. The day after Garang died, 150 Southern Sudanese joined thousands of their brethren around the world by taking to the streets to call attention to Garang's death, which many understandably believed was not an accident. After gathering in downtown Sioux Falls, the mourners participated in a prayer service and then walked to the offices of elected officials. Protesters called on those officials to support the political agenda that Garang had been trying to establish in his first weeks in office, especially the process of seceding from the North, strengthening the global position of the South, and healing the region after decades of war, crippling poverty, and underdevelopment. In the days following Garang's death, so many Southern Sudanese missed work to mourn Garang that Morrell's, a meatpacking plant, was forced to shut down a processing line, resulting in a purported loss of $100,000. Many employees lost their jobs in those two days, but leaders negotiated with employers, and they ultimately got their jobs back.

A critical part of the CPA was a 2011 referendum on South Sudanese independence from Sudan. In 2011, more than 3.8 million Southern Sudanese voted, and nearly 99 percent chose secession. On July 9, 2011, the Republic of South Sudan (ROSS) became a country, and Salva Kiir Mayardit, Garang's second-in-command, became its first president. In 2013, long-standing tensions within the SPLA/M violently reemerged in Jonglei state, central Equatoria, and elsewhere.[6] Military forces led by President Kiir and opposition fighters led by Riek Machar, commander of the SPLA/M-In-Opposition (SPLA/M-IO) clashed, resulting in the killing of thousands of civilians. More than a half-million civilians have fled the country since 2013, and it remains politically, economically, and socially fragile.

On September 12, 2018, Salva Kiir and Riek Machar signed a peace agreement in Addis Ababa, the capital of Ethiopia, the twelfth agreement between them. It was brokered by the Intergovernmental Authority on Development. The agreement facilitates the sharing of the country among major tribes, such as the Nuer and Dinka, and lesser ones. In short, South Sudan has become an "informal protectorate of Sudan and Uganda," with Ugandan troops there to support Kiir's faction and Sudanese troops to support Machar's faction. Mahmood Mamdani, professor of government at Columbia University and the director of the Makerere

Institute of Social Research in Kampala, Uganda, believes that "South Sudan will likely turn into a tribally fragmented society. The state will reflect this fragmentation and will in turn deepen the societal fragmentation" (Mamdani 2018). The only way that South Sudan can forestall tribal fragmentation and violence is to recognize the agreement's deficiencies and build a pan–South Sudan political process that will trump military conflict.

Oil will once again serve as the blood running through the Sudanese body with a pending agreement to share oil between Sudan and South Sudan. South Sudan has the third-largest oil reserves in Africa, but the oil fields were destroyed during the most recent conflicts. PBS news reports that five oil fields will be operational again by the end of 2018, promising $5 billion over the next five years (Mednick 2018). Because oil accounts for 98 percent of the country's budget, some attribute the peace deal to oil, which is shortsighted and could bring more corruption. In focusing on oil and ushering South Sudan into the global economy without addressing the history of interethnic violence, corruption, and competition, peace will remain elusive.

Above, I noted work by Larisa Kurtović (2015), who argues that we are all, in various ways, living in a postsocialist world order because, since the fall of communism in the 1990s, there have been no large-scale alternatives to capitalism. Similarly, South African artist and curator Gabi Ngcobo (2017) argues that "we are all postcolonial," though some contexts are more postcolonial (or postsocialist) than others. Sharad Chari and Katherine Verdery (2009) encourage scholars to think "between the posts" in order to better understand contemporary forms of imperialism and capitalist accumulation, including neoliberalism and state-sanctioned racisms. For example, communist activism is part of Sudan's twentieth-century history (Hale 1996), and the former Yugoslavia was impacted by Western European forms of colonialism and global processes of racialization (Baker 2018). Separating histories of postsocialist and postcolonial regions diminishes the wider, overlapping, and ongoing impacts of these processes that resulted in profound global, political, economic, and social changes that extend all the way to North Dakota. Bringing them together allows us to better challenge newer forms of empire, capitalism, and racism that result in dispossession, war, and forced migration. Decolonization, warns Ngcobo, "means creating new configurations of knowledge and power—and that can be a messy procedure" (Ngcobo 2017). Some envision alternative political and economic formations as a challenge to capitalism, but Tsing and others point to a more practical stance: "One works with what is available" (Tsing 2015, 278), even if that means within the system, in the ruins of capitalism, in the corridors of state government, or in a refugee resettlement office.

Refugee Resettlement (1948–1999)

Fargo is an assemblage of histories and people that have converged on the physical landscape of the eastern Great Plains, thereby creating a unique city; and refugee resettlement is an assemblage within an assemblage. Resettlement assemblages are comprised of governing bodies from localities all over the world and massive governing bodies, such as the United Nations High Commissioner for Refugees (UNHCR), the International Organization for Migration (IOM), and other humanitarian aid organizations and governments. Refugee resettlement coevolves with other assemblages, which then mutate into something else, something that New Americans and members of the dominant population in Fargo cocreate. As Tsing describes, "Patterns of unintentional coordination develop in assemblages" (2015, 23). In the rest of this chapter, I explain the recent history of resettlement to Fargo and how and why refugees get to Fargo, which thereby changes the cultural landscape of the city and affects the everyday lives of those involved in the process.

Refugees are persons who have been persecuted in their own country, have crossed a border into another country, and are unable to return home due to fears of persecution. The United Nations (UN) established the first definition of "refugee" in 1951 to accommodate the needs of displaced Europeans after World War Two. Prior to this time, people fleeing political situations were considered to be in "exile." In 1967, the definition of "refugee" was expanded to include more people fleeing persecution, including those in postcolonial countries, but the definition remains limited. For example, gender and sexuality are not specifically mentioned as criteria for which someone might be persecuted. A refugee is defined as "a person who is outside his or her home country, or if he or she has no home country, then outside of the country in which he or she last habitually resided, and who is unable or unwilling to return to his or her country of nationality because of persecution or well-founded fear of persecution based on the person's race, religion, nationality, membership in a particular social group, or political opinion" (UNHCR 1967, 16–18).

Before World War Two, the U.S. government had no formal domestic policy regarding refugees. Refugees and immigrants found assistance through religious and ethnic organizations. After the war, following the admission of over 250,000 displaced Europeans, Congress enacted the Displaced Persons Act of 1948, the first refugee legislation. This legislation provided for the admission of an additional 400,000 displaced Europeans who had been allies during World War Two. Demonstrating the role that global social and economic politics played in defining and resettling refugees, in the 1950s and 1960s, U.S. resettlement practices almost exclusively admitted persons fleeing communist regimes (Hungary, Poland, Yugoslavia, Korea, China, and Cuba). Most of these waves of refugees were assisted by private ethnic and religious organizations, which formed the basis for the public/private role of contemporary refugee resettlement (Wright 1981).[7] It was during this time that the idea of *refugeeness* emerged as a juridical category. Randy Lippert (1999, 304) explains: "Both in the intensifying international Cold War with the so-called Second World [like the former Yugoslavia], and in the nationalizing Third World [such as Sudan] (which, of course, were not mutually exclusive historical events), therefore, refugeeness became a Western moral-political tactic within broader objectives. It became a way of relating to and intervening into that which was deemed illiberal and uncivilized."

The Refugee Act of 1980, signed by President Carter, incorporated the UN definition of "refugee" and standardized resettlement services for refugees admitted to the United States. The Refugee Act of 1980 requires annual consultations between the Office of the President and Congress to determine refugee admission numbers for the fiscal year (October 1 to September 30). Representatives of the executive branch, state and local officials, and nongovernmental organizations (NGOs) testify before each house of Congress, and then the State Department proposes the nationalities and groups to be identified for resettlement. The president determines the admission ceilings for the coming year. In the 1980s and 1990s, the United States accepted about 100,000 refugees per year. The Refugee Act of 1980 was supposed to diminish the role that formal politics played in admitting refugees, especially politics that discriminated against humanitarian aspects of resettlement. It aligned more with international standards of human rights than the ideological and geographical bias of previous eras—for example, the emphasis on admitting refugees from communist countries, who "voted with their feet" against what the United States deemed to be repressive and/or anticapitalist regimes (Loescher and Scanlan 1986).

Despite the Carter administration's desire to uncouple refugee resettlement and formal politics, resettlement continues to be a barometer for national and international politics. Since World War One, the government and military of the United States have been involved in diplomacy, wars, and violence all around the globe. Since World War Two, some of these engagements have occurred overtly, such as the wars in the Middle East and Asia (Korea, Vietnam, Iraq, and Afghanistan), and others more covertly, such as wars in Central America (El Salvador, Guatemala, and Nicaragua) in the 1980s and in Africa (Somalia, Kenya, and Niger) in the 1990s. Refugee resettlement has served as a way of rewarding allies and demonstrating goodwill to the survivors of those wars and thereby building international diplomatic relations.[8]

Refugee resettlement relies on partnerships between states and NGOs, from the local to the global.[9] First, refugees must meet the UN definition of a refugee (see above) and then apply for refugee status in the United States via UNHCR. The U.S. State Department processes applications for refugee status submitted to UNHCR. Preparation for citizenship in the United States begins before refugees arrive. Funded by the State Department's Bureau of Population, Refugees, and Migration (PRM) and conducted by the IOM and other organizations abroad, cultural orientations provide information about predeparture processing, travel, the role of the resettlement agency, housing, health, employment, transportation, education, money management, cultural adjustment, and rights and responsibilities (laws relating to driving, rape, and domestic violence). Before they arrive and after they are admitted, refugees are provided with orientations to American culture and are encouraged to attend the sessions, but attendance is not required for admission into the United States.

The IOM provides refugees with interest-free travel loans for their transportation costs to the United States.[10] Before traveling to the United States, refugees must sign a promissory note to repay their airfare. This means that refugees arrive in the United States already in debt, and they must begin to repay their loan three months after their arrival. If they are unable to begin paying, they are responsible for contacting IOM to set up a payment plan. Failure to comply with the established payment schedule can result in legal action.

The State Department and the Office of Refugee Resettlement (ORR) determine where refugees will be resettled based on housing availability, job possibilities, family reunification cases, and levels of community support. ORR partners with state refugee offices and the agencies involved in the U.S. refugee resettlement program known as Voluntary Agencies, or VOLAGS. About half of these VOLAGS are religious organizations that include resettling refugees as part of their core mandate. Others are state-based, as in Iowa, or related to ethnicity, such as the Ethiopian Community Development Center.[11] ORR also looks for "preferred communities" to resettle refugees, which are cities that "allow ample opportunities for early employment and sustained economic independence. In addition, they support special needs populations" (ORR 2016).

Lutheran Social Services began resettling refugees in 1948, mostly Protestant Germans and Eastern Europeans fleeing the post-Nazi regime and communism. From the 1940s until the 1980s, churches volunteered to sponsor families on a case-by-case basis, and families took turns supporting refugees. Most refugees resettled to North Dakota during these decades came from Southeast Asia and Eastern Europe, with a few families from Africa and the Middle East.

Larry Olson became involved with refugees in the 1970s through his church's sponsorship of Cambodian and Vietnamese families. Larry was trained in social work and was strongly motivated by social justice. In the 1970s, Larry said, "every church had a refugee family." It was considered "trendy." Churches provided daily, hands-on mentoring that included driving families to and from appointments or to work, helping with food, clothing, and other household products, and acculturating to Fargo. During these years, Larry noticed a spectrum of motivations among churches sponsoring refugees, from a "Christian passion" to help the less fortunate to a desire to evangelize, on the assumption that "this is our chance to save not only their bodies but their souls." He recalled examples of Vietnamese and Cambodian families who complained about sponsors pressuring them to baptize their children, forcing them to go to church, or failing to provide information about obtaining a divorce. While many VOLAGS have a religious affiliation, as of 2017, the State Department explicitly forbids them to proselytize. During the time when individual churches sponsored refugees, there was no training for sponsors, orientation for refugees, or oversight in general. Larry recalled significant variation in approaches to sponsorship and feelings of burnout, or "compassion fatigue" (Loescher and Scanlan 1986, 198; Ong 2003, 82).

In the 1970s and 1980s, the resettlement office consisted of just one staff person, who completed paperwork and acted as a liaison in the community. Larry advocated for a transformation in refugee resettlement that facilitated more training and accountability. In 1981, he started the Unaccompanied Refugee Minors (URM) program through LSS, which was separate from the main resettlement program. The URM program places refugee children under the age of eighteen in foster families and provides case management. After that, Larry moved to Bismarck to work as the state refugee coordinator for a few years but returned to LSS in Fargo to oversee the transformation of refugee resettlement from a church-sponsored program to a more formal, bureaucratic agency.

New American Services (NAS) is one of dozens of programs under the umbrella of LSS of North Dakota. Founded in 1919 as an adoption agency, a century later LSS has more than three hundred employees across the state. About a third of them work in Fargo. Other LSS programs focus on housing, youth, adoption, disaster relief, poverty alleviation, rural communities, and addiction. LSS programs receive their funding from different sources, and they mostly have separate staff for each of their programs. Funding for NAS mostly comes from the Department of Health and Human Services, but NAS also receives mandates and funding from the State Department via the Bureau of PRM, from national VOLAGS, and from other grants and in-kind donations. The two VOLAGS that monitor NAS are Lutheran Immigration and Refugee Services and Episcopal Migration Ministries. "Though the scope of its service is broad," reports a *Forum of Fargo-Moorhead* article on LSS's centennial celebration, "LSS is perhaps most often associated with refugee resettlement" (Huebner 2019). As such, I use NAS and LSS interchangeably. Most people refer to the resettlement agency simply as "LSS."

Although some individuals supported refugee resettlement early on, Larry said there was no institutional, systemic support for refugees. In fact, in the 1970s and 1980s, many agencies, including public schools and medical clinics, refused to cater to the specific needs of refugees. For example, Larry reported that in the 1980s, when LSS began resettling Cambodians, teachers in the school district protested having to teach Cambodian children. They said they had made accommodations for Vietnamese students but did not have the resources to serve a new group of undereducated, non-English-speaking students. Schools argued that because churches had brought refugees to Fargo, churches should be responsible for them, even their education.

Schools and some other public institutions sometimes defied Section 601 of Title VI of the Civil Rights Act of 1964, which requires all programs or activities receiving federal financial assistance to provide language interpreters.[12] The law states that providers are required to make reasonable, documented efforts to provide information and services in a language or medium that the person served can understand, free of charge to the client. If possible, in order to ensure that the individual does not feel threatened or misguided, the provider should avoid using family members as interpreters. With few qualified interpreters in Fargo, a lack of will to find funding for interpreters, and fewer refugees compared to larger cities, family members, including children, often acted as interpreters.

In the meantime, Larry attended national resettlement conferences and discovered what programs in other states and cities were doing, what services they were offering, and what kinds of support they were receiving. He became more outraged at the lack of support for refugees in Fargo. He told me that other resettlement agencies were not seeing the kind of resistance that he was seeing in Fargo. In the 1980s, LSS resettled 100–250 refugees per year at most. In 1992, LSS resettled 572 refugees, more than twice as many as the previous year. As the numbers of refugees coming to Fargo increased, voices of resistance to resettlement and anti-immigrant attitudes became louder, but in keeping with its Christian mission, "Guided by God's love and grace [to bring] healing, help and hope to those in need," LSS persisted.

Larry and Norman Swenson, CEO of LSS, organized a meeting with the superintendent of schools. What they thought would be a small, intimate meeting to ease interagency tension turned out to be a "tense and intense" meeting of about fifteen people, including school principals, who wanted to know the exact number of arrivals. In short, schools viewed resettlement as a local issue that required advanced planning, and they believed that LSS was withholding information that was necessary for schools and students. In line with its local and (inter)national mission, LSS saw resettlement as a global, local, and moral issue. Larry said they tried to explain to school officials that "this is not LSS . . . withholding [numbers] from you. This is the situation in the world." Larry continued: "At one point [Norman] said, 'You have to realize, we're responding to the people in camps and if they don't get out, they could die in the camps.' And the vice superintendent—I just remember—he *slammed* his notebook down on the table and he said, 'Well, then let them die!' . . . I was in total shock. It's like, I can't believe I just heard this."

Larry and Norman left the meeting. It was difficult for them to hear what they viewed to be cold-hearted lack of support and no attempt to understand, much less respond to, how global politics were playing out—or not playing out—in Fargo. Larry approached refugee resettlement as a Christian and an activist, a way to support people who suffered from war that included harmful U.S. foreign policies and practices. Regardless of who or what kinds of policies produce refugees, it must be acknowledged that schools, public assistance programs, and others who had to work with refugees felt frustrated by the lack of transparency that overwhelmed their organizations and required a new approach to their work, an approach that required interpreters and knowledge about war, migration, and cultural differences. These organizations were required to provide for the needs of the whole community, not only refugees. At the same time, there was ugliness directed toward refugee kids who were different from the majority population and plenty of racism and xenophobia in Fargo that was hard to separate from the organizational hurdles required to work with refugees.

In the meantime, church sponsorship waned as compassion fatigue grew and fewer congregations were willing to sponsor refugees. With a few sponsors, LSS could not secure or maintain high numbers of new refugee arrivals. Larry further explained that overinvolvement, and then waning support by churches and underinvolvement by state agencies—in addition to an anti-immigrant climate among some in the larger public—resulted in

> refugee families . . . getting out of here as fast as they could. . . . They were hearing, in California, you can go to a doctor that speaks their own language! . . . They'll help you . . . and you don't have to be tightly controlled by other groups [e.g., churches]. And so there got to be kind of a real swinging door here. Refugees were coming in and moving out within three to four months. . . . And everyone could say, "Oh yeah, it's the weather, it's this and this and this and this." . . . [But] the systems as a whole were resistant.

The situation in Fargo in the 1990s supported Steven Vertovec's (2007) claim that top-down efforts to promote and embrace diversity are unlikely to succeed. A group of people accustomed to a particular reality, who may be mourning the loss of that reality or who are required to change their labor practices as a result of new forms of diversity, were unlikely to embrace a new one, particularly when those practices were imposed on them. As a result, Lutheran Immigration and Refugee Service briefly considered closing the North Dakota program. Larry told me that he went to speak with the governor about the plan to end the resettlement program and the governor responded emphatically that North Dakota needed to keep its resettlement program because "it was the most Lutheran state in the country." This posited a humanitarian approach to resettlement, which was different from the economic approach that future advocates would take in defending resettlement in North Dakota's booming economy.

Though public institutions in Fargo continued to resist resettlement, Larry said that he and other refugee advocates "started circling the wagons. . . . We felt under attack, and then we just decided, damn it, you know, if nobody else is gonna do it, we'll do it. . . . We started developing . . . this complexity of services." Larry continued: "Change was not gonna come voluntarily. . . . Systems do not change of their own accord. They change when they absolutely have to." Speaking angrily at times, tearing up at others, Larry recalled what the resettlement program meant to him personally and what he felt the program meant to the city of Fargo. He summarized the program's relationship to the city with a quote from Gandhi: "First they ignore you, then they laugh at you, then they fight you, then you win." Enough volunteers, teachers, human service workers, and neighbors had the experience of getting to know refugees personally and as individuals, not clients or forms of diversity to be managed, and so acceptance of New Americans grew little by little. However, while Larry and others felt that New Americans made Fargo better, others believed that his methods were confrontational and abrasive and that he and other advocates were forcing humanitarianism down the city's throat.

The Surge (1999–2001)

Native Americans, Euro-American whites, and refugees and immigrants from around the world have been entangled in separate and overlapping historical assemblages, like European colonialism. These historical processes, along with individual agency, eventually resulted in the copresence of—and encounters between—these groups in Fargo. If an assemblage, or a city, is like a ball of yarn connected to countless other balls of yarn around the world, then there are bound to be knots: "To learn about an assemblage, one unravels its knots" (Tsing 2015, 83). This chapter ends with a thick description of a big knot: the surge in resettlement to Fargo at the turn of the century.

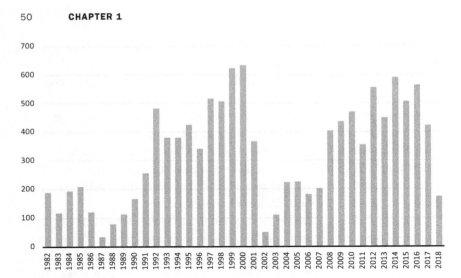

FIGURE 1.1. Refugee arrivals to North Dakota, 1982–2018. Data compiled from the Office of Refugee Resettlement's annual reports to Congress (ORR 1982, 1996, 1999, 2006b, 2009, and 2018), Lutheran Social Services of North Dakota (LSS) for the years 2000–2001, and reports to the *Grand Forks Herald* for 2017–2018 (Chaduvula 2018).

Resettlement to Fargo increased throughout the 1990s, peaking in 2000 with 633 new refugee arrivals, though nearly as many were resettled in 1999 (figure 1.1). According to the 2000 census, the foreign-born population of Fargo was 6 percent of the total population, and the local newspaper reported that refugees comprised 76 percent of that foreign-born population (*Forum of Fargo-Moorhead* 2001). Based on interviews with different ethnic group leaders and statistics kept by LSS, Cass and Clay counties (Fargo and Moorhead welfare agencies, respectively), and schools in Fargo-Moorhead, the *Forum of Fargo-Moorhead* estimated that there were about 6,000 refugees in Fargo in 2001. The U.S. census does not track refugee populations, and LSS does not track all secondary migration, so determining the number of refugees in a given city requires some guesswork, and the number of refugees in Fargo was likely larger. The *Forum of Fargo-Moorhead* reported that the largest ethnic groups in Fargo-Moorhead in 2001 were Bosnians (2,000), Vietnamese (1,000), Sudanese (800), Somalis (700), and Kurds (500).

In December 2001, after six months of investigation by several reporters, the *Forum of Fargo-Moorhead* published a series on the impact of refugees on the region and how they were adjusting to life in the United States. "Valley to the World" appeared in three eight-page special sections. Its purpose was to educate the public about the influx of refugees into the city and was published at a timely moment—three months after 9/11. In May 2001, a white father and son were convicted of assault after beating a twenty-one-year-old Sudanese man with a club. Fargo police urged the FBI and the U.S. attorney's office to consider it a hate crime, as the perpetrators used racist epithets in describing the incident. Shortly after the attack, regional social and religious leaders issued a statement imploring residents to make the area "'a place of acceptance and warmth that values its diversity in cultures, colors and different views. We can and will thrive and grow as we respect and honor our differences, our diversity'" (*Forum of Fargo-Moorhead* 2001). This appeal became a catalyst for the "Valley to the World" project, after which the introduction to this book is named.

Articles focused on heart-wrenching human-interest stories, with histories of the wars in Somalia, Sudan, Liberia, Bosnia-Herzegovina, and Nigeria. They featured local agencies serving refugee populations and disagreements between them and gave accolades to volunteers who mentored refugees. These articles also featured businesses that employed refugees and the labor that refugees contributed to the city. Questions framing the series were: "So who are these people? Why did their compasses point to F-M [Fargo-Moorhead]? How do they benefit the community? Are they too much of a burden? How much are they being helped?" (*Forum of Fargo-Moorhead* 2001).

"Valley to the World" highlighted North Dakota's labor shortage and the cost of increased human diversity to city institutions, such as schools and welfare offices. Some employers reported that "without refugees they couldn't fill jobs, and that they're a necessity to keep businesses going" (*Forum of Fargo-Moorhead* 2001). One business that benefited from refugee resettlement was Cardinal IG, a glassmaking plant. Dave Pinder, the plant manager, came to Fargo in 1998 after attending West Point and then managing a paper factory in northern Maine. More than half his workforce was refugees and immigrants. In a 2007 interview, he told me that he expected workers to show up on time and work hard and did not permit fighting or racist or sexist jokes at his plant. All positions were full-time with benefits, and the plant ran twenty-four hours a day, five days a week. Workers earned $10.20 per hour but could make up to 52 percent profit sharing, which is a retirement plan that gives employees a percentage of a company's profits based on its quarterly or annual earnings and which Pinder said required "working very smartly, eliminating waste, and working their tail off." Pinder knew the first and last names of all of his workers, which he demonstrated on a tour of the plant. He confidently waved, shouted over the noise of machines, and shook hands as he told me each employee's name. In 2005, Pinder supported local photographer Meg Luther Lindholm in chronicling New American workers at the plant, and her photos were displayed at the Plains Art Museum (Pantera 2005). In 2011, Pinder became president of the company.

Ted Hardmeyer of Dakota Molding, a rotational molding plant that opened in 1996, told journalists that without refugees his company would be "out of business." In 1996, refugees comprised nearly two-thirds of its workforce. In 2001, it had seventy employees, twenty of them recent immigrants. He also said that turnover was high due to monotonous entry-level work. He wondered aloud "if he exploited new Americans with low wages," but hoped that the plant offered them "a chance to move up." He noted that the company faced communication challenges with New American workers but that it readily worked around them because it was worth it to the company to "make those accommodations" (*Forum of Fargo-Moorhead* 2001).

Out of 328 major employers in the region, 117 responded to a 2000 Fargo–Cass County Economic Development Corporation survey about employment trends. Of those 117, 35 percent said they had hired refugees or other New Americans, but they did not see refugees as significantly reducing the region's labor shortage due to language barriers (*Forum of Fargo-Moorhead* 2001). Fifteen years later, the Development Corporation reported a positive work ethic among New Americans but added that English language acquisition and orientation to culture in the workplace continued to pose challenges for New American workers (GFMEDC 2015).

LSS used this information to argue that resettlement was economically beneficial for the region. In 2000, the regional economy was rapidly expanding and diversifying while also attempting to maintain its industrial and agricultural base, which proved to be challenging, as two of every three young people were leaving the state. According to North Dakota State University sociologist Richard Rathge, the state of North Dakota needed workers to compensate for a significant drop in its entry-level workforce of twenty- to thirty-four-year-olds, a group that declined 16 percent in population from 1990 to 2000 (*Forum of Fargo-Moorhead* 2001). They left in search of more opportunities and better jobs. These were the years before the oil boom. It was not until 2009 that North Dakota, which had begun to reverse a long-term trend of young people leaving, had the highest rate of in-migration of any state, making the state younger than it had been in years (North Dakota Census Office 2009). In the early 2000s, however, the swelling immigration to North Dakota of both refugees and Latin migrants was a major reason that North Dakota showed any population growth at all in the 1990s and contributed to Fargo's 22 percent population rise over the same time period (*Forum of Fargo-Moorhead* 2001). At the same time, New Americans were putting a strain on the city because some of them had different needs and desires than U.S.-born residents, which required new forms of labor and sociality on behalf of the dominant population—for example, using language interpreters to communicate with the newcomers and understanding that frequent smiling and making small talk was not the way that everyone preferred to communicate, particularly with strangers.

In the face of criticism from all sides, LSS struggled to keep up with the demands of so many clients. Unlike previous church sponsors, who volunteered their time and had few reporting requirements, NAS staff were required to document case management and employment services. According to staff who worked for NAS at that time, few files were completed, though reporting requirements were not strict enough at the time to warrant agency sanctions. In the mid to late 1990s and into 2001, caseworkers had dozens, sometimes hundreds, of cases at any given time, and they received little to no training. Sometimes, as I chronicled in the introduction, staff failed to meet new arrivals at the airport or set up the apartment before the client arrived. Alma, a resettlement worker, recalled,

> Because we had more than double [the] clients each year than what we are receiving right now [in 2008], I think that at that time we are only providing for their basic needs. . . . As long as we know they have apartments set up, that's great. And we just didn't have time, that we do have now, or services, to be able to spend more time in one-on-one on clients. . . . And over the last ten years . . . I had over twelve different supervisors, so (laughs) . . . turnover is always [high]. . . . It's always been a problem. . . . Everybody has a different style, everybody kind-of interprets things [i.e., policies and procedures] differently. So that [was] kind-of rough.

Like Alma, Anna Overgaard came as a refugee and worked as a case manager. She recalled this period as "insane" and "a total shock." She explained that the expectations from clients, the agency, and the city were unreasonable and unmanageable. According to Anna, caseworkers simply did not have the time to do all that was asked of them, not with such high caseloads. Many resettlement staff—particularly those who came as refugees—lived in the same apartment buildings as their clients, which made for an uneasy, if not impossible, separation between work and home life. As such, they were essentially expected to be working constantly, while also integrating into U.S. culture at the same time as their clients. Many resettlement staff told me that it took years to learn how to tell their clients "no" and instead to help them do more for themselves. All of this resulted in insufficient attention to clients, high rates of turnover and burnout, and strained relationships with community partners. Kristi Johnson, a county welfare worker, recalled,

> I quite honestly don't know how the LSS worker was communicating with these people. [Refugee clients] didn't speak *any* English, none whatsoever. . . . They are trying to show me that they don't have enough food and they're in this house with all these kids and that they had all these canned goods when they didn't know how to open them (laughs). . . . What sticks out in my mind in that case is that my idea of what priorities and needs are for families is so different from the volunteers, from the church, and LSS. 'Cause here I am talking about the food for the family [and] there's volunteers coming in putting up curtains (laughing).

NAS relied heavily on volunteers for assistance with day-to-day responsibilities. Without volunteers, the program would have likely collapsed, but volunteers had even less accountability than resettlement staff (Erickson 2012). State workers often mentioned the lack of accountability standards of both resettlement workers and volunteers. LSS became a pariah among state agencies, other nonprofits, and the wider public. It was a target for a broad range of persons with anti-immigrant attitudes, advocates who felt refugees needed more support, and state and nonprofit organizations that saw LSS as the epitome of organizational mismanagement. As one welfare worker put it, the general attitude was this:

> Clients weren't being served, they were being dumped . . . by LSS. And it was real hard for us to manage, but we're such a tiny piece of it. They come in, they apply, they go. You know we're not on the front lines with case management and finding housing and jobs and teaching skills and orienting and networking and all of that. Clients were falling through.

A director of another nonprofit organization explained:

> I think they have forgotten how to collaborate. They can't do it all by themselves. Nobody can. However, are they asking others to interact? Uh uh. . . . I talked to the director of Cass County Social Services, and she said she was ready to bring criminal charges against LSS for the way they were misusing their funds. She didn't, but I mean there's been a long history of not liking each other and not sharing. I don't think you can survive without collaborating. I don't think there's anything you can do all by yourself.

Everyone had an opinion about what LSS was supposed to be doing ("more!"), but many stakeholders were angry at the lack of transparency and communication with other agencies and actors. By the early 2000s, the formal rhetoric of human service organizations in Fargo included partnerships, networks, and collaboration, with the ultimate goal of economic self-sufficiency for their clients. However, different agencies had different definitions of economic self-sufficiency and different notions of how to achieve it and what these collaborative networks should look like. A unifying factor among different stakeholders in refugee resettlement was their critique of LSS. Kathy Hogan, former director of Cass County Social Services, argued,

> The whole community needs to be involved in the decision-making process regarding how many to take—if we are all mutually responsible. So I don't like the idea that we have the responsibility with no voice. And you know, after 9/11, when there was a significant decrease in [arrivals], this community can manage that. And the systems are placed to manage that resettlement population. But when we were at six hundred, we did not have the capacity, and . . . my concern was that we were seeing so many unmet refugee needs during those few years, that it was . . . wrong.

While Hogan acknowledged that refugees had unmet needs, she did not believe that it was the welfare state's responsibility to address all of those needs. She felt the resettlement agency especially had a responsibility to define refugees' needs and then work on addressing them. Hogan told journalists that while many refugees found jobs within the first few months, "most of them don't stick with the same company." Some were dealing with depression and trauma. The Fargo Health Center reported that 50 percent of its refugee patients suffered from depression and virtually all of them had some kind of mental trauma (*Forum of Fargo-Moorhead* 2001).

After September 11, 2001—though none of the 9/11 terrorists were classified as refugees—the largest drop, proportionally, in any category of immigrant admission to the United States was in refugee resettlement. In 2001, the United States resettled an average number of refugees, about 70,000, because by September, many of them had already been resettled. In 2002, the United States resettled one-third that number, the fewest since 1977 and until 2018, as demonstrated by North Dakota's resettlement figures over time (figure 1.1). The dramatic decrease in new arrivals to Fargo after 9/11 could have allowed LSS to recoup and reevaluate its program, address its relationships with other agencies and organizations in the region, and build a better reputation in the city. Instead, the organization seemed to fall into more disarray. Just weeks before 9/11, longtime NAS director Larry Olson resigned. Between 2001 and 2006, there were more than ten different directors of NAS, with high turnover rates for many case management staff, though a few intrepid caseworkers and employment staff remained at the organization. One staff member told me that staff would place bets on how long a new director would last. For about a year, in 2001–2002, the director for the Center for New Americans in Sioux Falls served simultaneously as the director for NAS in Fargo. It was not until 2006 that Christian Novak became director of NAS. Serving until 2012, he provided stability to the once-fledgling agency.

Conclusion

Refugee resettlement brought postsocialist and postcolonial people and practices to Fargo, where they encountered new and different assemblages of settler colonialism, race, neoliberal capitalism, and Christianity, as well as progressive practices that challenged the dominant culture and that could lead to new forms of commoning in Fargo. The surge in refugee resettlement at the turn of the century made refugees more visible and shed light on these global assemblages. To explain the seemingly sudden presence of new people in the city, many turned to Lutheran Social Services for answers and explanations, which is why I focused my ethnographic gaze first on the resettlement agency, the subject of chapter 2.

THE NGOization OF REFUGEE RESETTLEMENT

Walking into New American Services (NAS) in 2007 felt like taking a trip to a secret place. The *Forum of Fargo-Moorhead* reported in 2001 that immigrants lived "a sort of subterranean existence in F-M," and it still felt like that six years later. Outside of English-language-learning classrooms, private gatherings, and the break room at some job sites, NAS was one of the few public places in the city where people of color might outnumber whites, and English was just one of many languages spoken. I went to my first NAS staff potluck in Fargo eager to make a good impression on my interlocutors. Smells from foods around the world greeted me: Somali staff brought *samosas* (a savory pastry stuffed with vegetables or meat); an Iraqi man brought homemade bread; a Bosnian woman brought *pita* (a traditional dish in the Balkans of thinly rolled filo dough filled with meat, cheese, or vegetables); a Croatian woman known for her extraordinary baking skills brought homemade *kolač* (cake); others brought cookies, *tabbouleh* (a mixture of parsley, tomatoes, barley, lemon juice, and oil), and sweet tea. Every potluck was different and reflected the cultural backgrounds and culinary interests of the staff. Due in part to the large number of refugees resettled in Fargo, spaces like this are no longer such an anomaly.

In this chapter, I explain the policies, politics, and everyday practices of NAS. To highlight tensions surrounding citizenship and the role that nongovernmental (or nonprofit) organizations play in Fargo under neoliberalism, I analyze these practices in terms of the "NGOization" of refugee resettlement. NGOization refers to the proliferation of NGOs under neoliberalism as extensions, or new faces, of the state.[1] There are tens of thousands of NGOs around the world; many of them proliferated after World War Two alongside the establishment of the United Nations in postwar Europe and in newly independent states emerging from decolonization. NGOs contribute to a global civil society sector that works alongside, and sometimes in opposition to, government sectors.

The term "NGO" usually refers to large organizations with global reach, such as the United Nations or Amnesty International, and to smaller organizations in the field of international relief and development assistance. NGOs have diverse and overlapping roles and responsibilities, from distributing charity to igniting and growing social movements and serving as the operational arm of government and multilateral assistance agencies. Because NGOs are most often affiliated with "international assistance" in the United States, similar organizations are more frequently referred to as "nonprofit organizations." NGOs are types of nonprofit organizations. Anthropological studies of NGOs are useful for understanding refugee resettlement in the United States because of the explicit international components of refugee resettlement and resettlement's ties with multilateral NGOs and governments, such as the UNHCR and IOM and governments in refugee-sending countries. The professionalization of refugee resettlement changed dramatically in the 1990s, driven by local, national, and global processes. During these years, the world witnessed unprecedented levels of humanitarian crises, including three times as many natural disasters as compared to the 1960s, and by the end of the decade, there were twenty-seven major armed conflicts raging (Forman and Stoddard 2002, 242). As NGOs became increasingly important vehicles for humanitarian assistance around the world, filling in gaps where governments failed, refugee resettlement agencies in the United States became extensions of and alternatives to these other forms of assistance.

Between 1970 and 1994, the number of international relief and development organizations based in the United States grew from fifty-two to more than four hundred (Forman and Stoddard 2002, 243). Refugee resettlement agencies are facing some of the same pressures that NGOs around the world are facing, including the pressure to become more efficient as well as "more exclusive, and rule-based or [to] remain subject to the competitive market forces that regularly overwhelm the cooperation ethic among NGOs" (256)—hence my application of the NGOization framework to resettlement agencies. Furthermore, due to historical and contemporary assemblages, such as those I highlighted in chapter 1, U.S.-based nonprofits are inseparable from the international NGO community as a whole (270).

I view NGOization through a feminist lens. In feminist scholarship, NGOization is defined as a steady increase in the number of NGOs run by and for women worldwide (Jad 2007, 177; cited in Hodžić 2014, 222). According to Saida Hodžić, "NGOization is not a descriptive, but an evaluative notion: it does not simply refer to the boom in NGOs, but understands this phenomenon as harmful for feminism. . . . The NGOization paradigm has become institutionalized as a master narrative and now serves as a normative theory that structures the feminist field of knowledge about NGOs" (2014, 222). Feminist critics of NGOization claim that NGOs have enabled the depoliticization of social and women's movements, their appropriation by donor-driven agendas, and a neoliberal co-optation of feminist practice (Adelman 2008; Schuller 2012). Hodžić refutes this claim by explaining how the NGO paradigm can "obfuscate power relations in feminist organizations as much as it reveals them, and that we need to pay close attention to the trips of failure, fall and contamination that haunt it" (2014, 222). In a similar fashion, Aradhana Sharma argues that NGOs "can simultaneously bureaucratize women's lives *and* unleash unexpected forms of empowerment" (2014, 95; emphasis mine).

In chronicling the transformation of refugee resettlement over time (1948–2018), I challenge desires to paint a master narrative about what refugee resettlement was or is—purely humanitarian or simply unaccountable—by building on the literature on NGOization. As Hodžić argues, master narratives of NGOs and social movements, such as the women's movement, are not uniformly progressive or radical. Advocates for refugee resettlement in Fargo were not uniformly progressive either. Some people desired more refugees to fill the robust labor market, while others looked to refugee resettlement as an extension of global human rights. As an NGO predicated on referral services, New American Services partnered with employers, state agencies and schools, churches, and other nonprofits, but members of these partner organizations were not always willing partners, and many of them critiqued NAS practices.

What was NAS mandated to do? What did it say that it did? What did it actually do? What could it have done better? In order to explain what NAS's organizational identity meant for staff, clients, and the city of Fargo, I provide an overview of everyday resettlement practices and beliefs about resettlement staff, and how I interpreted their work in regard to the larger social issues I have laid out in this book: race, citizenship, and diversity. As to what caseworkers are mandated to do, the Cooperative Agreement between the Government of the United States (the State Department and the Bureau of Population, Refugees, and Migration) and VOLAGS outlines the responsibilities of VOLAGS. This includes what constitutes "basic needs support," "core services," and "performance standards."

Professionalizing Refugee Resettlement

By the 1990s, nationwide, resettlement programs began to shift to more bureaucratized, state-level management agencies marked by the increase of paid staff over volunteers and more stringent reporting requirements than in previous decades, including management of individual case files, which early sponsors were not officially required to keep. Many societal changes and movements begin in this haphazard way and are consequently disorganized but also more flexible, for better and worse. Only once they generate sufficient momentum, whether from a local or national level, or some combination of both, are organizational systems put in place to make them more orderly. This comes with a different set of costs and benefits and a different "politics of need interpretation," a phrase coined by sociologist Nancy Fraser (1987) to describe a two-tiered welfare state in which men are not stigmatized for accessing social welfare (in North Dakota, men access farm subsidies), but women, especially Black women, are considered social failures for accessing social welfare (see Roberts 1997).[2]

Refugee resettlement in the late twentieth century was administered on a local level, often through religious institutions that sought to provide humanitarian assistance to poor refugee families. The primary goal was to provide only modest temporary relief, to facilitate economic self-sufficiency, and to help refugees navigate the job market, new social institutions, and new forms of accountability and professionalism. The development of refugee resettlement was contingent on public/private partnerships among actors with competing ideas about the needs of their clients, staff, and the general public, and these relationships were shaped by neoliberalism.

Partnerships in the context of neoliberalism correspond to an advanced liberal rationality that specifies a reduction in the reach and power of the state while demanding alignment with other authorities and experts to accomplish the work of government. The idea is that there are many roles to fill, that the government should not be doing all of them, and that private organizations play different but nevertheless important roles than public and governmental bodies. Such partnerships are seen as "flexible business ventures[,] . . . investments where everybody wins, undertakings where the parties involved do not remain silent, subsist and survive, but consult, prosper and thrive." In such relationships, "notions of culture, emotion and oppression are, of course, absent" (Lippert 1998, 393). Staff in refugee resettlement agencies navigated national policies, local cultures, and different ideological terrains on an everyday level. They were also among the first people that newly arrived refugees met in Fargo. In this way, refugee resettlement agencies serve as gateways to citizenship. They perpetuate some hegemonic cultural ideals, but challenge others.

According to Italian philosopher Antonio Gramsci, civil society and the state have many complex faces that collude in promoting and upholding hegemony (Buttigieg 2005). Hegemony is another way of discussing the process of "manufactured consent," or the process of getting people to believe in their own oppression—for example, labor and consumer practices, certain beauty standards and regimes, and the idea that those in power deserve to be in power despite the fact that the playing field is uneven from the start. The concept of "civil society" encompasses a broad range of nonstate actors, such as NGOs, churches, and social movements. Some argue that the strength of civil society can serve as a crude index for the health of a democratic society, but under neoliberalism, this is misleading (Stubbs 1999). Instead, as Lynne Haney (2010) argues, many civil society institutions are simply new faces of the state; they do not challenge state power, but uphold it. In her work on refugee resettlement in California, Aihwa Ong contends that "studying power in the United States, perhaps more than in other societies, requires that we think not in terms of an overarching state apparatus, but in terms of a multiplicity of networks through which various authorities, nonprofit agencies, programs, and experts translate democratic goals in relation to target populations" (2003, 80).

Like many NGOs, New American Services is neither strictly public nor private. It receives most of its funds and mandates from the federal government, but its services are carried out by private agencies in partnership with other nonprofit organizations and state actors. As I mentioned earlier, "NGOization" refers to the proliferation of NGOs under neoliberalism and, in feminist terms, a coopting of progressive politics by said organizations. Feminist scholars have begun to question sweeping criticisms of NGOization and instead have shown how NGOs can foster as well as hinder progressive politics. Building on Donna Haraway's metaphor of the cyborg—an early, groundbreaking response to humanism that challenged traditional notions of gender, feminism, and politics by rejecting rigid boundaries such as those between "human" and "animal"—Hodžić suggests that NGOs "also embody 'transgressed boundaries, potent fusions, and dangerous possibilities'" (Hodžić 2014, 231, citing Haraway 1991, 154).

"Like cyborgs," Hodžić argues, "NGOs have ambivalent origins" (2014, 231). Feminists presume the parents of feminist NGOs to be the paternal and patriarchal (and neoliberal) state and the women's movement, but, like cyborgs, NGOs "are not always faithful to their origins" (232). As such, Hodžić urges us to consider NGOs as "productive" in their capacity to "foment new spheres of political activism." But, she continues, "they are not innocent, and their effects are unpredictable and ambivalent" (232). One reason for this ambivalence is that some NGOs are structured to mirror the state, with increased performance standards and bureaucracy, while others emerge out of social movements, for example, domestic violence shelters (Morgen 2002). Refugee resettlement has more flexibility and room to accommodate differences and diversity than many state institutions do, but it is increasingly structured like the state and as such faces some of the same limitations.

Bob Sanderson was the CEO of LSS of North Dakota from 2005 until 2016 and worked in state welfare administration for thirty years before that. He used the following analogy to describe the similarities and differences between private and government sectors:

> The analogy that I always used was government was sort of this big cargo ship in the middle of the ocean that would take you about two weeks to turn the thing around to go in the other direction. The private sector was a little speedboat that could just do what it wanted. And I really have found out that that's not so true. We [in the private sector] operate under a lot of the same . . . rules, employment issues, and many of the same kinds of restrictions that government does. So it isn't anywhere near the speed that I thought it was. I think the one thing that is really much nicer about the private sector is that you really can go out and start new things without having to ask a bunch of people for permission. You know, in government you are going to go through layers of bureaucracy and politics . . . to get something done. . . . So in that way, it is much easier and much better and much more creative.

There are similarities and differences in the governing structures and social practices of public and private institutions, though neoliberalism has blurred these distinctions. There is more bureaucracy at LSS than there was in the church sponsorship era, but less bureaucracy—and accountability—than most strictly government agencies. However, NGOs have more flexibility and room for creativity, which can result in better services.

A "Standard" Refugee Resettlement Case

The following is a hypothetical, composite refugee resettlement case based on hundreds of cases that I have been a part of, either as a former case manager or as a researcher and volunteer.[3] Using this "standard" case allows me to protect confidential information about clients while giving a sense of what refugee agencies are mandated to do according the Cooperative Agreement.

The forecast for the weekend includes a low temperature of minus 27, not including wind chill, which will make it feel like minus 50. On tonight's five-o'clock news, words to describe this weather included "bitter," "dangerous," "frigid," and "bone chilling." The lead story of this morning's paper was entitled "Why Do We Live Here?" and the gist of it was that there is more to Fargo than the cold weather; if nothing else, living in such a climate was something to be proud of. The article was not very convincing. Today it was clear and sunny and around 20 below when we met at the storage house next to LSS to do another apartment setup. Most of the employment staff and case managers were there. We complained about the cold but joked with one another and did the job. We took breaks inside the truck's cab to warm our painfully cold hands. In between talking to clients on cell phones, staff quickly loaded mattresses, bed frames, sheets, couches, tables, chairs, and boxes of mismatched dishes into the truck. Once the truck was loaded, we caravanned to the apartment buildings in the neighboring town of West Fargo, where many new families are placed. On other days, we went to south Fargo, to another low-income apartment block that LSS works with. Later, I helped Qualili buy food and toiletries for the new family at Walmart. He reminded me that I was to always choose the cheapest product because the family would buy nicer things once they got jobs.

If there was help from volunteers or interns, once we started unloading, we usually set up the apartment in an hour or less. That includes washing and putting away dishes, setting up the bed frames and making the beds, putting away linens and toiletries, and arranging the sparse furniture. There are multiple guidelines from the Cooperative Agreement and U.S. occupancy laws that can be confusing for families. For example, each child in the family must have his or her own bed, and only two siblings of the same sex are allowed to occupy each bedroom. It's impossible to find four- or five-bedroom apartments that the refugee cash assistance stipend will cover, so LSS places large families in adjacent apartments, even though they will likely use the space how they deem fit, for example, all sleeping in one apartment.

Before a family arrives at the Fargo airport, the resettlement agency receives an e-mail and a fax alerting it to the impending arrivals. The agency knows roughly how many refugees it will be responsible to resettle in a given quarter, but plans can change quickly. Sometimes staff know a week in advance before a new arrival comes; other times they have less than twenty-four hours to prepare. In any case, they must make arrangements for the family or individual. From 2006 to 2016, about 90 percent of refugees resettled to Fargo were family reunification cases, which means that the people coming had family members in Fargo who agreed to provide support and guidance. Such cases are required to have an "anchor," a relative who lives in the same city or within one hundred miles. Refugees who come to the United States without family sponsorship are referred to as "free cases." A "free case" must live within fifty miles of a resettlement agency affiliate for the first four months; however, if refugees who are part of a free case move more than fifty miles away from a resettlement affiliate, they can file for a "placement exception form," which must be approved by the state refugee coordinator.

Staff are responsible for finding, securing, and furnishing the family's apartment. They might begin by searching the storage unit for items donated to the program, such as chairs, mattresses, couches, lamps, baby strollers, or car seats,

TABLE 1 Sample Reception and Placement Evaluation and Safety Checklist

PA name:		Case #:	Home safety check conducted by:
Case size:	DOA:	# of occupants	Date home safety check conducted:
Address:			Temporary (T) or permanent (P) housing:

Compliant housing and all required furnishings must be provided <u>upon arrival</u>.

ACCEPTABILITY	COMPLIANT	FOLLOW-UP NEEDED. SEE CASE NOTES.	DATE FOLLOW-UP COMPLETED/ INITIALS
Housing is decent, safe, and sanitary based on federal housing standards or local or state standards if they are higher.			
Both the housing site/complex and neighborhood appear safe.			
SPACE			
Local minimum standard for habitable area requires a minimum of bedrooms/sleeping areas for the people living here.			
SAFETY			
All areas and components of the housing (interior and exterior) should be free of visible health and safety hazards and in good repair. Complete a thorough check of the house to ensure the following:			
There is no visible bare wiring.			
There is no peeling or flaking interior paint or plaster.			
There is no visible mold.			
There are no detectable dangerous or unsanitary odors.			
Emergency escape route(s) have been identified and are accessible.			
Fire extinguishers can be easily located and are accessible where required.			
All windows and outside doors have working locks.			
Appropriate number of working smoke detectors; assure that it has working batteries.			
Windows are in working order with no evidence of broken glass.			
Heat, ventilation, lighting, and hot and cold running water are adequate.			
Electrical fixtures are in good repair (check for light bulbs, check electricity).			
LEAD SAFETY CHECK			
Residence either built after 1978 or meets all lead safety requirements.			

ACCEPTABILITY	COMPLIANT	FOLLOW-UP NEEDED. SEE CASE NOTES.	DATE FOLLOW-UP COMPLETED/ INITIALS
APPLIANCES AND FIXTURES			
Kitchen: residence equipped with a stove, oven, and refrigerator in good repair.			
Bathrooms: residence equipped with sink, flushing toilet, and shower or bath in good repair.			
GARBAGE AND EXTERMINATION			
Easily accessible storage or disposal facilities for garbage			
No evidence of current rodent or insect infestation			
DISABILITY ACCOMMODATION			
In cases of refugees with disabilities, housing should be free of, or permit the removal of, architectural barriers and otherwise accommodate known disabilities, to the extent required by law.			
Identify disability:			
AFFORDABILITY			
To the extent possible, the family should be able to assume payment of the rent at the end of the R&P period, based upon projected family income from all sources. The family should be left with sufficient resources for other essential expenses (food, transportation, utilities, etc.) after rent payments are made.			
Length of lease agreement:			
Monthly rent: $	Security deposit: $		Waived: Yes / No
FINAL ASSESSMENT/COMMENTS:			
Based on the above finding on this date, I find this housing meets the basic minimum standards set forth in the Cooperative Agreement.			
Signature:	**Print name:**		**Date:**

and load them onto the truck. What staff cannot supply with donations, they purchase at Walmart. (Table 1 provides examples of the checklists that staff are mandated to follow when receiving new clients.) Most refugees live in one of three apartment complexes in Fargo and West Fargo. Staff bring furniture, assemble bed frames, make beds, and put dishes and food in the kitchen. On a nice day, one can see children and families walking about and playing in courtyards and in parking lots. The agency receives $950 from the federal grant that it uses to pay the family's first month's rent and down payment and to purchase furniture, household supplies, and clothing.

FIGURE 2.1. The author with NAS staff after an apartment setup.

Photo by Tracy Kuchan, 2008.

Apartment setups were taxing but usually fun. They were especially trying when case managers had high caseloads and tight schedules and no volunteers or interns to help. When time allowed, apartment setups were an occasion to build staff camaraderie (figure 2.1), even friendships and romantic relationships. For example, friends of mine met while working at the resettlement agency in Sioux Falls, and today they are married with five children.

On spring days in 2008, three or four staff members and an intern would regale me with life stories and tales of previous apartment setups. In turn, I would share stories with them about my caseworker days in Sioux Falls or my life in Bosnia. We would engage in races to see who could set up a bed frame faster, we would pay attention to small details such as putting up curtains, and smokers might have a cigarette when the setup was complete. In 2000, at the height of resettlement to Fargo, with so many new arrivals, high caseloads, high staff turnovers, scarce donations, and a paucity of volunteers, many people, including New Americans, told me that LSS did not always fulfill its obligation to fully furnish the apartments, for example, with chairs, dishes, sheets, or other necessities (*Forum of Fargo-Moorhead* 2001).

Before 9/11, caseworkers would meet families at their arrival gate at the airport, but since 9/11, they must wait until the family passes through airport security. The case manager is ultimately responsible for picking up the new family at the airport, but if the case is a family reunification, then family representatives accompany the caseworker to the airport. If the caseworker does not speak the language of the new arrival, and no family is present, then they try to bring an interpreter. Watching family and friends reunite after months, even years, of separation was one of my favorite parts about refugee resettlement.

Witnessing individuals who had walked from villages in South Sudan to Ethiopia, back to South Sudan, and who eventually found a modicum of refuge in the Kakuma Refugee Camp in Kenya embrace in a sterile airport is an emotional experience. I witnessed young men hug each other, at once crying and laughing, hysterically, incredulous at their fate after surviving so many forms of violence and abandonment. Per cultural practices in Sudan (and until they became aware of the assumptions of homosexuality of such practices in the United States), reunited men would hold hands and embrace as they walked out of the airport and into their new life.

From the airport, a representative from NAS, usually the caseworker, takes them to their new home, an apartment complex filled with other refugees and low-income residents, where they eat a meal ideally prepared by someone from their home region. Within twenty-four hours of arrival, the caseworker provides an orientation to the apartment. The lack of tailored orientations was a source of tension among some New Americans. As I explain more in chapter 5, Bosnians came from a semi-industrialized country and most (but not all) had access to electricity and plumbing in the former Yugoslavia. When caseworkers explained to them how to flush a toilet or turn on a water faucet, they felt deeply insulted. There was a similar attitude of disdain among others from semi-industrial countries or those who had lived in urban settings, for example, Iraqis. On the other hand, I met refugees who did not know how to open a car door and had no experience with multilevel buildings, electricity or running water, and heating or cooling appliances. Some Southern Sudanese, as well as some Liberians, Somalis, and Burundians, were among this latter group. In the beginning, they struggled to keep warm in the winter, understand the difference between the refrigerator and freezer, or why there were so many different kinds of soap and detergents.

The next step in resettlement is paperwork. Caseworkers gather information on family history and background, previous residences, wartime experiences, and medical and educational history. Once the resettlement paperwork is complete, the caseworker, case aid, or volunteer escorts the newcomers to appointments around the city. One of the first appointments is the Social Security Office, where refugees show their I-94 Form, a travel document from the Department of Homeland Security that is an admission record to the United States and proves they are permanent legal residents and able to work legally. New arrivals also meet with someone from Cass County Social Services, where they apply to the Supplemental Nutritional Assistance Program (SNAP) and for Refugee Medical Assistance

(RMA), a form of Medicaid, government healthcare for eligible low-income families, which is available to refugees upon arrival and for up to eight months after arrival, unless they obtain health insurance through an employer.

Caseworkers help to make medical and dental appointments for the family, enroll children in school, and act as liaisons with housing managers and other social service providers. Families with prominent healthcare concerns, including mental and/or physical problems caused by war, poverty, disease, displacement, or age—and families with children—typically require more time and resources than smaller, healthier families. Some resettlement agencies assign these more challenging cases to specific caseworkers who only deal with clients with medical problems or who are on welfare. I was an "impact case manager" at LSS in Sioux Falls, which meant that I worked with clients who were not able to become self-sufficient in the first eight months, mostly single mothers and elderly persons. In some agencies, there are medical caseworkers to help refugees with medical problems and, more recently, resettlement agencies have developed a team-based approach to case management, with different caseworkers for health, education, and social services. Some refugees arrive already speaking English, have work experience, and need little case management, if any at all.

In addition to SNAP and RMA, refugees receive Refugee Cash Assistance (RCA), a monthly stipend from the federal government based on family size and income. Most of this money goes back into the local economy for rent and other housing expenses. There are two different funding sources for distributing RCA: the Reception and Placement Grant, which gives individuals or families a monthly stipend for up to eight months, or until they get a job, and the Match Grant program, which is a fast-track program with a higher monthly stipend but lasts only four months, with the understanding that the individuals will be able to find a job quickly. Those in the Match Grant program might have had formal employment experiences, speak English, or are single and able-bodied and do not have children or elderly family members to care for.

In order to receive RCA, adults are required to attend English-language-learning (ELL) classes upon arrival. There are barriers for adults to learn English, especially those who are employed or who care for children or elderly family members. In Fargo, the classes were located away from the resettlement agency, the welfare agency, job sites, and the apartment complexes where most refugees lived upon arrival. New Americans are responsible for getting themselves to and from class, but public transportation in Fargo was inefficient, and few could afford a car, especially in the first year, when ELL courses were mandated. Sometimes caseworkers drove clients to classes or found a volunteer or family member to drive them, but this was not sustainable. ELL programs in Fargo do not provide childcare.

In the initial months, refugee clients meet with employment specialists, who assesses where they might work, provide assistance in filling out applications, and accompany clients to interviews. Most refugees, regardless of educational or employment background, begin work in hotels, restaurants, and factories. Those who speak English have more options, for example, in retail or the nonprofit sector, but those with higher education or professional training struggle to find work in their field or to have their education easily acknowledged or certified in the United States, and most ended up in low-skill jobs or the nonprofit sector. In addition to basic needs, reception, placement, and employment services, within thirty days of arrival, resettlement agencies are responsible for providing refugees with an orientation to the community. These classes proved an ideal place to learn how refugee resettlement worked with the city and what values it espoused and promoted. Moreover, they showed the many faces of refugee resettlement, the state, and citizenship.

Cultural Orientation

Cultural orientation took place four hours a day, four days a week, for two weeks. Guided by the Cooperative Agreement and led by resettlement staff and staff from the public and private sectors, cultural orientation included the following topics:

1. The role of the resettlement agency in sponsorship (What is LSS mandated to do?)
2. Public services and facilities (welfare agencies, healthcare clinics, and education)
3. Personal and public safety (the police, driver's education)
4. Public transportation
5. Standards of personal and public hygiene
6. The availability of other refugee services (NGOs and nonprofits)
7. The importance of learning English
8. Personal and household budgeting and finance
9. Information on permanent resident-alien status and family reunion procedures
10. The legal requirement of each adult refugee to fully repay his or her IOM transportation loan
11. The legal requirement to notify the U.S. Department of Homeland Security of each change of address and new address within ten days[4]

12. The legal requirement for males between the ages of eighteen and
    twenty-six to register for the Selective Service within thirty days of arrival

The Cooperative Agreement states that the local resettlement agency shall carry
out its responsibilities in cooperation with ORR and the Department of Health
and Human Services, with state and local governments, and with other publicly
supported refugee services programs, so NAS invited staff from other agencies
and institutions to be a part of the orientation. Cultural orientations are among
refugees' first formal introductions to U.S. forms of citizenship and offered a lens
on how the resettlement agency and other official institutions in Fargo viewed citizenship, but they also reflected what refugees wanted to learn.

Classes were predicated upon pragmatic aspects of everyday life, such as how
to dress in the winter, ride the bus, shop for groceries, and apply for jobs and welfare, and they were designed to minimize misunderstandings. For example, a
New American went grocery shopping one day and did so by putting her goods
into a bag rather than a shopping cart. Someone in the store witnessed this and
called the police on her for shoplifting. As a result of that incident, some orientation sessions mention that most people in Fargo use shopping carts or baskets to
gather their food, only putting groceries into bags after they have been purchased.

The first week of cultural orientation in Fargo focused on key aspects of social
citizenship by emphasizing rights and duties in the United States: educational, resi-
dential, legal, health, and welfare systems, as well as citizenship as a legal process
that comes with rights (Miranda, voting) and responsibilities (Selective Service, being a good renter or homeowner). British sociologist T. H. Marshall (1950) argued
that social citizenship under advanced capitalism necessitated a strong educational
system to act as an equalizer, and a strong welfare state to act as a safety net in a
society that advocated for full equality among its members but also promoted capitalism, an inherently unequal economic system. Under neoliberalism, however, social citizenship has come to be thought of as the responsibility of individuals to
reduce their burden on society, especially on the welfare state (Ong 1996 and 2003).

The second week of orientation primarily promoted economic citizenship.
Economic citizenship in advanced capitalist nations places the most worth on
property ownership, wage work, and consumerism (Cohen 2003; Collins 2008;
Kessler-Harris 2003). Promoting wage work and consumerism above all else
means placing less emphasis on family, neighborhoods and friends, spiritual values and religious practices, not to mention forms of activism and leisure that do
not revolve around economic imperatives. Under neoliberalism, economic citizenship and social citizenship work hand in hand to support entrepreneurialism,
individualism, an unfettered free market, and smaller government, especially a
dismantling of the welfare state.

NAS staff wanted their clients to be successful in the United States. Doing so meant introducing them to forms of neoliberalism and ways of controlling or governing oneself and others that promoted worthy social and economic citizenship. Barbara Cruikshank describes this form of governance (in Foucauldian terms, "governmentality") as "forms of action and relations of power that aim to guide and shape (rather than force, control, or dominate) the actions of others" (1999, 4). Governmentality views the state as more than an apparatus of government; instead, it is a way of ruling and accessing power through everyday interactions and social relations through various institutions that do not automatically fit under the rubric of the state, such as NGOs, schools, and religious bodies (Foucault, Burchell, Gordon, and Miller 1991). These autonomous sites are not part of the formal state and tend to be guided by neoliberalism and enterprise logic, not communal or humanitarian interests (Sharma and Gupta 2006). Cruikshank argues that the making of citizens occurs through "technologies of citizenship: discourses, programs, and other tactics aimed at making individuals politically active and capable of self-government" (1999, 1). NAS introduced refugees to technologies of employment, education, social services, housing, and healthcare. Like NGOization, this "will to empower," as Cruikshank puts it, "contains the twin possibilities of domination and freedom" (2). Orientation classes at NAS offered these twin possibilities as members of different agencies and organizations introduced refugees to basic rules of conduct for living in Fargo but also offered the possibility of more and different kinds of freedom, and the possibility for commoning, for seeing beyond differences and building new solidarities.

While there were many differences among resettlement staff and their clients in terms of gender, race, ethnicity, religion, age, ability, and so on, a significant dividing line between resettlement staff and many of their clients was socioeconomic class, as demonstrated in orientation classes. Classes promoted hegemonic aspects of worthy citizenship that aligned with middle-class values defined in neoliberal and consumerist terms. NAS staff used themselves as examples for how refugees could obtain middle-class status, including jobs, homeownership, English language skills, the ability to send remittances to family "back home," and purchasing consumer goods such as televisions and cars. In this way, staff elevated their own status as professionals in the hierarchy of racialized citizens in Fargo. Like social workers in the 1950s, as described by Walkowitz, resettlement workers "probably never fully realized the consumer dream, [but] like many other 'middle-class' Americans, they were susceptible to the popular media's idealization of this consumerism as a standard experience" (1999, 214). At the same time, staff offered progressive voices and spaces against discrimination on the basis of race, ethnicity, and religion. Though middle-class status was actively promoted as the most desirable, staff also addressed homesickness, responsibilities to family far away, struggles with language and new customs, and feelings of being a stranger in a strange land. Below, I describe two orientations that I observed in Fargo but also draw upon eight orientations that I participated in as a case manager in Sioux Falls in 2001–2002. First, I explain what was said at orientations, and then I provide my interpretations about deeper, underlying messages that presenters sent to newly arrived refugees and how refugees responded.

Observing Orientation

The room is crowded but quiet as people speak in hushed tones in different languages. Some are more animated than others, but most look tired. Two people sleep with their heads on the long tables in front of them; others nibble on donated snack food or drink tea or coffee. Interpreters sit among them, speaking quietly. On a given day in 2000 or 2001, the group would have included dozens of new arrivals from Europe, Asia, Africa, and/or the Caribbean. They would have been Bosnians, Albanians, Southern Sudanese, Somalis, Kurdish Iraqis, Cubans, Vietnamese, Haitians, with maybe a few persons from Burundi, Djibouti, Sierra Leone, Eritrea, Rwanda, or Togo. I remember presenting at the cultural orientations in Sioux Falls in 2001–2002, when the basement room was packed with ripe, warm bodies and the smell of cigarette smoke after breaks. In 2007–2008, when I observed the classes in Fargo, it was a small group of seven, from Sudan, South Sudan, and Iraq.

Orientation Schedule

Week 1: Legal, Social, and Educational Rights and Responsibilities
Day 1: Laws and the role of the police
Day 2: Public health and wellness programs and the welfare state
Day 3: Schools for children and adults; the roles and responsibilities of NAS
Day 4: Driving, housing, and weather
Week 2: Employment
Day 1: Overview of entry-level employment
Day 2: Tips for how to succeed at entry-level jobs
Day 3: How to fill out a job application
Day 4: How to interview

The Law

As more refugees arrived in the 1990s and stayed in Fargo, the city appointed a refugee liaison officer to prevent misunderstandings, explain laws, and create communication and trust between the police force and refugees. Amy Swenson was the first refugee liaison officer. She approached LSS about coming to orientation classes, largely because refugees requested more information from her about what the laws were. Her first presentation was thirty minutes long. The longer she worked with New Americans, the longer her list of things to address grew, until the law-enforcement orientation day included a four-hour presentation with breakout sessions. Amy based her orientation topics on conversations and experiences with New Americans. In an interview in 2007, she told me that "too often people in power decide what other people need." She wanted to hear what New Americans needed. When she first started working with New Americans, one of the biggest problems was domestic violence, so that became a key topic at orientation.

In 2007, Swenson stepped down, and Alex Gangstead took the position. She came to her first orientation dressed in her police uniform and presented on driving laws, alcohol and drugs, rape, early marriage, domestic violence, child discipline versus child abuse, policies and procedures for police officers, and what to expect from encounters with police, including Miranda rights and the right to an attorney. Using a series of scenarios, Swenson slowly explained each topic, gave examples, and stressed short- and long-term consequences for not obeying the law—for example, jeopardizing housing, employment, cash assistance, and applications to become legal citizens, and, in some cases, risking deportation.

Swenson explained that the government requires two pieces of information about every automobile: registration and license plates with updated stickers. I imagined how some of the participants interpreted this information, as I had recently seen a newly arrived woman struggle with how to open a car door. I wondered how she interpreted the information about how to obtain an updated sticker for a license plate. I thought about the refugees I had known over the years, who saw driving as a prominent symbol of freedom and independence but who did not want to attend driving classes and felt that insurance was a waste of hard-earned, much-needed cash—hence the emphasis on driving laws on the first day of orientation. Misunderstandings or different interpretations of law left some refugees, like Southern Sudanese, feeling that they were being racially profiled, whereas police officers felt that they had evidence of Southern Sudanese driving without a license or insurance and wanted to protect people from accidents involving inexperienced drivers. To address these concerns, cultural orientations also featured a representative from the Department of Motor Vehicles, who reiterated some of the same points Swenson made and outlined the necessary steps in obtaining a driver's license and the importance of insurance. The driving test in Fargo in 2008 was offered in six languages: Arabic, Spanish, Vietnamese, Somali, Bosnian, and Russian.

Participants were encouraged to ask questions; most did so through an interpreter. Presenters spoke for a minute or two and then paused so that interpreters could share the information. Once participants stopped talking, presenters continued. Sometimes participants fell asleep; at other times, they engaged in discussion. For example, some chuckled when Alex recommended not lying to police officers or making them nervous when they pull you over, saying with a smile, "You don't want us to be nervous." In another scenario, Alex explained that one must be twenty-one years old to drink alcohol and explained that many refugees have problems with alcohol, especially drinking and driving. Some laughed when Alex said regarding rape, "No means no, even if you're already in bed." I surmise that people laughed at this comment due to (1) discomfort, (2) lack of familiarity and possibly disbelief and even disagreement with the concept of "No means no," or (3) an acknowledgment of personal experience with the scenario (refusing sex or being refused sex, for example).

One man asked, "A woman hits herself to fool the police. What happens?" Alex answered, "We don't know who is lying, so police have to uncover the truth. Just because you're arrested doesn't mean you will be convicted. Details help. Remember that domestic violence also affects housing, RCA, and other financial matters." Another man proposed the following scenario: "Kids hit other kids and someone calls the police. Then what?" Surmising that parents were worried that they would be accused of abuse and the state would remove the children (which did happen), Alex dryly answered, "We're not idiots. We talk to people, look at evidence, look at the whole situation, like marks and handprints. We know there are misunderstandings [between kids and other kids and between kids and parents]. You have the right to discipline your child in appropriate ways." A Liberian woman said that she knew "rebellious kids, African kids, who don't want to listen and want to be like American kids." Alex explained that the police can help parents by explaining how to take away privileges, such as not allowing kids to go out with friends, talk on the phone, or play video games, and they could try to help parents figure out why kids rebel and get parents the help they need. She stressed that parents who do not speak English fluently should ask for an interpreter when speaking to the police, not pretend to understand what is happening or allow children to interpret, or misunderstandings could occur. (I address the relationship between police officers and New Americans more in chapter 4.)

Public Health and Welfare

A representative from public health, Mary Miller, spoke on the importance of getting tested for tuberculosis, which she described as "a very, very serious disease," and other chronic diseases (e.g., AIDS) and, when applicable, to take the prescribed medication. The refugee health nurse from the Family Healthcare Clinic, Maureen Fernandez, introduced health prevention and a program that paired new arrivals with more established New Americans. Such mentors made home visits to help refugees adjust to life in the United States and, when applicable, to administer medication. Maureen also discussed preventative care by explaining that staff at the Family Healthcare Clinic "want to see you *before* you get sick."

Judy Hendricks, the caseworker from Cass County Social Services who worked with all newly arrived refugees in 2007–2008, explained SNAP and Medicaid at the orientation. Judy was rather cantankerous. Before getting into the structure of the welfare state, she began by shouting, "You have two *very different* casework-ers: LSS and me. Don't call me if your check isn't big enough. Call me about food and medical, only food and medical." At orientation, Judy begins to demarcate the responsibilities of welfare workers from LSS workers, which serves to delin-eate an arbitrary line between the state and private sector, a space that neoliber-alism has blurred.

Judy spoke quickly about what Medicaid would and would not cover: "Medi-cal begins *only* the day you arrived in this state, so if you got sick on your way here, in New York, we can't pay." She described copayments for medical visits and medications, and when to dial 911 or take a taxi to the doctor ("if you're *very* sick, life threatening, bleeding, having a heart attack") and when not to dial 911 ("for a toothache"). All newly arrived refugees' primary doctors were at the Family Healthcare Center in Fargo, and Judy explained that they should not go to any other doctors without a referral from the center or they would pay a lot of money.

Judy summarized welfare programs from Temporary Assistance to Needy Families (TANF), Medicaid, and Supplemental Security Income (SSI) to heating and childcare assistance, and the eligibility requirements for each program. In doing so, she explained paperwork, a fundamental aspect of citizenship in ad-vanced capitalist countries, as the need "to prove *everything* you tell me." She continued: "If there is a pregnancy, a baby, you move, get work, everything must be proved on paper, not just verbally. For example, you must show pay stubs, a lease, pregnancy letter from the doctor, a birth certificate." Laughing, she said, "It's not that I don't believe you; it's just those are the rules." "Those are the rules" was a common phrase I heard among county welfare workers. Briefly, "follow-ing the rules" was shorthand for enforcing the conduct of welfare "equally" on all clients, regardless of background, which I discuss in more detail in chapter 3.

Climate

A local meteorologist, Bob Novak, explained Fargo's climate. His presentation in-cluded videos of the notorious 1996 blizzard with quotes like "We in the Mid-west pride ourselves on dealing with blizzards. . . . Killer wind chills . . . made this storm one to respect." After the video, he demonstrated on both himself and his eight-year-old son how to dress warmly for the winter using boots, scarves, mittens, hats, and winter coats. He then showed a black-and-white VHS tape of the legendary tornado in Fargo on June 20, 1957, during which more than three hundred homes were destroyed and more than a thousand homes and businesses were damaged. I watched the awestruck faces of New Americans watching these films, people who had lived near the equator all of their lives, and listened to their questions about how to stay safe during tornados. They seemed more afraid of tornados than blizzards. To laughter, one man asked if there were places in the United States that did not experience tornados so that he could move there.

Homi Bhabha argued that the weather was one of many markers of England's colonial status, the mention of which invoked "the most changeable and immanent signs of national difference" (1990, 319). Unlike the cool, dreary, green English countryside, people who moved to Britain from former colonies came from "the heat and dust of India; the dark emptiness of Africa; the tropical chaos that was deemed despotic and ungovernable and therefore worthy of the civilizing mission" (319). These postcolonials, Bhabha argued, arrived in cities such as London with new and different voices, and carried with them different symbolic and imaginative geographies, thereby changing the concept of the English nation. Not unlike the postcolonials whom Bhabha references, New Americans changed Fargo's cultural landscape and symbolic geographies. Weather brought people from diverse backgrounds together on an everyday level, but it also highlighted the kinds of differences that Bhabha wrote about. Images of Southern Sudanese, Liberian, and Somali women dressed in colorful prints, wearing sandals while waiting in dirty snow by a windy bus stop, once strange, have become commonplace. The weather was more than idle chatter among people living in Fargo; it served as a point of comparison and departure between the region, the nation, and the rest of the world. It also served as a means of social control over people who did not understand its power. The climate was also seen as a way of discouraging "riffraff," and surviving it was a means of evaluating cultural toughness and belonging.

De León (2015) chronicles life and death on the U.S.-Mexico border as migrants attempt to cross the dangerous Sonoran Desert. He demonstrates that the federal policy of Prevention Through Deterrence is a strategic plan and policy that kills. Violence, he writes, "is constructed in the desert" (16) and used to do the "dirty work" of the Border Patrol (43). Migrants who came to the United States seeking asylum and who fear deportation are also trying to cross the border into Canada in subzero temperatures. Journalists report that cab drivers have taken migrants unfamiliar with the climate to the border, charging obscene amounts of money (one article reports a taxi driver stripping a passenger of $700 for the drive) and leaving them in minus forty-degree temperatures without advice or support. According to the *Forum of Fargo-Moorhead*, about one thousand asylum seekers crossed into Manitoba in 2017, and not all of them came out alive (Chase 2018). Orientation to the climate is necessary for survival.

Education

Connie Miller, an ELL teacher in the Fargo school system, introduced New Americans to the K-12 school system of education and ELL programs for adults. She explained grades, testing, privacy and permission acts, the importance of school attendance, and the consequences of truancy. She described expected behavior of children on buses and in the classroom and stressed that bus drivers and teachers are not allowed to physically punish children in the United States. Some children interpret this as an invitation to push their teachers beyond reasonable limits, to which an Iraqi father exclaimed, "God help you!" Connie laughed and responded, "God help *you*! I don't believe how much you have to learn!" She explained a general philosophy of teaching, including the desire to teach skills for life, critical thinking and facts, cooperation and teamwork, and parental involvement in children's education. On the last point, Connie explained that this was not necessarily true in all cultures, and the Iraqis in the group laughed. Southern Sudanese told me that they could be beaten in school for not correctly answering a question and that their system was predicated on memorizing facts and not challenging authority, as was the former Yugoslav system of education.

Housing

Two middle-aged white women explained housing rights and responsibilities, with a heavy emphasis on responsibilities. They were housing managers for two of the largest real estate development agencies in the region, which rented to low-income families, including those living in Section 8, government-subsidized housing. The women explained tenants' responsibilities for signing and upholding a lease agreement, rental upkeep including apartment hallways, parking lots, and playground areas, how to install and change fire-alarm batteries, and the importance of maintaining a reasonable noise level and respecting one's neighbors.

A Somali woman, Anna, who worked for NAS, told me that she lived on the second floor of an apartment complex with her husband and two young children. A white woman who lived beneath them complained that the children were loud, and Anna insisted that it was nothing out of the ordinary for young kids. The woman complained so often that the management told Anna they should "just leave," so they did. They found another apartment and then received a bill for $2000 for breaking their lease and not paying rent. The company refused to take her calls or call her back. She and her family moved to another country within a year of the event. I do not know all of the reasons why Anna and her family moved, but certainly everyday acts of prejudice and microaggressions did not help them to feel welcome in Fargo.

The Role of New American Services

The LSS immigration lawyer walked new arrivals through some of the legal steps required to become a citizen, including the law requiring all men between the ages of eighteen and twenty-five to register for Selective Service, as well as how to file for family members to come to the United States. NAS workers explained RCA, including how to fill out monthly report forms on employment status, but they explained the process more slowly and carefully than Judy did. NAS staff gave pep talks. Alma testified to a group of new arrivals that when she first came to Fargo, she cried every day. She explained how she hated Fargo and wanted to go home to Bosnia but that now she likes it ("it's normal"). She concluded her talk by saying, "Be patient, work hard, and the freedom is here. It's up to you how far you want to take it, but it's hard. You've already proven that you are a big survivor—by moving all the way across the world. Most of us have been there and we know how hard it is, but you can do it!"

This is a different approach to speaking with new refugees than pragmatically telling them to "document everything." Christian, the director of NAS, concluded the orientation by listing reasons to love Fargo, including low crime rates and low unemployment. He explained the importance of learning English and obeying the laws in gaining acceptance in the United States. He added that gainful employment was the best way to become like other Americans: "Americans work hard, and when they see that refugees are working hard, they are more likely to accept you." When Christian asked the group what they would most like to learn in the United States, they responded "how to find work" and "how to go to school and work." In practice, however, New Americans embraced a range of desires, from an enthusiastic embrace of neoliberal, middle-class values like those espoused by resettlement staff, to a rejection of them and a desire to forge a different path toward citizenship.

Employment

The second week of orientation was devoted to employment and job training. NAS employment specialists facilitated the week, and the schedule focused on the financial and social capital that employment was purported to bring. Staff explained the existence of different kinds of jobs but focused primarily on entry-level positions in hotels, factories, restaurants, and hospitals. They explained part-time versus full-time work, shift work, how benefits are determined, how to punch a time card, transportation options, how and why taxes are configured, and the difference between needs (a place to live, food, water, and transportation) and wants (a cell phone or flat-screen TV).

Staff also explained *why* it was so important to work. Work, they explained in a PowerPoint presentation, brings "personal satisfaction" in that one can use one's skills, knowledge, and abilities in a satisfying way; make a financial contribution to one's community; and establish a good quality of life. "Good quality of life" was most often described as one's ability to work, stay off state welfare assistance, pay the bills, and participate in the consumer economy. Staff even advised families on how to save on childcare costs by having two-parent households work different shifts. Orientation and case management in both resettlement and welfare placed work over community building, at least for low-income parents who could not afford to stay home to raise children or pay for childcare. To boost confidence in refugees who had never participated in wage labor, staff explained that they already had some of the skills they would need to work in entry-level positions; for example, managing a family could translate to managing a team of workers. The importance of being on time was stressed, but so too were vacation time, sick time, and how to resign from a job.

Staff told refugees that they had the same rights as workers as U.S. citizens but that they must follow the same set of laws, such as those regarding sexual harassment. A young female intern and a middle-aged male caseworker demonstrated scenarios that could be considered sexual harassment, which resulted in uncomfortable laughter and questions about other potential scenarios. The staff person and intern explained that supervisors should not, for example, sit too close to an employee, say anything inappropriate such as calling someone "Sweetie," or hug, touch, or try to hold an employee's hand. The staff member recommended keeping an arm's length away from other employees, if possible, and added, "If you can smell someone's perfume or cologne, you're too close!" A participant claimed, "But some perfume might be strong and the whole building can smell it!" The group laughed, demonstrating they were not passive learners.

Tips for economic success included (1) be on time for work, (2) be friendly (but not too friendly) with supervisors and coworkers, (3) be productive at work, (4) ask questions if you don't understand, (5) take initiatives to learn new tasks and responsibilities, and (6) give your current employer two weeks' notice before moving to another job. On the last two days of orientation, participants practiced workplace English and, using interpreters, held mock job interviews and filled out job applications, a significant feat for those who could not read and/or write in their first language, much less in English. The goal of orientation and eventual employment, according to one employment specialist, is to help you to do many things for yourself. . . . You don't want to sit at home all day long! Work will make you less tired and sleepy. Overall you will be happy while working. You will pay taxes to the state, which will use that money to *help people*! . . . In the first stage, you could buy a little TV, but after two years, you can buy a big screen TV, or a car to get you to work or shopping. In two to four years, you can buy a car to take you to other states (to visit family and friends). Life is like a ladder to the roof. You can't just get to the roof; you need to go step by step.

The subject of employment and "hardworking" Americans came up throughout orientation and in everyday conversations with staff about the most important aspects of citizenship and success in the United States. During one orientation, a staff member stated, "It doesn't matter where you work, only that you make money, but there are appropriate and inappropriate jobs for your health." This statement describes the mixed messages sent by NAS. As one of the few institutions that consistently brought new forms of diversity to Fargo, NAS was charged with the responsibility of incorporating "diversity" into the city. Finding employment and promoting self-sufficiency and consumerism to mold refugees into model citizens was the most effective way to do this, but the jobs that NAS promoted, and that most refugees obtained initially, were in the service sector, and most of them did not provide a living wage or benefits, thus contributing to underemployment. (See Haines 2010 for a longer discussion on self-sufficiency and refugee resettlement in the United States.)

Historian Lizabeth Cohen outlines the post–World War Two message that mass consumption was not a personal indulgence but rather a responsibility designed to improve the living standards of all Americans. This message continued through 9/11 when President George W. Bush encouraged Americans to respond to the terrorist attacks by shopping. Cohen points out that the success in marketing consumerism and homeownership has resulted in Americans asking themselves, "'Am I getting my money's worth?' rather than 'What's best for America?'" (Cohen 2003, 239).

How these orientation messages were received varied depending on the background of the individual or group and personality. Some refugees seemed interested in the material, asked questions, and even cracked jokes. Others sat without betraying any emotion whatsoever, staring into space, seeming to not pay attention, but I could never be sure. At one orientation, a middle-aged Iraqi man was especially gregarious, and the classes felt more like a conversation. In the same group, however, was a shy woman from South Sudan, who struggled at one point to ask a question. The whole group encouraged to her to "speak up and not be shy!" First, Jane attempted to ask her question in English, then Swahili, and when she was not yet able to convey the question, she engaged the Arabic interpreter.

> JANE: What happens if you want to move after eight months [when the RCA checks end, but you still have a lease agreement]?
> GRETCHEN [A HOUSING REPRESENTATIVE]: It can be very expensive!

Another woman in the room knowingly made eyes at another woman as if to say, "Yes, good question—one that I too have considered." Jane continued:

> JANE: I want to move closer to family.
> GRETCHEN: It's best to wait until the [one-year] lease is up and then move closer to family. . . . We can check the file, but it's better to wait until the lease is done, because she [addressing Jane through the interpreter] would have to pay rent on her apartment until the lease is up. If you have ten months left on your lease and your rent is $465 a month, that means you would have to pay four or five thousand dollars.
> JANE: No! Okay, I'll stay. [Lots of laughter.] [In English] It's good, it's good.

Orientation was not the first or last place that refugees learned about the discourse and practice of American citizenship. They learned some of this discourse before arriving in the United States—in refugee camps, for example—and then it was reinforced at orientation and again during the process of filling out countless applications, going to interviews, enrolling children in school, and various other appointments. What made LSS different than some other agencies was that the organization and many of its staff knew better than most that, in Shahram Khosravi's words, "refugees have to perform refugeeness" (2010, 73). Khosravi explains that to even "have a chance of getting refugee status, one must have the ability to translate one's life story into Eurocentric juridical language and to perform the role expected of a refugee" (33). The performance begins when refugees first apply for asylum status and continues as they move from one country to another. Staff at NAS know this. They also know that many refugees are highly capable people, but they can also see through some of the performances. They know that an "invisible border keeps immigrants strangers for generations" (76). Staff want to help refugees succeed and know that there is more than one path to success.

A Closer Look at NAS

From 1952 until 2012, Lutheran Social Services (the whole, umbrella organization, not just New American Services) was located in a brick building adjacent to Olivet

FIGURE 2.2.   Old Lutheran Social Services building (1952–2012).

Photo by author, 2010.

Lutheran Church on Eleventh Street South in Fargo (figure 2.2). From NAS's inception in the 1980s until 2008, and with the exception of a year when the organization briefly moved to downtown Fargo, its offices were located in the basement of this LSS building. Resettlement staff joked that their subterranean location symbolized their position in LSS and in the city. Most of the staff worked out of the basement, but the director's office was on the first floor. In 2008, due to structural problems in the basement, LSS moved most of the NAS staff to the main floor. Only the assistant director remained in the basement.

In both Fargo and Sioux Falls, in the NAS office buildings during the late 1990s and early 2000s, it was difficult to keep clients from walking into caseworkers' offices without an appointment. Of course, this can be viewed as exemplifying agency or resilience on the part of clients seeking services. It was difficult for caseworkers, though, and they developed strategies to avoid walk-ins, such as leaving the building or learning to say no. There were quiet days in the office, certainly. Other days, though, caseworkers ran around the office looking for files or clients. The waiting room might be filled with families, children, men, women, young people and old, from all over the world, waiting for information and clarification on any number of topics. Some days case managers were barely in the office at all because they were too busy driving clients around to appointments or conducting home visits.

There were days when I was a caseworker in Sioux Falls when I ran out the back door of my office building to avoid clients who persisted in coming without appointments and who demanded money and other services from me that were beyond the purview of my job. Southern Sudanese male caseworkers in Sioux Falls told me they learned to never make home visits to Southern Sudanese women alone or that rumors would spread that they had a sexual relationship, thereby negatively impacting their clout in Southern Sudanese social and political circles. When including another Southern Sudanese male caseworker for these visits did not end the rumor mill, they began to make home visits with a white female colleague. Even that sometimes resulted in unseemly rumors about those involved.

In 2012, when forced out of their old office to make way for a larger church and parking lot, LSS in Fargo dispersed, and NAS moved into a temporary office across town on Forty-fifth Avenue South, while LSS organized a five-million-dollar capital campaign to build new offices that would house all of its Fargo programs and staff. The building was erected at a prominent location at the intersection of Interstates 29 and 94, and in 2015, all LSS programs moved into the new structure (figure 2.3). The new building symbolizes the powerful role of LSS in the city and is an example of assemblage, where emergent forms of commoning can take

FIGURE 2.3.   New Lutheran Social Services building (2015–present).

Photo by author, 2016.

place. Architecture can facilitate and inhibit forms of commoning and division. Resettlement offices in both Sioux Falls and Fargo are now modeled more on welfare offices, with doors and an administrative desk separating the waiting area from caseworkers' offices, which prevents clients from walking in unannounced. While more beneficial for workers, allowing them more time to keep up with case files, phone calls, and scheduled appointments, it may also be seen as another step in surveying or controlling clients.

In 2007–2008, NAS staff consisted of a director, an assistant director, four case managers, three employment specialists, a supervisor who oversaw case managers and employment staff, two program assistants who helped with reporting and maintained the front desk, an immigration lawyer, and three full-time caseworkers employed by the Unaccompanied Refugee Minor (URM) program. I did not include the URM program in my study due to the complicated nature of conducting research with minors. In 2007–2008, nine of eleven core staff were New Americans, but those numbers fluctuate as staff leave and new staff are hired.

In evaluating the success of a local resettlement program, the ORR asks local resettlement agencies to report which languages the staff speaks, as it prefers that staff speak as many of the languages of the communities being served as possible, thereby saving on interpreter costs. Thus, staff at resettlement agencies often reflect the racial, ethnic, cultural, and/or religious diversity of refugee communities. In 2007–2008, both employment specialists were middle-aged men—one white American and one New American from Iraq. The supervisor was a middle-aged Bosnian woman, and the four caseworkers included a white American woman in her mid-twenties and three New Americans in their thirties—one Somali man and two women (one Somali, one Bosnian). Both administrative staff were women from the former Yugoslavia. In addition, there was one college-student intern, a white woman. Each year that I returned to NAS, the staff had changed. For example, within in a year of my time at NAS, three of four case managers had left.

The director's job was to manage staff, work with LSS's CEO and board, report to the VOLAGS and state refugee coordinator, handle monitoring visits from the VOLAGS, write grants, serve on community boards, and network in the wider community. NAS had more than ten different directors between 2001 and 2006, after which Christian Novak served as the director from 2006 until 2012, providing much-needed stability to the agency.

Novak came to Fargo as a refugee. In 1991, he and his wife fled the former Yugoslavia to escape escalating violence. After living in Germany and Switzerland for seven years, where they had a child, the family moved to Fargo in 1998. They already knew English, and Novak soon began working for LSS as an employment specialist and education coordinator. Then from 2000 to 2004, he served as the director of a different LSS Program, which involved extensive travel around the state of North Dakota. He also acted as executive director of a non-profit in Fargo, and he earned a master's degree in public and human service administration in 2006, just before becoming the NAS director.

Novak told me about the challenges he faced in balancing different scales and scopes of resettlement. For example, he needed to demonstrate his program's success on the state and federal levels by proving that refugees in Fargo could become economically self-sufficient within the mandated 180 days. To stay in good standing with ORR, agencies had to maintain an employment rate of 75 percent of new arrivals in the first ninety days. Novak educated the public about refugees and addressed supporters of resettlement who argued for better long-term mentorship of refugees but did not understand the mandates of the program (economic self-sufficiency) or budgetary constraints. He met with business leaders throughout the state, who wanted a statewide resettlement program in order to provide a steady stream of workers for the then-burgeoning oil and service industries but who did not consider the social service, medical, and educational needs of those potential workers and their families.[5] He also addressed the needs of a multicultural staff with a high rate of turnover.

Until 2011, North Dakota was the only state agent, and the Department of Human Services was the state agency that received funding from ORR to carry out refugee resettlement. In this model, the state employs a state refugee coordinator, who has oversight for the programs that ORR funds. In consultation with a statewide Refugee Advisory Committee—which includes representatives of state social services, adult learning centers, school districts, healthcare providers, public health agencies, NGOs, and city governments—the state refugee coordinator confirms the number of arrivals coming to the state in a given year, keeping in mind that cities must (ideally) have the capacity to manage the entire resettlement process, not only reception and placement. For example, schools must be able to accommodate refugee children and adult education learners; welfare agencies must be able to accommodate those who cannot become self-sufficient within the first 180 days; and medical clinics need resources for addressing health problems unique or prevalent among refugee populations, including mental health services. Interpreters are vital in carrying out these services.

Under this resettlement model, in North Dakota, the Department of Human Services and the division of Children and Family Services was the coordinating agency. Brenda Jacobsma, the state refugee coordinator from 2005 until 2010, explained that many states placed their resettlement programs in the economic assistance or medical services division of the state government, because resettlement was viewed much like welfare, that is, as economic assistance. Brenda worked with staff in multiple human services divisions, especially the economic assistance division, because there was a strong relationship between RCA and TANF, the national low-income cash assistance program. Both of these assistance programs are based on eligibility—for example, being a newly arrived refugee or a single parent and legal state resident living below the poverty line. As the state refugee coordinator, Brenda oversaw between twelve and fifteen contracts throughout North Dakota. Contracts entailed managing refugee health, education, and social services. She worked most closely with LSS, but also with schools and health departments throughout the state, as well as the state finance division that distributed funding.

In 2011, North Dakota became one of thirteen states to be a part of the ORR-sponsored Wilson-Fish program, which is "an alternative to traditional state administered refugee resettlement programs for providing assistance (cash and medical) and social services to refugees." The program "emphasizes early employment and economic self-sufficiency by integrating cash assistance, case management, and employment services and by incorporating innovative strategies for the provision of cash assistance" (ORR 2015). The purposes of the Wilson-Fish program are to

- increase refugee prospects for early employment and self-sufficiency;
- promote coordination among voluntary resettlement agencies and service providers; and
- ensure that refugee assistance programs exist in every state where refugees are resettled.

According to Novak, the reason that North Dakota transitioned from being a traditional resettlement state to a Wilson-Fish state was because LSS was the only resettlement agency operating in the state. In some states, there are many VOLAGS, and local resettlement agencies resettle thousands, not hundreds, of refugees to multiple cities throughout the year.

In addition to full-time staff, NAS hired part-time case aides. Case aides are language interpreters for newly arrived families who do not speak English. They often did more than interpret. All case aides in Fargo were New Americans, and they were in high demand from multiple sources for their language skills and cultural expertise. They were busiest with new arrivals, high-needs clients, and large families. In addition to interpreting, LSS asked case aides to transport clients to and from appointments, and to make phone calls and home visits. Such responsibilities made the differences between "case aide" and "case manager" nearly indistinguishable. Some New Americans began working as interpreters, then became case aides, and were eventually hired as caseworkers or employment staff. Both case aides and case managers were paid by the hour; both worked closely with clients getting needs met; and sometimes both interpreted. However, case aides had less job security and fewer responsibilities than the average caseworker. In 2007–2008, there were Afghan, Burundian, and Bhutanese case aides, because those were the populations being resettled at the time.

Caseworkers and case aides uniformly stressed that their motivations to work in resettlement stemmed from wanting to improve the lives of refugees and because they understood the process and the emotional and physical strains of being a refugee. Dženana, a caseworker from Bosnia-Herzegovina said, "I feel for those people. . . . I understand it in the soul, when they come to me and they're having a hard time." Alma, also Bosnian, expressed similar thoughts: "Well, I'm former a refugee myself, so I know what our clients go through. . . . I can relate to them and I know . . . the expectations. . . . They might not be the same, but they could be similar. So that kind of prepared me to work with the clients that we serve, having to go through that myself."

Being a refugee who had survived that journey mattered. Peter Loizos writes about the politics of storytelling among refugees. A Greek Cypriot refugee told him, "Those who aren't refugees do not understand the pain of those who are—it cannot be shared. But the refugee can talk about his suffering to another refugee, and between the two of them, the suffering is controlled. The one understands the suffering of the other, but the non-refugees don't feel things, they aren't affected in the least" (Loizos 1981, 127; cited in Jackson 2002, 97). "This is why," argues anthropologist Michael Jackson, "refugees are the best qualified people to work with refugees. Even if others are prepared to listen, there is often such a manifest discrepancy between the world they inhabit and the world the refugee has survived, that the sharing is inhibited" (Jackson 2002, 97). In this way, resettlement agencies push the boundaries for what constitutes professional training, namely, lived experience.

Workers at other agencies complained about the lack of qualifications, training, and accountability of LSS workers. One county welfare employee said, "Just because you speak another language doesn't mean you're a good caseworker." Despite the high-needs case management required for some refugees that includes language barriers, lack of formal education or work experience, gender- and age-related challenges, mental and physical challenges, and reporting requirements, LSS did not require experience in social work or counseling, and it provided little training for new staff. Some staff held college degrees, but a college education was not required. Staff told me they learned their job as they went along by asking questions. Some U.S.-born resettlement workers disagreed with the emphasis on refugee status and language ability as qualifications for resettlement work. Courtney, a young white woman who was raised in North Dakota, had recently earned a bachelor's degree in psychology, and worked at NAS for less than a year before quitting, said, "Cass County would never hire workers with no education and no background . . . just because they had been on food stamps." She went on to critique the lack of training she received when she first started at NAS:

> I was told that I wouldn't get training. . . . I didn't follow anybody around for any cases or anything. There was a first case—you're gonna go to the airport. Here's what you do, here's the person you need to contact. . . . So more like a little pushing in the right direction. . . . I'm usually not a person to ask a lot of questions, 'cause I think I can handle a lot, but I did have questions. I asked, but honestly there wasn't adequate training and it's terrible because I think there should be at least . . . a two-month training process. Because . . . I made mistakes and I had to fix them.

A supervisor told me that different types of trainings were offered to new staff. One kind of training was local but not standardized. It involved conversations between the assistant director or supervisor and the new staff person. New caseworkers were also encouraged to shadow other caseworkers, but this was not required and, according to Courtney, did not always happen. Another staff member told me that trainings comprised in-house team-building exercises, which I did not personally witness. There were also regional trainings sponsored by the VOLAGS, in this case, Lutheran Immigration and Refugee Services (LIRS) and Episcopal Migration Ministries. Staff from UNHCR, ORR, the State Department, and LIRS presented on best practices in case management and how to document in case files, and offered panels about the resettlement process, political situations in refugee-producing countries, and information about the populations of refugees being resettled that year. New staff were encouraged to attend these trainings but not required to do so. The agency could not afford to send its entire staff to regional trainings, but the turnover rate was so high that sometimes staff members came and went in less than a year without the opportunity to attend such trainings. The director attended annual trainings sponsored by ORR, but the agency could not afford to send more than one or two people to these meetings.

I attended an LIRS training in Minneapolis as a caseworker in 2001 and as part of this research in 2008. At these conferences, I met resettlement workers from all over the country, many of whom were New Americans from Vietnam, Burma, Sudan, South Sudan, Cuba, Ukraine, Somalia, Iraq, and the former Yugoslavia. I learned about differences in resettled populations and program management. For example, I discovered that many Bosnians from the city of Zenica, where I lived from 1998 to 2000, lived in Florida, whereas more Herzegovinians and Roma from eastern Bosnia lived in Fargo. A common theme at these conferences was that refugee resettlement was decidedly not social work—they were *referral agencies*.

Staff from different institutions and professions in Fargo (the welfare agency, volunteers, other nonprofits, journalists) called for more, better case-management skills among resettlement staff, even as the resettlement agency stressed that it was only a referral agency. The pressing questions were: Whose responsibility were refugees? Were they best left to fend for themselves? Or did they need—as one long-term volunteer called for—"a twelve-member team, preferably for a lifetime," to help them adjust and thrive in the United States? Were refugees the responsibility of the federal government, cities, or agencies?

NAS workers wanted more accountability for clients, but they had a difficult time enforcing rules, such as sanctioning clients from RCA if they did not attend English classes. Many caseworkers personally understood the difficulties of being a refugee, the challenges of navigating the public transportation system in Fargo, and the short four- to eight-month period that refugees were eligible for cash assistance, and it was simply not worth their time to sanction clients. Others made the case for sanctioning. Alma argued,

> I think that if we sanction one [client], they will listen. And I don't think we have done that. . . . I always used to tell my clients[,] . . . "We're here to teach you to help yourself. We're not here to do things for you, because that is not going to help you in the long run, that's not going to do anything for you, that's just gonna enable you to be more codependent. . . . We're here to teach you to become independent. . . ." Self-sufficiency, that's our goal. So I think it's important to emphasize that. But when you're under a lot of stress and you have so many clients, you don't have that much time to spend one-on-one on clients . . . as much as you would like to, to be able to get that message across.

Clients were not sanctioned because, staff told me, "by the time you do the paperwork and have a hearing, the 120 days of reporting is up anyways." Not sanctioning clients can be considered a form of resistance within an oppressive neoliberal political economy (Morgen, Acker, and Weigt 2010).

At the same time, note the references to "self-sufficiency" and the conjuring of terms such as "help yourself" and "codependent," which have been keywords in the proliferation of neoliberal, antiwelfare discourse in the United States since at least the 1960s, when influential social scientists argued that people living in poverty displayed individual pathologies rather than attributing poverty to large-scale structural inequalities (Greenbaum 2015; Moynihan 1965; Lewis 1966). On one hand, resettlement workers espoused self-sufficiency and gave their clients "tough love" when it came to some forms of assistance, such as refusing to chauffeur clients around the city and forcing them to find their own transportation to classes, appointments, or work in a city with weak public transportation and a harsh climate. On the other hand, workers had empathy for clients and wanted to facilitate success in the best ways they knew how.

In terms of overall adjustment during those first few months, those who came from industrialized or semi-industrialized countries—such as Bosnia-Herzegovina, Ukraine, or Iraq—and especially those who had a trade skill, fared better at the beginning than those from developing nations with no employable skills or those with higher education, whose degrees would not be acknowledged in the United States. Such individuals were most likely to work as resettlement staff. One accountant I met earned money by privately doing taxes for other refugees. He would have preferred to work in a firm, but as a middle-aged man, he was not interested in the training required to become a certified public accountant in the United States. Another man was a trained tailor and earned good money working for a local laundry company, but he did not speak English, which limited other employment options or mobility in the company.

Conclusion

The NGOization of refugee resettlement from the church-sponsored era to the agency-sponsored present day has resulted in the increased professionalization of refugee resettlement. This transformation, along with neoliberal policies emphasizing economic self-sufficiency, flexibility, and increased bureaucracy, has, for better and worse, resulted in more accountability from workers and clients but has also, arguably, diminished—though not extinguished—the potential for political engagement and social justice. Walkowitz explains how Cold War politics replaced social activism among social workers with "a new disciplinary social policy . . . one that made productivity and efficiency the measure of service" (1999, 220). Refugee resettlement professionalized in an age of terrorism, and like social work in the age of communism, the same might be said about resettlement's turn to work that is more disciplinary and less about social justice. Modeling resettlement after the social work profession runs the risk of depoliticizing resettlement in ways that could lead to more scientific and psychological treatment, catering to the state and other funders, and preserving the status quo (Abramovitz 1998, 519–520).

Ilcan and Basok argue that "the greater demand for voluntary agencies to be accountable to the state for publicly funded activities . . . have forced voluntary agencies to move even more in the direction of service delivery and away from social justice–oriented advocacy work" (2004, 136). The professionalization of refugee resettlement resembles the professionalization of social work (Abramovitz 1996 and 1998; Gordon 1994; Walkowitz 1999). Social work began as advocacy for struggling single mothers after World War Two, then professionalized and became more quotidian, bureaucratic, and draconian, but it has returned to some of its earlier social justice work. At the historical conjuncture in which refugee resettlement is situated, in which it could turn down the road to bureaucratic practices or toward social justice, resettlement agencies can follow their mandates while also being creative about ways to incorporate social justice and participatory citizenship in their practices—for example, by asking refugees what they need and offering different opportunities or information based on those answers and feasibility, rather than primarily promoting middle-class values and conservative interpretations of the Cooperative Agreement.

Like so many other NGOs, NAS is paradoxical in that it reproduces hegemonic functions of the state and everyday bureaucracies but has the potential to engender commoning by bringing people together from different backgrounds into a common space with a common message that can be interpreted in different ways, resulting in new practices in the city. Besteman refers to people who work with refugees as "helpers in the state-funded neoliberal borderlands" (2016, 171). In some cases, these helpers were highly adept at traversing these multiple sectors; in other cases, poor case management resulted in strained relationships with clients, coworkers, and other agencies and resulted in a high rate of turnover. In any case, most staff viewed refugees as agents who had some control over their lives. As compared with county welfare workers who sought to always "follow the rules" or some volunteers who treated refugees paternalistically and ever in need of assistance (Erickson 2012), resettlement workers saw the complexities of refugees' lives.

One approach to facilitating more social justice would be to make commoning a more explicit part of refugee resettlement. Resettlement agencies could, for example, channel their power to foster more citizenship as participation and encourage more conversations among clients from diverse backgrounds and between the majority population and refugees. Orientation could include, for example, not only information on hegemonic forms of social, legal, and economic citizenship, but also an open-ended dialogue. Refugees could be asked what citizenship (or more simply a "good life") means to them and what tools and services they would need to attain it. New Americans can be very resourceful, especially when given the space and time to do so. Resettlement agencies could work together with state and private agencies to broaden the discourse on worthy citizenship rather than funnel refugees into jobs or the welfare system. Orientations and referral services might include representatives from New American groups who have been in Fargo for a longer period of time, other nonprofit organizations and associations, and city officials. A map of commoning areas in the city, not just social service agencies and employment sites, might go a long way in offering hospitality and alternatives to mainstream citizenship practices.

SIBLING RIVALRY
Welfare and Refugee Resettlement

Public and private agencies are important sites for understanding citizenship, labor practices, social service relationships, and changing social relations in the twenty-first century. This chapter provides an overview of the role of the welfare state as part of the assemblage of refugee resettlement in Fargo. Assemblage, in this context, "draws attention to the ways in which welfare states are composed of multiple elements: policies, politics, places and personnel" (Clarke and Newman 2012, 150). Welfare states comprise multiple, and sometimes contradictory, objectives and injunctions. They are, according to Clarke and Newman, "embedded in sets of techniques and technologies. Such elements are combined—or assembled—together in more or less coherent and stable forms. As a result, they are rarely reducible to a single organizing principle or political character" (150).

This chapter highlights practices of welfare workers in Fargo and compares them to practices of refugee resettlement workers in order to better understand how these institutions have shaped citizenship as well as local race, class, and gender formations in similar and different ways by framing them as siblings in the kinship of neoliberalism. Like siblings, workers in both sectors have competed and cooperated as they have worked with New Americans in the city. These institutions and their locations in the public/private borderlands are important loci for understanding varying approaches to citizenship, immigration, race, labor and class, and gender.

Scholars have documented well the history of the social work profession and the ways in which it has contributed to racial, gendered, and class formations across the United States and Europe. Here is not the place to summarize this rich

scholarship or to address the ways that social work has structured political conflict and participation on the national and international levels. In short, the history of refugee resettlement, which I outlined in chapter 1, mirrors that of social
work in the United States in the early to mid-twentieth century, which was inextricably tied to private charities but became more dependent on state aid beginning in the 1930s. Throughout the twentieth century, social work became more
professionalized as it transformed from private, religious-based charity work into
a more quotidian, scientific, secularized, bureaucratic, state-sponsored and "objective" profession (Abramovitz 1996 and 1998; Gordon 1994). In so doing, social workers learned to establish and police class borders between themselves and
people on welfare (Walkowitz 1999) but also exercised political agency and se-
cured some social rights for women, especially for poor women (Kingfisher and
Maskovsky 2008). Over the course of the twentieth century, especially under neoliberalism, the welfare state became a lucrative path to white-collar work for
African American women but, beginning in the 1970s, sought to limit access to
welfare and to promote welfare-to-work programs, especially targeted at poor
women of color (Acker 2000; Davis 2006; Fujiwara 2008; Goode 2002; Mullings
2001; Piven 2001; Roberts 1997). As Walkowitz (1999) explains, "The language
of class came to take on an enhanced political and racial rather than socioeconomic meaning. After 1970, 'middle class' became an established way of talking
not about class but about social respectability coded as the consuming behavior
of white people" (210).

Historic and contemporary welfare regimes in other regions of the country influenced welfare policies and practices in Fargo, which intersected with local assemblages of welfare workers, welfare recipients (including New Americans), and
the city. In what follows, I first explain the basic structure and responsibilities of
Cass County Social Services. Next, I provide a contemporary policy background
to refugee resettlement and welfare in Fargo and then describe everyday practices
of welfare workers, including the ways in which workers, who were mostly white
women, confronted new forms of racial and gendered diversity among New
Americans. In conclusion, I examine the politics of welfare in Fargo.

Cass County Social Services

Cass County Social Services (CCSS) is a state-supervised, county-administered
public welfare agency located in Fargo, the seat of Cass County. The command-
ing presence of CCSS's large brick building in downtown Fargo (figure 3.1) differed dramatically from the old offices of Lutheran Social Services, which were
located in a church parking lot for fifty years. Exacerbating these differences in

FIGURE 3.1.   Cass County Social Services.

Photo by author, 2008.

spatial design is the presence of security guards and a metal detector greeting visitors at the entrance (likely because there were also courtrooms in the building).

In 2008, CCSS served 14,000 people per month with a budget of $90 million per year. CCSS was divided into programs or units according to the kinds of assistance provided. The Economic Assistance division employed about fifty staff in 2007–2008, and included

- Temporary Assistance to Needy Families (TANF);
- General Economic Assistance, which includes childcare, Medicaid, heating assistance, and Supplemental Nutrition Assistance Program (SNAP; popularly known as "food stamps"); and
- Adults, Aging, and Disabled Services, which distributes Supplemental Security Income (SSI).

TANF was eligible to families with children who did not have parental support or care due to parents' death, continued absence from the home, incapacity, or disability and who met certain criteria, such as legal citizenship or immigration status and income level. Calculated in the same way as RCA, the amount of the benefit was based on the number of eligible household members, available income, allowable work expenses, and childcare expenses. There were other economic assistance programs affiliated with TANF, such as the Diversion Assistance Program and Pathways to Work, a transitional program to assist former TANF recipients who had found a job that paid them enough to get off welfare but essentially made them a part of the working poor. The Diversion Program was created to give people more time to meet participation requirements after they began working. People using the Diversion Program are not part of the federal participation count so, unlike with TANF reporting requirements, states are not punished for having people on Diversion, because those people have jobs.

North Dakota had some of the highest rates of two-parent working families in the country, but it was one of seventeen states that did not have a two-parent family TANF program—only single parents were eligible. Most people who qualified for TANF also qualified for other Economic Assistance division programs such as SNAP, childcare, and heating and housing assistance, which I describe here to illustrate the complexity of TANF operations and the scope of what workers do. Within the Economic Assistance division, there were five program supervisors who were each assigned eight to ten eligibility workers who carried a specialized caseload and determined which people were eligible for which programs. For example, three clusters of staff administered SNAP, family Medicaid, childcare assistance, and the Low-Income Home Energy Assistance Program (LIHEAP). Another cluster carried SNAP and aged/disabled Medicaid; still another SNAP, TANF, family Medicaid, and LIHEAP; and the last included foster care. One eligibility worker processed all SNAP and/or Medicaid applications for new refugee arrivals. She retained the cases through the first eight months and then transferred anyone who applied and was eligible for economic assistance programs after eight months to another worker. According to former CCSS director Kathy Hogan, the refugee caseload consistently made up about 10 percent of the total caseload for CCSS. After their initial eight months in the country, refugees were divided among the direct service staff.

Other state and county programs that worked closely with Economic Assistance staff were (1) Family and Children Services, which was part of CCSS and included adoption, foster families, and child protection services; (2) Southeast Human Services, which was located in a separate building in south Fargo and offered mental health services, substance abuse, disability, aging, and vocational rehabilitation services; (3) North Dakota Job Service (referred to as JOBS), a state-run program located in its own building in south Fargo; and (4) Section 8 Housing, which was also located in its own building, in downtown Fargo, and was funded by the U.S. Department of Housing and Urban Development. Because the latter two agencies were not located in the CCSS building, representatives from Southeast Human Services and North Dakota Job Service colocated weekly at CCSS in order to work with people needing services, especially TANF recipients, who were required to work with Job Service.

I attended three Economic Assistance monthly meetings referred to as "TANF cluster meetings," where workers met with a representative of Job Service and discussed transition and referrals to and from JOBS, Diversion, Pathways to Work,

TANF, drug and mental health counseling services, and other state and county programs. Like New American Services (NAS) staff meetings, there were somber discussions about the people they were serving and the limited amount of agency workers felt they had in assisting low-income people within the welfare state structure, but there was also laughter and cookies. I interviewed fourteen workers at CCSS and Job Service, including direct staff, eligibility staff, supervisors, and the former director of CCSS. To protect anonymity, I refer to CCSS and North Dakota Job Service workers as "county workers" or "state workers" without differentiating between the agencies, units, or clusters.

Welfare Reform and Refugee Resettlement: A Policy Background

In 1996, Congress passed the Personal Responsibility and Work Opportunity and Reconciliation Act (PRWORA), or simply "welfare reform." PRWORA replaced the previous low-income family cash-assistance program of Aid to Families with Dependent Children (AFDC) with Temporary Assistance to Needy Families (TANF). It ended the individual entitlement to public assistance and gave states unprecedented flexibility in program design. It also coincided with the surge in refugee resettlement to Fargo in the late 1990s. Unlike previous welfare programs that supported poor families in caring for their families at home and promoted education and job-training skills, TANF put a sixty-month lifetime limit on welfare cash assistance and enforced a work-first attitude by encouraging economic self-sufficiency. It severely cut the educational and work-training components of welfare and imposed mandatory labor in exchange for limited public assistance, also known as "workfare." In short, work became a social duty (Collins 2008).

Whereas AFDC gave a state money based on its number of clients, under TANF a state received a block grant based on a mid-1990s calculus and was required to meet an overall work participation requirement or face a potential financial penalty. Since 2002, the statutory requirements are 50 percent for "all families" (most of which are classified as single-parent) and, in eligible states, 90 percent for two-parent families. In other words, since 2005, states have had to engage half of their TANF cases of work-eligible individuals in productive work activities leading to self-sufficiency. A work-eligible individual is defined as an adult (or minor-child head of household) receiving assistance. If a state fails to meet the requirements, it risks a federal penalty. In the past, states could have received federal funding by using a broader definition of "work" that could accommodate harder-to-serve populations such as refugees who come with fewer employable skills than the average able-bodied American or an ability to speak English. The renewal of TANF in 2006 changed this policy to enforce an even stricter "work first" approach. This approach defines human worth on the basis of one's ability to work, not on family, parenting, education, community building, or the common good.

Loren Schmidt, a veteran county staff member, believed that AFDC badly needed to be reformed and that limitations on lifetime state assistance needed to be implemented but felt that "PRWORA [was] a joke." He recalled explaining the new program to clients in 1996:

> We brought seventeen families together . . . just before Christmas, and said, "Effective January 1, you can't go to school . . . under TANF 'cause you're gonna have to do all job responsibilities." And I think it was seventeen folks in the office. . . . I remember sitting in the room; it was kind of a surreal experience. It's kind of like you were on a drug or something and you remember the room, you remember the people, and I remember my voice, sort of like an out-of-body—you know when you hear your voice talking? And I just couldn't believe what I was saying to these people. . . . Our jobs, welfare reform, lifetime limits, that would all work really well, and it would complete the circle nicely if there were the opportunity to educate people. But there isn't an opportunity to educate people. It's a maximum twelve months. . . . Work opportunity? Well, I can't say it out loud anymore and feel good about it because there are no opportunities. . . . Personal responsibility? The person who's responsible is the worker making sure that they get the checks to the right person who's owed. . . . The federal reporting requirements are Neanderthal. They do nothing more than prove that lawmakers don't have clue 1 about what goes on in families' lives.

National welfare policies, like PRWORA and its renewal, trickled down to Fargo, but carrying out welfare policies is not a straightforward, objective practice. It has local variations and interpretations.

Unless exempt, TANF recipients must complete a minimum number of hours each week in one or more of the following approved work-related areas: job readiness, job search, high school/GED or education directly related to employment, paid employment, job skills directly related to employment, on-the-job training, vocational training, unpaid work experience, community service, or childcare for another participant involved in community service. The differences between JOBS work requirements and an actual job is that the income earned from JOBS is part of a temporary agreement between the client and the state. As such, people enrolled in TANF and JOBS do not earn retirement or other benefits that come with some paid work. The work requirement is meant to be temporary and does not guarantee a paid position after the workfare requirements end. Refugee resettlement is predicated on this model of economic self-sufficiency.

Carey Frye, a supervisor of the JOBS program, told me in 2008 that there were about 25 JOBS work sites around Fargo. Most of them offered low-skill jobs that did not require much training or education. Unless they were responsible for the care of a child younger than six years of age, participants had to complete a minimum average of thirty hours per week in one or more of the above work activities. If caring for a child under age six, a single parent had to complete a minimum average of twenty hours per week. State-supported education and training via TANF was limited to no more than twelve months in a lifetime. Carey said she continued to try to work with people who wanted to go to school for longer than twelve months. If a client completed twelve months of vocational education, she told me, "that doesn't mean that I'm not going to move mountains to help you continue to go to college and meet the requirements for participation and jobs." She said she would work with people on finding a part-time job or work-study. She told me that one of the biggest challenges to implementing the renewal of PRWORA in 2006 was the twelve-month limit on educational and training hours for approved work activities.

Due to challenges with English, different economic and subsistence patterns in home countries, psychological and physical trauma, and different attitudes toward welfare, some newly arrived refugees posed challenges for county workers, who found it difficult to support refugees in meeting work-participation hours. Loren exclaimed: "What refugee is going to learn the English language in four months? . . . I'd like to see the feds change the TANF rule with New Americans to say that you're like anybody else; you have a lifetime limit of sixty months. Right now their eligibility ends sixty months from *the date of their arrival*. . . . Talk about being on the fast track!" Other workers I spoke with agreed with Carey and Loren that four to eight months was not enough time for many New Americans to become economically self-sufficient.

CCSS began to track where newly arriving refugees worked, because NAS was allegedly not keeping such information. The 2000–2001 study followed 110 newly arrived refugees and found that thirty of them became employed within the first few months; of these, seventeen worked in manufacturing at jobs that paid from $7 to $9.30 per hour, and the other thirteen were in service sector jobs, restaurants and motels, that paid $6.50 per hour (*Forum of Fargo-Moorhead* 2001). The study cited language as the biggest barrier to ongoing employment. Those who did not become employed and were not eligible for social services were at the mercy of family or public and private agencies in Fargo. The *Forum of Fargo-Moorhead* (2001) reported that refugees were about 6 percent of Fargo's total population in 2000–2001 but that 10 percent of approximately 4,000 welfare cases were refugees.

Refugees who opted for an education over a job were not counted as "economically self-sufficient" in NAS reporting. TANF policies made it difficult for people, refugees or not, to attend school or training programs. This is why Cindy Mueller faced criticism when she started a skills training program for refugees. The project purportedly placed graduates in jobs with higher pay and benefits than they might have had without the training. It included an eighty-hour course that prepared New Americans for manufacturing skill training and certified nursing assistant courses. Emphasis was placed on workplace vocabulary, safety, math, critical thinking skills, teamwork, interpersonal skills, work ethic/attitude, time management, and conflict management in the workplace. Cindy sometimes tried to recruit newly arrived refugees into this program with the goal of getting more refugees better jobs faster, but the training course interfered with NAS's reporting requirements, which measured economic self-sufficiency in terms of jobs, not educational or training programs. Staff at NAS said the program was promising, but asked that Mueller wait until after the initial eight-month reporting requirements ended to recruit refugees. Both NAS and CCSS staff critiqued Mueller for not providing proof that her recruits found better, higher-paying jobs. In any case, most refugees worked in low-wage, service sector fields such as consignment stores, nursing homes, restaurants, hotels, and daycare centers, but some also found living-wage jobs in factories.

JOBS and TANF workers understood that low-wage jobs do not lead to self-sufficiency for refugees or U.S.-born citizens. Carey noted that while North Dakota had a lot of available jobs, many of them did not pay a living wage, and clients had to understand that they would need additional training to find a job that paid a living wage and provided benefits. Programs were purportedly created to train future workers for more competitive jobs, but the reality looked much different. In a study by the Center on Budget and Policy Priorities, researchers found that the share of state and federal TANF spending used for basic assistance (cash welfare grants) has fallen significantly. States spend only about a quarter of their state and federal TANF dollars on childcare and work activities combined. According to Schott, Pavetti, and Floyd (2015), in TANF's early years, when the economy was booming and welfare caseloads were shrinking, states used their block grants for childcare and welfare-to-work programs. Over time, however, they began to redirect those monies to other programs, for example, "to fill state budget holes, and in some cases to substitute for existing state spending" (Schott, Pavetti, and Floyd 2015, 1). Even during the Great Recession, "states were often unable to bring the funds back to core welfare reform services and instead made cuts in basic assistance, child care, and work programs" (2015, 1). Most people who reach their lifetime limit of TANF benefits become part of the working poor (Morgen, Acker, and Weigt 2010).

Welfare reform was not only about reducing individuals' reliance on the state; it was also about reducing particular groups' reliance on the state, especially poor women of color. Welfare reform impacted women more than men, because women generally bear more responsibility for children and, as such, work more part-time or temporary jobs and have a greater need for welfare to supply or supplement other economic means (Brodkin 1988; Fraser and Gordon 1994; Mink 1990; Piven 1990). Lynn Fujiwara (2008) explains that antiwelfare and anti-immigrant reform measures in the 1990s were inextricably tied to race, class, and gender. TANF barred noncitizens (but not refugees) from receiving welfare. This decision was not predicated on differentiating between "citizen" and "alien"; rather, these policies were about race: "In the case of welfare reform, where the two largest immigrant groups were Asian and Latino/a, *citizenship* was defined by 'race'; citizenship thus became the innocuous demarcating line in lieu of the odious race" (Fujiwara 2008, 40).

Scholars argue that welfare reform had several problems: it assumed that adequate jobs existed, that single parents could manage work and family, that those without necessary human capital or structural support could obtain the skills necessary to get a decent job, and that parents who rely on welfare do not face significant barriers to employment; rather, they became "dependent" upon the system (Fraser 1989; Kretsedemas and Aparicio 2004; Morgen and Maskovsky 2003; Susser 1986). In addition to increasing levels of poverty, welfare reform has wreaked havoc on welfare workers, on the ways in which they view and carry out their jobs, and on their relationships with their clients (Morgen 2001; Kingfisher 2002).

Everyday Practices of Welfare Workers

In CCSS's Economic Assistance division, workers processed new applications three mornings per week, with two appointments each on those days, and an average of three to four new cases per week. Periodically workers did recertifications or redeterminations with their clients and assisted with walk-in appointments, but the bulk of their time, outside of formal interviews, was spent processing cases. When describing their job, county workers used terms such as these: *meeting, evaluating, recommending, complying, following up, screening, testifying, verifying, proving, contacting, training, pushing, making ends meet, reviewing, re-dating, re-signing,* and *dealing with federal guidelines.* They lamented spending more time on "paperwork" (or, more aptly, computer work) than with clients. The primary responsibility for many caseworkers revolved, in large part, around quantifying and verifying need and "punishing individuals who entered the territory of the welfare state . . . separating the normal from the abnormal, the good from the bad refugees, the responsible from the 'welfare cheat'" (Ong 2003, 126). Loren explained that welfare reform shifted their job from trying to help clients get off welfare to "maneuvering" the system for sixty months, until a client's lifetime limit was reached.

Michael Lipsky (1980, 3) calls state employees who deliver the everyday services of the government "street-level bureaucrats." This includes social workers, teachers, police officers, and legal-aid lawyers, whose job is to interpret government policies to the public on an everyday level. Others call state workers "experts of subjectivity" (Rose 1996) or "middling modernizers" (Rabinow 1989). In this line of analysis, the job of government employees is "to teach clients to be subjective beings who develop new ways of thinking about the self, acting upon the self, and making choices that help them to strive for personal fulfillment in this life" (Ong 2003, 16). These workers represent and translate government policy on an everyday level while working with high caseloads, unclear goals, and discretion in how they carry out policies, often on a case-by-case basis. They also lack training in cultural competence, by which I mean understanding that people around the world are at once similar and different, connected through global assemblages such as colonialism, neoliberalism, and human rights discourse, but in different and inequitable ways.

How do street-level bureaucrats explain the goals of the welfare state under neoliberalism to those from a formerly communist country, like Bosnians, or to those who have not experienced a modern representative government, like Southern Sudanese? How do state workers, who are mandated to serve everyone who is eligible for their services, incorporate new forms of diversity and equity into their programs? How do power and governing practices coalesce into concrete governmental regimes with locally situated patterns of inequality (Kingfisher and Maskovsky 2008, 115)? What does it mean for workers and clients?

"Those are the rules" was a common phrase during the year I spent in Fargo (2007–2008), along with "We treat clients all the same," but how can workers treat clients from different backgrounds the same? How might language impact the interpersonal relationships between workers and clients? Or gender? Or education levels? In my first week in Fargo, I began making phone calls to set up meetings with interlocutors, and I called CCSS. I explained to the woman answering the phone who I was and what I was doing in Fargo (studying refugee resettlement and its impacts on the city), and I requested a meeting with director Kathy Hogan. The woman sounded perturbed but gave me a meeting time, adding curtly that I should know that "we treat all of our clients the same." Treating clients, students, or citizens "the same" is about equality, which is different from equity. An equitable approach understands that societal structures are built on historic and contemporary forms of oppression and resistance to oppression. A bottom-up approach to equity would incorporate the perspectives of marginalized groups. Treating clients "the same" does not acknowledge that different groups of people have been and continue to be treated differently within societal institutions, that is, by policies and staff in those institutions.

In a study on intercultural knowledge and skills in a welfare agency in a small city in an Upper Midwestern location that resembled Fargo, Katherine Phillips found that county welfare providers relied on program policies and rules, their personal value systems, and a generic set of helping attitudes to guide their work with refugees. She argued that welfare program rules "were seen as an Americanizing force, encouraging self-sufficiency, a work ethic and training refugees in the behaviors necessary to deal with bureaucracies" (2004, 115). New Americans told Phillips they wanted more "human connection" in their interactions with county workers. Her findings indicate that county providers relied minimally on cultural competence skills and that, in the absence of these skills, county programs and workers served primarily to indoctrinate refugees into dominant American cultural norms and practices, which points to the need for more training in cultural diversity.

In 2007–2008, county staff were almost all white, female, monolingual English speakers most of whom identified as practicing Christians. Out of a total staff of about 135 employees that served 12,000 to 14,000 clients every month, fewer than ten CCSS staff members were male, and fewer than five were people of color. By 2016, the staff had grown more diverse with at least eight staff members who were people of color, but it remained overwhelmingly white and female. Most had grown up in small towns or on farms and told me that outside of their job, and sometimes their church, they had had little contact with people from other races or cultures. Some had previously moved to Minneapolis–St. Paul or another part of the country but had moved back to be closer to family or because they preferred living in smaller, safer, less crowded areas.

All Family and Child Services workers were required to have degrees in social work; most of the TANF and Aged and Disabled Services program workers had college degrees. Many of the eligibility workers in the Economic Assistance division did not have college degrees, but new workers received systemic training. In examining welfare offices in Oregon, Morgen, Acker, and Weigt argued, "Training was an important vehicle for promoting organizational change, including 'nuts and bolts' workshops and other workshops designed to address the values, beliefs, and expectations of welfare-to-work programs" (2010, 53). As Kathy Hogan explained about CCSS, "We have regular performance reviews, and if you're not doing your job, you get terminated. . . . We have a pretty sophisticated performance management system."

Compared to NAS caseworkers, who used arbitrary, flexible interpretations of policies, county workers viewed state policies as objective and straightforward, if not also complicated. As mentioned in chapter 2, Judy, the caseworker who presented on CCSS at the cultural orientation for new refugee arrivals, explained the rules to a new group of arrivals: "You have to prove everything you tell me. It's not that I don't believe you, it's just those are the rules." Yet county workers also acknowledged that there was room for interpretation. Loren explained: "They're diverse rules. They're contradictory rules. They're competing rules. They're nebulous regulations."

County workers expressed frustration with implementing ever-changing rules while also maintaining large caseloads. "We provide services to *people*, but the state wants us to be automatons," one staff member explained. At one TANF cluster meeting, workers discussed their fear of taking vacation only to return to piles of work. Staff complained that high caseloads and overwhelming amounts of paperwork made it nearly impossible to accomplish everything within the state-mandated forty-hour workweek. Loren told me in 2007, "I can't do it. I can't do it. I can't keep up. . . . This morning I was in at six o'clock. Last month I worked forty-eight hours of overtime. I'll work another twenty-five to thirty hours of overtime this month." I asked about how much time the average worker spent on paperwork, and he said, "I'm all over them because they're working more than forty hours and not claiming them. And that's the death . . . of any organization. So if we start doing that, we're in deep—[shit]. That happened once before at Cass County and it cost them almost $100,000 . . . because people were working off the clocks and administration knew it."

In order to get clients services that they needed, workers routinely described having to "be creative" when implementing state policies. Rather than holding clients accountable, CCSS staff reported feeling that the state held them, not clients, accountable for making clients self-sufficient. Drawing an arbitrary line between the state and private sector was important to CCSS and NAS staff and was part and parcel of managing new forms of diversity in the welfare state. I describe their relationship as siblinglike because they have a common progenitor in the state, the Department of Health and Human Services, which funds both programs. The agencies also have increasingly similar structural makeups, including policies aimed at self-sufficiency, but different temperaments and training, as well as racial, gender, and religious differences among the staff. To welfare workers, the elder sibling in this scenario, it seemed that the state was being tougher on them and their clients, and much more lenient on the younger sibling, the resettlement agency and its refugee clients.

Siblings: Cass County Social Services and New American Services

Despite the high-needs case management required for some refugees, NAS did not require computer training or experience in social work or counseling, and it provided little systemic training for new staff. Cultural knowledge and language skills were preferred over other qualifications. Resettlement agencies often reflect the racial, ethnic, cultural, and/or religious diversity of the resettled refugee communities. NAS staff reported spending about half their time with clients as opposed to doing paperwork, which is a marker of accountability, and they are paid about two-thirds the salary of state workers. When I asked NAS staff about the differences between their program and the county's in terms of attitudes and policies toward New American clients, they described theirs as more accommodating, empathetic, and flexible; they viewed state welfare workers as uncompromising, "fake nice," "cold," and even discriminating against refugees.

During new-refugee orientations, Judy explained when to call CCSS and when to call NAS: "You have two very different caseworkers: NAS and me. Don't call me if your [RCA] check isn't big enough. Call me about food and medical, only food and medical." Both CCSS and NAS workers complained to me that they felt it was the other's job to ensure that refugee clients correctly filled out their CCSS report forms and in a timely manner. If a client failed to do so, NAS workers sometimes blamed the CCSS worker for being lax, cold, or discriminating, and CCSS workers blamed the client and the NAS worker for not being responsible. This feeds into the argument articulated by Sharma and Gupta: "The boundary between state and non-state realms is thus drawn through the contested cultural practices of bureaucracies, and people's encounters with, and negotiations of, these practices" (2006, 17). Ana, an NAS worker of Somali origin, told me in 2008,

> [County workers] don't care about clients. I interpreted for people there, and they don't explain. We think a little more about our clients—we think about where the money is going to come from. We try to find interpreters and communicate with our clients. [CCSS workers] tell their clients to call their case manager [at NAS] every time [the clients] call Cass County because they say they can't understand them. Well, we don't understand [the clients] either, and then we have to call an interpreter to do their work—the same with filling out their paperwork. Why should I have to fill out paperwork for their services? If I can teach a client how to fill out those forms, then why can't they?

Negative depictions of social workers are neither new nor unique to NAS workers. "Working out of increasingly rationalized and impersonal bureaucracies,"

Daniel Walkowitz argues, "social workers have been vulnerable to being stereo-typed as heartless investigators" for decades (1999, 101). Part of the issue is that social workers are positioned ambiguously between the many publics they serve. New Americans are just one of these publics, but they have an outsized role in influencing social workers' everyday lives in Fargo due to the relative lack of ra-cial, religious, and gendered diversity present in Fargo before the 1990s.

Judy told me that the county had administered RCA in addition to Refugee Medical Assistance and SNAP, but then NAS began administering RCA. Judy ex-plained why the county should have continued doing it:

> *We* have more controls than they do. We have better *training* than they do. . . . I'd be the one having to do it, so why would I be wishing more work on myself, but . . . over the years, I've seen what *I think* are a lot of mistakes, because they didn't train anybody (chuckles). They're there for a week and they're thrown into "the shakes." . . . But we pretty much fig-ure the new worker [at CCSS] is worthless for a year [until they get properly trained]. Six months is pure training and then *very gradually* a caseload is added. NAS doesn't do it that way! . . . They're just attached at the hip to their lead worker for quite a while. . . . A worker gets better training here.

When NAS took over the RCA administration, it eased some of the labor burden on CCSS workers, but there was less training and oversight for resettlement work-ers, and according to CCSS staff, NAS workers made more mistakes. Unlike at NAS, a county worker would likely be fired for not meeting his or her benchmarks. Judy, like other social workers I spoke with, stressed that they were professionals who had training. Walkowitz studied the ways in which the professionalization of social workers in the twentieth century was inextricably tied to their desire to be seen as trained and respectable members of the middle class: "This tortuous path to respectability, however, would continue to be strewn with category pit-falls; for another fifty years, debates raged over who was and who was not a social worker and whether being a social worker conferred professional status" (1999, 30). Another crucial aspect of their job as "gatekeepers of public and private re-lief aid" was "the patrolling of class" (10). By the twenty-first century, social work had become a middle-class profession, not viewed as relatively low-paid charity work like what the frontline staff did at NAS. Maintaining a distinction between the *profession* of social work and the labor practices of other kinds of human ser-vice work, in this case with refugees, remained important to social workers in twenty-first-century Fargo.

NAS workers believed that county workers had more power than county work-ers felt they had. NAS workers did not understand the complexity of services, large caseloads, and diverse needs of clients who used the services of the welfare state. A more diverse clientele meant more labor for already stretched-thin welfare workers. However, NAS workers understood, as Loren stated, that the rules are more flexible than county workers believed them to be. In their work on welfare in Oregon, Morgen, Acker, and Weight argued that caseworkers have "considerable discretion in deciding what levels of noncompliance to tolerate before initiating a sanction," and thus "they wielded a great deal of power over clients" (2010, 127). NAS workers believed that refugee clients received fewer discretionary case management services from the county. State workers, for example, have discretion in referring clients to other social service providers, in how much information they provide to clients about other organizations and agencies, and in how much they are willing or able to assist the clients personally in accessing those services, which was challenging with the amount of paperwork they had to do. County workers reported spending from 30 to 90 percent of their time on paperwork and did not feel they had much power in changing this.

When I asked her if she felt that she had power in interpreting policies, Kathy Hogan said, "We have very little control. Local entities have very little control. . . . Ninety percent [is] regulated by someone else." She knew that the U.S. State Department made the ultimate decisions regarding resettlement, but she also knew that NAS had a role in deciding how many refugees it could accept each year, which gave it a stronger voice than she had in accepting welfare clients. A key difference between private human service agencies and state human service agencies is that private agencies have a greater degree of power and flexibility in choosing whom they serve. The state is supposed to serve everyone who is eligible for its services.

During my first meeting with her in the fall of 2007, Kathy told me she *loved* New Americans but that in 2000–2001, county staff and administration were frustrated because they were unprepared for such large numbers and for the new needs of refugee clients, who lacked English or job skills and had different approaches to government than U.S.-born citizens. Kathy explained that refugees from the former communist bloc believed that welfare was a right, an unpopular perspective in neoliberal America, where the welfare state was under attack. Increased workloads and new forms of diversity among clients were hard on her staff. She told me that refugees "have had a dramatic impact on social services: on economic assistance programs, on child welfare programs, on disabled services."

To prevent burnout among the CCSS staff, supervisor Nancy Jordan tried to adjust caseloads by determining the percentage of New Americans on welfare, a process that started by tracking the number of "foreign" names on the lists:

> I go through it by hand, and I highlight people I think might be refu-
> gees, and then I check them in the system and look how many people
> are in that household that month, verify that they arrived as refugees,
> even if they have become citizens. . . . I am pretty liberal in how I count
> those, even if they've become citizens, or they've had babies since they've
> been here that are U.S. citizens right away. I still count that family because
> they still . . . have special needs. . . . Part of the reason I do it is so I can
> keep my caseloads even, so that one individual doesn't get a whole bunch
> of people who don't speak English.

This quote shows that legal citizenship is too narrow a lens for understanding belonging and the everyday practices of citizenship. Even after they have become
"legal" citizens, New American welfare clients are treated differently. If everyone
were treated equally, then why were refugees tracked differently than U.S.-born
clients? Different clients have different needs and require different case management practices. Of course social workers have subjective practices. They work with
people, and people are different from one another; they come from different backgrounds and have different social locations even within the same city. Case management must be flexible in dealing with these differences, especially if they want
more equity. Achieving a modicum of equity in a beleaguered welfare state under
pressure to incorporate new forms of diversity meant relying more on public-
private partnerships, which is why Hogan believed that

> the whole community needs to be involved in the decision-making pro-
> cess regarding how many [refugees] to take—if we are all mutually re-
> sponsible. So I don't like the idea that we have the responsibility with
> no voice. And you know, after 9/11, when there was a significant decrease
> in [arrivals], this community can manage that. And the systems are in
> place to manage that resettlement population. But when we were at six
> hundred, we did not have the capacity, and . . . my concern was that we
> were seeing so many unmet refugee needs during those few years, that
> it was . . . wrong. . . . If we're gonna resettle New Americans and refu-
> gees, then we need to do it well.

Hogan spoke publicly against resettlement and helped to find funding for new
nonprofits in the city in order to better support refugees, whom she felt were not
getting the services they needed and who were disproportionally draining state
services and staff. The welfare state wielded power in Fargo, and it operated beyond the walls of CCSS. As Sharma and Gupta write, "We can begin to concep-
tualize 'the state' *within* (and not automatically distinct from) other institutional

forms through which social relations are lived, such as family, civil society, and the economy" (2006, 9).

Walkowitz argues that welfare workers have had ambiguous and heterogeneous relationships with the state: "The state is represented by many different players, and they do not speak with one voice" (1999, 19). There are different levels of state workers, from politicians and policymakers to supervisors and frontline workers. At each level, continues Walkowitz, there are "competing agents of state policy . . . at various bureaucratic stages. State hegemony therefore contains numerous interstices and possibilities upon which to build alliances or resistance, both for clients and, as workers, for social service staff" (19). Just as there are different interpretations of state policies, so too are there different perspectives on citizenship, race, gender, and class. Like other professionals, social workers share racial prejudices that are deeply ingrained in American culture, but they can also be some of the most progressive voices against various forms of discrimination in a given location. Since most welfare recipients in Fargo were white, and almost all welfare workers were white, the influx of New Americans, many of whom were people of color, called attention to race as a new category of difference between and among workers and people who received welfare, but it was not the only difference.

Race-ing Welfare

Clarke and Newman argue that "diversity forms one of the critical points around which relationships between state and citizen have been reconstructed." "Diversity," they continue, "has been used as a threat or challenge to established national universalism and as the means of reworking liberal universalism" (2012, 164). They critique scholars who argue that migration makes European white societies more diverse and that diversity undermines social solidarity that has sustained welfare states. This is problematic, they say, because it collapses diversity, minorities, ethnic groups, and nonwhite races into one social category and in so doing normalizes white people as the dominant, privileged group against which all "ethnicized" others are compared. This process results in perpetuating "claims to treat ethnic differentiation as either pre-social or pre-political facts. To do so ignores the economic, social and political histories of the construction of difference and inequality; it represses the histories of white American and European privilege; and it fails to recognize the ways in which racialized or ethnicized differences (and inequalities) were intimately bound up in pre-existing welfare policies and politics" (156–157).

In other words, arguing that refugees *brought* diversity to Fargo dismisses the violent history of European settlers in the United States, who also came as immigrants, who settled the land by killing or forcibly removing Native Americans, and whose white descendants continue to benefit from that history while at the same time continuing to challenge the sovereignty of Native Americans. The idea that refugees bring diversity overlooks forms of diversity within the dominant population, for example, differences with regards to sexuality, political ideologies, and religious practices. New Americans, of course, have brought *new forms* of diversity, and how welfare workers approach this diversity can help us to better understand the role of welfare in perpetuating and challenging dominant understandings of citizenship, the state, and diversity, which privilege wealthy and upper middle-class whites more than other groups.

Lisa Smith was a white woman in her thirties, married with two children, who lived in a small town and commuted to Fargo for work. Lisa seemed excited to discuss with me her take on the wider public's anxiety surrounding "foreigners." Lisa grew up in a small "conservative, racially homogenous" town in the Upper Midwest where, she said, most people, including her grandparents, were prejudiced against Native Americans. She had traveled to Europe and appreciated learning about other cultures and hearing how people in other countries viewed the United States. Lisa believed that too many people in the Midwest were closed-minded toward foreigners. Lisa's husband was critical of refugees and immigrants because he believed they were getting benefits—such as a Habitat for Humanity house that was given to an Iraqi family—that he believed should go to a U.S. citizen, even though the father of this Iraqi family was killed while serving with the U.S. military in Iraq. To rationalize her husband's stance on foreigners, she stressed his civic engagements and desire to give back to his (presumably white) community.

Lisa thought it was important to educate people to understand that many refugees work hard: "Not all refugees are bad. They're not all sitting around." As our conversation went on, she provided more examples of racism and xenophobia among people she knew. She reasoned that their beliefs arose due to little education or experience with people from other cultures. They needed more exposure, Lisa explained, but in the same breath, she told me she believed it was best to have a daycare provider that "looks like your kids." Then she passionately described her outrage when a young girl in her daughter's elementary school expressed "anger" toward white people for injustices against her Native American ancestors. Since Lisa did not want me to record our interview, the following comes from my field notes:

> *Lisa began the story with "Since we're talking about race . . ." (Though I mentioned race, I was asking her about refugees. She repeatedly brought the conversation back to race.) Lisa came home from work and her daughter told her that "Katy" said white people enslaved Native Americans. Lisa*

stressed how upset her daughter had been. Lisa felt Katy's statement had been an "accusation, not a fact." She was confused because Katy's father is white; only her mother is Native American. Lisa wondered where this conversation happened: Was it in the classroom or on the playground? She hoped that if such a conversation happened in front of a teacher, then that teacher would dispel some of the anger. Lisa wondered what Katy's family talked about at home, where she got "that idea." Lisa didn't know what to say to her daughter. She explained that she didn't know if their ancestors had participated in those kinds of things, but that things are so much better now; people are not enslaved anymore. And maybe some of the people who did that in the past, "like the people who participated in the Holocaust," were "good people." Maybe, she said, they were "working families" and some of them might have thought it was necessary for survival. Lisa said she tries not to talk about opinions about "other people" around her children (presumably by "other people" she means refugees, Native Americans, racial minorities, and anyone who is not white), because she wants her kids to form their own opinions.

This story shows the ways in which some whites in Fargo acknowledged some forms of prejudice against some groups, especially in the past, but rejected what it meant in the everyday lives of contemporary people who face discrimination. This is white privilege (Jensen 2005; McIntosh 1988; Moraga and Anzaldúa 2002; Rothenberg 2005). Lisa's comments echoed the sentiments of early Norwegian settlers that Karen Hansen chronicles (see chapter 1) in that despite some progressive political leanings, "the shared geographic space was divided by a gaping social chasm" (2013, 240) more than a century after Europeans colonized the region.

Bell hooks has argued that whites must educate their children in the ways of the dominant population in order to cope and survive in a white supremacist society (hooks 1995). Lisa's interaction with her daughter is an example of this. Denying the multigenerational trauma and anger experienced by Native Americans due to dispossession and genocide—or characterizing people who participated in the Holocaust as "nice people"—is to further white Christian supremacy. Racism, classism, and sexism are hereby perpetuated by placing historical acts of violence in the past, naming them as "ideas" rather than facts, and ignoring contemporary structural inequalities that are tied to those previous systems of violence and oppression, for example, the violence and discrimination against Native Americans that occurred at Standing Rock against the water protectors in 2016 (though I spoke with Lisa before this event).

When I asked another state worker, Nate, how his background shaped his views about his job, welfare, and refugees, he explained, "I like to think I'm not a prejudiced individual. I grew up in an atmosphere, you know, it was white America and . . . some Native Americans, but generally speaking it was a white population, and I really got to know what it was like to be a minority when I played college basketball." Nate said he was one of the few white players on the team and felt discriminated against on the basis of race. He "was pissed" that he "wasn't playing" but comforted himself by knowing that he went to college to get an education, and most of those players "weren't there getting an education," but were there "to play ball and have fun." Then he told me that he was the only player from that class to graduate from college. A key word above is "individual." Morgen, Acker, and Weigt (2010) argue, "Many [welfare] workers valorized self-sufficiency and linked it to ideals associated with individualism in US mainstream culture: self-respect, choice, accountability, and responsibility. An unspoken neoliberal assumption underlies these values: that the individual is solely responsible for her- or himself in a world of self-interested choice-making others" (86). Nate saw himself as an individual, not connected to larger structures. He did not mention feeling discriminated against off the court, for example, in the classroom or the employment sector, an experience his fellow players likely had. Nate seemed to attribute his own successes off the court to hard work, without recognizing the structural inequalities that kept his teammates from realizing comparable successes off the court, stating they only went to college to have fun.

Nate said his parents had been "racist" but that they "instilled some good values and . . . you take that a step further when you go to school. You really get to experience some things and I'm pretty tolerant and . . . I will accept a lot of things." Nate actually mentioned white privilege, but not his role in having it. He later said, "I know that you're going to find prejudice wherever you go. . . . You can do all the education that you want, [but] if you've got somebody that was raised prejudiced, unless they make a conscious effort to change that, you're going to be stuck with this type of a person to deal with." Nate seemed to believe that he had overcome the racism of his parents, but he also believed that prejudiced people could not unlearn racism. Based on my experiences teaching college students, I have more hope than Nate that people can unlearn racism and prejudice.

Diversity in Fargo was almost always viewed through the lens of race, but neither "race" nor "culture" were clearly defined and were often collapsed into one social category. Kristi Hansen was married to a man, had two children, and lived in a small town near Fargo. She grew up in a different small town than she lived in and was the daughter of blue-collar workers. During my interview with Kristi, she often evoked "ethnicity" to describe people who were not white. Toward the end of our conversation, I asked her a question that I asked everyone I spoke with: "Do you identify with a certain ethnicity or religion?" The question seemed to catch her off guard. After a long pause, whispering to herself for a time, and stumbling over her words, she said,

> I think I was raised—my . . . parents weren't prejudiced, really. You know my dad was in the service; he had Black friends and, you know, I just, it was, just really never a big deal. It wasn't really an issue. . . . Actually, both sides of the family, there have been times . . . when they've married, to the inter-race, you know black, Native American, we have Hispanic. I don't know. . . . It was never really an issue (laughs). Never really been, yeah, never really been an issue.

Kristi interpreted my question about her ethnic background as "an issue" and seemed to feel the need to explain that she knew people who were not white. The idea that citizens of Fargo are white Christians is so deeply engrained in the culture that most discussions about race, ethnicity, or culture meant discussions about people who were not white or Christian. When I asked questions about ethnicity or race, many people assumed I was talking about refugees and immigrants, likely and understandably due to the topic of my research. However, when I asked about refugees or immigrants, people also assumed I was talking about race and ethnicity and about people who were *not* white. There is more to refugee identity than their race. When I asked Kristi to describe her own ethnicity, she answered by explaining that she had known Blacks and Hispanics.

Sociologist Eduardo Bonilla-Silva relates this type of incoherent speaking about race to the ideology of color-blind racism. In his research with whites about race, he found that

> almost all respondents exhibited a degree of incoherence at some point or other in the interview. Digressions, long pauses, repetition, and self-corrections were the order of the day. The incoherent talk is the result of talking about race in a world that insists race does not matter, rather than being a tool of color blindness. However, since it is so preeminent in whites' race talk, it must be included as part of the linguistic modalities of color-blind racism. (Bonilla-Silva 2014, 119)

Color-blind racism explains how "whites have developed powerful explanations—that have ultimately become justifications—for contemporary racial inequality that exculpate them from any responsibility for the status of people of color" (2). We should not assume that racism is limited to the Klan or to overt forms of violence—though such forms of violence continue to occur at alarming rates—because "racial domination is a *collective* process (we are all in this game) and . . .

the main problem nowadays is not the folks with the hood, but the folks dressed in suits!" (xv). Color-blind racism is an ideology and a practice that "has become a formidable political tool for the maintenance of the racial order" (3). It exists because it benefits whites, the dominant race (9). Color-blind racism—or as Dána-Ain Davis calls it "muted racism"—developed in conjunction with neoliberalism. "Muted racism" or "muted racializing" occurs when "white privilege is generated in the absence of blatant racism" (Davis 2007, 354).

Some welfare staff I interviewed brought up race and culture on their own terms by explaining how they were more educated and experienced about racial issues than the average white citizen, which means they likely were more progressive than other citizens in the region. Lisa, Kristi, and Nate seemed to anticipate accusations of prejudice and responded by giving examples of other people who were more prejudiced than they were, a defensive move. They spoke to me of their "prejudiced," "close-minded," "conservative," and/or "ignorant" families, but seemed anxious and grateful for the opportunity to explain to me why people were this way. Bonilla-Silva characterizes such "stories of disclosure" as part and parcel of color-blind racism, not just stories, because they are so formulaic as to be predictable, part of a pattern not replicated by progressives or anti-racists. Like in Bonilla-Silva's interviews with whites, CCSS workers I spoke with discussed racist family members as a sort of confessional "structured around a trinity formula: confession, example, and self-absolution" (2014, 140). This relates to color-blind racism because "successful domination (racial or otherwise) requires making the dominated believe, participate, and process their standing as normative" (xiv). This happens in many ways, including the (re)telling of histories. Many whites believe, for example, that if racial and ethnic minorities "would just stop thinking about the past, work hard, and complain less (particularly about racial discrimination), then Americans of all hues could 'all get along'" (1). Decreasing racism must include a critical lens on both individual *and* systemic racism, on past *and* present forms of racism, and addressing how race continues to influence and limit equal access to rights, resources, and respect.

We cannot talk about race without also talking about racism, because racism is a social practice that historically preceded the social construct of race. Race was developed to justify racism, colonialism, and slavery. This is why many whites do not like to talk about race (Bonilla-Silva 2014). In Fargo, "race," "ethnicity," and "culture" were often evoked to describe refugees, but not whites from the Upper Midwest. Ruth Frankenberg shows that many discussions of whiteness and Americanness have tended to be "unmarked markers," an "absence of color" (Frankenberg 1994, 69). By valorizing difference in terms of racial diversity, white actors evade power differentials. "White" becomes "implicitly equivalent to self, norm, and nation. Nonwhites are marginal, the differers [sic]. Their inclusion in the nation . . . is construed here as optional: the nation does not require their presence in order to be fully formed" (69). In reality, this country was built by immigrants and slaves, not only white Euro-Americans. Thus, the categories of nonwhiteness/non-Americanness and whiteness/Americanness have come to be seen as mutually constitutive categories (70). It is also likely that people do not have a clear understanding of terms like "race," "ethnicity," and "culture" and use them interchangeably because, as long-time members of the dominant white population, they have not recognized the differences between them as important, and because they want to use inoffensive terminology. When CCSS's caseloads ballooned to include nearly 10 percent of New Americans, staff began to notice racial and cultural differences among their clients but did not have the vocabulary to describe them.

Individuals engaging in color-blind racism might argue that critiquing a Native American child's version of the past, as Lisa did, is less damaging than the actual murderous rampages against them historically. Nevertheless, language is power, and history matters. According to anthropologist and historian Michel-Rolph Trouillot, "Human beings participate in history both as actors and as narrators" (1995, 2). "We are all amateur historians with various degrees of awareness about our production. We also learn history from similar amateurs" (20). History is not a straightforward story written by historians; history is an active process shaped by a variety of sources and a diverse cast of narrators, from academics to pop culture icons, religious and cultural leaders to amateur historians, and the general public to social workers. "History," Trouillot writes, "reveals itself only through the production of specific narratives. What matters most are the process and conditions of production of such narratives" (25). In all likelihood, descendants of white settler colonialists will have a different perspective on the past than Native Americans. Rather than demonstrating color-blind racism, Lisa's approach to the history between white Euro-Americans and Native Americans reveals a "history-blind colonialism," a desire to put the violent colonial past in the past, rather than deal with the ongoing effects of settler colonialism on Native American populations today. Through these different perspectives on history, we can "discover the differential exercise of power that makes some narratives possible and silences others" (25). Lisa appeared to want to silence (or at least she wanted a teacher to silence) the child who spoke a Native American version of history. The stories we tell ourselves about ourselves are shaped by diverse sources and narratives, collective and individual, and by power. Just as racism is a collective process that we all participate in, so too is settler colonialism. Both are maintained in part by promoting some versions of history while silencing others. To alter the path of white racial domination and settler colonialism, dominant histories and narratives must be called into question, while alternative histories must be (re)constructed.

While some CCSS staff had little contact with refugees or people of color outside of their jobs, others had more experiences with racial differences and seemed more comfortable talking about them. Dot, an eligibility worker, was a married white woman in her thirties who had two children and lived in a small town outside of Fargo. She told me that she heard complaints from U.S.-born white clients about refugee clients. U.S.-born clients believed that they had to "jump through more hoops and give more information and get slower service than refugees." Dot told them that "no one has preferential treatment," but the U.S.-born clients were nevertheless "very, very angry." Dot said she almost called security on one white man because "he really felt that he was being exploited." According to such clients, jobs and wages in Fargo suffer because refugees are willing "to work for nothing." Dot believed that some Americans were jealous because refugees were working harder, even starting their own businesses, which made some U.S.-born clients angry. Unfortunately, Dot said, she heard more negative things about refugees and immigrants in Fargo than positive things. Judy said that all county workers put up with such attitudes "almost on a daily basis." Staff picked up the phone to hear, "If I was Black or I didn't speak English, you'd give [welfare] to me! The general public thinks that minorities get more benefits than the white Protestant American. . . . That has never changed."

Katherine Fennelly has studied the relationship between immigrants and white, rural Minnesotans. She writes,

> People viewing immigrants as a threat commonly view society as a "zero-sum" competition in which resources are finite, so that gains by immigrants necessarily imply equivalent losses by natives. People of low socioeconomic status are most susceptible to the perception of immigrants as a competitive threat. . . . Perceptions of economic threat are also particularly strong among those who adhere to an interpretation of the "Protestant work ethic" that attributes low status to a lack of self-reliance and hard work. (Fennelly 2008, 153)

I asked Dot what was needed to make Fargo more welcoming and inclusive, and she said New Americans and longtime residents needed a two-way street for understanding each other: "We have to understand what you [New Americans] are and where you come from, and you also have to understand us. You have to understand that we're Norwegian and German immigrants. This is our lifestyle. This is what we're accustomed to." I asked her to elaborate on what it meant to be "Norwegian and German immigrants," and she said,

> Well I think for the most part, probably "hardworking." And they're [a] very, take-care-of-yourself kind of culture. Not very . . . open at first, you

know probably reserved and kind of standoffish. And you might think people are kind of snobbish, but I tell you what, if you're in trouble, they're the first ones to give you the shirt off their back. I mean I see that time and time again here—that people are very, very generous. So I think that you know we might get a bad rap too. . . . But I think that . . . folks . . . [are] maybe a little more reserved until you get to know them, and then you're their friend for life.

The belief that people in the Upper Midwest are nicer and harder working than people in other places (big cities, other parts of the country or other parts of the world), even if they are cold at first, was a common theme among people in Fargo.

Not all caseworkers approached New Americans or nonwhites in the same way, of course. Dot told me that she had not been exposed to people of color growing up in a small North Dakota town. She remembers two Vietnamese students but had never met a Black person until she attended Moorhead State University, where she "had exposure to other cultures and other people" and "loved it." Dot had friends from El Salvador, Pakistan, Saudi Arabia, and Aruba. She was pleased to learn that "they're just like us"—that is, just like white North Dakotans. Dot learned about her friends' culinary and cultural practices and discovered that they had "the same dreams and hopes and . . . the same sense of humor." I had a similar feeling when I moved away from small-town Minnesota and my Iowa college town to study at the State University of New York at Stony Brook for a semester. I was enamored by the forms of diversity I encountered and vowed to learn more.

Other caseworkers I met expressed a desire to learn more history about the violence that forced refugees to flee, about life in refugee camps, about relationships between men and women in refugees' home countries, and about cross-cultural ideas regarding work, parenting, and government. This desire to learn more about "culture" was sincere, and it can be an important step in overcoming prejudice and learning to listen to people who receive welfare. However, refugees in Fargo represent dozens of different languages and vastly different socioeconomic backgrounds, religions, and customs. In a diverse city, it cannot be in the purview of already stretched-thin workers to know everything about every culture. Moreover, knowledge about refugee camps, cultural customs, and violence abroad can exacerbate structural inequalities already at play. Unless conveyed in a thoughtful manner that teaches about culture as a system of power, such knowledge would likely flood white workers with pity without any mechanism for harnessing these emotions toward a productive outcome. Learning how structures of inequality operate, both locally and globally, would go further to decrease discrimination, prejudice, and cross-cultural misunderstandings. Such education and training would include the influence of colonialism on populations around the world and how global empires created social categories such as race and then exploited people on the basis of those categories. Such education could lead to greater political consciousness and participation among workers and people who receive welfare from all backgrounds.

Gendered Aspects of Welfare and Refugees

Gender is important in these discussions because gender intersects with race, ethnicity, and culture. There was a strong desire by some female caseworkers to better understand how women in particular were (mis)treated in other countries; this further strengthened hegemonic ideas about gender relations in Fargo and worked to establish hierarchies based on race, class, and gender (Abu-Lughod 2002; Mullings 2005; Stoler 2002). Prefacing a desire to know more about gender, something that could potentially unite women, was arguably another way to avoid discussing race. Ong shows that "feminist" caseworkers in particular had a tendency to view Asian cultures as "patriarchal" without understanding the ways in which patriarchy also operates among U.S. cultures. "Feminist agents identify 'culture' as the basis of problems in Asian families," Ong argues, "and thus tend to ignore the way that Asian women exercise power, and the effects of wider institutional forces on families trying to cope in a violence-ridden environment" (2003, 144–145). The Cambodian men that Ong worked with faced racism and class-based discrimination in wider society. The desire for welfare workers to empower women, but not men, led to the disempowerment of men and contributed to problems between the sexes. I found similar attitudes toward gender and culture, particularly among female caseworkers. As Kristi told me,

> I think we've come a long ways in this agency to *really* educate ourselves about the culture, not to necessarily excuse behaviors, because things are things and rules are rules, But just to really help *us* understand the complexity of things . . . I'm very interested in how women are treated in the different cultures, [because I'm] a woman, probably (laughs). I'm always very interested in refugee camp experiences. . . . I don't think we have as an agency a good understanding about the refugee children that are coming here—and parents, the impact of posttraumatic stress disorder that they're bringing with them because of the things that they've experienced.

There are forms of violence against women and men in other parts of the world that do not exist in Fargo; they are historically particular and culturally specific but connected to one another in global assemblages that include colonialism, patriarchy, globalization, kinship, and war. I met refugees in Fargo who survived concentration camps, forced conscription into state and/or rebel armies, rape, ethnic cleansing, and systemic attempts to exterminate them and their families. Kristi, and workers like her, also heard such stories. They genuinely wanted to understand what life was like for women in other countries and to support them, but without training, such knowledge about recipients of welfare can serve to reinforce the idea that refugee women are weaker and more susceptible to violence and discrimination than white women in the United States. U.S. women experience sexism too, though the forms that sexism and misogyny take and the services available to victims vary across race and class (Crenshaw 1989 and 1991).

Workers sought to find the right approach for people who survived violence while also meeting strict participation requirements for the state. One worker told me,

> I hate to focus on the past, even with . . . a New American. I mean, their stories are all very interesting and they're actually very heartbreaking. I have a recent New American in our workshop right now. The other day we were talking about whatever, and one of the other clients in there asked her a question that led her to tell her story, and I was just like "Noooo! Don't tell it!" I mean, I didn't know what it was, but I didn't *want* to know it, . . . but it was too late and she told it. So, anyhow, everyone's all teary eyed and sick to their stomach about how women are treated in other countries and that whole thing like that, so I don't necessarily like to focus on the past so much as where they came from. And I know that they will always have a piece and part of that with them, but what do they see now and what do they see as going forward with their culture, and really what does it mean to hang on to your culture but yet be an American? And is that really conflicted, or is it really not conflicted?

Listening is an act of compassion that can go a long way in establishing trust and building rapport. Pity without compassion serves the worker more than the client. Social workers do not have time to research the history of all the countries from which their clients come, but they can assist people who are from different backgrounds by understanding how structures of oppression operate to create and reinforce inequality cross-culturally. Finn and Underwood explain that the welfare worker "does not unilaterally impose new rules of order on a passive recipient; rather, the two are bound together in a complex interplay of impression management, where application of impersonal, bureaucratic rules is mediated through a personal relationship" (2000, 126). Stories of violence impact that relationship. U.S. women are not immune to violence and patriarchy, though they may not experience the kinds of brutal and systemic violence that women surviving war have (which is also debatable when analyzing the treatment of Native American women, Black women, and Latinx women, especially).

Loren gave examples of the kinds of violence that some of his clients experienced in their home countries, and then said, "I'll never forget that. This is why people act the way they do!" He emotionally explained that he had found cases of welfare fraud among "*some of the nicest people*, and it's because . . . there is no trust [in government], or getting over on government [i.e., trying to outsmart government workers] is such a natural part of their daily life." In her work with Cambodian refugees in California, Aihwa Ong argued that the primary responsibility for many caseworkers revolved, in large part, around quantifying and verifying need and "punishing individuals who entered the territory of the welfare state[,] . . . separating the normal from the abnormal, the good from the bad refugees, the responsible from the 'welfare cheat'" (2003, 126).

To address the constraints under which he and his staff worked—including draconian federal welfare policies and a state social services board and commission that included "some people who did not trust Cass County Social Services"—Loren and other welfare service administrators worked to orient staff toward "service, not numbers." This meant building more alliances with partners outside of the welfare state, in addition to establishing good case management practices, which Loren explained were "necessary to energize and uplift people." Kathy Hogan told me, "Cultural differences make a lot of people uncomfortable, because anything new makes a lot of people uncomfortable. . . . And the issue is, so what do you do with that?" I asked her whose responsibility it was to educate people about refugees and New Americans in Fargo, and she quickly replied, "Well, it's everyone's. It's everyone's. . . . You learn it in your neighborhoods, you learn it in your churches, you learn it in your schools. But it is hard, you know. . . . To think that this is gonna be a simple thing is unrealistic." After years of critiquing resettlement, in her farewell speech to her staff before her retirement in 2008, Hogan said that working with New Americans was one of the top ten things she would miss most about her job at CCSS. Hogan served as a North Dakota state representative for District 21 from 2009 to 2018. In 2018, she was elected to the North Dakota Senate.

Since Hogan left as director of CCSS, some administrative practices have changed at both CCSS and NAS. In addition, Judy retired. Loren has been serving as the point of contact for newly arrived refugees, and he presents at NAS cultural orientation sessions. He works to build trust with welfare recipients, case management staff, and interpreters, but building these relationships has proved challenging with a rotating NAS staff. For years, Loren said, one person at NAS handled all of the refugee TANF cases and served as the point of contact with CCSS. The NAS worker served as the protective payee for TANF payments, but NAS changed its practices and began dividing TANF cases among all eight workers, which has caused more labor for state workers.

Conclusion: The Politics of Welfare

The relationship between CCSS and NAS is indicative of larger patterns between the state and civil society more broadly. Their differences and similarities speak to different ways of defining, managing, and interpreting diversity and the common good. The welfare state is supposed to serve everyone who qualifies for its services, but the state is not objective or neutral. Welfare policies are carried out by "street-level bureaucrats" (Lipsky 1980) who use—and *should* use—subjective practices in carrying out their work with a diverse clientele. In Fargo, a challenge for people in need of CCSS services is that staff are mostly white Christian women who have demonstrated a range of feelings and approaches to New Americans, from interest to disdain, pity to annoyance, and support.

The state does not serve everyone equally *or* equitably. Race and gender inform interpersonal relationships between welfare workers and recipients, but these were not acknowledged or discussed by many of the workers, at least not to me. While state workers had more training and accountability measures than workers in the nonprofit sector, this training was mostly about the "nuts and bolts" of the job, not cultural competence. While the nonprofit sector lacked training and accountability, and suffered from high turnover rates and burnout, nonprofit workers seemed to provide a more human connection and flexible case management practices with fewer restrictions, which softened the caseworker-client power dynamic. One way that workers at both agencies accommodated the demands of their difficult jobs was to blame staff at other agencies for not doing more.

Better, more standardized training for all new resettlement staff and volunteers at NAS could prevent staff burnout and high turnover rates and decrease resentment toward state workers. This might include a map and list of organizations and agencies in Fargo, both state and private, and what each organization does. The training could include brief histories of the populations being resettled, with guest speakers from those countries, when available, as well as scenarios based on real examples for caseworkers to discuss before they work with New Americans. The annual Building Bridges conference does some of this work, but it happens once a year, attendance is not mandatory, and new staff need training before beginning case management. A challenge is finding a time and space in their stretched-thin budget. A similar training would be useful for new CCSS staff.

According to Loren, the state legislature wanted CCSS's 2017 budget to be 90 percent of what the 2016 budget was, which would allow no room for growth or accommodate exploding caseloads. Such a request forces concerned caseworkers and welfare administrators to work harder and more creatively with their nonstate partners in order to find poor people the services they need. This relationship can be beneficial for workers and users of services, but it is also fraught due to unclear training and accountability measures in the nonprofit sector, and a lack of diversity and cultural-competence training among state workers.

Scholars have been decrying the end of welfare for decades as politicians continue to dismantle policies aimed at alleviating the suffering of the poor; meanwhile, economic inequality continues to grow, and people across the United States have grown angrier at government. John Clarke argues that we should "'think again' about welfare states—and . . . we should think better" (2004, 2). Rather than choose between the "end" of welfare and the "survival" of welfare, or between the state and the market, as scholarship on neoliberalism so often does, Clarke encourages us to view the welfare state as more than "one thing." Instead of proclaiming that neoliberalism has resulted in the end of welfare, he challenges us to see the resilience of welfare states and their relationship, for example, to nonstate practices and programs, (such as refugee resettlement). The relationships between welfare states and other actors are variable, contested, constructed, and constitutive. Approaching welfare as a structure in constant flux, never entirely stable or unstable, allows us to envision a new and different kind of welfare state in an age of globalization and neoliberalism, one that goes beyond simple income distribution.

My work in Fargo supports Clarke's assertion that welfare states change. People and practices shape welfare states through their knowledge, norms, identities, and power (2004, 37). They are shaped by top-down policies, such as PRWORA, but also by bottom-up everyday practices, such as the influx of refugees to Fargo.

New American Services and Cass County Social Services are key stakeholders in refugee resettlement, especially in the initial period when refugees first arrive in Fargo, but they are only pieces of the city's total structure. In my experience, not all refugees needed these services, especially after the first four to eight months. Some refugees in Fargo have little, if any, contact with these institutions. The next chapter analyzes the beliefs, practices, and discourse about refugees and race beyond resettlement and welfare agencies in order to provide a deeper, richer context for why members of the dominant population reacted to refugees in the ways that they did. It describes responses to refugees by schools, police, nonprofit organizations, (social) media, the public, city planners, and politicians, as well as programs designed to educate the public about resettlement.

DIVERSITY AND INCLUSION IN FARGO

Fargo is more geographically isolated than most parts of the country in terms of its proximity to larger urban centers and the low population density surrounding the city, but people in Fargo are part of assemblages that connect them to others around the country and the world. These assemblages are built through social, economic, political, and religious relations with family and friends, news media and social media, music, literature, popular culture, and through travel and education. The identity of a person, a group of people, or a city does not develop in isolation. This chapter provides data on the beliefs, practices, and discourse about refugees and race beyond refugee resettlement and welfare agencies. My aim is to provide a broader, richer context for refugee resettlement in Fargo by highlighting a spectrum of tensions between those who welcome refugees and those who do not. Primarily, I use the lenses of race and sociality as markers of difference. In doing so, I explain what tensions indicate about the structures within which resettlement work is done—for example, education, police, media, politics, and civil society, and a range of practices surrounding and shaping refugee resettlement in the city. I make the case that diversity is good for a city, if not also difficult for the trailblazers who embody and support it.

Learning Race and Racism

Most people begin learning about race and ethnicity from family members. In a city comprised mostly of whites, it is most likely that individuals will learn about race from other whites, which provides an incomplete picture of race relations in the United States at best, and a lesson in white supremacy at worst. My earliest recollection about race and racism occurred when I was five years old. I was playing a game, which began, "Eeny-meeny-miny-mo, catch a n— by the toe. If he hollers, make him pay fifty dollars every day, eeny-meeny-miny-mo." My mom overheard me, and her unusually quick, almost explosive, response was memorable. She sat me down firmly and told me that "the n-word" was a "very bad word." Naturally, I asked why. She explained that it was a negative word associated with people with darker skin colors, that it was not nice, and that I should never use it again, and I didn't. Others' first memory about racism is the first time they were on the receiving end of this word. Language can hurt.

A few years after this conversation with my mom, I read my first biography of Martin Luther King Jr. and became instantly enamored by him and by stories of the civil rights movement. I read as much as I could about King, but also about race and racism. I read *Black Like Me* by John Howard Griffin, then *Roots* by Alex Haley and *The Autobiography of Malcolm X*, all of which forever changed the way that I viewed the world and my place in it. I give my own example here to show one of many ways that people learn about race. There are countless other ways in which we learn race and racism, and my aim here is to offer examples of how race was constructed in and through Fargo, and shaped by its historical and contemporary assemblages and structures, from refugee resettlement to *National Geographic*.

In January 2008 *National Geographic* published "The Emptied Prairie," an article about North Dakota's disappearing small towns (Bowden 2008). When the author Charles Bowden described lands occupied by North Dakotans as "empty," white people in North Dakota got angry. The article included photos of haunted-looking abandoned farmhouses with broken-down furniture, rusty cars, a naked doll without eyes, a cat, a horse, and sweeping views of prairie and big sky. Only one of the fourteen photos portrayed a person, her middle-aged white face obscured by a reflection of a snow-covered landscape. The article outraged North Dakotans. Scott Olsen wrote a letter to the editor of the *Forum of Fargo-Moorhead* that he had been "betrayed by a love of my life." For him, *National Geographic* had been "*veritas*—unassailable, unshakable truth" (Olsen 2008).

In *Reading National Geographic*, Lutz and Collins (1993) argued that readers like Olsen viewed *National Geographic*'s portrayal of "third world" people as unproblematic, objective, even scientific. The article challenged Olsen's conservative humanism and middle-class values by turning the lens on his own culture. Olsen was not alone in his anger and disappointment. People from across the state wrote letters to local newspapers and to the magazine. The story dominated local newscasts. Citizens asked incredulously, "Why didn't the author mention our growing economy, low unemployment rate, cosmopolitan centers like Fargo and Bismarck, outstanding small-town leadership, and the oil boom in the west?" Longtime readers threatened to cancel their subscriptions. North Dakota's Senator Conrad called the magazine to say that he felt the piece was an "especially egregious representation of the state," a preposterous, unfair, and inaccurate, representation that "left an inappropriate image of an entire state and that the people here are quite resentful, *tired of the constant belittling*" (cited in Olsen 2008; emphasis mine). The article caused so much controversy that ABC News made the entire state of North Dakota its "person of the week" (Gibson 2008). Some North Dakotans, like those who responded to the *National Geographic* article, felt belittled because they were so often portrayed as more backward and less cosmopolitan or modern compared to other Americans.

The reactions of North Dakotans to the *National Geographic* piece explains further how refugees race-d Fargo. Readers were accustomed to seeing a juxtaposition of "the West" and "the rest" in *National Geographic*. This "juxtaposition of articles on New Guinea rituals with articles on orderly farms in New England or shiny new factories in the South underscored evolutionary themes in the articles and photographs themselves" (Lutz and Collins 1993, 26). The portrayals of the United States in *National Geographic* were usually of sophisticated middle-class, privileged, white families and communities. "Generally speaking," Lutz and Collins explain, "*National Geographic* helped white, upwardly mobile Americans to locate themselves in a changing world, to come to terms with their whiteness and relative privilege, and to deal with anxieties about their class position, both national and international" (38). For example, *National Geographic* did not report on civil rights movements in U.S. cities. Instead, in the 1950s, the magazine featured Asian and African people attending to white explorers. In the 1960s, *National Geographic* portrayed the "third world" as "a safe, comfortable space, where race was not an issue and where white people did not have to reevaluate the sources of their privilege" (159). The magazine "averted its eyes from anything that suggested interracial or intercultural conflict," (40) including potential threats from people of color or formerly colonized peoples (164).

By showing photographs of a declining North Dakota countryside, including just one photo of an "average-looking" middle-class white woman—not the typical image of the upper-class suburban cosmopolitan homemaker that the magazine often portrayed—the magazine disrupted a well-established tradition of representing whites in the United States as upwardly mobile, shining examples for "the rest" of the world. Lutz and Collins showed that "*National Geographic* magazine is the product of a society deeply permeated with racism as a social practice and with racial understandings as ways of viewing the world. It sells itself to a reading public that, while they do not consider themselves racist, turn easily to race as an explanation for culture and for social outcome" (156–157). *National Geographic* was one of countless sources of ideas about race and culture in North Dakota that informed local understandings about those coded as other, in this case non-Western people and people of color.

Muriel McDonald and her husband moved to Fargo from the East Coast in the 1960s. Muriel was a retired language instructor, mother, active member of the Catholic Church, and an outspoken advocate for refugees, the poor, and other disadvantaged groups. She exuded patience, openness, and compassion. She started the Giving Plus Learning Program, which paired elderly volunteers with New Americans for English classes, driving lessons, and tutoring for the citizenship test and certified nursing assistant exams. On the first day I met her, she granted me immediate access to all of the program's files, including the phone numbers of all mentors and mentees, and a list of other people in the community who worked with refugees. In one of our many conversations, she told me,

> What I see quite often is there is . . . pretty hidden racial prejudice. It's been focused before on American Indians because that's the only minority we've had. And it's pretty deep. So that you may not even be aware that you're doin' it, and I hear it over and over again, such as . . . "I can't tell you where they're from, but they're dark." Because everybody here *isn't* dark. And I notice it myself. I mean, anytime I'm in a group anywhere, everybody's white, so I think to pretend it isn't here is pretty unrealistic.

Diversity is relative. For those North Dakotans and Minnesotans who came from small towns or even more rural areas, Fargo felt diverse. Some whites had never seen a person of color or a woman wearing a hijab until they came to Fargo. For whites moving to Fargo from more diverse parts of the country, however, even cities like Minneapolis or Chicago, the lack of racial diversity in Fargo was palpable.

In the *High Plains Reader*, journalist C. S. Hagen wrote a series on racism in North Dakota and how race relations have changed over time (2017a, 2017b, 2017d). In the first installment of this series, Hagen claims that North Dakota is "a perfect place for white supremacists" because of its history of violence and forced removal of Native Americans, the prevalence of whites who believe in their superiority over other races, and antagonism toward New Americans. In addition to writing about a history of violent settler colonialism, he draws attention to twenty-first-century white supremacists in North Dakota and compares them to members of the KKK and Nazi sympathizers in North Dakota in the 1920s. For example, on April 24, 2017, Holocaust Remembrance Day, someone posted white nationalist flyers around the city. One flyer said, "This country is your birthright.

Don't give up." Another read, "Trump was the first step. We're the next" (Hagen 2017g). Hagen ties local forms of racism to national forms, such as the killing of activist Heather Heyer by Nazi sympathizer James Alex Fields at the "Unite the Right" rally in Charlottesville, Virginia, on August 12, 2017.

Heralded as one of the largest white supremacist gatherings in U.S. history, at least one of the thousands of whites at the rally was Peter Tefft of Fargo, whose father, Pearce, garnered national attention for disavowing his son's practices in a letter to the *Forum of Fargo-Moorhead* (Tefft 2017). He wrote the letter in order to "loudly repudiate my son's vile, hateful and racist rhetoric and actions. We do not know specifically where he learned these beliefs. He did not learn them at home. . . . We have been silent up until now, but now we see that this was a mistake. It was the silence of good people that allowed the Nazis to flourish the first time around, and it is the silence of good people that is allowing them to flourish now." According to his father, Peter did not learn racist values at home. We do not know where Peter Tefft learned to be racist, but sources on white supremacy abound. We can learn a lot from conversations between adults and children about race, culture, and diversity. My desire to be antiracist began with conversations with my parents. African American writer James Baldwin explained his perspective on racism in a letter to his fifteen-year-old nephew, which is worth quoting at length:

> There is no reason for you to try to become like white people and there is no basis whatever for their impertinent assumption that *they* must accept *you*. The really terrible thing, old buddy, is that *you* must accept *them*. And I mean that very seriously. You must accept them and accept them with love. For these innocent people have no other hope. They are, in effect, still trapped in a history which they do not understand; and until they understand it, they cannot be released from it. They have had to believe for many years, and for innumerable reasons, that black men are inferior to white men. Many of them, indeed, know better, but, as you will discover, people find it very difficult to act on what they know. To act is to be committed, and to be committed is to be in danger." (1962, 292–294; emphasis in the original; see also Coates 2015 and Ward 2016)

Pearce Tefft acted by repudiating his racist son, and he was not alone in doing so in Fargo. Local activist Luke Safely argued in the *High Plains Reader* that more whites need to stand up against white supremacy because remaining silent is "willful ignorance, and it's North Dakota nice." Safely began putting up posters naming local Nazis, like Peter Tefft (Hagen 2017a).

Mary Jane Miller, a white woman in her eighties who volunteered with refugees, spent much of her interview with me discussing sexism and racism in North Dakota. Mary Jane and her husband had six children and lived most of their lives in Grand Forks, about eighty miles north of Fargo. To earn some extra income and meet new people, they took in University of North Dakota student tenants. Their first tenant, in 1960, was not able to live on the UND campus, because he was Black. Mary Jane told me about the racism she witnessed after welcoming David into her home:

> Educated people—my bridge group—would say, "Does he get the sheets black?" . . . When my mother, my own mother, came to visit me in Grand Forks, she came in, and she crossed paths with David, and she . . . grabbed me and she took me into the dining room and she says, "Oh, you've got to get that man out of the house, he's going to rape you!" And I said, "Mother, if any one of my sons grows up to be as fine a gentleman as David, I will feel I'm really successful." He was a polished English person from the Bahamas.

Mary Jane also spoke about feminism and her prochoice beliefs. Her apartment in the retirement home in 2008 featured stickers for U.S. presidential candidate Hillary Clinton. Mary Jane ran as a Democrat for the North Dakota House of Representatives in 1980 but lost in a Republican landslide.

Mary Jane told me that refugees were discriminated against in new and different forms than her former tenant was discriminated against as a Black man in 1960, or than she was discriminated against as a woman running for elected office in 1980. Refugees, she explained, were discriminated against on the basis of language as well as "how they dress and how they think and maybe the food they put on the table." Mary Jane understood cultural components in the social construction of race, and that racism was more than physical appearance and skin color. Refugees were differently included in Fargo on the basis of language, skin color, food, and everyday cultural practices, like clothing.

Another volunteer for the Giving Plus Learning Program, Joan, was a New Jersey native who was shocked at the ratio of whites to people of color in Fargo and discussed with me decades' worth of prejudice and discrimination that she had seen leveled against immigrants, refugees, and Native Americans in the region. Another woman, Shirley, grew up in south Chicago in the 1960s, where she learned to fear African Americans and developed narrow views of urban Black families. Shirley told me that she was scared of Black men but learned about American Indian and African American history through a graduate class and decided to do something about inequality by writing her dissertation on English language acquisition among refugees. First, she had to overcome her fears and prejudice. She tried working with Roma but was unable to find any Roma who would speak with her. She met some Southern Sudanese men who agreed to speak with her, which she told me, changed her life completely. She saw their homes, and their humanity, and admitted to me that she was at first afraid of Southern Sudanese because she negatively equated them with African Americans, based solely on their skin color. She learned to unlearn racism through the course of her research and learned that not all Black people were the same. Her empathy stemmed from lessons she learned from Southern Sudanese about their journey to the United States and their desire to integrate into U.S. society. Whether her acceptance extended to African Americans, I am not sure.

Doug Johnson met New Americans through his job as a driver for Handiwheels, a nonprofit organization that provided transportation to people who used North Dakota Medicaid. Doug was a tall, wiry white man and an amateur nature photographer. At our first meeting, Doug spoke of his deep appreciation for the prairie and nature and then slowly began to tell me about his friendship with Simon, a Southern Sudanese man who rode his bus regularly. As they rode, they discussed topics as wide ranging as food, transportation, jobs, and dating. He found it strange that Simon wanted to get married but that he refused to marry the woman he was dating because he wanted to go back to Sudan to find a wife who would be more subservient than the Sudanese women in America, who were "spoiled" (see chapter 6 and Shandy 2007 for more on men looking for wives in Sudan). One Thanksgiving, in a gesture of friendship, Doug brought Simon a deer that he had hunted. Unlike some whites, who appeared to be drawn to refugees because of their suffering and need for assistance, Doug stressed that he preferred to learn about New Americans' ideas and cultural practices, not about their suffering. Talking to people on a bus was another way people learned about diversity, not only about race or refugee status but about cultural differences in dating, marriage, and hunting practices.

Glen Gunderson learned about structural inequality, especially racism, through his volunteer work with refugees that began in retirement. Before that, Glen said, he did not know anyone from another country. Then he started volunteering for Cultural Diversity Resources. Glen's ancestors came from Norway and Sweden, and he referred to his ethnic roots often. When I asked him to explain what it meant to be Scandinavian in Fargo, Glen said, "Eighty percent of the people around here say one thing to your face, something politically correct, and then turn around and believe something else." Glen also told me that he felt racism was a big problem in North Dakota. Glen was "a closeted Democrat" at work. He was afraid that, as a Democrat, he would not be accepted by his coworkers or might even be fired. He saw well-qualified men, mostly from Asia, interview for positions, but they were always turned down for the job. Glen "didn't have proof," but he suspected that race had something to do with it.

After he started volunteering at CDR and later at the Giving Plus Learning Program, where he tutored refugees in English, Glen began to notice structural inequalities. He explained that a friend of his, a Black woman, had been pulled over by police for speeding. She had been driving her boyfriend's car, and her boyfriend had a criminal record. Glen went with her to court to fight the ticket and could not believe the differential treatment he witnessed between Black and white defendants. He saw "a white kid with three prior convictions of drunk driving get off." Glen's friend had to pay a seven-hundred-dollar fine for speeding. The difference, he said, was "skin color and having a lawyer." Glen went on to describe how "bitter" and "outraged" he was at "the system."

I have argued elsewhere (Erickson 2012) that volunteers like Glen, perhaps more so than resettlement or welfare workers, have served as foot soldiers of citizenship, a citizenship that has privileged whiteness, Christianity, a Protestant work ethic, and gendered practices of care but also has challenged some of these same ideals, as was the case with Glen and Mary Jane. Everyday interactions between volunteers and New Americans in Fargo—whether through programs such as the Giving Plus Learning Program or LSS—served to form and solidify social hierarchies in ways comparable to the missionaries that Jean Comaroff and John Comaroff (1992) described in their work in colonial South Africa. By working with refugees in homes, schools, stores, clinics, and social service organizations, on an everyday level, volunteers consciously and unconsciously have changed the ways that New Americans view and are viewed by the city.

North Dakota Nice

People I met in Fargo, especially those who grew up in the region, viewed themselves as nicer, friendlier, and harder working than people in other parts of the country. I asked everyone I interviewed (sixty formal interviews) to tell me what it meant to them to be a "good person" as well as their most and least favorite aspects of the region. A pattern emerged that had to do with niceness, work ethic, and climate, and it was prevalent across generations. Roy Elenika, a fifty-something white man from North Dakota, believed in niceness as a force for social change: "I'm convinced it doesn't really matter where you come from, anywhere in the world. People are basically the same. And [if] you start from there, it's easy [to communicate with people from other cultures]. I think it's easy if you're friendly and open and honest with people, establish a relationship with them. [You can relate to] just about anybody from anywhere if you're willing to do that."

Being "friendly and open and honest" has to do with power and trust, something refugees and other historically marginalized groups are wary of giving, especially to (white) people in positions of power. When refugees were not "nice"—for example, when they did not smile, volunteer personal history, or make small talk, some in Fargo interpreted this as their being mean, difficult, or unwilling to assimilate. A twenty-something white woman who worked at Walmart told me that she did not like "foreigners" because they did not smile, and that intimidated her. She felt particularly uncomfortable around "Africans." Southern Sudanese told me that they found it strange and annoying when strangers smiled at them.

Courtney, another white woman in her early twenties who worked briefly at New American Services, told me that her parents moved back to Fargo from Colorado because the work ethic was stronger in North Dakota. Work ethic also defined Courtney: "I worked when I was twelve and had my first real job when I was thirteen, and I've always worked, and when I see [refugee] clients who are like nineteen, and . . . [they ask], 'How can I work?' and I'm like, 'Well, I worked at *thirteen*!' I had four jobs in college. I worked sixty-plus hours . . . but somebody who's never had to work . . . who's never had the importance of *why* to work . . . I mean, that's more of my background." By "work," Courtney meant waged labor in an advanced capitalist society, a twenty-first-century version of the Protestant work ethic, the idea that one does not work for income alone but to fulfill a moral, if not also spiritual, imperative of self-improvement and community building (Weber 1958).

In one conversation, Alison Baker, a middle-aged white woman who worked for a nonprofit organization, complained about her workload, sometimes incompetent staff, and how it was easier simply to do everything herself. She asked me if I was "a farm girl" and then followed with: "On the farm, you just do it. You do everything. You sweep when things need to be swept! But not everyone has that attitude!" When I asked Susan, a white woman in her mid-fifties who worked for the welfare state, about her favorite aspects of the region, she said, "I just think the Midwest is so friendly. . . . And they have a good work ethic. I like the four seasons. I think I'd miss that. Even though I hate winters, I still would miss the four seasons, but I think it's to our benefit. This is gonna sound terrible, but I think it keeps a lot of the riffraff out, when we have the winters and the four seasons." Jean Walters, a white woman in her eighties who volunteered with refugees, told me, "Well, *I* would say . . . the people are friendly here. They're hardworking. I think they really have a work ethic. . . . For the most part North Dakota is kind of a safe place, and we don't have perfect weather, but we don't have hurricanes." Work ethic, niceness, and abilities to withstand the weather contributed to forms of sociality that were present in institution after institution that I worked with, and arose in everyday conversations with cashiers at the grocery store, postal workers, and the president of the Fargo-Moorhead Chamber of Commerce, who explained:

[The work ethic is] a strong part of our culture. . . . We *do* compare favorably nationally with our work ethic here. . . . We don't have a magic formula for it, but . . . people here grow up knowing how to work, wanting to work, willing to work. [That's] maybe not true in other parts of the country. . . . We're pretty darn lucky that it is true here. And I think it's a good match between our dominant original culture [meaning whites, not American Indians] and our enhanced culture through diversity [New Americans].

Many people in Fargo *were* nice. Take, for example, the story of a Haitian man who came to Fargo as a refugee and walked to work, even on frigid winter evenings, because public transportation was not available evenings or Sundays. One night, a white woman saw him, a Black man, walking alone and stopped to pick him up. She then drove him to work every day until he could afford to buy a car. Their families became friends and remained so years later. Others volunteered with apartment setups for newly arrived refugees, made curtains for them, took them grocery shopping, tutored them in English, and drove them to appointments, school, and work. According to a longtime resettlement worker, refugees attributed their success to the support they received from "American friends."

Education

Along with refugee resettlement staff, welfare workers, and volunteers, teachers are on the front lines of refugee resettlement. Dozens of languages are represented in Fargo, Moorhead, and West Fargo schools. In Fargo alone, there are seventy-one different languages spoken and sixty nations represented (Schmidt 2016). According to its 2016–2017 annual report, the Fargo Public Schools English Learner program served 815 K–12 students. About 70 percent of these were refugees, and 30 percent were immigrants. The largest groups of students who speak languages other than English at home are Nepali (17 percent), Somali (13 percent), Arabic (13 percent), Creole/Pidgin (10 percent), Spanish (9 percent), and Swahili, Bosnian, and Native American Indian (each 5 percent), in addition to Vietnamese, Chinese, Dinka, French, Kinyardwanda (2–4 percent each), and other (9 percent). Across the three school districts, Somali is the most common language, with 675 students speaking it at home (Schmidt 2016).

Connie Miller, an English language learning (ELL) teacher in the Fargo school district, explained the challenges of having the number of refugee children in her school grow from two or three to more than three hundred over the course of just a few years. The 2002 No Child Left Behind Act (NCLB) (Pub.L. 107–110, 115 Stat. 1425) made these changes all the more difficult because of its thesis that high standards and measurable goals alone could improve individual outcomes in education. Rooted in racialized, neoliberal beliefs, the law worked against schools with rapidly changing demographics. In order to receive federal funding, NCLB required states to develop assessments in basic skills and required that they be given to *all* students, regardless of first language or ability. NCLB forced many teachers to view their students in terms of test scores. Due to language barriers and lack of formal education in home countries or refugee camps, refugee students impacted these scores negatively.

In the 1990s, there were few ELL teachers and few ELL students. Seemingly overnight, three hundred new students began arriving annually. It was tough on teachers, who had high performance goals to reach but scant support to accommodate the changes taking place in their classrooms. Connie's school had to hire more teachers, aides, and social workers, and the change was, according to Connie, "slow in coming." Adding to the challenges was the fact that most ELL curriculum focused on Spanish-speaking children, who have knowledge of U.S. culture and some literacy in the home. Many refugee children in Fargo, however, did not have basic cultural knowledge about the United States or literacy in the home. ELL teachers do not just teach English; they also help integrate students and their families into the community. When the school did not provide enough support, she turned to the chamber of commerce, which helped her design a curriculum for mentors to work with ELL students. They calculated that they needed about three hundred mentors. They got just twenty in the first year. She also worked with nonprofit organizations to develop after-school programs for refugee children.

I asked Connie to explain the challenges of incorporating new forms of diversity in her classroom, and she said that she wished she could learn more and quicker about the cultures of her students. Doing so would have resulted in different approaches to students and different pedagogical practices. In college, she learned that teachers should have authority in the classroom, to set up rules and require that students abide by them, which means not talking when the teacher talks. She found it personally insulting and a challenge to her authority when students did not listen. She explained:

> You don't learn culture by reading a culture-gram. You learn culture by viewing what the people living in that culture [are doing], and then [view] it up against my culture. . . . I don't mean to be—to do something wrong or hurt anybody. . . . It's just that my culture doesn't match up with theirs. And as far as a specific instance, I think of the Somalis,

when they first came, and they [were] loud. They're just a lot louder people than we are. We are Norwegian up here, you know, pretty quiet, and they talk all at once. And that doesn't really fit in well to what an American teacher's expectations are. But then I learned that . . . that's what they do. Actually what happened is . . . I saw the parents doing that. We'd have meetings in the principal's office, and the parents were talking at the same time. I'm like, holy buckets, this is what they do. You know, something I would have considered rude in my culture . . . it just affected the way that I was able to relate to the kids and know, okay, they're not meaning to be rude to me.

Connie recognized how different cultural practices and approaches toward talking and listening played out in her classroom. She realized that she had been judging the practices of Somali students negatively, taking their cultural norms as a challenge to her authority. When she realized that "being loud" was not a personal attack, she adjusted her pedagogy.

Police

In 1994–1995, Amy Swenson was assigned to patrol the region of south Fargo, where most new refugees were being placed in apartment buildings. Language barriers, fear of law enforcement, and other cultural differences made her job increasingly difficult. Basic law enforcement tasks became more time consuming, but she enjoyed working with New Americans. In 1995, an incident occurred that would make her job harder. It was referred to as "The Kebab House Incident." According to the *Forum of Fargo-Moorhead* (1995, A1), three teenage boys allegedly accosted Stephanie Sarabakhsh outside of the Iranian restaurant she owned and managed with her husband and sister-in-law. Stephanie's husband, Mort, and his sister Zhaleh were Iranian-U.S. citizens who had lived in the United States for more than twenty years. The boys allegedly circled Stephanie's car on bikes and shouted that it was "'her and her kind ruining America'" (*Forum of Fargo-Moorhead* 1995).

Over the next days and weeks, several incidents followed: a swastika was carved in the restaurant's back door with threats against the family, fake body parts with additional threats were allegedly sent to the family, and the restaurant was set on fire. As the restaurant burned around her, police found Zhaleh bound with tape at her ankles and hands with a crude cross resembling a swastika carved in her stomach. After the incident, one thousand people attended a march against racism and xenophobia at North Dakota State University, where Mort Sarabakhsh,

Stephanie's husband and Zhaleh's brother, was a professor. On October 25, 1995, Peter Jennings reported the alleged hate crime and the rally on the nationally televised *ABC Evening News*. Two hundred people attended a follow-up rally. Local banks, churches, and families donated thousands of dollars to rebuild the restaurant. Then the thirty-eight-year-old Zhaleh Sarabakhsh was accused of committing the violence against herself. She was arrested on charges of committing arson, insurance fraud, endangering herself and the family business, and making a false report (*New York Times* 1995). On June 7, 1996, after undergoing psychiatric evaluations, Sarabakhsh was found to be suffering from psychotic depression and not criminally responsible for her actions. The circuit court judge ruled that she presented a risk of harm to others and ordered that she be committed to the North Dakota State Hospital for a period not to exceed two years (Arson Case Briefs 1996). Amy Swenson told me that Sarabakhsh was "culturally homesick."

The National Crime Bureau heard about the story and reached out to the Fargo police to offer training for them in best practices with New Americans. Amy had already been envisioning such a program, one that would build trust and teach New Americans about the laws in the United States. She attended the best practices workshop in Washington, D.C. In 1997, she became Fargo's first refugee liaison officer. She then approached LSS about giving a presentation at orientation sessions. Her first presentation was just thirty minutes long. It grew to one hour, then two, and now is a four-hour presentation.

Amy took a proactive stance to her position by learning about various cultural practices, asking elders or leaders in New American communities for advice and cooperation about specific cases, and mapping the names and relationships of families whom she saw as real or potential criminals. She worked to prevent refugees from committing violations because they did not understand the laws. Once they were in the system, it was very difficult for them to get out, which could eventually impact their access to legal citizenship. Many refugees did not realize that, for example, violating a restraining order or driving drunk could impact their job status, housing, and long-term legal status. According to Amy, the program "created a different trust level between refugees and law enforcement and that [was] the biggest difference."

Amy accompanied some New Americans to court in order to explain what was happening and to support them. They sometimes told the judge that they understood and then turned to Amy and whispered, "I didn't understand." Language barriers remained a problem for law enforcement, so Amy supported the development of the Metro Interpreter Recourse Center, in 1994, in order to provide training and certified interpreters in the city. Amy remained the refugee liaison officer until 2007, when she left for another position and Alex Gangstead became the new liaison.

In 2008, the "refugee liaison officer" became the "cultural liaison officer," which expanded the position to all groups in Fargo that did not fall into the category of "white, U.S.-born, English-speaking citizens." The City of Fargo website describes the position as follows:

> The Fargo Police Department created this position in 2008 to provide Fargo's large new American population with a familiar face in law enforcement that they could reach out to with questions and concerns. The new American population consists of refugees, immigrants, and asylees. The Cultural Liaison Officer also serves our diverse Native American population. The Native American community in Fargo represents more than 21 federally recognized nations from the US and Canada. Each nation has its own beliefs, practices, traditions, cultural values, protocol, history and language. (City of Fargo, n.d.).

Alex worked to bring as many New Americans and Native Americans to the table as possible, because, she argued, "if you're not at the table, you're on the menu." Alex also said that there are considerably more services for New Americans than when she first started her job, across the public and private spectrum—services offered by interpreters, school social workers, and healthcare providers—which has made her job easier. Also, the Fargo Police Department is becoming more diverse, with more women, people of color, and those from underrepresented populations, such as Bosnians and Latinos, but it is still predominantly a white male department. The department is also training its officers to deescalate situations verbally rather than through physical confrontation, but that poses a challenge among people who do not speak English.

Another part of Alex's job is to educate the public about New Americans and to explain U.S. culture and laws to New Americans. Local news station Valley News Live (KVLY), an NBC-affiliated television station licensed to Fargo that serves eastern North Dakota and northwestern Minnesota, has not made Alex's job easier. In an effort to boost ratings, KVLY began airing provocative and misleading information about refugee resettlement to the city. After one particularly erroneous report about the prevalence of tuberculosis among refugee populations, and harassment of refugees following these reports, Alex spent an entire day at a local adult learning center trying to reassure New Americans that most people in Fargo wanted them in the city.

Police officers in Fargo also respond to hate crimes targeted at New Americans and other minorities. From 2012 to 2017, the Fargo Police Department reported forty-eight hate crimes, in addition to the kinds of harassment mentioned earlier: white supremacy posters and Confederate flags. In 2014, a client bit off the nose of a Somali cab driver who had intervened in a domestic fight in his cab.

In 2017, a man in Moorhead followed a Somali woman around a grocery store, demanding that she remove her hijab (Johnson 2017). Between 2010 and 2015, North Dakota was one of the top five states for the number of reported hate crimes and actions per capita (Majumder 2017; see also Hagen 2017f, 2017h, and Hagen and Gonzalez 2019).

On July 25, 2017, what started as a parking dispute in Fargo turned into a verbal altercation between Amber Hensley, a white woman from Mapleton, and three Somali-American women, sisters Sarah and Leyla Hassan and Rowda Soyan. Personal insults about one another's appearance were hurled, and then Amber said, "We're gonna kill all of ya. We're going to kill every one of you fucking Muslims." Twenty-one-year-old Sarah Hassan recorded the incident and posted it online. The accounting firm where Hensley worked reported hundreds of calls to complain about her behavior, which resulted in her termination. Amber apologized on Facebook, and then Fargo police chief David Todd facilitated a reconciliation meeting between Hensley and the Hassan sisters (McFeely 2017). Hensley learned that the Hassans endure ongoing prejudice based on their dress (both wear hijabs) and on their native country, and the Hassans learned that Amber's father was killed in Iraq. The women accepted Amber's apology, and they embraced. The Hassans and local civil rights activist Hukun Abdullahi of the Afro American Development Association tried to help Amber get her job back (Hagen 2017a). *Forum of Fargo-Moorhead* reporters claimed the incident "thrusts Fargo into the nation's culture debate" (Tran, Hyatt, and Schmidt 2017). The story demonstrates the tensions and the work that must be done to facilitate acceptance of diversity but also that such work can bring about change and diminish prejudice (Erickson 2017b). There is clearly more work to be done to make Fargo welcoming and to increase inclusivity, particularly in regard to representation of minorities in structures throughout the city, including media.

Publics and (Social) Media

In August 2015, Damon Ouradnik started a petition on Change.org that called on the Cass County legislature to end refugee resettlement to the region. Nearly 3,300 people signed it. Of the 1,099 people who reported their location on the petition, 82.5 percent of them were from North Dakota or Minnesota, and about half were from Fargo, West Fargo, or Moorhead. There appeared to be nearly equal numbers of men and women. One problem with online petitions like this is that the identities of the signatories are not verifiable. In the comments section of this petition, opinions about refugee resettlement were infused with opinions about crime and safety, legality, Islam, alleged poor health and hygiene among refugees, and rude behavior. Rhetoric about refugees taking jobs from well-deserving Americans reflects national sentiments about immigrants, not the reality in Fargo, where thousands of jobs are unfilled and there is a labor shortage. This nativist us-versus-them attitude portrayed refugees as accessing undeserved services and goods that U.S.-born residents cannot access, and it viewed refugees as "illegals" who "hated America." Anti-resettlement activists continue to target LSS as a reckless organization for bringing refugees to the area. There was a deep concern that tax money was supporting noncitizens and that refugees needed to assimilate faster. "Help Americans first" was the most common theme in the comments section of the petition. A counterpetition was created to bring *more* refugees to the region, which was signed by 163 people, mostly locals from Fargo, West Fargo, and Moorhead.

In 2016, the City of Fargo applied for and was chosen to be one of twenty communities in the United States selected for a "Gateways for Growth Challenge," a bipartisan program that partners with Welcoming America and that seeks to welcome and integrate New Americans into communities around the country. (Welcoming America is a national organization that provides tool kits in social entrepreneurship to make cities across the country more inclusive.) Gateways for Growth, which launched in December 2015,

> invited communities across the US to apply for research, technical assistance, and matching grants to support the development and implementation of multi-sector strategic plans for welcoming and integrating new Americans. These communities are part of a national trend in which local government, business, and civil society leaders embrace research showing that being inclusive toward immigrants helps cities and counties thrive economically. They are working proactively to ensure an environment where all residents can contribute and succeed. (Dormegnie 2016)

Gateways for Growth cities promote citizenship through entrepreneurial enterprises, seek to improve public safety and access to services, and advance education and workforce goals to help metropolitan regions compete in the global economy. The ultimate goal of this program is to prepare immigrants and cities for employment and economic development.

Upon becoming a "Welcoming City," Fargo received technological support and materials to collect data in order to help the city better support New Americans. The focus was primarily on language (developing better interpreter services, for example) and inclusivity. From a planning perspective, inclusivity meant increasing accessibility to the city, to its public spaces and institutions, as well as to provide a more welcoming tone. When it was announced that Fargo would become a Welcoming City, KVLY news anchor Chris Berg represented this recognition as controversial, arguing that the program promotes "open borders" and a recruitment strategy for immigrants and insinuating that it was a reckless move.

These petitions and programs speak to the changing methods and contentious politics of commoning—that is, finding common ground across multiple demographics. Political theorist Benedict Anderson (1983) showed that the nation is often experienced as an "imagined community," because members of the same nation will never all meet one another. This imagined community has been created and maintained primarily through media and has never been representative of all its members. Feminist sociologist Nira Yuval-Davis contends that Anderson's definition of the nation is misleading, because "the politics of belonging is all about potentially meeting other people and deciding whether they stand inside or outside the imaginary boundary line of the nation and/or other communities of belonging" (2004, 218). Both approaches to the nation were at play in Fargo as local news media, KVLY in particular, provided scathing reports on refugee resettlement as more refugees arrived in Fargo. Whites saw the changing demographics, and some of them developed a crisis of identity.

The Change.org petition symbolized a revitalization of a homogenous local culture in Fargo based on an imagined, whitewashed past. It's unknown whether any of the signers of the petition had ever met a New American, but their comments make it clear that they did not welcome the opportunity. "Nation" evokes ideas about ethnicity, race, class, gender, and religion. Using the media to create and maintain particular communities—in this case, U.S.-born white Christians— arouses individual attachments, interests, aspirations, and fears that crosscut those of the larger nation-state (Appadurai 2001, 10). Using media as a forum makes it possible to move from shared imagination to collective action. Both traditional media and social media have been used to incite collective action in Fargo.

In November 2015, Valley News Live commissioned a controversial Mason-Dixon poll to gauge the public's opinions about refugee resettlement, and more than half of the 625 respondents stated they were "opposed to" ongoing resettlement. Misleading questions asked for opinions on education, crime, and Lutheran Social Services. More than any other mainstream news outlet, KVLY served as a one-sided megaphone for antirefugee sentiments. The *Forum of Fargo-Moorhead* opinion editor, Jack Zaleski, said of the station, "They have no standards at all. . . . They tilt [so] heavily towards the sensationalism that they often get caught doing unethical stuff" (quoted in Johnson 2016).

In November 2015, KVLY ran a four-part series on refugee resettlement to the region. Chris Berg interviewed Jessica Thomasson, the CEO of LSS from 2014 to

2019, as well as City Commissioner Dave Piepkorn, who has been an outspoken critic of refugee resettlement to the city due to its purported costs and burden on taxpayers. In an especially egregious example of sensationalism, in his interview with Thomasson about the possibility of resettling Syrian refugees to Fargo, Berg played a video of presumably undocumented migrants running across the border from Mexico into the United States. Not only was this false reporting, but it also painted undocumented migrants one-dimensionally, more like animals than humans, and as a threat. Migrants face dangerous, often deadly, journeys to get to the United States after escaping violence and poverty (De León 2015; Stuesse 2016). There is more to their story than the media usually portrays. Due to her efforts to resettle refugees and decrease the stigma around them, the *Forum of Fargo-Moorhead* named Thomasson its 2015 Area Person of the Year.

Before becoming the CEO of LSS North Dakota in December of 2014, Thomasson was part of the City of Fargo's planning department; before that, she served as Fannie Mae's senior deputy director for North Dakota. More than the previous CEO of LSS, Thomasson spoke about the organization in public. She talked about the working poor, affordable housing, and making Fargo a welcoming and growing city. A city cannot grow, she said, without migration, without people who come for jobs. Thomasson became the face of refugee resettlement in the city. In November 2019, she stepped down as CEO of LSS to become the director of community inclusion for the North Dakota Department of Human Services. She told me in a 2016 interview that when she was asked to speak about refugees, she required at least ninety minutes, because it took time to explain resettlement in a way that allowed people to move beyond fear: "There is a disconnect between opinions and reality," she explained. "Refugee resettlement cannot be a conversation only about numbers. It's about emotions." People feel that resources are scarce, even if that is not true, and "even people of faith feel like refugees are going to physically harm them," she said. "It's not an intellectual argument; it is visceral, unnamed, and emotional."

I asked Thomasson what role she felt that LSS played in refugee resettlement, and she said, "We are at the end of a long line of people from the country refugees flee on their path to Fargo. We have partners and make connections. We integrate refugees into the community. . . . We are changing the understanding of what community is." Thomasson said she had been thinking a lot about community and diversity and what they mean to different people. Diversity in North Dakota, she explained, is a new experience for local companies. "Authentic diversity" would mean attending to employees' different holidays, food preferences, religious practices, and the like. When local conversations become juxtaposed with a "noisy national and international conversation," this becomes all the more challenging. "Things get tangled up in people's minds: migration, immigration, refugee resettlement, homegrown terrorists—all of them are seen as terrorists."

Sometimes people act on their anger. In December 2015, arsonists set fire to a Somali-owned café in Grand Forks, causing $90,000 worth of damage. Soon after, more than five hundred people donated nearly $25,000 to help the owners rebuild (Berry 2015). Hate crimes, the Change.org antirefugee petition, and arson are just some examples that speak to the ongoing, divisive nature of refugee resettlement to Fargo. Each example becomes fodder for a broad range of contentious themes such as diversity, race, community, nation, citizenship, fiscal responsibility, and terrorism. Just as there are people in Fargo trying to push the discourse in more authoritarian and nativist directions, so too were there people like Thomasson and Miller pushing the discourse toward inclusivity by offering programs and support to New Americans and trying to decrease misinformation and prejudice. As James Baldwin wrote, whites fear a loss of identity. Understanding this fear is central to facilitating a move through and beyond it.

In many parts of the country, the rallying cry against immigration of any kind is the notion that immigrants are taking jobs from more deserving Americans. Fargo has some of the nation's lowest unemployment rates. Unlike in many other small, postindustrial cities, xenophobes and critics of immigration have not been able to claim that refugees and immigrants are taking jobs from better-deserving Americans. Instead, they began creating false panic about the prevalence of tuberculosis among refugees. On May 16, 2016, Chris Berg reported that the "health risks of resettlement include rising rates of tuberculosis infection" (Arick 2016). The report states that rates of tuberculosis (TB) were rising for the first time in twenty years and that the rise was likely attributed to foreign-born populations, especially refugees. The report prompted a protest against the station, and organizations and individuals spoke out harshly against the tactics of KVLY to incite fear in the general public against refugees (Walker 2016). Similar reporting methods continued in another report by Berg, who claimed that health officials in Cass County were putting the public at risk for not being open and transparent about the prevalence of *latent* as well as active TB (Berg 2016a). There were just four reported cases of active TB in the county in four years. In 2015, there were nine active TB cases in the state of North Dakota. A person with latent TB has been exposed to the bacterium that causes TB but is asymptomatic and noninfectious. In response to the Berg reports, LSS responded that it did not see active TB as a health risk and praised local health officials in their handling of TB cases among refugees.

Spreading fear about refugees got easier after the news broke of Kenyan-born Somali national Dahir Ahmed Adan, who claimed allegiance to the Islamic State and was accused in 2016 of stabbing ten people in a Minnesota mall before an off-

duty police officer shot and killed him. This was the first case of a refugee committing an act of terror against the United States. Adan had lived in Fargo as a
one-year-old. Berg reported:

> So here you've got one on US soil from Somalia that was settled here in
> Fargo. Goes out and stabs ten people in the name of Allah in St. Cloud.
> This radicalization thing that everybody thought would never come here
> is right now right here in our backyard. I'm hoping that some of you can
> see now why a lot of people in our area are asking questions to Lutheran
> Social Services and others about costs. Of course, also safety that's as-
> sociated with refugee resettlement. Wait 'til you hear this. Speaking about
> you and your family's safety, more shocking news tonight. (Berg 2016b)

There are many examples of sensationalist journalism at KVLY fueling already
well-established animosities and fears against refugees. Not surprisingly, fear and
anger also have reached the political sphere, where politicians have begun to call
for more transparency and less support of refugees.

Politicians

City Commissioner Dave Piepkorn has been targeting refugee resettlement for
years, calling it "an unfunded mandate" for local governments (Tran 2016). As in
years past, in the 1990s and early 2000s, LSS took the brunt of criticism because it
has been the primary institution for bringing refugees to the region, even though it
is not responsible for secondary migration. Piepkorn (2016) targeted his criticisms
at LSS and portrayed refugees as potential criminals and security risks. He began
raising concerns about the cost of refugee resettlement to local governments after
the St. Cloud mall stabbing. Refugees are more heavily vetted than any other group
of immigrants coming into the country, more than those coming on tourist, business, or student visas. (Of the nineteen 9/11 hijackers, one came on a student visa,
and the rest arrived on tourist and business visas.) Refugees have suffered at the
hands of terrorists and war criminals in their own countries, and then they often
become the targets of prejudice and discrimination in the United States.

Such a critique of refugee resettlement is predicated on the notion that refugees take more from cities than they give. This notion is demonstrably false. In
October 2016, Piepkorn requested a report to determine the costs of refugees to
the city, which he claimed could be in "the millions" (Hagen 2017e; Tran 2016).
Cass County Commissioner Chad Peterson told the *Forum of Fargo-Moorhead*
that he, too, was interested in knowing more about the cost of refugee resettlement
on local communities and was frustrated that such inquiries were interpreted

as xenophobic and racist. "Government shouldn't be in the business of feelings and hugs and kisses," he said, which is why he wanted "a cost figure" to allow local government to ask state or federal governments for more money to help in resettling refugees (Ingersoll 2017). Peterson's comment is in contrast to Jessica Thomasson's perspective that resettlement is about emotions, not numbers.

In February 2017, State Representative Chris Olson of West Fargo sponsored House Bill 1427, which sought "to provide for a legislative management study of refugee resettlement in North Dakota." At the hearing, more people testified against the bill than for it, which resulted in the transformation of the bill into a two-year study to research the fiscal impact and "absorptive capacity" of refugee resettlement in North Dakota. A Senate legislative committee did not pass the first reading of the bill, saying that it was too "unwieldy" (Emerson 2017; see also Berg 2017). The original bill would have allowed local governments to seek a moratorium on resettlement if the city or town lacked "absorptive capacity," and the governor would have been able to issue a statewide moratorium with an executive order. The second reading of North Dakota HB 1427 was more focused, calling on the study to examine any effect refugees may have on wages or working conditions, housing, law enforcement, and government services. The new version of HB 1427 passed the Senate, and Governor Doug Burgum signed it on April 11, 2017.

After a six-month investigation on the financial impact of refugee resettlement to the city, the Fargo Human Relations Commission presented its results (Ingersoll 2017). More than one hundred people attended the meeting at city hall, including all of the city commissioners except Piepkorn, who was purportedly on vacation. The report showed that the costs of refugee resettlement to the city were not significant (New American Economy 2017). In fact, in 2014, foreign-born residents contributed $542.8 million to the metro area's GDP, including $13.8 million in state and local taxes. This group also wielded $149.4 million in spending power (New American Economy 2016). The report continued: "Because of the role immigrants play in the workforce helping companies keep jobs on U.S. soil, it's estimated that in 2014, the 10,663 immigrants and refugees living in Fargo helped create or preserve 490 local manufacturing jobs that would have otherwise vanished or moved elsewhere" (New American Economy 2016).

The Human Relations Commission presented this information but also explained the drawbacks of putting a one-dimensional numerical value on individuals' and families' contributions to the city (see also Hagen 2017c and 2017e). Doing so, they argued, challenged their mission "to promote acceptance and respect for diversity and discourage all forms of discrimination." Piepkorn dismissed the report and questioned the credibility of those who created it. The local report also focused on figures from national studies that suggest immigrants provide benefits, not only costs, to local economies. Citing a 2016 study by the National Academies of Sciences, Engineering, and Medicine, the commission reported that, "on average, a first-generation immigrant is cost positive in North Dakota by approximately $3,250 per individual" (Ingersoll 2017).

In July 2017, the Department of Health and Human Services found that refugees bring in more government revenue than they cost in social services over time. This contradicts local narratives that refugee resettlement is too expensive and echoes other studies regarding the economic contributions of refugees. The report never saw the light of day, however, because the Trump administration suppressed it (*New York Times* 2017). In another report, from June 2017, *From Struggle to Resilience: The Economic Impact of Refugees in America*, researchers argue that while resettlement policy is usually framed as a humanitarian issue, "it is often the economic impact of refugees that leave the most enduring impression" (New American Economy 2017, 2). Their six key findings were:

1. Refugees contribute meaningfully to the economy as earners and taxpayers earning a collective $77.2 billion in household income in 2015, contributing $20.9 billion in taxes, and leaving them with $56.3 billion in disposable income, or spending power.
2. While refugees receive initial assistance upon arriving in the US, they see particularly sharp income increases in subsequent years. In their first year in the United States, refugees earn roughly $22,000 but after 25 years, their median household income reaches $67,000, more than $14,000 more than the median income of US households overall.
3. Refugees have an entrepreneurship rate that outshines even that of other immigrants. They start new businesses and generate billions of dollars in doing so.
4. Refugees make particularly meaningful contributions to the economies of several large states, like Michigan, Georgia, California, and Minnesota. [It is worth noting here that the development in Fargo contributes to the Minnesota economy as well.]
5. Even more so than other immigrants, refugees take steps to lay down roots and build lives in America. More than 84 percent of refugees become US citizens compared to roughly half of immigrants, and more than half of all refugees are likely to own their own home.
6. In an era when the country faces unprecedented demographic challenges, refugees are uniquely positioned to help. One way they can do this is by lessening the anticipated strain that an aging population will have upon the country because 77.1 percent of refugees are working-age compared to 49.7 percent of the United States-born population. [In Fargo, refugees are a valuable workforce.]

These national reports suggest that refugees contribute more to the U.S. economy over time than they take from social services, disproving a claim that refugees are a drain on states and cities that resettle them (see also Evans and Fitzgerald 2017, and Hagen 2017i). City Commissioner John Strand, a former Fargo school board member and owner of the independent newspaper the *High Plains Reader*, said the extra costs to schools is "not that quantifiably significant compared to what most people think" (Tran 2016). These reports also show that social safety nets work. Giving refugees something to build on results in their giving back to the economy later. Most of them give back more than they initially receive from the government.

Mayor Tim Mahoney, a former city commissioner, approaches resettlement as an economic boon to the region. He told the crowd who gathered to hear the Human Relations Commission report on refugee resettlement that Fargo needed "to embrace people of all backgrounds so the city can keep growing. We have a lot of jobs out there. We can't get them all filled" (Ingersoll 2017). Mahoney told me in an interview in 2016 that he sees New Americans recruiting other New Americans to the region because there are jobs here. He is pleased with the number of New American–owned restaurants and grocery stores. It used to be that people who wanted to eat international cuisine had to go to Winnipeg or Minneapolis, but thanks to New Americans, "that's not true anymore." Fargo is becoming a destination city, which poses challenges as well as benefits. Mahoney was keen on urbanizing the city in the best way possible while keeping it "safe, comfortable, and welcoming." For refugees, this meant working in the service industry that catered to a blossoming knowledge industry.

A city employee reported to me that a 2016 Gateways for Growth study found that refugees in Fargo are underemployed and have fewer businesses than New Americans in other cities. Some people, like Chris Berg and those opposed to resettlement, blame this on refugees' lack of skills and motivation. Others blame it on racism and a lack of willingness for members of the dominant population in Fargo to give New Americans a chance. The study also showed, however, that refugees are a relatively small portion of the foreign-born population in Fargo. A city employee told me that four in ten people in Fargo are foreign born and that many of them are "affluent and educated." It would seem that refugees are no longer the majority of foreign nationals in Fargo, as they were in the 1990s and early 2000s, but they continue to receive a disproportionate amount of negative publicity.

There is reason to doubt the validity of these economic impact studies, even when their data supports a prorefugee/prodiversity argument. The sample size of New Americans in Fargo is significantly smaller than in large cities. In small cities, as I have shown throughout this book, individual New Americans have an outsized impact. Likewise, the challenges that people opposed to refugee resettlement can have also have an outsized impact and could explain why New Americans in Fargo are underemployed.

Unlike in the 1980s and 1990s, when Larry Olson was pushing for acceptance of refugees on humanitarian grounds (see chapter 1), the debate surrounding refugee resettlement to Fargo in the 2010s, for both antirefugee and prodiversity camps, centered on economics: How much does refugee resettlement cost the city? At its core, though, the debates were about emotions and feelings towards others, with humanitarianism, diversity, and inclusivity on one side of the continuum and insecurity, loss of white identity, racism, and xenophobia on the other. While economics is not irrelevant, I do not think either side of this debate has been particularly swayed by economic data that challenges their position. The studies give legitimacy to both sides of the resettlement debate by centering the analysis on numbers, on economic citizenship as the primary means toward worthy citizenship, not emotions, social citizenship, or equity.

As important—or necessary—as research on New Americans' economic contributions is to challenging narrow-minded economic approaches to refugee resettlement, it still focuses on neoliberal conceptualizations about citizenship that privilege wage work, property ownership, economic entrepreneurialism, and individualism. Not mentioned in the above studies on New American economic contributions to cities is how refugees contribute to schools, neighborhoods, faith communities, and social circles. Rarely mentioned are the ways in which New Americans strengthen the fabric of civil society and communal action, and they do so in the face of racism, xenophobia, learned ignorance, and false reporting about them. However, as demonstrated by the large number of people who protested HB 1427, and the stories that I have shared and will share in the next two chapters, there are local people working hard to challenge one-dimensional portraits of New Americans as either economic costs or benefits. Such people work to portray New Americans as complicated, interesting, if not also flawed, people—as we all are—who bring more than just labor, capital, or problems to a city.

Diversifying Civil Society

Social integration is key for new city residents, not just economic integration. While Fargo has become more diverse over the last twenty-five years, white people and those born in the United States still decide what kind of relationship they want with people of color and foreign-born citizens. Many people in the dominant population in Fargo consider themselves descendants of pioneers, rugged Scandinavian individuals, with little acknowledgment that their ancestors took the land from Native Americans and that they themselves continue to deny public space to both Native and New Americans. However, people have been seeking to change this for decades.

In the mid-1990s, as more refugees arrived in the region, state agencies and schools felt overwhelmed by new forms of racial, religious, gendered, and linguistic forms of diversity that refugees represented. To address these news forms of diversity, government agencies began building a stronger civil society sector to support New Americans in order to act as a safety net for families who were not being served well by the beleaguered LSS or CCSS. For example, in 1994, city and county government officials created Cultural Diversity Resources (CDR) with a mission to "embrace [Fargo-Moorhead's] increasing ethnic diversity and assist diverse populations in overcoming barriers to community participation" (from the website, accessed in 2015). In 1998, CDR became a city-, grant-, and corporate-funded 501(c)3 organization with three full-time staff, nine board members, and an on-the-job training program with a mission "to increase the understanding and value of diversity in our communities and to create opportunities by eliminating barriers to community participation" (from the website, accessed in 2015). The city concurrently developed the Metro Interpreter Resource Center (MIRC) to provide coordinated training and administrative support for a decentralized network of interpreters that operated in the Fargo-Moorhead area. MIRC was a City of Fargo project but housed in the CDR offices.

Also founded in 1994, Charism was designed to address the city's low-income population, but it grew to include programs for underserved youth, including New American children. In 2000, a working group that would become the People's Diversity Forum formed "to educate New Americans on the legal system and to provide support on legal issues and concerns" (from the website). The People's Diversity Forum and CDR were both run by New Americans, who worked with city and county government officials, including CCSS, the police department, and the judicial system. According to Glen, the aforementioned volunteer with CDR for many years, the city supported CDR so that it could say that it "did something about diversity," but it did not deal with diversity in a comprehensive way. The leaders of these organizations were often the only New Americans to serve on other boards. They spoke for large, diverse refugee populations but did not seek to represent the diversity of their demographic, especially women.

Frustrated by a lack of support and representation by New Americans among the city's decision-making bodies, and by the duplication of services around the city, in 2014, a North Dakota State University professor, Kevin Brooks, received a grant and used the funds and his university sabbatical to reboot the Giving Plus Learning Program, which closed in 2011. The mission of the reformed organization is to match volunteers with English language learners in order to foster a welcoming community for newcomers to the Fargo-Moorhead area. The program offers in-home tutoring as well as drop-in sessions on weekends, help with citizenship test preparation, driver's permit test preparation, and GED test preparation.

In 2015, Brooks led discussions to create the New American Consortium for Wellness and Empowerment, or the WE Center. The WE Center brought together leaders from three ethnic community-based organizations in order to streamline funding and provide a structure to maximize resources for community organizations. Organizations included in the WE Center in 2016 were the Giving Plus Learning Program, the Djibouti Community, and African Initiative for Progress. Competition for local resources and clout as well as different leadership styles prevented more organizations from joining. In 2016, the staff of the WE Center included a New American director as well as a former employee of New Americans Services, who worked without pay. The WE Center stands for wellness and empowerment and a shared identity. It was designed as a commoning project in the hopes of building bonds and creating community, and it builds on a triangular model of needs, with safety, citizenship, and one-on-one connections between individuals and groups. Using "commoning" as a verb highlights how people are fighting to create new, different, more equitable public spaces as the state and market encroach upon them (De Angelis and Stavrides 2010). Programs at the WE Center include tutoring, a summer art program, diversity training, and collaboration with CCSS on some case management programs.

The WE Center also organizes "Welcoming Week." Welcoming Week is part of the national networking organization Welcoming America, which is guided by the principles of inclusion and helps nonprofit and government partners transform their communities into more welcoming places for all people, including refugees and immigrants. The organization was established in 2009, and by 2017, there were Welcoming Weeks in over 160 cities and towns across the United States. The goal in bringing Welcoming Week to Fargo was to raise the visibility of nonprofit organizations that work with New Americans and to facilitate better social and economic integration. The week has included an international potluck and "Community Table," featuring meals made from produce grown by New Americans with the help of Growing Together, a community gardening group that works primarily with New Americans and is affiliated with LSS (figure 4.1). Growing Together donates five hundred pounds of food to the event. There is a "World in Fargo-Moorhead" diversity exhibit and Facebook page, which illustrate the power of community building through photographs and stories about New Americans, "one portrait and story at a time." There have been cultural presentations by New Americans about their home countries, an immigrant entrepreneur panel,

FIGURE 4.1. Community table.

Photo by Ronald Albert, Amu Production. Used with permission.

fundraisers, and volunteer orientation sessions. Sponsors include local government entities, such as Job Services and schools, and nonprofits such as LSS. The YMCA led a discussion about race in Fargo-Moorhead, and Charism sponsored a family movie night.

Narrative 4 is a North Dakota State University–sponsored storytelling program that facilitates a two-day story exchange between New Americans and U.S.-born Midwesterners. On the first day, partners tell each other a story from their own lives. The next day, each partner tells the other's story to the larger group as if it were that person's own. The central idea is that by exchanging stories, people can develop radical empathy that goes beyond political, socioeconomic, and cultural divides (Lussenhop 2017). BBC reports that Damon Ouradnik, the man who started the Change.org petition against resettlement to North Dakota, reluctantly agreed to participate, though he felt like he was "jumping in a shark tank." A friend encouraged Ouradnik to participate in the program because he thought Ouradnik might "learn something." Ouradnik was paired with Arday Ardayfio, a Ghanaian who came to Fargo in the late 1990s and started an IT consulting business. Ardayfio did not know at first that Ouradnik was the person who started the antirefugee petition in Fargo. Once he found out, he felt he "had to show [Ouradnik] immigrants are not here to take" (Lussenhop 2017).

We learn from the BBC article that Ardayfio and Ouradnik shared stories about how they overcame difficult circumstances to become economically self-sufficient. Ouradnik insisted that he was concerned about the *costs* of resettlement, not about race. He left before the Narrative 4 event was completely over, so another participant, a Somali-American activist, reached out to him because she felt there was more to his story. He invited her to his home, where she discovered that he had grown up in a small town in northern Minnesota in a family that practiced a strict religion within a small sect, and with abuse and alcoholism. He emancipated himself at the age of sixteen, spent time in a foster family, and then got into drugs and alcohol and spent time in jail. When he was in his thirties, he quit drugs and alcohol, returned to school, and became a manager at his company. For people like Ouradnik, who suffered violence and abuse and overcame difficult circumstances to become economically successful, it felt like adding insult to injury to be called racist when all he wanted to do (purportedly) was to hold people to high standards of accountability. Considering his difficult childhood and young adult circumstances, it's interesting, but not surprising, how much emphasis he placed on economic self-sufficiency, rather than on the need for a social safety net—for programs serving people who suffer from physical and emotional abuse and from addiction, and those who need a place to go when home isn't safe. Such a view is consistent with conservatism.

In Fargo, the Jefferson School Project is a pilot project funded primarily by United Way that seeks to engage more people in their local neighborhoods. The Jefferson School is an elementary school in a neighborhood where many New Americans reside. It is located centrally, about a mile and a half from downtown Fargo and a mile from the Islamic center. The Jefferson School Project includes representatives from the city, health centers, schools, homeownership organizations, CCSS, and nonprofits—in other words, an array of both public and private stakeholders in the city. The goal is to better support refugees in Fargo and West Fargo by addressing barriers to good jobs, education, homeownership, public transportation, and childcare. Despite its good intentions and recruitment strategies, I was told that few New Americans attend the meetings.

Scholars such as Nina Glick Schiller and Garbi Schmidt have argued that addressing "multiethnic" neighborhoods where migrants live addresses only part of their web of sociality: "Left unexamined are other kinds of sociabilities enacted within these migrant-dense neighborhoods and within other urban places"—for example, stores, factories, and institutional settings "to which mobile people from various class backgrounds and statuses contribute their sociabilities" (2016, 5). The Jefferson School Project is attempting to address sociabilities, it seems, by its diverse membership, including the welfare state, schools, police, and other state entities. It seeks to create commonalities and opportunities through place-based neighborhood connections.

Diversity and Inclusion in Downtown Fargo

Between 1876 and 1892, Fargo's population grew from 600 to 8,000, and downtown Fargo became a thriving center of commerce. In 1893, thirty-one blocks of downtown Fargo were destroyed in an epic fire fueled by strong prairie winds, but the city was quickly restored. Within a year, more than two hundred buildings had been erected, some of which still stand today. In the 1960s and 1970s, the downtown deteriorated as developers abandoned it in favor of more modern facilities at the periphery of the city, such as the West Acres Regional Shopping Mall. Built in 1972, the mall was located four miles from downtown, at the crossroads of Interstates 29 and 94. In the 1990s, developers renewed their interest in the downtown. The iconic Fargo Theater, built in 1925, was renovated in 1999. Hotel Donaldson, built in 1893, had fallen into disrepair until it was bought in 2000 and renovated into a modern hotel and restaurant with a rooftop bar and view of the city.

Downtown Fargo (figure 4.2) has again become an urban destination and center of commerce and social life. There is a palpable pride in local culture

FIGURE 4.2. Downtown Fargo.

Photo by author, 2016.

and history in downtown Fargo that shows in recent revitalization efforts and businesses offering "I love Fargo" T-shirts and other place-based promotional goods and locally made products. When I visited Fargo in 2019, the downtown felt significantly more urban and cosmopolitan than it had when I lived there in 2007–2008. New restaurants, boutique stores, breweries, a farmers market, and a food co-op are now part of the city center. It does not, however, mirror the diversity in the greater Fargo metropolitan area, in spite of efforts to amend this. Downtown Fargo has been shaped by substantial renewal efforts, but it is still coded as "white public space," a term coined by Enock Page and Brooke Thomas to describe "the *places* where racism is reproduced by the professional class" (1994, 111). White public space provides privileged people with implements and infrastructure to maintain their power. This is accomplished through the "generalized locations, sites, patterns, configurations, tactics, or devices that routinely, discursively, and sometimes coercively privilege Euro-Americans over nonwhites" (111). White public space sends a message to nonwhites that they are not welcome. This can occur through overt segregation, such as Jim Crow laws, and in covert and subtle ways, such as gentrification. New Americans from different countries told me that one of the things they missed most about their home countries was a public space, in the center of town, where they could stroll, have coffee, and meet friends. In 2007–2008, downtown Fargo did not provide this.

In Bosnia-Herzegovina, for example, city centers are more vibrant, affordable, walkable, and approachable than in comparably sized cities in the United States. In warmer months, city centers are a constant hub of activity, with open-air markets selling fruits and vegetables and row after row of outdoor cafes packed with people of all ages. They come to the center for the experience, a walk, the noise, and the people. A cup of coffee at a café, affordable to most people, serves as a means for connecting with neighbors and participating in the life of the city. Even during cold months, when outdoor tables and chairs have been put away for the season, the center is alive with families walking their young children, dogs roaming, and people looking for a table inside one of the many smoky cafes. When I was in South Sudan in 2008, I observed sprawling marketplaces filled with clothing, cigarettes, car parts and gasoline, music, household wares, food, and other items from around the world. Goats run wild and cities are dusty because there are relatively few paved roads compared to cities in the Global North. Few people own cars; thus, cities in South Sudan are built around pedestrians. Downtown Fargo has become significantly more walkable over the last decade; revitalization efforts are bringing upscale apartments and hotels to the downtown area, but it remains a car city, and public transportation to and from downtown Fargo is weak.

Since the early 2000s, Doug Burgum has had an especially strong influence in downtown Fargo. Burgum became governor of North Dakota in 2016. An entrepreneur and philanthropist, he founded Great Plains Software, which Microsoft bought for $1.1 billion in 2001. In that same year, Burgum spared his first historic building from demolition by transforming a former farm-implement warehouse into a North Dakota State University facility that houses offices, studios, academic departments, and classrooms. In 2006, Burgum founded Kilbourne Group, a company committed to renovating and repurposing Fargo's historic structures and, according to its website, "creating smart, healthy cities through vibrant downtowns." Since 2006, the group has renovated and repurposed more than two dozen buildings for offices, apartments, hotels, and other commercial and retail purposes, developing approximately $350 million of real estate projects in downtown Fargo as of 2019. Kilbourne Group asserts that property values have more than tripled since 2001. As property values increase, so too does the exclusion of residents with limited means.

Kilbourne Group has coopted the language of commoning to frame its values. Its website explains, "Kilbourne Group believes vibrant downtowns create smart, healthy cities. We seek to be a leader in the evolution of downtown Fargo and to help shape that evolution in a way that benefits the *common good*" (emphasis mine). The company purports to do this not only by creating "smart, healthy cities" but through its philanthropic efforts that center on "workforce attraction efforts, downtown events, tenant support, etc." and "housing, health activity initiatives/events, art, diversity, etc." "Diversity" has become a buzzword, as ambiguous as it is popular. Kilbourne Group's approach to diversity connotes that it is separate from the central mission of a "smart, healthy city," an afterthought. In theory, the company supports a common good. In practice, it is developing a *private cosmopolitanism* that caters to businesses, entrepreneurs, the high-tech world, and high-class diners and consumers—the "creative class" that Richard Florida (2002) once argued was necessary for urban growth (he has since critiqued his own concept; see Florida 2017)—not to a *public* space that welcomes all people and represents multiple forms of income and diversity, or the *common* good.

Scholars have researched the ways in which cities have been designed through global, neoliberal processes that construct, devalue, and reevaluate real estate in various urban localities (Harvey 2006; Smith 2002). They have demonstrated the ways in which "actual existing neo-liberalism" (Brenner and Theodore 2002) materializes through governance policies and the restructuring of specific places by privatizing services and public spaces, reducing public services, and state withdrawal of funding city-based services and programs. In this mode of urban governance, city centers and neighborhoods serve to revalue land, thereby increasing disparities of wealth and power. In theory, neoliberalism was supposed to result in trickle-down economics, benefiting all. In practice, it has served to dramatically increase the gap between the wealthy and the poor. In other words, "smart, healthy cities" are for those who can afford them, and increasingly few people can. Under neoliberalism, explain Woods and Landry (2008), experts in regeneration advised city leaders to develop their local economies based on high-tech, creative knowledge industries, and financial services. As a result, city leaders and urban developers are forced to compete globally for flows of capital, corporate offices and professionals, and the creative classes. Fargo is no exception.

Creating a stronger, healthier downtown by renovating historic buildings, capitalizing on pride in the local culture, and creating a walkable city center with more retail and recreation opportunities can be attractive to residents and visitors alike, especially to those who can afford those opportunities. However, treating diversity as an afterthought rather than as a foundational part of the downtown renewal process serves to create more income inequality and stifles diversity and inclusivity. An especially egregious example of this is the federal Tax Cuts and Jobs Act of 2017 that is designed to provide significant tax benefits to investors, like those of Kilbourne Group, who reinvest capital gains into long-term investments located in "Opportunity Zones," which are designated by each state and approved by the Treasury Department. In the meantime, the cost of living in these Opportunity Zones rises while wages stagnate and poor people struggle to make ends meet as they are forced to live farther from these zones but commute to work in them. Kilbourne Group offers investors several Opportunity Zone real estate projects, such as Block 9.

When I visited Fargo in summer 2019, the construction of Block 9 dominated the downtown. A partnership between Kilbourne Group and other companies, Block 9 is a complex that will feature office space, condominiums, a hotel, a parking ramp, ground floor retail, and a community plaza. The community plaza will include a band shell for outdoor performances, interactive water features in summer, an ice skating rink in winter, and a central lawn with flexible seating. The project broke ground in September 2018 on a site that had previously been a parking lot and is expected to open in 2020. It will include the tallest building in Fargo, designed by SOM, an architecture firm that has designed buildings all over the world. Time will tell whether Block 9 will be welcoming to people who are not wealthy or white.

Contrast this to the International Market Plaza, which was created as a space to make it easier for immigrants to open their own businesses. The International Market Plaza features stores selling clothing from different parts of the world, a beauty shop with beauty products for all types of hair, jewelry, home décor, and restaurants. The goal is to encourage immigrant entrepreneurialism. It was under development for more than ten years, and though it finally opened in 2016, International Market Plaza has not yet become the thriving marketplace that developers and supporters had hoped it would be. International Market Plaza and other "ethnic" stores in Fargo feature more and different kinds of goods than most other stores in Fargo. They look, feel, smell, and sound different than stores downtown or in the mall. International Marketplace, the African Market grocery store, the Bosnian grocery store (which, in 2019, was owned by someone from Somalia), the FM International Food store (owned by a Vietnamese family), and many other immigrant-owned stores and restaurants are easy to miss if you are not looking for them. Customers at these places quickly learn that they are not coded as white space. It is likely that people will be speaking languages other than English and the goods offered will not be represented in English. The goal of customer service is not to make the (white) customer feel comfortable, to engage in small talk, or to educate. If customers do not know what they are looking for, they could become easily disillusioned. The same might be said for New Americans in downtown Fargo, though for different reasons. Of course, some New American businesses are accommodating to the white majority and use their businesses as a way of educating. Likewise, some white-owned businesses are more welcoming and accommodating to diversity than others. My point is that for downtown Fargo to be inclusive, entrepreneurs, investors, and their partners in the public sector would need to expand their ideas of what diversity means and engage different groups of people, such as New Americans, racial and sexual minorities, people with disabilities, and people from different faiths, and address income inequality as a barrier for building inclusive communities. I asked B. Smith, a person who had ties to city government, if downtown Fargo is welcoming to a majority of Fargo's residents. "It's *not*," Smith replied. "It's for middle-class white women to go shopping and for young entrepreneurial hipsters."

Organizations such as Emerging Prairie are beginning to recognize barriers to business success for New Americans and other minorities in Fargo. Emerging Prairie focuses on helping startups and on building a stronger entrepreneurial network in Fargo. One of its core values is radical inclusivity. B. Smith's assessment of Emerging Prairie in 2016 was that it was for young white people with technology degrees to hang out and drink coffee and that the offices were not welcoming to those who did not fall into this category. However, Emerging Prairie made diversity, equity, and inclusion a strategic priority in 2019. A report it published in conjunction with this priority found that less than 3 percent of small businesses were immigrant owned and only 5 percent were minority owned as of 2019. The report outlined areas where Emerging Prairie could improve its commitment to diversity, equity, and inclusion—for example: better accessibility to its programs for people with disabilities and those who do not speak English; opportunities for capital investment for immigrant-owned businesses; more multigenerational collaboration between baby boomers and young adults; mentorship and technical assistance for New American entrepreneurs; and more diverse, authentic partnerships with more diverse groups of people (Emerging Prairie 2019, 6). How these findings will impact the organization's programing and events remains to be seen. Businesses can approach diversity as an asset, not only as a system for using people as tokens, charity cases, or barriers to overcome. Doing so allows for a more diverse array of businesses, the development of new consumer bases, less dependence of one or two key employers, and a positive feedback loop between businesses, consumers, and the city.

Changing the Narrative

In her work with Somali refugees in Lewiston, Maine, Catherine Besteman explains how focusing on the cost of refugee resettlement rather than the social, cultural, and economic benefits refugees bring to a city "allows people who are unhappy about black refugees in their city to avoid accusations of racism and silences dissenting voices as out-of-touch softies and tax-and-spend liberals" (2016, 200). Besteman says that the "hostile treatment of refugees reveals much about the hostile treatment of others in the neoliberal borderlands who struggle with idealized requirements for economic self-sufficiency and identities marked by cultural or racial difference" (198). "Racism uses neoliberalism as a rhetorical smokescreen" she argues, "turning xenophobia and fear of foreignness or difference into an economic argument. Neoliberalism also makes use of racism. . . . By utilizing the slippage between poor people and people of color, neoliberalism taps into racist fears to push economic reforms that hurt all of the poor in the name of worthiness" (199). In this chapter, we see that refugee advocates—or helpers in the neoliberal borderlands, as Besteman refers to them—recognize these racist and neoliberal tactics and are fighting to change the narrative.

One of the ways some in Fargo are trying to bridge opposing sides of the refugee debate is collaboration and storytelling, whereby people encourage and facilitate tolerance, inclusion, diversity, and equity by choosing which stories to tell, where and how to tell them, and whom to tell them to. Tsing argues that we might encounter our best hopes for survival by "listening to the cacophony of trouble stories" (2015, 29). "The diversity that allows us to enter collaborations emerges from histories of extermination, imperialism, and all the rest," she explains. "Contamination makes diversity" (34). Storytelling, however, is at once radical and risky. Anthropologist Michael Jackson, who writes about the politics of storytelling, explains that in crossing borderlands that ordinarily demarcate different social domains, such as those between U.S.-born whites and refugees, or between social conservatives and progressives, "stories have the power to take us in two very different directions":

On the one hand, they may confirm our belief that otherness is just as we had imagined it to be—best kept at a distance, best denied—in which case the story will screen out everything that threatens the status quo, validating the illusions and prejudices it customarily deploys in maintaining its hold on truth. On the other hand, stories may confound or call into question our ordinarily taken for granted notions of identity and difference, and so push back and pluralise our horizons of knowledge. (Jackson 2002, 25)

The goal for Narrative 4 and other diversity advocates in Fargo is, of course, the latter, for people to recognize that "as much difference may be 'found between us and our selves, as . . . between ourselves and others'" (Jackson 2002, 25, citing Montaigne 1948, 298). Jackson continues: "Storytelling is, in the final analysis, a social act. Stories are composed and recounted, their meanings negotiated and renegotiated, within circles of kinsmen and friends" (2002, 112)—or, in this case, strangers. Stories "bind people together in terms of meanings that are collectively hammered out" (103). Sharing stories with strangers gives stories power, "not to forgive or redeem the past but to unite the living in the simple affirmation that they exist, that they have survived" (112). The goal in sharing stories is to help people move beyond ignorance and fear to knowledge and acceptance, which becomes a set of potentialities that can be actualized in ways that are connected with a politics of hope. With this in mind, I now turn to stories of Bosnians and Southern Sudanese in Fargo.

RESETTLED ORIENTALISMS

Bosnian Muslims and Roma in Fargo

One cold, gray January afternoon in 2008, I arrived fifteen minutes early to the apartment building where I was to meet Hajro. Chilled and sleepy on this gloomy winter day, I sat in my car and closed my eyes for a moment of rest before my next fieldwork step. My eyes were closed for only a minute when I heard a tapping at my window. I hesitantly rolled down the window, and a man asked if I was Jennifer and then introduced himself as Hajro. Though we had never met, he guessed correctly that I was the anthropologist. I got out of my car and followed him to his apartment.

Muslim by ethnicity, Hajro was a soft-spoken man in his mid-fifties, his face carved with wrinkles from years of smoking, poverty in childhood, communism, war, and migration. He sat across from me at a small kitchen table, chain-smoking and drinking Diet Coke. Crying intermittently, he told me about his poor childhood, life under communism when he worked for an oil refinery, the 1992–1995 war, and how he had gotten used to fighting and watching people die. He witnessed a man shoot his disabled brother in the head. In 1995, Hajro survived a gunshot wound and then fled to Germany to be with his wife and children, only to find his wife with another man.

Hajro came to the United States in 1998. Within two months, he began working in the chicken plant in a nearby Minnesota town, where he remained for more than a decade, until he was laid off because he refused to take on more responsibility without more pay. Before Hajro met Tracy, his girlfriend, he "didn't have a life." Hajro told me he "worked, went home, worked, went home, worked, went home." He met Tracy at a casino and after two years of friendship moved in with her. After he lost his job, he filed for unemployment while he looked for another job. In the meantime, he cleaned the house, cooked, and waited for Tracy to get home from work, something, he told me, he never would have done in Bosnia, where men don't wait on women, but he loved Tracy, and helping her made him happy. Hajro became a U.S. citizen in 2007.

When I left the apartment that afternoon, Hajro gifted me three small coffee spoons, a symbol of Bosnian hospitality, and told me to come back again. A week later I ran into Tracy. She told me that Hajro appreciated telling his story to an American in his own language but that he had discovered I was tutoring a Bosnian Romani (Gypsy) man for the U.S. citizenship test. Because of my association with Roma, and that family in particular, Hajro did not want to see me again. Hajro was not alone in his disdain for Roma. This opening scene speaks to a key theme in this chapter, a concept I call "resettled orientalisms."

"Resettled orientalisms" builds on the work of Milica Bakić-Hayden, who coined the term "nesting orientalisms" (1995). She claimed that Western European discourse and political maneuvering designated the Balkans as more "oriental" than Western Europe; in turn, ethnic groups in the Balkans developed their own scales of orientalizing the other. In this configuration, Muslims were construed as the least civilized, most "othered" ethnic group in the former Yugoslavia. I expand this concept to include Roma (Gypsies) and examine how "nesting orientalisms" played out in Fargo, where Roma outnumbered Muslims. There were other differences among them, beyond ethnicity, that served to divide Bosnians in the city. For example, those who lived in cities in prewar Bosnia-Herzegovina (BH) grew tired of being grouped together with "villagers" (*seljaci*), people who lived in rural and mountainous regions, whom urbanites viewed as less cosmopolitan than themselves. Herzegovinians, people from the western and southern part of the country, distanced themselves from Bosnians, believing their culture and geography to be superior to those of Bosnia.

For nearly twenty years, Bosnians were the largest refugee group in Fargo, and they had one of the worst reputations, which impacted their experiences with housing, employment, welfare, education, and healthcare. Reasons for this poor reputation had to do with the assemblages and politics of ethnonationalism and citizenship in the former Yugoslavia and how they intersected with local understandings of race, ethnicity, and refugees in Fargo. Before the 1992–1995 war, 44 percent of BH's population was Muslim, 31 percent Bosnian Serb, 17 percent Bosnian Croat, and 8 percent other, which included Roma, Hungarians, and Jews, among others. In Fargo, two-thirds of the Bosnian population were Roma; the rest were Muslim, with some exceptions, such as people in ethnically mixed marriages. Lutheran Social Services resettled more than 1,300 Bosnians between 1992 and 2004. It's hard to know how many Bosnian nationals and naturalized

U.S. citizens of Bosnian descent there are in Fargo today, because they are free to come and go as any legal residents in the United States. Staff at LSS and some Bosnians told me that there were an estimated 3,000 Bosnians in Fargo when I was there in 2007–2008, while the *Forum of Fargo-Moorhead* reported fewer than five hundred Bosnians in a 2015 article (Lyden 2015). Census data tracks a broad category of "white," which can include refugees and immigrants from Europe and the Middle East. Schools track children, and the welfare agency tracks people on welfare, but missing in these counts are employed adults without children, who were not initially resettled to Fargo.

In this chapter, I highlight challenges Bosnians faced, obstacles they overcame, and ways in which they pushed the boundaries of "normal" in Fargo. In so doing, I describe relationships between and among Bosnian Muslims, Roma, other people, and institutions in the city. I argue that relationships between Bosnian Muslims and Roma were of mutual misrecognition and that this misrecognition made it more difficult to form a "Bosnian" coalition that could liaison—as other refugee groups did—with the city for more rights, recognition, and entitlements.[1] The case of Bosnians in Fargo challenges the idea that the nation or the state is the primary means of establishing group identity. Instead, I encourage us to think more about everyday practices as a means to initiate and form greater solidarities.[2]

The Arrival Story

Two common stories circulated among Bosnian Muslims in Fargo. The first was the arrival story. Refugee resettlement staff worked with people from a wide variety of backgrounds—from rural people who had never experienced electricity, running water, or multistory buildings (for example, some Southern Sudanese, Liberians, and Burundians), to those who came from semi-industrial parts of the world (former Yugoslavs and Iraqis), to city-dwellers, such as Bosnians resettled from Western European cities. Part of the required training and orientation of new arrivals involved explaining how to use appliances, utilities, and public transportation, as well as social topics such as how to behave during a job interview.

Over Bud Lights at a backyard barbeque that a friend brought me to, Sabina, a Muslim woman in her thirties, told me that what she regretted most about those early days in Fargo was the inability to tell her caseworker in English, "Go fuck yourself" (*jebe se*). Another woman, Aida, said she and her husband and children were met by a volunteer, who showed them an apartment, turned on the faucet, and said slowly, "water," then brought them to the bathroom and said "toilet." Shouting and gesturing excitedly, often reaching across the table to touch my arm to make a point, Aida said, "People here have *no idea* what it's like to go from here (demonstrating high) to here (demonstrating low) and how hard it is to get to that high place again. Because when you go from high to low, it's absolutely the worst thing in the world." Dženana, another Bosnian Muslim woman, said that Fargo felt to her like the end of the world (*kraj svijeta*). She hated the cold weather and found the lack of public transportation and walkability of the city appalling. She missed the layout of European cities, where people met in centers to stroll, have coffee or ice cream, and window shop (she lived in Switzerland before coming to Fargo). I told her that such places existed in the United States, but she did not have the energy to move again and found Fargo to at least be safe.

The second common narrative had to do with drinking coffee: a Bosnian arrives in Fargo and finds herself in a conversation with a "friendly" American neighbor. The neighbor says nonchalantly, "We should have coffee sometime." The following day, the Bosnian knocks on the neighbor's door and says she's come for coffee. Looking perplexed, annoyed even, the neighbor explains that in America you call before going to someone's house. Laughing as they told me this ten years after they had arrived in Fargo, Bosnians had since learned that "time is money in America. People here don't have time to relax and drink coffee. Here you have travel mugs and fifteen-minute breaks, barely enough time to smoke a cigarette" (see also Croegaert 2011).

Aida told me she learned to tell the difference between "real" nice and "fake" nice. She found people in Fargo to be cold, even mean. I told her that people in the Upper Midwest had a reputation for niceness and considered themselves warm and friendly. Aida made an exaggerated face of disgust as she told me that she found Fargoans to be "close-minded." People in Fargo, she said, knew little about the rest of the world, hardly traveled outside the region, and did not like strangers, not even people who moved to Fargo from other parts of the county. Mersiha, a middle-aged Bosnian Muslim woman, was the only foreign-born staff member at her place of employment. Any person of color or person who had a pronounced accent was sent to her to answer questions. She regularly overheard caseworkers (all white) saying to clients, "I can't understand a word you're saying!" She translated from English to English so caseworkers and clients could understand one another. Mersiha felt that her coworkers disliked refugees and other foreigners but would never say so because they had to be "politically correct." At a previous job, Mersiha had experienced prejudice as one of her coworkers commented on refugees abusing the tax and welfare system and made nationalistic, racist remarks. According to Mersiha, this coworker was lazy, whereas Mersiha worked hard. Mersiha found another job. Before leaving, she showed her paycheck to the woman and pointed to the amount of taxes taken from it.

Sabina, Aida, Dženana, and Mersiha were from different parts of BH and had had different experiences with war and migration, but they were similar in age, had children, and felt disappointed by what Fargo had to offer them and their families. Others loved Fargo. Kokan, a Herzegovinian Muslim, came to Fargo with her husband and three daughters and proudly called Fargo her home. She cried when expressing the gratitude that she felt toward her employers and doctors for helping her to recover from the wartime violence she had experienced, the suicide attempts, and the physical and psychological hardships that came with war and migration. "This is my country [*moja zemlja*]—North Dakota," she told me, "and believe it or not, I feel like I was born here."

Nediha Kolaković came to the United States from Germany and was worried how she, her husband, and her son would acculturate. Lutheran Social Services sent her a volunteer, a woman in her twenties, who helped the family learn English and get to know the city. Years later, Nediha invited the woman to go to Germany with them, which fulfilled a lifelong dream for the woman. The story was featured in the "World in Fargo-Moorhead," a photo-essay series initiated in 2016, in which Nediha explained how she created lifelong friendships in Fargo (Heinold 2016).

Whether they felt like they belonged in Fargo or not, Bosnians in Fargo faced challenges and discrimination on the basis of their nationality or "outsider" status (see Halilovic 2013). A family with three children held a high school graduation party for one of their children and invited around forty people to the celebration. A car drove by their house during the party several times, and the students saw a man get out and urinate on the neighbor's lawn. The neighbor blamed the Bosnian family for the incident and called the police. After an explanation, the neighbor apologized for calling the police on the party, and the police left. The mother of the family told me that she had heard people say it wasn't fair that "refugees don't have to pay taxes," which is not true. This family opened a Bosnian grocery store and restaurant while continuing to work other jobs. They owned their own home, three cars, and a boat, and enjoyed traveling around the country. The family told me that a neighbor had once asked them how they were able to achieve so much, while also remarking that refugees "should have to pay taxes." The family explained to the neighbor that they worked hard for what they have and that, like other Americans, they do pay taxes. Many in Fargo refuse to believe this, however.

Generally speaking, it was especially difficult for Bosnians who had lived relatively well before the war—who were adults in Yugoslavia during the 1960s through the 1980s—to experience the loss of their home, social status, nation, and sometimes family members, and then to come to a place so cold, literally and metaphorically. Those who came from poorer backgrounds in BH before the war and who were able to succeed economically in the United States were more grateful for their opportunities. Dženan opened his own business in Fargo and told me that he grew up with modest means in prewar BH. He had not traveled much until coming to the United States, but now he travels to Chicago "like it's nothing." He spoke about how many Bosnians have succeeded and done well for themselves in Fargo, buying homes and traveling back to BH to visit family, but others continue to struggle and, after ten years in the United States, still rely on food stamps. Some were still reeling from wartime violence they had experienced. Across these differences, a common theme that emerged among Bosnians I met in Fargo was the desire for a "normal life" (*normalan život*).

How Bosnians Survived Fargo and Even Laughed

A common phrase in the former Yugoslavia before the war was that "you could sleep on the street and not be afraid." Among people of all backgrounds, discussions about prewar Bosnia included a deep sense of safety and love for Tito because he curbed ethnonational violence and punished those who engaged in it. For most, life in the former Yugoslavia offered a sufficient level of economic security, including state-sponsored education and healthcare, and for those in the Communist Party, free housing and paid summer vacations to the Adriatic coast. Kokan told me, "I finished school in economics, my husband had a job, he worked for a company, we had a completely normal life before the war. . . . I had a flat, the children went to school, [we had a] car, everything [was] normal—like the most normal a person could live. . . . In the former Yugoslavia, no one went hungry. In the old Yugoslavia, we had such a beautiful country that had everything: some more, some less, but there was no poverty."

A "normal life" meant a beautiful life, a good life, a safe and secure means of making a living (Halilovic 2013; Jansen 2006, 2007a, 2007b, and 2008; Coughlan and Owens-Manley 2005 and 2006). In her article on everyday life in Sarajevo at the end of the war, Maček (2007, 39) explains that the concept of a "normal life" was "charged with a sense of morality, of what was good, right or desirable. A 'normal life' was a description of how people wanted to live, and a 'normal person' was a person who thought and did things people found acceptable. Thus, 'normality' . . . communicated social norms according to the person using it, and as such also often indicated her ideological position." Muslims in Fargo described a "normal life" in Yugoslavia as having a steady job; time to relax with family and to visit with friends and neighbors; not having to think about ethnicity, nationalism, or politics; and freedom to travel to other republics, even internationally (Čolić-Peisker and Tilbury 2006; Čolić-Peisker and Waxman 2005; Korać 2005).

For many Bosnians in Fargo, homeownership and enough economic security for oneself and one's family to make the neighbors jealous were important aspects to establishing a "normal life." Alma explained to me that "Bosnians view success based on material things, based on what kind of car you drive, how much money you have in the bank, what kind of furniture you have. . . . Even though they might be struggling, [out of pride] they don't want to show that to others." For those who had secure socioeconomic status in prewar BH, a loss of status and respect in the United States added further insult to injury. They did not like to be grouped with Roma or, in some cases, with people from rural parts of BH who had little education or experiences with urban life before the 1992–1995 war, when they were forced to leave their homes and find refuge in cities. There was little desire to foster a national or ethnic community due to differences that were described in terms of "culture" (*kultura*).

Kultura "refers to a whole set of ideas associated with sociological oppositions, such as town versus village, educated versus uneducated, poor versus rich, modern and Western versus backward and Balkan" (Bringa 1995, 58; see also Stefansson 2007, 60–63). In Fargo, *kultura* was evoked to designate whether a person's actions were respectable, proper, and *pošteno* (honorable). Alternatively, Bosnians used the concept of *mentalitet* (mentality). *Mentalitet* refers more to ideas, beliefs, practices, and habits, a way of thinking and seeing the world. Because of my experiences in the former Yugoslavia and knowledge of the language, Bosnians would sometimes stop explaining something to me and say matter-of-factly, "*Pa, ti znaš Bosanski mentalitet*" ("You know the Bosnian mentality"). I asked them what it meant to them and received more clarification on BH ways of seeing, differences between people from Bosnia and from Herzegovina, and between men and women (see Franz 2005).

Rahima, a Muslim woman in her fifties, explained to me the socioeconomic and regional differences in BH: "In Bosnia, you could tell just by looking at someone if they were from the village, but here every [Bosnian] looks the same and you really can't tell where they're from. So if someone says they're from Mostar, you ask, 'Are you from Mostar or the *area* of Mostar?'" Nusret did not want to be associated with people from his own country, especially those whom he jokingly referred to as "hillbillies" (*seljaci*), or Roma. Many Bosnians, he said, "say they're from Sarajevo, but really they're from mountain villages around Sarajevo, where they spent their lives chopping wood to keep warm and came to the city during the war" (see Stefansson 2007 for an analysis of these urban/rural differences in Sarajevo). Nusret wanted to be seen in U.S. society the way he had been seen in the former Yugoslavia before the war: as an educated, professional, urban, hard-working family man. For Nusret, *seljaci* negatively impacted the representation of Bosnians in the city.

Sanja fought in the Bosnian war and served as a commander. She met her husband during the war. In 2000, Sanja, her husband, and their son were resettled to Pelican Rapids, Minnesota, a small town about fifty miles east of Fargo. In the 1990s, Pelican Rapids (population 1800) saw an influx of over seven hundred refugees, mostly Bosnians and some Somalis. Most of them worked in the turkey plant, and many eventually moved to Fargo-Moorhead. According to Sanja, she and her family arrived in the middle of a cold, gray, dismal winter, and they had a poor resettlement experience. The agency did not provide the mandated furniture. When they arrived, a man drove them to an empty apartment that looked like "barracks" in the middle of nowhere. Soon after, a Bosnian family from a neighboring apartment came to greet them and to make coffee, and they relaxed. Then they met their caseworker, a Bosnian from a rural background, who explained how to use toilet paper. This angered Sanja, who said to him, "Listen . . . I don't know where you're from, but I come from the capital city of our beautiful Bosnia-Herzegovina! . . . You might have come a few years before me, and you think you're a big man, but you're not. And you never will be." Sanja was accustomed to being respected as a commander and a member of a well-to-do family who lived comfortably before the war. She found the transition to life in the United States difficult because she had lost her means of garnering social respect from fellow Bosnians and U.S.-born citizens. Sanja worked in the turkey plant in Pelican Rapids for a short time, and then the family moved to Fargo.

I asked Kokan to explain to me what the Bosnian mentality was. Here's the dialogue that ensued:

> KOKAN: The Bosnian mentality? I wouldn't know how to answer what the Bosnian mentality is because I'm not Bosnian. They have, let's say, different tastes than we do.
>
> JEN: Sorry. How about a Herzegovinian mentality?
>
> KOKAN: I can tell you about the Herzegovinian mentality. We are cheerful southerners. We're very laid back! But we're especially loyal to our family, work hard, and we don't like when someone messes around with us. . . . We're famous for our jokes (laughs). . . . We are especially vulnerable. A Bosnian is stubborn. . . . He doesn't compromise. And a Bosnian, if he gets drunk and you provoke him—right in the nose (gesturing a punch). We're not like that. It's not like that with us [Herzegovinians].

Many Herzegovinians in Fargo distanced themselves from Bosnians because they felt that Herzegovina had a more honorable and educated culture. They also considered it more beautiful than Bosnia because it was closer to the Adriatic Sea. Moreover, Roma in Fargo were from Bosnia, not Herzegovina, and non-Roma did not want to be associated with Roma.

Kokan also mentions being "laid back" and "vulnerable," both of which tie to *sevdah*, a concept that cannot be adequately translated into English but that speaks to enjoying the moment, relaxing, and not stressing out. It is also a form of resistance against domination, an attitude that says we will survive, we will find humor in the situation while doing it, and there is more to life than work. *Sevdah* is an Arabic word incorporated into the Bosnian language during the Ottoman Empire that means love, desire, or ecstasy, and it is also a form of music (*sevdalinka*) (Imamović 2017). Sevdah signifies deep existential longing and enjoyment. Vulnerability is an important emotion in a country that, in the twentieth century alone, experienced three major wars (both world wars and the 1992–1995 war), localized wars in the early part of the century, and rule under two empires (Ottoman and Austro-Hungarian). Part of this vulnerability also translated into cultural narratives of suffering and complaining, or melancholy. By complaining, I mean expressing everyday dissatisfaction with life that speaks more to existential vulnerability and insecurity than the details of the complaints. Of course, Bosnians are not the only people in the world to experience empires, wars, or melancholy, but sevdah is the local expression to describe such feelings in BH. Sevdalinka might be compared to the blues in the United States.

Osman, a Rom from Kosovo, described sevdah as living in poverty but sharing a cigarette with friends and not worrying about tomorrow. The concept does not fit the historical or cultural foundations of the dominant population of white Euro-Americans in the United States, which centers on the Protestant work ethic, the American dream, advanced capitalism, neoliberalism, and individualism, which are predicated on slavery, genocide of Native Americans, and forced labor of ethnic minorities and systemic discrimination. Osman told me that when people called him from abroad and asked what life in the United States was like, he would say in a melancholy voice, "It's all right. There are jobs, nice houses, cars, good schools, ways to make money . . . but there's no sevdah." American culture is anti-sevdah. Alma said, "Everything is so hectic, you know. . . . It's like run, run because you have to go to work because you have to pay the bills, and if you don't pay the bills . . . then that makes us sick and we end up paying even more. . . . I think that people are overworked, overwhelmed, stressed, there are so many diseases that people are being affected by . . . because of that stress and because of the overwhelmness [*sic*]."

Like Alma, Rahima stressed the connection between working, paying the bills, and feeling stressed out, but Rahima also contrasted this to the Bosnian mentality about work: "Everything here is about money. You work and work and work for money and you may not even have time to enjoy it. It's like the turtle and the hare—America is the hare—you run, run, run but don't enjoy life. In Bosnia [the turtle], you have time to enjoy things, go out for coffee or ice cream, and see people. Here people sometimes have coffee together, but everyone has such different work schedules that it can be hard to find the time. Everyone's busy." Renata, who was in her early to mid-twenties when she came to the United States in 2005, missed the slower pace of life in BH. A slower pace of life changes the nature of sociality, work, and family relationships. At one point or another, most Bosnians I met in the United States mentioned the lack of free time to enjoy the fruits of their hard work. Dženana appreciated that I had seen life in BH and that I understood that life could be slower and more relaxing; there could be time to enjoy a slow cup of coffee, to take a walk in the center of town, to window shop but not buy anything.

When I lived in BH, there was forced relaxation time in my office. Every day at four o'clock was coffee hour, something I looked forward to at the beginning of my time in Bosnia because I was often bored during the first few months and coffee time allowed me to interact with others, to try to understand their conversations. By the end of my time in Bosnia, when I was frantically trying to finish the Roma research project (Medica Infoteka 2001; Erickson 2017a) before going back to the United States, I sometimes wanted to skip coffee and keep working, but my colleagues would not have it. "Jenny!" they would say. "Leave that computer right now and come drink coffee with us!" If I protested, they repeated, "Come over here right now! Light a cigarette and relax!" I appreciate that now. At the time, it perturbed me. Sevdah is not about work per se; it's about community. Drinking coffee by oneself in the former Yugoslavia is a painstakingly lonely practice (Drakulić 1991). Traditional Bosnian coffee is made with finely ground beans that settle to the bottom of the *fildžan*, a tiny cup without a handle, that Bosnians could spend hours drinking (it's sometimes called Turkish, Greek, or Arabic coffee in the United States). We discussed how travel mugs and drive-through coffee shops in the United States were epitomes of anti-sevdah (see also Croegaert 2011).

Part of the BH mentalitet was openness, boldness even, to critique the American mentality, knowing that this process made Fargoans uncomfortable. Some Fargoans appreciated hearing different perspectives and critiques about the United States. Generally speaking, North Dakotans preferred those who expressed deference to and appreciation for American culture and opportunity, who told stories that highlighted the problems in other countries, not in the United States.

In her book *How We Survived Communism and Even Laughed*, Croatian writer Slavenka Drakulić wrote, "Sometimes humor is the only way to overcome depression" (1991, 16). Joke telling is ubiquitous in the former Yugoslavia. Jokes fall into a variety of categories, from blond jokes to "black humor," from political to sexual, from animals to sports, war, ethnonationalism, and communism. Popular jokes in BH involved the characters of Mujo, Suljo, Huso, and Fata.[3] These unambiguously Bosnian Muslim characters are portrayed in jokes as simple, happy-go-lucky, alarmingly direct, self-deprecating, and sexually promiscuous. Jokes situate individuals and groups within particular social and political worlds and can help in understanding relationships between ethnicities, races, and cultures (Apte 1985; Davies 1990 and 2002; Vucetic 2004). Jokes featuring Bosnian Muslims allude to self-deprecating dolts and mimic the kind of "nesting orientalisms" that constructed Bosnians as less intelligent than their northern or western neighbors. Here is an example:

> Mujo came back to Bosnia from America. Suljo asked him, "Well, how was it?"
> "They're twenty years behind us," answered Mujo.
> "How's that?" asked Suljo.
> "They've still got it good."

In this joke, Mujo compares war-torn Bosnia to the world's military, socioeconomic, and cultural superpower. "Still" alludes to the dream and dissolution of the former Yugoslavia. Self-deprecation, naiveté, and a sense of bravado are key components of such jokes. Jokes also speak volumes about the relationships between ethnicities, between men and women, between nation-states, and between urban and rural people. Because everyone is a target, Bosnians justify racist and sexist jokes as all in good fun, nothing more. For twenty years, non-Romani Bosnians have reveled in telling me Gypsy jokes: "Jenny!" they would say. "What does a Gypsy do with a computer? Go through the recycling bin!" I would roll my eyes and not laugh at the jokes, which would result in more raucous laughter from the tellers. On the one hand, joke telling served to welcome me, an outsider, into the group; on the other, it was a way of challenging my Roma advocacy efforts.

Joke telling among Bosnians demonstrated cultural vulnerability, a way of coping with poor representations, and could at once highlight and ease tensions between and among them and wider societies. Jokes revealed a gullible Bosnian as more than simply a victim. Sometimes the jokes turned their supposed simplicity into a virtue, or at least a likable characteristic (Jansen, Brković, and Čelebičić 2017, 1). Nusret, who suffered from depression, told me that he spent hours looking for new jokes online to cheer himself up when he felt down about the war, life in the United States, or nostalgia for his prewar life. Humor helped him forget problems for a moment. At the same time, joke telling reinforced "nesting orientalisms" and provided another means for fueling mutual misrecognition, not only among Bosnians but also between Bosnians and the dominant population.

While joke telling was not as common among the dominant population as it was among Bosnians, humor was nevertheless an important aspect of the folklore. Like the different ethnicities in the former Yugoslavia, Midwest humor included comparisons between ethnic Norwegians, Germans, Swedes, Finns, and Poles. The Norwegian characters Ole and his wife Lena, and their friends Sven and Lars, bear striking resemblances to Mujo, Suljo, Huso, and Fata: fun-loving, sexually promiscuous, self-deprecating dolts, usually farmers, loggers, or fishermen, traditional occupations in Scandinavian countries.

Though they emerged from different political, economic, and cultural histories, stereotypes of people from the Upper Midwest, like those of Bosnians in the former Yugoslavia, portray small-town, rural people in simplistic, less civilized terms. The following joke alludes to the stereotype that people from the Midwest are not as intelligent or capable as those from more cosmopolitan areas or the coasts:

> After having dug to a depth of ten feet, New York scientists found traces of copper wire dating back one hundred years and decided that their ancestors had a telephone network more than a century ago. Not to be outdone by the New Yorkers, California archaeologists dug to a depth of twenty feet; shortly afterward, a story in the *Los Angeles Times* said, "California archaeologists found traces of a two-hundred-year-old copper wire and concluded that their ancestors had advanced high-tech communications one hundred years earlier than the New Yorkers." One week later, a local newspaper in North Dakota reported, "After digging as deep as thirty feet in his pasture near Fargo, Ole Olson, a self-taught archaeologist, reported that he found absolutely nothing." Ole concluded that three hundred years ago, North Dakota had already gone wireless.

In this joke, the New Yorkers and the Californians were portrayed as "real" scientists, whereas Ole from Fargo was a "self-taught" archaeologist. Comparing Ole with "real" scientists is similar to Mujo saying that America was twenty years behind BH. In both cultural contexts, the butt of the joke is perceived as provincial, rural, and backward, in contrast to the modern, cosmopolitan ideal (Vucetic 2004). I told this joke to a friend, and she had already heard it from former Yugoslavs using the Bosnian character names. Jokes reveal assemblages.

Despite some important similarities in how Bosnian Muslims and Scandinavian Americans are viewed in their respective national imagined communities (Anderson 1983), there are important differences in telling jokes that allude to cultural and historical differences. Two Bosnians, one man and one woman, told me the same joke about hunting big game in "Africa" that involved killing local people after mistaking them for animals. Both people who told this joke had been reprimanded and advised not to tell such jokes because they were offensive. Both seemed disappointed when I did not laugh at the joke either.

In the former Yugoslavia, ethnonationalism and corresponding religions were the means by which people differentiated and judged one another. Racism was seen as a problem between blacks and whites in the United States or South Africa, but nothing that they contributed to or benefited from in Bosnia or in the United States. The Yugoslav region has not been immune to the global processes of racialization (Baker 2018), but the Bosnian (or Serbo-Croatian) language does not have a word for "race." They use "rasa" when speaking about race. Though Bosnians have faced their share of prejudice by virtue of being refugees, BH Muslims are white and benefit from white privilege more than Roma, who are more likely to be racialized as people of color because of their sometimes-darker skin color and, even more so, by their cultural practices.

Resettled Orientalisms

In Europe, people from the Balkans are viewed as less civilized than their Northern and Western European neighbors. Maria Todorova argues that due to their location between the socially constructed categories of East and West, "balkanism" is a more apt way of describing the constructed otherness of the Balkans than "orientalism" because the Balkans were not colonized by Western Europe (1997, 17; see also Bakić-Hayden and Hayden 1992; Helms 2008). Nevertheless, there are similarities between the Balkans and regions colonized by Europeans, for example, in the various ways in which members of these regions internalized colonial-like mentalities. Bakić-Hayden argues that as a result of Northern and Western European treatment of the Balkans, populations within the former Yugoslavia constructed "nesting orientalisms" whereby the classification of other "has been appropriated and manipulated by those who have themselves been designated as such in orientalist discourse" (1995, 922). Grounded in an imagined pre-Yugoslav past, "nesting orientalisms" place those once ruled by the Western European Hapsburg monarchy (Slovenians and Croats) higher than those once ruled by the Ottoman Empire (Serbs, Bosnians, Montenegrins). Within this latter group,

Orthodox Christians are portrayed as more sophisticated than European Muslims, who further differentiate themselves from "the ultimate orientals, non-Europeans"—which can include Roma and people of color, for example (922).

Many Bosnian Muslims came to Fargo hoping to shed these orientalisms; they wanted a life free from political manipulation, violence, and ethnonational affiliations. They did not expect or want to be the minority to Roma, or grouped with refugees who had never experienced electricity, running water, or formal education. Some Bosnians in Fargo felt solidarity with other refugees; others did not. One man said that he did not want to be associated with "black cow herders from the bush." Some Bosnian Muslims identified as "Europeans," "former Yugoslavs" or "Herzegovinians" rather than "Bosnians," which became associated with Roma, who had one of the poorest reputations among refugees in Fargo.

Scholarship on balkanism and nesting orientalisms rarely attends to Roma, focusing more on European Muslims. The field of Romani studies argues that Roma are the ultimate orientals in Europe, a long-standing "Other within" (Lee 2000, 132). Roma ancestry originated in northwestern India. Based on linguistic evidence, scholars believe that the Roma left sometime during the twelfth century, probably as a result of repeated attacks by Muslim warriors (Hancock 2005; Matras 2004). They traveled through Persia, Armenia, and the Byzantine Empire, and finally into the Balkans during the thirteenth and fourteenth centuries (Crowe 1995). Historical documents illustrate anti-Gypsy attitudes and subjugation, including slavery, since their arrival in Europe. Roma are a diasporic people with historical and cultural commonalities, but they inhabit many contexts with different norms, traditions, dialects, and beliefs. Roma live all over the world but in highest concentrations in Eastern and Central Europe. Despite the wide variety of differences in the Romani diaspora in terms of language, phenotypic variation, religious affiliation, and other cultural practices, the one thing that all groups have in common is discrimination, prejudice, and violence inflicted by the *gadje* (non-Roma) who surround them (Crowe 1995). However, justification and forms of discrimination and responses to them vary from place to place (Engebrigtsen 2007; Stewart 1997 and 2012; Turgeon 1990; Van de Port 1998).

The enslavement of Roma (and some non-Roma) lasted in southern Romania until 1865, the same year that the Civil War ended in the United States, a war fought over slavery. In the twentieth century, the internment of Roma in Nazi concentration camps and the Gypsy Holocaust were some of the most extreme forms of anti-Roma violence. Roma in Europe face exclusion from healthcare, housing, education, employment, social services, political representation, and social life (Stewart 1997). Since 1989 and the fall of communism, Romani settlements have been targeted for violence all over Europe. Doctors in the Czech Republic practiced forced sterilizations on Romani women. Though abolished in

1993, the practice continued throughout the 1990s and 2000s; the last known case took place in 2007 (ERRC 2016). As the European Union has expanded and loosened the borders and travel restrictions between countries, Roma from Eastern and Southern Europe, especially Romania, have fled to Western Europe in search of more economic opportunities and safety. They have been met with disdain, discrimination, and forced removal, for example, in France and Italy (ERRC 2014 and 2015). Throughout the world, structural forms of inequality and marginalization continue to deny Roma human rights and full citizenship (Barany 2002; Crowe 2008; Fraser 1995; Guy 2001; Hancock 1988 and 1999; Lemon 2000; Silverman 2012; Stewart 1997, 2012, and 2013; Van de Port 1998).

While they often comprise a separate, sometimes defiant social group in all societies in which they live, Roma "are also simultaneously dependent on and part of that society" (Engebrigtsen 2011, 124). Romani ancestry is rich and diverse but not well known, because Roma have not controlled their own narratives. Gadje have written Romani history, using stereotypic representations. Lee (2000) argues that Roma are "orientalised" in Said's (1978) classic sense of the term. Roma everywhere, including in the United States, have been construed as pariahs (Hancock 1988; Okely 1996). Representations commonly take two forms: Roma are portrayed negatively as dangerous, dirty, lazy people to be feared and controlled, or positively as exotic travelers without the burdens that gadje face. Gadje have appropriated Romani culture in a way that, as Romani woman Ethel Brooks writes, "mixes fantasies about and hatred for our actual existence" (2012, 3).

Many criteria factor into Bosnian Romani identity. Some forms of employment in the former Yugoslavia were negatively associated with Gypsies, such as street cleaners, janitors, miners, and scrap metal collectors, while others were positively associated with Gypsies, such as musicians. Some Roma have a darker skin color than the majority population, but they have lived in the Balkans for centuries, married and had children with gadje for as long. Some Roma pass as gadje, especially those with light skin, good jobs, and no pronounced Gypsy accent.[4] The study my colleagues and I conducted in central Bosnia in 1999–2000 found that 66 percent of Romani women spoke the Bosnian language, but only 34 percent of their children did (Medica Infoteka 2001, 13). All of the Roma I met in Fargo spoke Romani, including the children; the adults, those who were raised in Bosnia, also spoke Bosnian, but their children did not. Other criteria used to identify someone as Rom were family name, neighborhood, and social customs, such as early marriage and celebrating Romani holidays. Roma in BH generally identify as Muslim (religiously and sometimes also ethnically), but few practice Islam (Erickson 2004 and 2017a).

It was difficult for Bosnian Muslims in Fargo to accept being outnumbered by Roma. Anti-Gypsy attitudes that so many gadje in Bosnia held also existed in

Fargo; arguably, they became more entrenched. Whereas Hajro did not want to talk to me again due to my association with Roma, others actively sought to engage me in order to debunk my supposed naiveté about Gypsies. Nusret explained, "Gypsies didn't like to work in the former Yugoslavia, and they don't like to work in America." By "work" he meant paid, formal jobs, the kind of jobs that required good social connections in the former Yugoslavia. "Wouldn't everyone like to do what they wanted?" Nusret asked. "That's how Roma are perceived even if that's not the full truth."

Bosnian Muslims felt that Roma complicated their own claims to citizenship and that Roma were unworthy of citizenship benefits afforded to those who "followed the rules." Aida said, "I'm not sure if I should hate them or respect them." Many Muslims saw themselves as hard workers, looking for a "normal" life that included a job, family, and time to relax with friends, and they did not identify with other refugees or Roma. Some Bosnians, like those who worked at the resettlement agency, identified with other refugees and sought to ease their transition to life in Fargo. Others expressed their anti-Gypsy attitudes to teachers, welfare workers, and police officers; still others discussed them on shop floors.

While tutoring English to Veranika, a Southern Sudanese woman, she told me that while she was at work, a Bosnian had told her there were "good Bosnians and bad Bosnians" and that the "bad" Bosnians were "Gypsies." Until moving to Fargo, Veranika had not known any Bosnians, much less been aware of the differences among them. Pointing in the direction of the next apartment, she told me her neighbor was Bosnian but "was one of the nice ones." In this way, anti-Gypsy attitudes that did not previously exist were fostered in apartment buildings and on shop floors. New forms of othering in the context of Fargo took root, but so too did new forms of commoning. I knew Veranika's neighbors, a Romani family, but I did not tell her this.

Race-ing Roma

Like other ethnic groups in Bosnia, Roma are not a uniform group (Acton and Mundy 1997). The Roma I worked with in Bosnia (1998–2000) were mostly Kaloperi, who lived in central BH and were mostly settled. Many of them were poor and supported themselves by begging and by salvaging garbage to sell at markets. Some Kaloperi valued formal education and sought good jobs, even as the educational system and job market excluded them. Many considered themselves Roma and Muslim and sought some degree of assimilation with gadje. Fewer Kaloperi spoke Romani than *čergari* (also referred to as *čergaši* in some regions of the former Yugoslavia), semi-nomadic Roma from eastern BH who were more conservative than Kaloperi (Erickson 2004; Medica Infoteka 2001). *Čergari* practiced early marriage (between the ages of fourteen and sixteen), avoided school, and desired less assimilation with gadje than Kaloperi. They were considerably wealthier than Kaloperi, as many worked in Germany as guest workers or owned their own businesses. Many also owned their own homes before the war forced them to leave (Erickson 2004 and 2017a; ERRC 2004). Most Roma in Fargo were *čergari* from the eastern city of Bijeljina. As in Europe, they were semi-nomadic, traveling often for business and family. Few graduated from high school, most practiced early marriage, and they rarely married non-Roma, though this was changing while I was in Fargo. These practices distinguished them from other Bosnians and the dominant population.

Like other refugees in Fargo, Bosnians, including Roma, worked in factories, hotels, restaurants, and retail. Few Romani families in Fargo were poor, certainly not as poor as the Kaloperi I worked with in BH. Many families owned their own homes and cars and would be considered middle-class. Some Roma had scrap metal businesses and traveled to other states for business and family. Few finished high school, and many practiced early marriage. Bošnjak and Acton (2013, 649) explain that early marriage customs among Chergashe Roma from Serbia and Bosnia secure political and financial ties between families. It is, the authors suggest, a practice that likely traces back to India and is largely influenced by Roma's enslavement in Romania and their marginalization and low status since arriving in Europe.

Family is central to the social and economic organization of many Roma because they have no central government or state institutions that resemble European or American societies. Family can provide behavior guidelines, emotional security, self-confidence, autonomy, and structures for passing on language and social values. At a rare wedding between a Romani man and a white North Dakotan woman, I met Salko, his daughter, and her son (figure 5.1). Salko married this daughter to a young Romani man when she was fourteen years old, and the couple had a child. When the daughter left her husband, the state took custody of her and her son. Salko went to court, and the state eventually awarded him custody of them, but years later he remained upset and wary of state control. A police officer told me that Roma used to invite teachers, police officers, and caseworkers to their children's lavish weddings only to discover that such invitations brought unwanted attention. Weddings then became more discrete. Bošnjak and Acton explain that because Roma are rooted "in host societies that are regulated by state mechanisms that often insist on uniformity and integration of minority groups, some Roma communities (such as Chergashe Roma) that continue with more conservative cultural practices provoke social stigma and non-acceptance" (2013, 650).

FIGURE 5.1. Bosnian Ramaden celebration.

Photo by author, 2008.

Roma told me they were tired of social workers lecturing them about early marriage, especially considering the high rate of premarital and out-of-wedlock sex,
divorce, and drug use in U.S. families. However, Roma did not show an interest
in educating the larger public about their history, beliefs, or practices. While some
Bosnian Muslims spoke about BH history and traditions in public, performed folk
dances or offered Bosnian cuisine at multicultural festivals, there were no Roma
booths at these celebrations or Romani representation at all, which bothered some
members of the dominant population, who wanted to build Roma-gadje alliances.
Additionally, Roma were seen as rude in a part of the country that considered
itself especially nice. For example, one shop owner told me incredulously that
Roma tried to bargain for better prices, an uncommon practice in Fargo.

I came to know one family of Roma in Fargo better than others. Our relationship began when I met Azra, a student in the ELL class I was observing, who was
in the seventh grade for the second time. By January, she had already missed more
than one hundred days of school. School bored her, she told me, plus her family
traveled too often for her to bother studying. Discovering I spoke Bosnian, she
asked if I could help her mother, Ramiza, study for the citizenship test. Ramiza's
husband, Mehmed, had already passed the test, and by default their children had
U.S. citizenship, but Ramiza did not. The family was eager for her to gain full,
legal citizenship so that they could travel outside of the United States as a family.
I gave Azra my cell phone number, and Ramiza called me that same day. Over
the next few months, I spent time with Ramiza in the family's apartment trying

to teach her English, but mostly we drank coffee, watched television (*Serbian Wife Swap* on satellite was a favorite), and spoke in Bosnian.

For years Ramiza worked at the Smucker's factory, but she lost her job when the factory closed, and she had not found another job. When I encouraged her to study English, she would bring me more food or coffee or change the subject, usually to my love life, health concerns (some of her family members and I have type I diabetes), and the importance of family. Ramiza's family was her life. Since she was the only one who was not eligible for a U.S. passport, the pressure to learn English was great. The family wanted to travel back to Europe, but they did not want to go without her.

One April evening, Ramiza called just after nine o'clock and told me to come over. I hesitated. She asked if I was alone, and I told her I was. She excitedly yelled into the phone, "You're home alone and going to bed at 9:00? What are you doing? You haven't come over in a long time! Why not come over?" I told her that she had not answered my phone calls in months. "Just come over!" ("*Hajde, doći!*"), she said. The wind had picked up, and a cold, wet snow was falling. I did not want to leave my warm apartment, but neither did I want to miss the opportunity to reconnect with the family, which lived in an apartment building just down the street. I arrived to find several "cousins" visiting from Switzerland. Laughing, Ramiza told me I could have any one of them for my husband and then asked me which one I liked best. They were hoping for U.S. citizenship. I told her I was not interested. She asked me if I wanted to go to the casino with them. I was curious about what the experience would entail, but declined because I did not want to encourage a marriage proposal. For the next hour or so, the men sat around the kitchen table speaking in Romani while I sat in the living room speaking to teenagers in English as they prepared to go out with friends for the evening. They told me they would quit school as soon as they turned eighteen. When the family went to the casino, I went home alone.

The goal of many Roma in Fargo had to do with economic and social autonomy, but they did not conceive of autonomy in the same way as members of the dominant population in Fargo. Neoliberal models of good citizenship rely on economic self-sufficiency, which means not relying on the welfare state and striving to achieve middle-class goals of education and waged labor. Roma models of autonomy might include relying on the state for welfare, but not for education, and striving to maintain one's own business, not working for another person.

Ramiza's husband, Mehmed, managed the family's scrap metal business with their sons, and said he preferred that his wife stay home. Ramiza told me she was bored and wanted a part-time job, but Mehmed was not supportive. Joking, she told me that she preferred to stay home anyway, since working at home was "easy," just a little cooking and cleaning, but she mostly watched TV and went shopping.

When I suggested that housework was work, too, she gave a knowing wink and said her job was easy compared to Mehmed's. To emphasize her point, she said that if a husband wanted a wife, children, and nice things, then he had better go out and work for them. Mehmed nodded assuredly. Mehmed and Ramiza's oldest son was in his early twenties and was married with three children. Their second son, who was sixteen, was engaged. At the time, they also had two teenage girls, Azra and another, who went to school sporadically.

During one visit, Mehmed came home full of dirt, looking exhausted after a long day's work of gathering scrap metal. In between joking and talking politics with me, he turned to his fifteen-year-old son, who had quit school to work in the family business, and spoke in Romani. I do not speak Romani, but I understood the word "copper," so I asked him to tell me about the business and if I could maybe go with him to work. He laughed hard and said that maybe his wife and I could start our own scrap metal business and then I could learn about it. After he cleaned up, he joined Ramiza and me and told me that "it's not good to work for another man" and that "America is a good place if you have a mind for business." I asked him what he thought about Fargo, and he told me that he has traveled all over the United States but liked Fargo best because it had low crime rates and was a good place to raise children to be well-mannered (*kulturni*). They had tried living in other states but had found other climates too warm. I asked him if he also liked Fargo because there were other Bosnians, other Roma, and he said, no, that was not a reason, because he was too busy working to socialize

FIGURE 5.2. Guest at a Romani wedding.

Photo by author, 2008.

(*društvo*). It was more important, he explained, to look out for oneself and one's family first.

There was infighting between some Romani families in Fargo, and between Roma and non-Roma, which occasionally became public. For example, at one Ramadan celebration, several men—Roma and non-Roma—got drunk and started physically fighting. I had heard that such fighting and destruction of property made it more difficult for Bosnians to book local venues for events such as weddings and Ramadan celebrations (figure 5.2). Some non-Romani Bosnians told me they avoided Bosnian events because the Gypsies drank too much and ruined the atmosphere.

During one wedding, two Romani brothers sat at separate tables, and when I asked why, they told me that they were not speaking with one another, but they did not elaborate. Ramiza asked for my help in trying to deport a Rom whom, she claimed, had beaten her son with a pipe over a business dispute. Another Rom was deported, after serving time in jail, for beating up a Latino man with a baseball bat at the county fair, a crime he claimed that another Rom had committed (Erickson 2012). These stories demonstrate a variety of relationships between Roma and state institutions. Though Roma in Bosnia often experienced second-class citizenship and were neglected by the state, Bosnian Roma in the United States, until they gained legal citizenship, faced discrimination by the state in addition to the possibility of being deported back to BH.

Police officers told me that Bosnians were stealing copper and conducting other ill-defined illegal activities. One police officer told me that a Bosnian [Romani] woman told him point blank that her husband stole copper from construction sites. Bosnian Roma have been prosecuted for these practices, but so too have white men from North Dakota. Welfare workers increased surveillance of Bosnian clients, believing they lied about marital status and income, and because some drove "nice cars." They added "scrap metal" as a category of income on their intake form. Teachers felt helpless in keeping Romani students in school. Child protection officers removed some Romani children from homes due to early marriage practices and on truancy charges. In the 1990s, when Bosnians first started arriving in Fargo, housing authorities grew weary of Roma breaking rental leases and hesitated before renting to Bosnians. In addition, Roma did not act as grateful as some other refugees did, nor did Roma appear to care what the dominant population thought of them, which included the belief that Roma were not "following the rules." All of these were egregious practices in a part of the country where people prided themselves on being nice. As such, Roma were not considered "worthy" refugees.

The stigmatization of Roma in Fargo stems from the relational categories of race, ethnicity, socioeconomic practices, and gender, but these intersections played out differently in Fargo than they did in postwar Bosnia or other parts of the United States, while at once being tied to them. This is how assemblages form and connect. Though some Roma in Fargo were poor, most were not. Many lived middle-class lives, owning their own homes or living in apartments alongside members of the dominant population. However, many in the dominant population did not see them as worthy citizens due to a combination of social and economic practices. Scrap metal businesses or early marriage alone would likely not justify social marginalization of Roma. It was the combination of nontraditional (male) business practices, (female) reliance on the welfare state, early marriage, the eschewing of formal education, refusing to engage with the dominant population on its terms, *and*, importantly, an attitude that disregarded assimilation. This challenged mainstream understandings about what refugees were supposed to be like: grateful, hardworking, poor, desirous of assimilation, and embodying a hegemonic citizenship status (well educated, formally employed, economically self-sufficient), maybe with help from generous, paternalistic patrons.

Social welfare benefits were stronger in the former Yugoslavia and in Germany, where most Bosnians lived before coming to Fargo. Some Bosnians, Roma and non-Roma, felt entitled to such welfare benefits in the United States. Welfare provided material support without challenging Roma belief systems of autonomy in the same way that courts and schools did. Due to centuries of persecution, and contemporary forms of discrimination against Roma, many Roma are wary of gadje institutions, such as courts and schools, that have taken their children, neglected to address Romani history and beliefs, and failed to protect children from harmful practices such as premarital sex, divorce, and drugs. Instead, for some Roma like *čergari*, family has been the most stable institution for social, economic, and psychological support. Bosnian Muslims also have expressed concern for their families, but in contrast to Roma, they have been less suspicious of institutions or people outside of their own ethnic group.

Non-Romani Bosnians, teachers, social workers, and others explained Roma practices to me in terms of "culture," a catchall term to explain difference. This version of culture has "no history, no politics, and no debates" (Mamdani 2002, 767). There are, in fact, debates among Roma about marriage practices. I knew of two cases in Fargo in which a Rom married a gadje woman, and there were different ideas among Roma about these relationships, ranging from support to anger to indifference. Ramiza told me that fewer Roma are arranging marriages and that many children have a choice in their marital partners. Both of her sons chose their own wives. In other words, marriage practices are changing, but how they are changing depends on where Roma are living and how they are responding to larger social, economic, and political structures (Bošnjak and Acton 2013)— for example, education, welfare, and economic systems. Oprea (2005) explains,

"'Cultural' explanations for child marriages and school drop-out rates do not suffice. Even in cases where poverty is not an issue—as in the case of some middle-class Roma's refusal to send their children to school—we must also keep in mind that educational institutions are aimed at assimilating minorities. They constitute the backbone of the state's socialisation project. Educational institutions are not neutral."

Viewing early marriage practices as "an internal, Roma-on-Roma offense," separate from state-sponsored inequalities, including attempts to assimilate minorities in the classroom, excuses the state's disengagement with such matters. Instead, says Oprea, we must view these practices as "a product of several factors operating together: gender roles within Romani communities, past and present state-sanctioned sexism and racism, and socio-economic instability" (2005). Overlapping historical and contemporary assemblages shaped the attitudes toward them. Such assemblages include slavery of Roma in Romania and of African Americans in the United States, discrimination against immigrants, and capitalism.

The practices described here were also gendered. Police officers surveyed Romani men working in the scrap metal business. A Fargo police officer told me that police tracked Romani genealogies, but when I pressed for more information, the officer admitted that they tracked "other cultures" too. The belief was that they needed to document "cultures' criminal records" and "relationships to one another" in hopes that refugees would believe that "the cops knew everything," which would ideally deter criminal activity. This police officer also told me that local residents would call the police station to report a crime and would say, "I'm not racist or anything, but I'm pretty sure they were Bosnian." Another officer listed a host of stereotypes about Roma, from a propensity to "steal copper" to listening to "rap music," which he associated with "hating America."

Some gadje in Fargo wanted to learn about Roma in order to facilitate better social relations with this group. I met English language teachers who worked hard to establish trust with Roma students and parents and felt defeated when Romani students dropped out of school. I witnessed an ELL classroom with several Roma and other refugees in it. Without Romani leaders to help them navigate Roma social landscapes and inform them about Romani histories and practices, some gadje lost interest in supporting Roma. I found that Roma were not interested in teaching gadje because they were more interested in preserving their families than teaching others about their "culture."

These need not be mutually exclusive. The tolerance—even celebration of—diversity in Fargo "requires a reciprocal commitment of 'becoming a citizen' on the part of the Other" (Clarke and Newman 2012, 162–163). It appeared that Roma were not interested in their part of the citizenship bargain, and the result was a poor reputation and increased surveillance, a race-ing of Roma. Roma in Fargo made new claims to citizenship that challenged the hegemonic, neoliberal model of economic self-sufficiency from the state, civic engagement, and politeness. The responses by people in the dominant population show the multitude of ways in which they managed and racialized refugee populations on an everyday level, ascribing racial or ethnic meaning to names, numbers, bodies, and practices in ways not previously used before refugees began arriving to the region.

In order to change the relationship between Roma and the city, members of dominant institutions could engage Roma in a way that demonstrates a desire for understanding how Roma depend on the city, keeping in mind that many Roma do not wish to assimilate. However, Roma would have to desire such a relationship, and many do not. Roma express strong family values. Using that as a starting point to engage with Roma, to understand what family means to them, would likely help. The rates of early marriage will likely decrease the longer that Bosnian Roma are in the United States, but Roma can still maintain their family values and businesses. Roma run legitimate scrap metal businesses, not only criminal ones, and they are capable of creative entrepreneurial practices in precarious neoliberal times, just as gadje are.

Conclusion: Mutual Recognition and Mutual Dependence

De Genova and Ramos-Zayas (2003) researched the ways in which Mexicans and Puerto Ricans in Chicago were racialized into a homogenous group of "Latinos" that denied the richness of legal, social, and historical differences between the groups. This homogenization thwarted Mexican and Puerto Rican efforts at self-identification while leading them to a racialized opposition toward one another. Despite important differences among groups racialized as "Latino," the authors argue, the persistence with which the category is used by hegemonic institutions such as the state might also be used to develop a pan-ethnic identity that could lead to more political, economic, and social rights for "Latinos."

This mutual dependence and mutual misrecognition between ethnic groups that might, in other circumstances, form solidarities, is also apparent between Roma and non-Roma in Europe. For example, in the Romanian village where Engebrigtsen (2007) conducted fieldwork, she found that relationships of dependence between Roma and non-Romani Romanians were misrecognized on an everyday basis, resulting in anti-Gypsy attitudes and policies. In all of these cases, the arbitrary nature of racialization, the slipperiness of ethnicity, the power of language, and state structures labeling minorities become more obvious and problematic, at least from an ethnographic perspective. Mutual misrecognition and mutual dependence pose challenges to forming and maintaining pan-ethnic identities—for example, "Asian Americans," "Latinos," "Gypsies," "immigrants," or "refugees"—that could be mobilized into political action.

Group membership—whether in terms of community, ethnicity, or nation—is key to social change. In this way, the broad category of "New Americans" could serve as an inclusive umbrella of different groups, not grounded in static understanding of ethnicity or community but in commonalities across nations, religions, ethnicities, and genders. For this to happen, a focus on commonalities is essential. Commonalities existed among Bosnians—for example, in language, food, religious and cultural celebrations such as Ramadan, and nostalgia for the prewar Yugoslav state. There were other commonalities across religious, racial, gender, class, and professional lines between Bosnians and other refugee groups and native-born citizens.

However, rather than come together as Bosnians or Roma, many people from BH displayed mutual misrecognition and little desire to identify similarities, much less make joint claims based on them to institutions. Because of their reputation as one of the more challenging groups of New Americans to work with in Fargo, they were arguably dependent on one another, and on other New Americans, to improve their status and social standing. "Resettled orientalisms" informed a new kind of anti-Gypsy agenda that discredited Romani ways of life and, perhaps unintentionally, acted as a mechanism to improve Bosnian Muslims' standing in the hierarchy of local racialized citizenship, where refugee groups competed with one another in a relatively homogenous dominant culture for social recognition, jobs, and respect. Bosnian Muslims challenged local ways of being, but only to a certain degree; many believed in the same hegemonic ideas of citizenship as people in the dominant population—homeownership, consumerism, hard work, and family values. Divisions among refugee groups, including Roma, posed challenges to forming and maintaining pan-ethnic identities—for example, "Roma," "Bosnians," or "New Americans"—that could be mobilized by disenfranchised groups for broad citizenship claims and for social and political capital.

BEYOND BARE LIFE
Southern Sudanese in Fargo

> **I will tell stories to people who will listen and to people who don't want to listen, to people who seek me out and to those who run. All the while I will know that you are there. How can I pretend that you do not exist? It would be almost as impossible as you pretending that I do not exist.**
>
> *What Is the What: The Autobiography of Valentino Achak Deng*

In 2008, Joseph Makeer brought his friend and fellow "Lost Boy" John Bul Dau to Fargo from Syracuse, New York, in order to help raise money for projects in Makeer's village in South Sudan. Makeer had recently published a memoir, *From Africa to America: The Journey of a Lost Boy of Sudan* (2008), about his journey from war-torn South Sudan to Fargo. Dau was one of three men featured in the award-winning documentary *God Grew Tired of Us* (Quinn 2007), which chronicles the journey of Dau, along with Panther Bior and Daniel Abul Pach, from South Sudan to the Kakuma refugee camp in Kenya to cities across the United States. There were five screenings of the film in the historic downtown Fargo Theater, with a question-and-answer period following two of the screenings.

The term "Lost Boys" refers to about 20,000 boys and young men, mostly Dinka and Nuer between the ages of six and eighteen, who fled war in South Sudan in 1987. Aid workers named them the "Lost Boys" after the orphans in the story of Peter Pan. In their treacherous thousand-mile exodus to Ethiopia, they faced disease, thirst, starvation, drowning, shelling, and bombardment. Lions preyed on them in the bush, crocodiles preyed on them in the rivers, and warring armies and rebel factions attempted to conscript them or force them into slavery. The Sudan People's Liberation Army (SPLA), the rebel army fighting the Northern Sudanese government (and each other), controlled the refugee camps in Ethiopia. John Garang de Mabior, the commander-in-chief of the SPLA and chairman of the Sudan People's Liberation Movement (SPLM), referred to the "Lost Boys" as the "Red Army" (child soldiers who were trained using communist ideology) and told them they were the seeds of the new Sudan, on battlefields and in classrooms. The SPLA gave boys older than twelve full military courses and sent them to the front lines, where they were slaughtered. The SPLA eventually learned that boys made for poor soldiers, but only after countless had died and many others had been trained to fight, kill, rape, and torture (Jok 1998).

After fleeing war in Ethiopia in 1991, the youth returned to Sudan with 250,000 other refugees on a long and brutal journey shaped by many quick and slow deaths, heavy rains, and fighting within the SPLA. Finally, the refugees made it to Kakuma, one of the largest refugee camps in the world, a sprawling settlement of mud huts and UNHCR tents near the Sudan border in arid northwest Kenya. By the time they arrived in Kakuma, more than half of the youth and countless others had died. Scott Peterson, a journalist and the author of *Me against My Brother: At War in Somalia, Sudan, and Rwanda*, described the group, whom he met several times during their years in flight, as "among the most badly war-traumatized children ever examined" (2001, 242). Peterson reported that psychologists documenting the group's extreme exposure to death and violence found that "up to 74 per cent of the boys were survivors of 'close' shelling or air bombardment; up to 85 per cent had witnessed someone starve to death; 92 per cent said they had been shot at; and 97 per cent had witnessed a killing" (238). In 1991, as the emaciated group arrived at Kakuma, the world was just beginning to hear about the wars taking place in Rwanda and Bosnia. Relatively speaking, media coverage of South Sudan barely registered on U.S. television channels or newspapers, at least until the United States agreed to resettle about 4,000 "Lost Boys" in 2001. The "Lost Boys" were less than 10 percent of the total number of Southern Sudanese refugees resettled to the United States, but they garnered a significant amount of attention, locally and nationally.[1]

The U.S. government began resettling Southern Sudanese refugees in the early 1990s. In the early 2000s, roughly 60 percent of all African refugees resettled to the United States were Sudanese, mostly from the South, but Sudanese numbered fewer than 25,000 total (USCIS 2004). In 1997, New American Services (NAS) resettled six refugees from Sudan. In 1998, they resettled sixty-six from Sudan, in 1999 seventy-six, in 2000 ninety-two, and, in 2001 sixty-five. NAS resettled 456 Sudanese from 1997 to 2008, but this number does not include secondary migrants who moved to Fargo, or those who left. NAS, schools, the New Sudanese Community Association, and the *Forum of Fargo-Moorhead* estimated that in 2001 there were approximately eight hundred Southern Sudanese in Fargo, about forty of whom were "Lost Boys" and a few of whom were "Lost Girls" (more on both groups below).

Southern Sudanese in Fargo identified as Kuku, Anjuak, Zande, Acholi, Latuka, Didinga, Bari, Madi, Dinka and Nuer, among others. Within these groups, there were wide variations in education and experiences with wartime violence and migration, such as rape, torture, conscription into the Northern Sudanese army or the SPLA, loss of family and home, and time spent in refugee camps or cities. Southern Sudanese came to the United States from countries as diverse as Egypt, Uganda, Kenya, India, and Cuba. The lingua franca among Southern Sudanese was English, Arabic, or Juba Arabic, a creole form of Arabic primarily spoken by those from the Equatoria region, or Dinka, the largest ethnic group or "tribe" in South Sudan and in Fargo. In Fargo, Southern Sudanese meetings were held in a combination of these languages. Those who attended school in Sudan were most likely to speak Arabic, the lingua franca of Sudan. The "Lost Boys" learned English in refugee camps but often did not speak Arabic or Juba Arabic.

Sudanese and Southern Sudanese scholars such as Rogaia Abusharaf (2002 and 2009), Jane Kani Edwards (2007), Nada Mustafa Ali (2015), and Jok Madut Jok (2001) explain that rich diversity in South Sudan poses serious challenges to making generalizations about its society, culture, laws, or contemporary nation-building. The one thing that all people from South Sudan have in common (along with many people in the North), however, is a long history of victimhood by the government of Northern Sudan, what Abusharaf calls the "twin processes of Arabization and Islamization," in addition to their marginalization by the North during the colonial Anglo-Egyptian Condominium period, resulting in "annihilation of their indigenous cultures and beliefs" (2002, 57).

Despite countless differences among them, Southern Sudanese shared three main characteristics in Fargo. The first was their blackness in a white city in a country where skin color shapes access to power, authority, safety, and everyday life. As one Southern Sudanese man, who arrived in the United States in the early 1990s told me, "We looked different. We felt different." Abusharaf explains, "Outside the Sudan, one is now transformed from being a Shaiqi, Nuer Beja, or Rubatabi to being a Black person. Racialization of Sudanese in North America is leading people in the [diaspora] to revisit long-held notions of skin pigmentation, ethnicity, and national identity" (2002, 164). The second characteristic among Southern Sudanese was their Christianity, a response to Islamization and Arabization by Northern Sudanese and to Christian missionization in South Sudan and refugee camps. There were at least five different Southern Sudanese Christian congregations in Fargo-Moorhead (Episcopal, Presbyterian, Lutheran, Catholic, and Assemblies of God). The third characteristic was their position in the low-skill workforce. Like other New Americans, most Southern Sudanese worked in factories, or as nursing assistants, home health aides, hotel maids, and dishwashers. They lived in apartment complexes across the city, and some owned their own homes.

Upon hearing that "Lost Boys" would be resettled to the United States, scholars, filmmakers, and journalists scrambled to record and study them. They have been the focus of countless studies in multiple fields, featured by journalists around the globe. They were the subjects of a feature film starring Reese Witherspoon and produced and directed by Ron Howard, *The Good Lie* (2014),[2] as well as a meticulously researched autobiographical and collaborative novel, *What Is the What: The Autobiography of Valentino Achak Deng*, written by best-selling author Dave Eggers with collaboration from Deng (2006). Though the book is fiction, the events are based on the real life of Deng, and the main character bears his name "Achak." Documentary films such as *God Grew Tired of Us* (Quinn 2007) and *The Lost Boys of Sudan* (Myland and Shenk 2003) recorded the lives of young men as they traveled from the Kakuma refugee camp to different cities in the United States, including their first time on an airplane and an escalator, trying to find their place in an American high school, working at demeaning low-skill jobs, navigating foster families, dating, urban life, and the intense pressure from kin and others in social networks in countries spanning the continent of Africa who expected them to swiftly send remittances. Of twenty-two films about Sudanese refugees, only one significantly features a girl or woman (Harris 2010, 56).

The "Lost Boys of Sudan"—and millions of other Southern Sudanese—are examples of philosopher Giorgio Agamben's *homo sacer*, one whose "entire existence is reduced to a bare life stripped of every right by virtue of the fact that anyone can kill him without committing homicide; he can save himself only in perpetual flight or a foreign land" (1998, 183). Homo sacer is at once bound to and excluded from the state. Southern Sudanese men and women were bound to and excluded from the violent state of Sudan, the violently emerging state of South Sudan, and as refugees to the United States, in all different ways. After being targets of killing and multiple forms of violence, being left to die, and living in limbo and precariousness in refugee camps for years, Southern Sudanese in exile were arguably not supposed to survive. Their remarkable stories illustrate that it is possible to come back from bare life and, even for some, to access rights.

Refugees and scholars who have worked with refugees explain that "one of the most arresting things about refugee stories—and more generally, the stories of people in crisis, in torture, and in flight—is that life all but ceases to be narratable" (Jackson 2002, 91). Of course, some survivors of torture and war *do* narrate their stories—for example, *testimonio* narratives speak to humanitarian issues in Central America. *Testimonios* are the result of a collaborative process in which a privileged outsider helps to write the account of a survivor's life in order to make it accessible to a wider audience. Older forms of testimonial literature include nineteenth-century African American slave narratives, in which a white author would authorize the former slave's account for a presumably white reader (Bex and Craps 2016, 38). Slavery has been endemic in South Sudan and Sudan for thousands of years (Jok 2001), and in fact there are slave narratives written about contemporary forms of slavery by Southern Sudanese (Bok 2003; see also Fadl and Lesch 2004). Testimonials are a form of public witnessing of shattering events in order to bring justice, accountability, and recognition to those who suffered from atrocities. There is humanitarian potential in testimonial literature (Bex and Craps 2016, 38), as I explain regarding the Lost Boys below.

Southern Sudanese Forms of Citizenship

Flores and Benmayor (1997) define cultural citizenship as everyday activities through which marginalized social groups claim recognition, public space, and eventually specific rights. Ideally, this can develop into full democratic participation (Rosaldo 1994). Social citizenship in an advanced capitalist society—which advocates for full citizenship among its members while also promoting capitalism, an inherently unequal economic system—necessitates a strong educational system to act as an equalizer, and a strong welfare state to act as a social safety net. Southern Sudanese worked to establish cultural and social citizenship in Fargo in a variety of ways and places. Simultaneously, they practiced diasporic citizenship. The diasporic citizen is, according to Victoria Bernal, "a key figure of global modernity; one that reveals the failures of postcolonial societies to provide peace, democracy, and welfare, and the failure of Western democracies to fully enfranchise populations marked as racially, religiously, or culturally different" (2014, 12). Diasporic citizenship calls attention to "the changing nature of relationships between people and states around the world" (11). Unlike the Eritreans that Bernal studied online, who "tend not to participate as active citizens in the politics of their adoptive countries" (19), Southern Sudanese were committed to establishing rights in *both* South Sudan *and* the United States. For example, they engaged in political, social, and religious online forums but also engaged in local politics by campaigning for Barack Obama or a new mayoral candidate. All of these practices challenge the sanctity and hegemony of the sovereign state by demonstrating that it is possible, if not easy, to belong to more than one country (Glick Schiller and Fouron 2001).

Southern Sudanese enacted multi-sited citizenship through religious, social, political, and familial assemblages, and they did so face-to-face and digitally. Southern Sudanese Christians connected with other Christians across the diaspora, in South Sudan, and with non-Sudanese Christians in the United States. The New Sudanese Community Association was a social organization that sought rights and resources for Southern Sudanese in Fargo. The SPLM chapter of Fargo was part of a large, well-established transnational political organization that sought to connect Southern Sudanese around the world to South Sudan. Kinship networks extended from South Sudan around the world to shape local family practices. In the following sections, I address each of these forms of citizenship in more detail.

Resettling Christians

Christian faith was a guiding force for most Southern Sudanese in Fargo and South Sudan (Pitya 1996; Shandy 2002; Wheeler 2002). One Southern Sudanese man told me that churches were an important "social service" for Sudanese because social service agencies were not providing enough support for Sudanese families in Fargo, just as the government and humanitarian aid organizations did not provide appropriate support during the wars. Churches, he argued, kept Sudanese from leaving the region. Below I describe some ordinary scenes that I observed in Southern Sudanese churches and with their white hosts. Though their approaches to Christianity were different, there were moments when whites and Southern Sudanese interacted in more than cursory ways, offering the possibility for more sustained and deeper connections in the future. Tsing reminds us that "assemblages, in their diversity, show us . . . entanglements that might be mobilized in common cause" (2015, 135).

There were at least five weekly Southern Sudanese services in Episcopal, Catholic, Lutheran, and Presbyterian churches in Fargo. The prevalence of different churches showed not only a diversity of Christian denominations and approaches to Christian faith, but also social divisions, primarily by ethnicity and language, among Southern Sudanese. For example, Dinka usually attended one church, Equatorians another. This is a pattern I first noticed in Sioux Falls and had to do with who had had contact with which missionaries in South Sudan or refugee camps, and it mirrored political antagonisms and geography in South Sudan— for example, between Dinka, Nuer, and Equatorians. In any case, writes Shandy, "Christian identity served as a vehicle for social construction and renegotiation" (2007, 105).

At the Episcopal church in Moorhead, Minnesota, there were three regular weekly services for Southern Sudanese, in Dinka, English, and Arabic. One Sunday of the month, there was a unity service, with white congregants, conducted in English with Arabic and Dinka interpreters. On a chilly and gray March morning, I attended a service with a Southern Sudanese friend and her two children. One white American man, who was likely in his sixties, arrived at the same time. He seemed eager to speak with me, but not my friend or her children. During the service, when the American pastor asked whether the Gospel reading should be translated into Dinka or Arabic, this same man said loudly, "We're in America. We should speak American." He was the only person to remain seated during the part of the service when you stand to greet other members and offer peace to one another. Eight white people attended the service, including the pastors and me, compared to about fifty Southern Sudanese. After the service, the man I had encountered earlier greeted me warmly, presumably because I am white, but no one else, and then left. Rather than the traditional post-church coffee and donut fellowship hour, Southern Sudanese food was served. A few white people sampled the food, but none of them interacted with the Southern Sudanese.

On the Sunday preceding Martin Luther King Day in 2008, I attended a Catholic service led by a middle-aged white priest who said a few words about King's "I Have a Dream" speech and then focused the rest of his sermon on the anniversary of *Roe v. Wade*, the 1973 landmark Supreme Court case that made abortion legal. He stressed the need to overturn the decision and to prevent women from having abortions. At the same Catholic church, on a different Sunday, a visiting priest from East Africa spoke to the crowd of Southern Sudanese on the importance of stories and journeys and encouraged members to incorporate the stories of Jesus Christ on their own journeys. The two messages reflect approaches to Catholicism that have been shaped by different political, economic, and cultural histories. After one evening mass, the Catholic church also sponsored "African Night" (figure 6.1). Most of the white Americans left after the service, but a few dozen remained to listen to Southern Sudanese speakers, dance to African music, and sample the food, which resulted in more interaction between Southern Sudanese and whites than I had seen at some other services.

FIGURE 6.1.   "African Night" at the Catholic church.

Photo by author, 2008.

These scenes demonstrate mixed responses and possibilities within white congregations to incorporate or interact with Southern Sudanese. Sociologist Pierette Hondagneu-Sotelo shows that faith-based activism has an important place in the field of immigrant rights and should be "understood in the context of the hostile reception that greets new immigrants, the deeply religious nature of both immigrants and the United States, and the changing role of religion in American public life" (2008, 7). In the United States, religion has been deployed to justify racism, xenophobia, and anti-immigrant nationalism, as demonstrated by the white man above who refused to greet or speak with Southern Sudanese worshippers—but it can challenge oppression and serve as a vehicle to move away from discrimination, fear, and prejudice toward "a more welcoming democratic, inclusive society" (8). The physical spaces of churches and Christian beliefs brought Southern Sudanese and white Christians together who may not have otherwise met. "African Night" and the offering of unity services are examples of possible roads toward commoning, in this case through Christian faith.

Social and Cultural Citizenship

The New Sudanese Community Association (NSCA) was the only Southern Sudanese–led organization registered as a 501(c)3 nonprofit organization in Fargo-Moorhead in 2007–2008 (figure 6.2). Its offices were located in a building with other nonprofit organizations in south Fargo. The organization provided rides to work and school, and disseminated information about education, social

FIGURE 6.2.   New Sudanese Community Association.

Photo by author, 2008.

services, and the legal citizenship process. Established in September 2004, the NSCA mostly relied on volunteers but eventually began to acquire local city- and state-funded grants, and it hired Chol (a pseudonym) as executive director in 2009. Chol was a former "Lost Boy" who earned his BA in political science from a local university. Because the NSCA was the only Southern Sudanese organization in Fargo, besides churches, it was also the target of complaints by other Southern Sudanese who wanted it to do more. NSCA meetings revealed the ways in which Southern Sudanese attempted to access social and cultural forms citizenship in Fargo and how social hierarchies influenced their goals.

According to T. H. Marshall (1950), in societies that advocate for full equality among their members but also engage in capitalism, an inherently unequal economic system, the state—in order to create more access to citizenship rights—should provide access to education and a social safety net (welfare) for those unable to work. Under neoliberalism, however, social citizenship has come to be thought of as the responsibility of individuals to *reduce* their burden on society, especially on the welfare state (Ong 1996 and 2003). As such, the burden of social citizenship falls to civil society and individuals, not on the state. Southern Sudanese discovered this lesson quickly. In addition to advocating for education and providing assistance to access social services, the NSCA also hoped to establish more cultural citizenship. They longed for a Southern Sudanese community center, a space to call their own in the city, but disagreements among themselves and lack of financial support, not to mention busy schedules and other responsibilities, made this dream difficult to achieve.

Southern Sudanese meetings or events began one to two hours later than the agreed-upon starting time, which they referred to as "African time," and lasted from two to four hours. From the beginning to the end of a meeting, the number of attendees waxed and waned. Unless it was a "women's meeting," there were always more men than women, usually at a ratio of about twenty to one, compared to the four-to-one ratio of resettled Southern Sudanese men to Southern Sudanese women. In addition to the gender imbalance, Dinka usually outnumbered representatives of other ethnic groups, resulting in arguments that mirrored politics in South Sudan, as Dinka comprise the largest social group and control many of the country's political organizations.

Below, I describe a typical meeting to highlight social hierarchies and citizenship practices among Southern Sudanese. One Sunday afternoon, a meeting was called to discuss two topics: (1) an emergency services fund (for deaths, medical bills, and other unanticipated costs for families), and (2) the role of the church in addressing wayward Sudanese youth. At the beginning of the meeting, there were about ten men and one woman, who spent much of the meeting in the kitchen. Ezekiel, a relatively young (mid-thirties) community leader from the Equatoria region, began the meeting by announcing that he planned to speak with nonprofit organizations and the city about these issues. He argued that these issues (the need for an emergency fund and for addressing wayward youth) related to issues facing *all* New Americans in Fargo. A couple of men protested that the purpose of the meeting was to address problems facing the *Sudanese* community, not all New Americans. They wanted to know why Ezekiel wanted to involve other people and organizations. For the next two hours, as more people arrived, discussion shifted from the original agenda to a debate about who was best qualified to serve the needs of Sudanese in Fargo: churches, Southern Sudanese organizations, nonprofit organizations that addressed the needs of all minorities, and/or the city of Fargo. These were a common topics at meetings.

After several hours of discussion, Achor, a board member of the NSCA arrived. Achor was angry that he had not received a formal invitation to attend the meeting. He demanded to know why the meeting was being held "behind closed doors." Someone explained the original intention of the meeting, which some did not view as the NSCA's responsibility. Ezekiel took this opportunity to attack the NSCA. He claimed that uninformed young people, such as Achor, led the organization. A man defended Ezekiel's accusation by giving three reasons why Sudanese organizations and committees fail: (1) lack of definition, (2) lack of planning, and (3) the need for more people with connections to the wider community and the city of Fargo, like Ezekiel, who came to the United States with a college degree and had worked for the UN. In 2008, Ezekiel was earning a PhD and working for a city organization. He had contacts with state and private organizations and had garnered public attention as an up-and-coming young leader in Fargo. He was on boards and committees throughout the city.

After more repetitive discussion, everyone agreed that there needed to be a meeting between the NSCA board and "the community."[3] The meeting would provide suggestions to the board as to how it could better serve the whole community. Achor encouraged everyone to come and to bring their wives and children. Someone asked if there would be childcare. Achor said a couple of women would have to "sacrifice" by watching others' children. The decision to have another meeting, instead of doing what they came to do—that is, create a protocol to develop emergency services and figure out how to best support Sudanese youth— was common. Lack of social cohesion among age grades and ethnic groups, as well as different approaches to citizenship in Fargo, ranging from conservative and traditional to more modern and progressive, made finding unity and common ground among Southern Sudanese difficult. Traditional Southern Sudanese approaches to citizenship included clearly defined gender roles and a gendered division of labor, respect for elders, and the desire to keep Southern Sudanese affairs within the community. Modern approaches sought more gender equity and more secular, democratic practices in community organizing. Sometimes disagreements about these different approaches spilled into the public sphere, causing unwanted negative attention, as demonstrated by a case of embezzlement within the NSCA.

In 2007, a man named Christopher who was then the secretary of the NSCA, embezzled nearly $12,000 from the organization. Christopher argued that the NSCA had told him he would be reimbursed for the driving he did for the organization. Also, his wife had been in an accident, and they had accumulated large medical bills that his family could not afford to pay, and the organization had already given him some money for that. He decided to take more. Once leaders discovered the missing money, they decided to press charges. A community meeting was called to discuss the situation.

The president of the NSCA, Chol, opened the meeting in a firm yet apologetic manner as he quietly explained to a crowd of more than one hundred what had happened. He seemed reticent to portray Christopher in too harsh a light. Apparently, there had been internal disagreement within the NSCA over the decision to press legal charges against Christopher, rather than deal with the situation within "the community." Chol explained the scenario in painstaking detail, providing a list of times and amounts of withdrawals made by Christopher from the organization's bank account. He stressed that they had *evidence* of these transactions. It appeared that the NSCA was on trial as much as Christopher, however. One man stood up and praised the organization for its high level of responsibility and argued that if Christopher were truly sorry he would have attended the meeting. Next, a young Sudanese pastor argued that pressing charges was "the American way" but that the Sudanese way was "to love, forgive, understand." He believed that the community should not be too much like the Americans: "Ten thousand dollars was nothing for the community, but a person is very important." Several people rushed to respond. One man said it was good to try to understand Christopher's perspective, but if they had not called the police, what would they have said to the donors about the missing money—"We forgave him?" The crowd erupted in laughter, including the pastor. Ayen seconded the point by saying that forgiveness in such matters "is worse than the Third World; it will make [us] zero. Sudanese used to be the best in Fargo-Moorhead. If someone asked you about Sudanese before, they would say, 'They are nice people, good people,' but now they say, 'They fight all of the time.' This needs to stop. That is bad. The Bosnians and the Somalis have organizations too, and the Sudanese also need to be organized and responsible."

According to political theorist Engin Isin, "The formation of social groups requires the presence and recognition of other groups, which give rise to solidaristic, agonistic, and alienating orientations simultaneously" (2002, 25–26). Put differently: groups distinguish themselves from other groups in order gain access to resources and power, and how they do this will be influenced by where they came from, the place they are living, and the populations they interact with. Southern Sudanese compared themselves with one another (Dinka and Equatorians, for example, and Southern Sudanese in other states), with other New American groups in Fargo (in this case, Somalis and Bosnians), and with the dominant population, especially donors. James Holston's research on citizenship in Brazil is helpful for understanding citizenship practices among New Americans in Fargo. Holston studies how residents in Brazil's urban peripheries have designed "insurgent citizenships," which demonstrate the ways marginalized and disadvantaged groups confront one another "in making decisions about their significance, assembling regulations for their management, and realizing them in practice" (2008, 32). "All citizenships," Holston argues, "engage this calculation of differences and equalities, and furthermore, are forced to reevaluate it periodically" (32). Doing so created feelings of solidarity, competition, and antagonism.

There was a palpable animosity especially between Dinka and Equatorians.[4] Ezekiel complained when meetings were held in Dinka rather than English or Arabic, languages that a larger number of Southern Sudanese had in common. Ethnic Dinka argued that Equatorians were trying to create a separate, competing organization for their own political power at the expense of a unified Southern Sudanese community. In his staccato way of talking, Ezekiel told me,

> The biggest challenges in Fargo for Sudanese is . . . Sudanese against Sudanese. They are bringing their tribes from their *old* country, from Sudan. They export them here. That's the *biggest* challenge! . . . You become narrow-minded, narrow focused. And once you bring the tribe here, you start bringing *all* those memories. Of hating this tribe. Loving this tribe. . . . They don't come together. These are some of the challenges. But we as community leaders are trying to *challenge* them by saying, "Think alike! Think bigger. Come out of your tribal cocoons. . . . You are in America. You are an individual person now; you are beyond that tribe." This is what we are trying to tell them. "Think bigger. We are all here as people with shared history. . . . When are we going to be *self-reliant*? We are not poor people! Look at our houses, our cars. We have jobs and make good money. We should not have to depend on others!"

The notion of community based on national origin is problematic for people from regions that have been engaged in civil war. For Sudanese, there was civil war first between North and South Sudan and then between (primarily) Dinka and Nuer, or the SPLM and SPLM-IO, in postindependence South Sudan. Calls for self-esteem and independence offer potential opportunities to move past these differences. Doing so could build unity by focusing on individual development, thereby eliding violent identity-based politics rooted in gender, age, and ethnoregional differences. Critics of this form of empowerment (Cruikshank 1999) argue that this can also act as a neoliberal technology of self-governance that works to shrink the role of the state and shift responsibility to nonprofit organizations such as the NSCA or churches, both dominated by men, or to other city institutions run by non-Sudanese. Feminist scholars have demonstrated the deeply gendered nature of this process whereby women and men experience the burdens and benefits of neoliberal policy in different ways—for example, the triple burden of wage labor, childrearing, and community work that women are often expected to engage in (Bernal and Grewal 2014; Erickson and Faria 2011; Sharma 2008).

Women's low participation in community organizing in Fargo was diminished by calls for more self-reliance by creating a double burden. Generally speaking, women take on more of the responsibility of childrearing than men. During one meeting, Ayen abruptly switched from English into Arabic and Dinka. She apologized to me in English but said that she expressed herself better in Arabic. During her speech, she mentioned, in English, "women," "welfare," and "ten years." Later I asked her why she did not want me to understand what she was saying about women and welfare. After expressing annoyance that I had understood her particular "Dinka dialect of Arabic" (she likely did not realize that she had spoken some English words), she explained to me that many Sudanese women were particularly vulnerable in the United States because of their low levels of education, their isolation in homes with children, and their lack of mobility. She lamented women's lack of interest in joining Sudanese organizations and men's lack of willingness to make the necessary accommodations to increase women's attendance, for example, by providing childcare at meetings. Ayen's desire to hide the phenomenon from me showed the ways in which Southern Sudanese internalized feelings of shame for relying on the state and not being self-reliant enough. Below, I expand on the ways in which some Southern Sudanese attempted to subvert more traditional age and gender hierarchies.

Political Citizenship

The Sudan People's Liberation Army (SPLA) and Sudan People's Liberation Movement (SPLM) (often referred to together as the SPLA/M) formed in 1983 to fight the military domination and political interests, respectively, of the ruling Northern Sudanese elite. Since its founding, it has been a fractured political organization and social movement (Jok and Hutchinson 1999) but has also been the largest public and international expression of Southern Sudanese identity, at least until 2013, when the Sudan People's Liberation Movement-in-Opposition (SPLM-IO) formed to challenge President Kiir and the hegemony of the SPLM. Ezekiel explained why politics mattered so much to Southern Sudanese before the 2011 referendum that resulted in South Sudan's independence:

> For Southern Sudanese . . . you don't get involved in politics, you don't get your life. You don't get your country. This is what they know. For them, politics is the gospel of the day. . . . They *love* politics! Because they know it's through politics that you can get independent . . . from the Arabs. You can become a nation, a Southern Sudan free nation. They *love* politics. Why they love politics? Because of social justice. The Arabs use politics to destroy Southerners, to oppress them. Very hard! . . . And then Southern Sudanese say, "Oh, wow! Politics is very powerful." You can use politics in order to really build people, even a nation.

With help from men and women in the diaspora, South Sudan did become its own nation, but it remains a precarious one. Politics can build a nation, but so too can politics destroy a nation, or a diaspora. Politics can be the continuation of war by other means. "Politics, in other words," argues Foucault (2003, 16) "sanctions and reproduces the disequilibrium of forces manifested in war. . . . We are always writing the history of the same war, even when we are writing the history of peace and its institutions."

There was a small chapter of the SPLM in Fargo, and SPLM meetings displayed hierarchies of gender, age, and social status. At one SPLM meeting, members discussed a controversial move by a youth regarding a May 16 celebration. Some leaders in the SPLM Fargo chapter argued that William Makuei had "improperly" used the SPLA/M flag to advertise his youth party. May 16, 2007, marked the twenty-fourth anniversary of the birth of the SPLA/M. The president of South Sudan, Salva Kiir Mayardit, declared it a "National Day" for the states of South Sudan, the Blue Nile state, Abyei, and the Nuba Mountains. The purpose of the day was to "keep alive the memory of those great sacrifices by our people and fallen heroes, and to acknowledge the tremendous contribution made by our gallant SPLA forces in the marginalized areas of Sudan" (Mayardit 2007). May 16 quickly became part of South Sudan's "mythico-history," a romanticized heroic past that served to justify violence and persecution against them (Malkki 1995). It also served as a symbol for "long-distance nationalism." Long-distance nationalism can be a potent personal and political identity, a relationship between transnational migrants and their home countries (Glick Schiller and Fouron 2001) that need not keep them from personal and political identities or commitments to their host countries.

The meeting began with three middle-aged men reprimanding William for flippantly using the SPLM flag to advertise his party. They argued that Southern

Sudanese should only use the flag and the holiday to talk about the long history of war and oppression in Sudan, which was why the SPLM was created. A long, repetitive speech by several men made the following points: If the youth wanted to have a party, it should be separate; May 16 celebrations were not to be taken lightly. May 16 parties should include formal invitations, speakers, and representatives of the SPLM. William argued that he had not used May 16 to promote his party and that he was aware of its importance. Someone showed a copy of his flyer to prove him wrong. Next the leaders reprimanded him for writing "no kids": "What kind of May 16 celebration does not include kids?" they shouted. "What kind of message is that?" Equally important, Ezekiel said, Sudanese in other states were bound to hear about this (Ayen confirmed the information was already in Sioux Falls), and the SPLM chapter of North Dakota would be shamed. William apologized and repeatedly stated that he understood the importance of the SPLM but that there had not been a party or celebration in several months and the youth wanted an excuse to get together and have fun.

Some defended William because he was "active in the community." The community could learn from his mistake that a youth party should not invoke "national issues." For such events, the national SPLM chapter would need to be consulted. Furthermore, they argued, when planning an event, an organizer must keep in mind what is happening in Sudan and South Sudan, like elections and the census, which the SPLM was preparing for in 2009–2010. Someone suggested combining the two parties, but, exasperated, the meeting attendees eventually agreed that it was too late to pull together enough resources to make that happen. At the end of the long meeting, they agreed that William would simply have to make a new flyer. Furthermore, he would have to make a speech at the party explaining that it was a *youth party* and *not* an SPLM party. Even though elders held William's actions in check, everyone agreed that he was a model youth because of his organizing capabilities. It should be noted that young men like William were encouraged to be involved in politics but would be held accountable if they challenged traditional age hierarchies or traversed boundaries between the social and political.

Southern Sudanese in Fargo also engaged in U.S. politics. In 2008, through the nonprofit organization that he worked for, Ezekiel created a program whereby he brought a group of New Americans to Obama's headquarters for political campaign training such as how to caucus. In the spring of 2008, I attended the North Dakota Democratic–Nonpartisan League Party convention in Grand Forks with two Southern Sudanese men, where we heard presidential hopefuls Hillary Clinton and Barack Obama. One of the men was an elder, who was earning his PhD. He wore a bright white suit, blue shirt, and U.S. flag tie to demonstrate his allegiance to the United States.

Gendered Citizenship

In addition to formal church services, community meetings, and SPLM meetings, there were also weddings, birthday parties, memorial services, and New Year's and Independence Day celebrations that offered opportunities for better understanding Southern Sudanese citizenship. At the beginning of a New Year's celebration held in a Fargo hotel conventional hall on December 31, 2007, elder men and women gave speeches on the importance of maintaining Southern Sudanese culture (figure 6.3). One elder woman spent at least fifteen minutes lecturing the crowd that women needed to obey men. I noticed some younger women rolling their eyes. In her work on global feminist knowledges, politics, and sexualities, Desiree Lewis explains,

> For older women, who are often the ones who police young women's bodies, customary practices can confer power, the authority to control the youth and the enactment of older women's dominance even under patriarchy. Such authority offers power and status where the old colonial and apartheid orders of 'tradition'—in the face of rapid urbanization and the breakdown of communal and traditional networks and belief systems—are fast eroding. For older men, the power is obvious. (2011, 213)

It was difficult to maintain Southern Sudanese customary laws or tradition in Fargo, and social hierarchies were turned upside down.

FIGURE 6.3.   Southern Sudanese New Year's celebration 2007.

Photo by author, 2007.

After time for eating and dancing, other guests were invited to give speeches. To loud applause, former North Dakota governor Ed Schafer commented how great it was that Southerners could live freely and not be persecuted for practicing their religion here. The crowd erupted in applause. To noticeably less fanfare, I explained my research and thanked them for inviting me. Then amid loud groans, the emcee told the deejays to turn off the hip-hop music and asked elders to lead a traditional dance. Dressed like stereotypical urban African American men—with low-hanging baggy jeans, large gold jewelry, baseball caps, and oversized jerseys—about a dozen young men stood in the corner and acted upset at the change in music. However, after a few minutes, they joined the crowds dancing to the traditional music. Men and women took turns caring for babies, and toddlers fell asleep and woke up throughout the party. Ayen told me that she had to be careful about whom she spoke with and for how long, or else rumors would spread quickly (she was divorced). If a couple was officially dating or married, then during a slow song, women gathered around the couple and ululated as they danced.

"Back in Sudan," a Southern Sudanese man explained, "the man controlled the household. They didn't learn to work as partners, [so] the man tries to control and manage everything here, too, including the money." Couples who came to the United States already married faced new challenges to traditional gendered divisions of labor. "In Africa," Nyakai and Nyariek told me, "everyone knows his position. But here men say, 'This country has made everyone like a woman'"—in other words, they explained, victims and dependents. Southern Sudanese men, they explained, believe that in the United States the order is reversed from Africa and that respect goes in the following order: children, women, dogs, and men. Nyaret said, "I think the man should still have the manhood, but they should at least see where they need to help. If a man loves a woman, then he needs to show his love and respect to her by giving her a hand." Despite the fact that both women expressed frustration at the lack of help by their husbands in the home, they were firmly against divorce and said that keeping families together was one of the biggest problems facing Sudanese in the United States. Over the years, however, their views have softened. One woman told me that she found it understandable why someone would want to get out of an unhappy marriage. Shandy argues that divorce was a "vivid example of how Nuer refugee women wield power and subvert the authority of Nuer males in America and Nuer elders in Africa" (2007, 118).

In order to prevent such subversions to the traditional social hierarchy from happening, some men returned to East Africa to find a traditional Southern Sudanese wife. They felt that Southern Sudanese women in the United States became too spoiled, and they worried if they brought their wives to the United States, they would demand more rights and freedoms (Shandy 2007, 111–112). I asked two men in Fargo who had gone to East Africa to find wives whether they had plans to bring their wives to the United States. Chol said he had never thought about it before but that it would be ideal because it was expensive to have a wife in Africa. During an English language tutoring session, a young Sudanese woman named Rose told me that her husband had come to Sudan to find a wife. Rose had not been in the United States very long and wanted to get out of the house more, learn to drive, and become more involved in the community, but she worried that if she became too active, it would be viewed as a challenge to elder women in the community. To avoid gossip and manage her family life, she stayed home.

Jacqueline had two children from two different fathers. Her boyfriend, the father of her second son, traveled for work, and she did not know the whereabouts of the father of her first son. I went to Jacqueline's house weekly to tutor her in English. She told me she loved our lessons because they made her feel smart and useful. Other than her neighbors, she did not interact with many non-Sudanese and was at the mercy of cousins, her boyfriend, and her boyfriend's family to get around. She used to work in a factory but quit after she had her second son. Jacqueline received government-subsidized housing benefits, but otherwise her boyfriend supported her. She told me she was frequently bored and wanted to go to school, but she did not have her driver's license or money to buy a car. She wanted to work in a bank, do something with papers, maybe become a nurse, but she needed more education. Jacqueline also faced challenges with her older son, who was getting into trouble in school and was suspended after threatening another student.

Rosa was born in 1957. She worked at one of the factories in town. I interviewed her one afternoon before she went to work. Our conversation centered on the extraordinary effort she made to attend school in South Sudan before the 1983–2005 war and while in exile in a neighboring country as the only Southern Sudanese in the class. She finished school, earned a degree in office management, and got a job as a secretary. Then violence broke out in that neighboring country, and she fled back to South Sudan. She found work for a nonprofit in South Sudan and helped to train other students in office management before war broke out again. She told me that her biggest challenges in the United States were education and language. Rosa had children in the United States but did not have a husband. During our conversation, two nephews came into the house, and she was clearly uncomfortable. She told me they gave her trouble. They used to live with her, but they moved out and now "hate" her because she yells at them to go to school, study, and not drink or make trouble. Another nephew was in jail.

In the United States, Southern Sudanese men and women work in order to save enough money to manage household affairs, send remittances to family in Africa, and have some disposable income. With such a strong emphasis on making money in the United States while also attempting to maintain Southern Sudanese ways of being, family relationships like that of Rosa and her nephews are strained. Marriages are tested. Divorce is uncommon in South Sudan. Southern Sudanese leaders worked at keeping Southern Sudanese couples in the United States together at all costs, even when domestic violence occurred (see Faria 2009, 138–139). Violence against women happens in all countries and subcultures, and I cannot say with any certainty whether Southern Sudanese women experienced *greater* degrees of domestic violence than other groups in the United States, but anecdotal evidence suggests that it is a grave problem.

Holtzman found that the causes of domestic violence and its implications differed substantially from what was true in Sudan (2000a, 400). In South Sudan, kin mediated domestic violence situations. In the United States, Southern Sudanese couples had to navigate a dizzying array of state and private organizations, as well as attempts by Southern Sudanese church leaders and transnational kin networks to keep the couple together at any cost. Root causes for family violence—such as new ideas about work, family, education, the role of government, lack of affordable childcare, emotional illness or trauma, or distance from extended kin networks—were not the focus of state interventions or of Southern Sudanese leaders, the latter of which policed traditional marriage and family patterns (Holtzman 2000b; Shandy 2007).

Based on my work with Southern Sudanese in Fargo, I could argue that Southern Sudanese women, like the Eritrean women Victoria Bernal writes about, are excluded from public life and politics and as such could "be understood politically as a form of 'bare life' (2014, 142). "In many historical contexts," Bernal continues,

> women have been denied political agency, social citizenship, and full legal status in their own right. Defined by their role as producers of life, women have been included in the nation through exclusion. Women as child bearers, and as reproducers more generally, while often excluded from political recognition and status, are regarded nonetheless as an essential part of the nation, almost in the way that a vital natural resource might be regarded or in the same way that territory is a sine qua none of any nation. . . . In fact, it seems to me that this is how it happens that the woman question comes to be posed *about* women by *men*. (142–143)

Discourse about women by men was spoken above by Achor, who encouraged women to attend NSCA meetings with their children. Achor, who had served jail time for beating his girlfriend, was not in favor of women's increased participation in the community as much as he was interested in promoting his own agenda and that of the NSCA and needed bodies to show him their support. Southern Sudanese women, as Bernal notes, "were defined by their role as producers of life," centered on their role as mothers. In South Sudan, "woman" is virtually synonymous with "mother."

Just as Eritrean women nurtured a sense of belonging to Eritrea, Southern Sudanese women nurtured a sense of belonging to South Sudan among their children. Referring to these practices as "parental nationalism," Caroline Faria explains that middle-class women especially "relied on a romanticized rendering of South Sudan, one complicated by accounts of disputes, hurtful gossip, and exclusions in the US-based community" (2014, 1058). However, I have found that Southern Sudanese women have more interest in politics and agency than Bernal observed among Eritrean women. Faria and I have written about the South Sudan Women's Empowerment Network, a transnational women's organization that sought to empower women in South Sudan and the diaspora (Erickson and Faria 2011). While these transnational women's organizing practices did not appear to take root in Fargo, women were leaders in planning social events, birthday parties, weddings, memorial services, and holiday celebrations. A few were part of the SPLM chapter, and they were in contact with women elsewhere who were more politically active, which could lead to more organizing in Fargo in the future.

Southern Sudanese used spiritual, social, political, and digital technologies of citizenship—as well as more traditional forms of social organization linked to age, kinship, and gender—to garner access to respect, resources, and power in Fargo and South Sudan. Their citizenship technologies cannot be separated from their Blackness in a white city. Their mere presence challenged dominant conceptions of who belonged in the city. Southern Sudanese tended to downplay the role of race in negatively shaping their experiences in favor of focusing on the opportunities the city offered them. They experienced racism but told me that they preferred U.S. forms of racism to Northern Sudanese forms of racism, or racism in other African countries. "White people," said Achor, "were the lesser of two evils." Northern Sudanese Muslims tried to force Southerners to be Muslims, but white people were "a little more polite" about their approaches to citizenship. Achor told me that he believed he was being paid less at his job in Fargo than his white coworkers, who had the same or less education and training. He found this unjust, but when I suggested he could fight it, he said he would rather focus on problems in Sudan. South Sudan was like a "shadow," he said, always with him, something he could not ignore. He told me that the battle for racial equality in the United States was someone else's battle. I asked him whose responsibility he thought it was to fight racism in the United States, and he said that it was mine and that of other Americans.

The "Lost Boys"

In April 2001, Sara Corbett wrote an article for the *New York Times* entitled "The Long Road from Sudan to America," which chronicled the arrival of a group of "Lost Boys" in Fargo. She describes three young men disembarking from the airplane on a January evening, when the temperature had dropped to fifteen degrees below zero with a wind chill factor that made it feel another twenty degrees colder. In Kakuma, where the young men had been living for a decade, temperatures averaged one hundred degrees. "Cold" had no meaning for them. The young men arrived in Fargo wearing thin gray sweat suits and flimsy white canvas sneakers that had been issued by the State Department. A caseworker from LSS, a white woman, met them at the gate with winter clothing.

Corbett followed the young men and the caseworker to their new apartment, where she saw a hodgepodge of donations, including basic food items such as milk, bread, and bananas, as well as cake pans and three-piece polyester suits. Another caseworker, a Somali man, who had been in the United States for five years, impatiently showed them how to operate appliances and the water faucet as the young men giggled and turned the water off and on. Like many former refugee caseworkers with whom I have worked, this man employed a sink-or-swim, tough love approach to newly arrived refugees, an approach that said, "If I can make it, so can you." According to Corbett, he told the young men, "Open your eyes. Don't think of Africa. Start your new life strong." Corbett writes,

> Watching young Maduk check the size of a rumpled shirt against his spidery shoulders, I was struck by an uncomfortable feeling, one I would have more than once during my time in Fargo. I fully understood that these boys were lucky, that there were thousands of Sudanese left behind in Kakuma—and millions of refugees stuck in camps across the globe—but still I could imagine, painfully, the small indignities and cultural stumbling blocks that lay ahead. As petty as this seems, the feel-good power of American charity was lost on me the second I imagined Maduk showing up for this first day of high school dressed in government-issue white canvas boat shoes and a shirt better suited for a retiree on a cruise ship.

Corbett soon discovered that the young men had never opened a box. She helped them open cornflakes for the first time. In Kakuma, refugees ate a monotonous diet of porridge and lentils, unreliably provided by humanitarian aid organizations, with few fruits, vegetables, or dairy products. When they arrived in the United States, they were not familiar with U.S. foods, food preparation, or food storage, including the difference between a refrigerator and freezer, or how to use a stove or microwave. They turned to convenience foods and soda (Willis and Buck 2007). The youth had never seen stairs or multilevel buildings before. They preferred—sometimes insisted—on living on ground-level floors. In addition to learning to live in a late capitalist country with new tools and technologies, the youth struggled with different social norms and customs, from women wearing pants and attending school, to working menial jobs, to modern medicine, and to being some of the only dark-skinned people in a city that was—in 2001—97 percent white.

Volunteers and state workers recalled the challenges faced by the "Lost Boys" when they first came to Fargo. One state welfare worker told me,

> There's one particular case. It was like three or four of them, living out in an apartment in West Fargo, and I think one adult there; he was kind of the in-charge guy. He was in his *very* early twenties, and he'd always had this group of boys that he was in charge [of], even coming from the refugee camp. And they were all in this apartment and, again, LSS was responsible for them, but they just didn't have the life skills to survive. . . . The people that were trying to help them were feeding them probably lots of American greasy, yucky food; one of them had horrible diarrhea 'cause the system couldn't handle that. And [volunteers and LSS] were . . . focusing on quick easy things . . . trying to teach them how to cook . . . macaroni and cheese and Hamburger Helper—all these things that their systems couldn't handle (laughing). . . . They had no concept of what winter was or the fact that you get frostbitten if you walk around with no gloves, and . . . they didn't have coats, so even education about the weather wasn't there.

One of the reporters who worked on the Valley to the World series for the *Forum of Fargo-Moorhead* in 2001 told me that their assignment was to follow a family from their moment of arrival at the airport and then for three to six months as they acclimated. She was assigned to follow some of the "Lost Boys." Like Corbett, this local journalist found a lack of support by LSS or by anyone else. She witnessed how the young men struggled to keep up with fast-talking nurses and doctors, how much they wanted to learn how to drive and to go to school, and saw how they struggled with the high costs of both driving and education. Driving lessons were expensive, so this local journalist began to teach some of them how to drive. Eventually she and her family adopted two of the young men.

An Office of Refugee Resettlement report to Congress in 2003 stated that 86 percent of the "Lost Boys" surveyed were employed, compared to 55 percent of non-"Lost Boys"; 65 percent were attending school; 79 percent were fluent in English; and none of the men surveyed relied solely on public assistance for their income (McKinnon 2008, 398). There were "Lost Girls" too, but girls were more likely to be abducted and taken to the North to be slaves and "wives" or to be incorporated into Southern Sudanese families along their journey or in the refugee camps. Due to the patriarchal, patrilineal, and patrilocal nature of Southern Sudanese, boys were more encouraged to get an education than girls. Girls were not recruited into the SPLA but faced violence by soldiers (Jok 1998). Once they reached a refugee camp, girls were placed in foster families and were less likely to be resettled (Deluca 2007 and 2008). Girls also brought a financial boon to families for their bride price (Grabska 2010; Hutchinson 1996).

Lily, a "Lost Girl," was first resettled to Mississippi but moved to Sioux Falls upon counsel from friends after just two months. After working briefly at a meatpacking plant, she quit to enroll in high school and then earned a scholarship to attend college. She told me when I interviewed her in 2012 that the biggest challenge when she first arrived was communication. She spoke only Dinka and a little Kiswahili but later became fluent in English. An anonymous donor paid for part of her college tuition, and she took out student loans and worked at Walmart to cover the rest. Lily met her boyfriend in the Kakuma refugee camp in Kenya, where they had lived for ten years, but he was resettled to Canada. She became pregnant with his baby while in college. Lily had no plans to return to South Sudan, because when she inquired about jobs there, men would tell her she could be a secretary. She wanted to earn a master's degree and saw a better future for herself as a woman in the United States. I asked her if she was involved in politics, and she said no because of "the mindset of men," who did not care about her opinion.

When Joseph Makeer's sister, Aju Galuak, also a "Lost Girl," was a sophomore at North Dakota State University in 2006, she decided to join the National Guard. She told the *Forum of Fargo-Moorhead* (2007) that the primary school completion rate for girls in South Sudan was about 1 percent, but in the United States "the only thing you need to do is just do it. . . . Work hard, and you'll achieve your goal." Galuak wanted the free college tuition but also the feeling of belonging that she never had in high school as well as a chance to change the world. Makeer tried to talk her out of it. He said, "In Sudan, normal women don't join the military," (*Forum of Fargo-Moorhead* 2007). He was also concerned about her safety. As the reporter summarized, the National Guard helped Galuak to realize that "she was running to get stronger, not to get away. She had come a long way. Besides, she found the shared trials of basic training brought her and fellow soldiers together in a way she never experienced in high school. She fit in." Makeer changed his approach to his sister's enlistment after having lunch with friends at a restaurant in south Fargo. The reporter describes how a group of men and women in National Guard uniforms entered the restaurant: One of [Makeer's] friends commented on the exclusively white group. Then Galuak walked in, and pride washed over him" (*Forum of Fargo-Moorhead* 2007).

"Boys" to Men

Like Lily and Aju, many of the young Southern Sudanese men who came to the United States in 2001–2002 arrived ready to work and to study (figure 6.4). It's all many of them would speak about when they first came, but they soon became disenchanted with how expensive and inaccessible U.S. education was and how much of their time they would need to spend working. In a group interview I conducted in 2008 (the group waxed and waned between three and six people as we spoke), they told me, "You work to get money, you go to school to get money, everything is about money. . . . [And] you send it all back [home]." Garang told me that he dropped out of college, because he had not been able both to attend school and to send enough money home.

Gabriel earned his bachelor's degree in natural resource management from North Dakota State University, receiving 162 credits along the way, and had plans to earn a PhD, become a professor, and perhaps go into politics someday. Gabriel had diverse academic interests, from civil engineering and emergency management to business administration, literature, and political science: "I cannot separate myself from books," he told me. "I have a lot of books. Most I got in college, and some I just buy in the bookstore. . . . Sometimes . . . over the weekend

FIGURE 6.4.   "Lost Boys" of Fargo (Garang, Jacob, and John).

Photo by author, 2008.

I can go to Barnes and Noble . . . you know, get the books I read." Gabriel spoke highly of the mentors who helped him get into college. He earned scholarships and qualified for student loans that allowed him to be a full-time student. With his loans, he supported family back at home. The success of some of the "Lost Boys" in Fargo becomes part of the American dream: overcoming all odds—even bare life—to make it. Valentino Achak Deng laments, "We were utterly dispensable to all—to the government, to the *murahaleen*, to the rebels, to the better-situated refugees" (Eggers 2006, 205).

Other "Lost Boys" told me, "Here in the U.S., everything is police and money." They explained to me how chiefdoms in South Sudan worked: The chief was responsible for all things, including elders, but elders would also be consulted on problems. Anthropologist Sharon Hutchinson explains, "Chiefdoms were ruled by common laws, which were different from the federal court in Juba" (1996). Wealth, for example, in the town of Bor, was determined by the number of wives and cattle a man had. A lack of proximate elders resulted in Southern Sudanese struggling with how to enforce social norms. As Shandy explains, "Gender and generation vie with each other for explanatory power in these situations" (2007, 116). The men told me that they viewed the police in Fargo as both chiefs and elders.

A neighbor woman had called the police on the men three times for being too loud. In exchanges like this, they found the police in Fargo "normal and human like" as compared to the police in Kenya, who were only called for "difficult cases, like fighting." However, they also told me they felt racially profiled by the police, especially when it came to driving, because they were stopped often for seemingly minor infractions, such as not stopping completely before turning right on a red light, or for no reason at all. Each of the men shared with me stories about negative encounters with the police. A police officer informed me that some of the men were driving cars without a license, registration, or insurance and that the officers were trying to ensure safety for everyone. A reporter told me that police had stopped one man six times in a matter of months. He had not done anything wrong, and he was never charged or arrested. They just wanted to check his license, headlights, and blinkers. The men told me they learned to write down the number of the police car in such situations in case they wanted to file a complaint.

Of course, not all police officers racially profiled people. One time, a group of Southern Sudanese men wanted to go to a popular nightclub in downtown Fargo. Because many of them did not have birth certificates in South Sudan, international agencies gave them birthdates of January 1. As such, January 1 is a comically common legal birthdate for many Sudanese. At this nightclub, the bouncer was checking IDs, and when he saw that more than one of the men had a January 1 birthday, he became suspicious that they were using fake IDs and refused to let them enter. They called the police, who explained the situation, and the men were allowed in. Upon hearing these stories, I asked them why they lived in Fargo, what they liked about it. They said that Fargo had a low cost of living and that it was smaller, easier to navigate, and safer than other U.S. cities.

After the screenings of the documentary *God Grew Tired of Us*, a question-and-answer period featured John Dau, Joseph Makeer, and other "Lost Boys" in Fargo. There were standing ovations at each of the screenings, after which a group of the men sang a song in Dinka entitled "We Believe in God." After one such performance, one of the men said, "We have to rely on ourselves and Jesus Christ, whether you are a Lost Boy, American, or Sudanese, you have to rely on Jesus Christ. God has also taken care of us. I know we have been through a lot, but that's why we survived, because we believed in God." The packed theater erupted in applause. An audience member asked them how they managed to maintain their faith amid so much adversity. They answered in the following ways:

> We were and are strong people, strong culture. We, the Dinka, or Southern Sudanese people, have to take care of each other. Let's say you have something small to eat—you share it. It was instilled in us, in our culture—don't need to be weak or stingy—share—it's the whole community, not his or hers. Ours is a culture that is really very strong.

> Our culture has a base which is the family—how you survive. When we didn't have one, we craved one. We made our own families in Kakuma, or we have a study group or go to church—it helped us. God is hardening us, disciplining us. We don't have a mountain of Zion in Sudan, but we do have the church.

These men highlighted their appreciation for new opportunities in the United States, especially education and employment, and the need to resist other aspects of U.S. culture. Dau explained,

> Your culture gives you an identity. In order to keep it [our identity as Sudanese], our dignity, we have to maintain our traditions. If you just jump into American culture—jeans dropping, then it's not good (laughter from the audience). America has a good culture too—like giving—we want to encourage ourselves to give to strangers, adopt to other cultures, but don't bring the bad things from Sudan here, like more than one wife. Bring the good Sudanese culture here and get the good American culture.

Dau and his fellow speakers used "culture" to explain their version of a "mythico-history" (Malkki 1995), a romanticized, heroic past, as part of the justification for violence and persecution against them. The speakers strategically and simply portrayed Southern Sudanese, and Dinka in particular, as pious Christians persecuted by evil Muslims, and as subjects of violence but never perpetrators. By unifying their Christian faith, cultivated long before their arrival in the United States, and their victimization by Muslims, Southern Sudanese were in a better position to garner support from the dominant Christian population than other groups of refugees in Fargo, such as Muslims from Bosnia-Herzegovina, Somalia, Afghanistan, or Iraq. The speeches from the impassioned "Lost Boys" brought people in the audience to tears.

Clarke, Coll, Dagnino, and Neveu argue that "culture provides the framing lens—a means of making citizenship visible in forms not always recognized in theory or in political life" (2014, 45). By framing their journey in terms of culture, "Lost Boys" were able to raise money for civic projects in South Sudan.[5] Their willingness to speak of their trials and triumphs publicly in a formulaic and compelling way served to unify themes into a collective testimonial. The "Lost Boys" used this narrative to collect funds for building wells, schools, and orphanages in South Sudan, and they elevated Southern Sudanese status in the United States, especially men's. Agamben's notion of bare life does not adequately reflect the political agency of those cast as bare life (see Darling 2013, 74).

An empowering aspect of storytelling is tied to the sharing and integration of one's experiences with those of others. In telling their stories and demonstrating gratefulness, "Lost Boys" salvaged and reaffirmed, in the face of dispersal, defeat, and death, the social bonds that bound them to a shared community in Fargo. As I listened to conversations of people walking out of the theater, I overheard praise for the film and the young men's courage, as well as curiosity as to why they had not asked for help sooner, because so many people in Fargo wanted to support them. Fargoans left feeling as though they learned something about South Sudan and about humanity. They were disheartened by the stories but pleased that they had been a part of the "giving" culture to which Dau had referred.

The stories of the "Lost Boys" allowed those in the theater to momentarily escape their lives and be transported to the cruel world of bare life, and then to reemerge in the United States with a new perspective. "This is why it is important," explains Michael Jackson, "to explore not only the ways in which stories take us beyond ourselves, but *transform our experience* and bring us back to ourselves, changed" (2002, 138). The men were able not only to tell their exceptional stories but also to "create a sense of self-esteem, agency, and control, not through the private reworking of lived events but through decidedly public enactments and negotiations of power relations in which men make 'themselves out to be' in the eyes of others" (Jackson 2002, 190, citing Gilsenan 1996, 231). Hannah Arendt argued that power "ultimately resides . . . not in what we may imagine for ourselves but in what we may make happen in the divided world we share with others" (Arendt 1958, 33). Storytelling is a powerful mechanism for trying to make sense of a divided world and calling for action. Jackson writes, "The politics of storytelling concerns the ways in which this passage from privacy to publicity is effected (Jackson 2002, 189). Two aspects of the political are implicated here. While the first involves a crossing between private and public spheres, the second involves relations between competing forms of discourse—the questions of *whose* story will be told, and *which* story will be recognised as true and given legitimacy" (Jackson 2002, 133).

Successful testimonials—those that seek to foster empathy and action while also helping narrators to rebuild the self—highlight the agency of an individual, rather than, for example, "appealing to the stock image of the civilized West aiding troubled Africa" (Bex and Craps 2016, 45). Though "Lost Boy" testimonials are relatively formulaic, their individual experiences are not: "The Lost Boys have become remarkably similar over the years. . . . But we did not all see the same things. . . . Survivors tell the stories the sympathetic want, and that means making them as shocking as possible" (Eggers 2006, 21). In further addressing particular characteristics of the wars in Sudan (North versus South, Muslim versus Christian) and explaining Dinka culture, they challenged some Western modes of representation about Africans as completely helpless, while also (understandably) downplaying the complicated history and intergroup conflicts at play in (South) Sudan and in Fargo, even between "Lost Boys" themselves.

In 2007, after meeting Joseph Makeer, Fargo supporters traveled with Makeer to his village of Duk Payuel and to Kakuma to make a film. Like traditional testimonials, Makeer's book and the film were aided by white benefactors who wanted to make a humanitarian difference in the lives of Southern Sudanese. The documentary *African Soul, American Heart* premiered at the Fargo Theater in 2008. That same year, Deb Dawson became the founder and CEO of a nonprofit organization of the same name as well as a school for girls. In 2011, the year South Sudan gained independence, construction began on the school, which welcomed its first twenty-three students the next year. In 2014, civil war forced the school to relocate to Uganda.

The success of Makeer's partnerships with white benefactors is likely what brought forth challenges to his claims as a "Lost Boy." Unlike many of the "Lost Boys" who came to the United States as unaccompanied minors, Joseph Makeer had sponsorship from an uncle and came with a family of his own, a wife and three children, in addition to his younger siblings, whom he had found alive when he reached Kakuma. Because of these kin relations, some "Lost Boys" in Fargo refused to accept Makeer's status as a "Lost Boy" and the social capital that came with it. They argued that even though his parents had died and that he had been with them on the perilous journey from South Sudan to Kakuma, because he had family he should not be entitled to "Lost Boy" status.

A group of about twenty "Lost Boys" publicly challenged Makeer's film project that sought to raise funds to build a boarding facility for orphans in Duk Payuel, South Sudan, Makeer's home village. The group sent letters to the list of donors calling Makeer's status as a real "Lost Boy" into question. When this form of discrediting did not work, in December 2007, while Makeer was in South Sudan with filmmakers, the men contacted the *Forum of Fargo-Moorhead* and made Makeer and themselves front-page news. In the article, they challenged Makeer's status as a worthy leader when his wife and three children relied on welfare. They argued that a good leader must first take care of his family and then his community (Koumpilova 2008). Such intergroup politics among Southern Sudanese occurred in other cities in the United States as well. In *What Is the What*, Valentino Achak Deng explains how the "Lost Boys" organization fell apart in Atlanta:

> There was jealousy though, plenty of it. . . . I do not think Sudanese are particularly argumentative people, but those in Atlanta seem, too often, to find reason to feel slighted by whatever is given to any other. It became difficult to accept a job, a referral. Any gift, from church or sponsor, was received with a mixture of gratitude and trepidation. In Atlanta there were one hundred and eighty pairs of eyes upon us all at any point, and there seemed never to be enough of anything to go around, no way to distribute anything equitably. (Eggers 2006, 155–156)

While the twenty men could have attempted to discredit Makeer in a variety of ways, they chose to highlight the fact that his ex-wife and children were on welfare. By drawing attention to his family's lack of economic self-sufficiency—a key aspect of "worthy" citizenship in Fargo—they hoped to earn social capital with more Americans and to discredit Makeer.

Southern Sudanese with whom I spoke in Fargo found the accusations against Makeer baseless. They explained that the accusers were from the same village as Makeer and were jealous because they were not receiving the recognition that Makeer was. I interviewed one of the men who signed the original letter to the donors but had not participated in drafting the letter to the newspaper. He said that ultimately "it was not [a] 'Lost Boy' issue . . . [but a] personal thing." Makeer was able to find empathy in a larger and influential public, and a distinct voice apart from the other "Lost Boys" in Fargo, who struggled to find recognition.

Though some "Lost Boys" have found success in the United States, others have not. Chol told me, "There's a lot of suicide going on. Some people, they feel their life's not okay." Suicides and murder-suicides among Southern Sudanese have been reported in news media across the country (Faria 2009; Bartnick 2011). Chol recounted some of these cases to me, adding that for others, alcohol and drugs were solutions to deep pain. (He said that women especially were not allowed to drink until they were considered elders. Those who abused the rule faced consequences, such as diminished chances for a good marriage or the ability to get married at all.) He explained that Southern Sudanese in the United States can drink a lot, but their families back in Africa will not know about it. Unlike in the villages, where everyone knew what everyone else was doing, there were few consequences for drinking in the United States. A man could drink a lot but still marry a "good" woman back in Africa. Chol added, "I still don't drink, and I don't want to do it. That's the part of culture that I'm still maintaining. . . . In the camp, we never drank."

I witnessed alcohol abuse, especially among men, as they drank more openly than women, but people informed me that women also had taken to drinking in the United States. A very drunk man at a party one night told me about his life as one of dozens of children of a father with multiple wives. He had a strong Christian upbringing, had gone to school, and spoke nine languages. He joined the SPLA when he was a teenager, experienced and carried out wartime violence, and found life in the United States challenging. He told me that he had nightmares and "loved cigarettes and beer too much." Valentino Achak Deng says,

> By many we have been written off as a failed experiment. We were the model Africans. For so long, this was our designation. We were applauded for our industriousness and good manners and, best of all, our devotion to our faith. The churches adored us, and the leaders they bankrolled and controlled coveted us. But now the enthusiasm has dampened. We have exhausted many of our hosts. We are young men and young men are prone to vice. Among the four thousand are those who have entertained prostitutes, [beaten, threatened, or killed their girlfriends], who have lost weeks and months to drugs, many more who have lost their fire to drink, dozens who have become inexpert gamblers, fighters. (Eggers 2006, 422–423)

The stories of the "Lost Boys" in the United States do not conform to one uniform narrative. While some have achieved extraordinary success, others continue to struggle. Their story is not over.

Conclusion

Ezekiel, Chol, Achor, and Makeer, among others, returned to South Sudan after the 2011 referendum. At least three of the women I spoke with who are mentioned in this chapter have also returned to South Sudan at least once since the referendum, but unlike the men, they have no plans to move back permanently. Instead, they prefer to practice parental nationalism and diasporic citizenship. Diasporic citizenship takes many forms, from the visits of priests and bishops from South Sudan to Fargo churches, to SPLM meetings, and from trips to South Sudan and other parts of the United States to meet with other Southern Sudanese, to sending remittances and participating in online forums and phone calls. Like Achor said, South Sudan was like a shadow they could not ignore. However, many struggled with dating and parenting in the United States as traditional social hierarchies based on age and gender disintegrated. They also faced racism. Their ability (the "Lost Boys" in particular) to narrate and translate their lives beyond bare life, in addition to their Christian beliefs, served to mitigate some of the racism leveled against them and to improve their standing in the hierarchy of local racialized citizenship where New American groups competed with one another in a relatively homogenous dominant culture for social recognition, jobs, and respect.

Southern Sudanese had an even longer list of differences than Bosnians in Fargo. They did not share a common language, as Bosnian Muslims and Roma did, though most identified as Christian and had been victims of attempts by the Northern Sudanese government and military (and sometimes other Southerners) to Islamize, kill, or exile them, to reduce them to bare life. Yet Southern Sudanese citizenship practices served as forms of commoning across these differences, although not always successfully. These practices gave them more clout and access to rights and resources, for example, through the New Sudanese Community Association and churches. Southern Sudanese, but not Bosnians, participated in the development of the Fargo World Garden Commons, a remarkable project of transforming one of Fargo's twenty water basins into a diverse, inclusive public space.

PRAIRIE FOR THE PEOPLE

Globalized capitalism has resulted in unprecedented amounts of goods, services, ideas, and people circulating the planet, which has provoked a range of responses at the local level, from excitement and acceptance of new forms of diversity, to fear, aversion, and panic, depending on one's experiences and point of view. Wars, violence, and climate change are forcing ever more people to flee their homes. As of June 2019, there were 25.9 million refugees in the world, and 70.8 million displaced people, the highest numbers since World War Two (UNHCR n.d.). Less than 1 percent of the world's refugees makes it to a country that provides them legal residency and a path toward full citizenship. The United States has been one of the few countries not only to accept refugees but also to provide full citizenship benefits for eligible permanent residents after five years. After being a global leader in resettlement efforts, the United States trailed the rest of the world in refugee resettlement in 2017 and 2018 (Krogstad 2019). In fiscal year 2019 (October 1, 2018–September 30, 2019), the United States accepted just 30,000 of the world's refugees, the lowest number since passage of the Refugee Act in 1980 (see chapter 1). The United States plans to admit a maximum of 18,000 refugees in 2020.

Ever-increasing numbers of refugees and immigrants around the world call into question the role of the nation-state and how citizenship has been defined and practiced at national and local levels. For some, there is a desire to double-down and isolate themselves and their country from "the other" and to narrowly define who belongs to the nation. For others, there is a desire to learn from refugees and immigrants and to expand the concept of the nation to be more inclusive.

For as long as the United States has been a modern state, there have been debates about immigration and who belongs to the nation, but the debates have taken different shapes and meanings over time and in particular places, framed by local interpretations. Though there are immigrants in Fargo from all over the world, the debate in Fargo has largely been about *refugees*. Refugees race-d Fargo by bringing new and multiple forms of diversity in terms of race, gender, and socioeconomic configurations to this white settler colonial population.

Urban life and diversity symbolize growth, creativity, and cosmopolitanism to some, and fear, danger, and contamination to others (Amin 2012). Cities offer opportunities for meaningful encounters with unexpected actors and new types of activity and agency. In an interview with Ignacio Farías, urban theorist Nigel Thrift argues that "cities can be powerful actors in terms of producing small changes that can move on to become big changes" (Farías and Bender 2010, 109). Such is the case with refugee resettlement in Fargo. However, due to their size and density, cities also host parallel assemblages, where even chance encounters with certain groups of people (for example, New Americans) are minimal and lack context and meaning, which can serve to fuel fear and hate.

Just as Fargo served as a mirror for struggles over abortion in the 1980s, it continues to serve as a mirror for struggles over citizenship and diversity in the country as a whole. Faye Ginsburg poignantly described how abortion activists in Fargo in the 1980s sometimes "crossed each other's boundaries, voluntarily or involuntarily . . . [and] acknowledged their common interest in helping women with unplanned pregnancies" (1998, 219). People on the front lines of refugee resettlement in Fargo during the surge of the 1990s and early 2000s also had to work together to make refugee resettlement function. Teachers, social workers, resettlement staff, volunteers, and police officers were on the front lines of this process, charged with integrating new cultural and religious practices and languages into their institutional designs. The various actors and agencies argued about the methods of doing this, and many believed that LSS should accept fewer refugees, but ultimately, most accepted a common interest in serving the less fortunate. During this time, refugees were viewed more as a population to manage than as actors in the city. However, as a result of collaboration, hard work, and persistence, New Americans have become part of the city and even codesigners in the planning process (see below).

Also, in the abortion debate, sensationalist media has shaped the contours of the refugee resettlement debate in Fargo. Ginsburg's prescient work on abortion in Fargo in the 1980s questioned "the symbiotic relationship between mass media and the efficacy of extreme political styles in the twentieth century" (1998, 117). Social media and the prevalence of choose-your-own-opinion-style news have only become more influential in the twenty-first century, driven by dramatic partisan politics and ratings. Like abortion activists, refugee resettlement proponents and opponents view their work as "part of a larger effort for full-scale social reform" and their work "offer[s] a frame for and interpretation and critique of the culture and one's place in it" (129). As racialized minorities, women, sexual minorities, Native Americans, and immigrants continue to make demands on the state and call for the rights and freedoms that have not yet been fully granted, thereby challenging a deeply embedded historical system of institutional power, those who have benefited the most from that system feel they are losing power that they have somehow earned as individuals, not as members of a powerful group.

In 2015–2017, another surge in refugee resettlement occurred in Fargo, but that was due to a prevalence of family reunification cases, not free cases, or those resettled without family anchors to help them adjust. During this latter surge, numbers did not reach year 2000 levels. Unlike the late 1990s, institutions had a stronger structure for working with refugees than they had previously, not to mention that family reunification cases require less case management and fewer social services than free cases. Another difference between these time periods lies in the political climate, the rise of populism on a global scale, and the more visible and louder presence of white nationalists around the country—and their challengers. In Fargo, populist and white supremacist beliefs have been created and maintained by settler colonialism, local sensationalist news media, the ubiquity of social media, and new forms of diversity in the city, which have made some in the dominant white population feel unsettled, even threatened, particularly those who have had little contact with New Americans (or Native Americans) but instead have gotten their information from right-wing media and similar such sources, which has had a profound impact on how they see the world.

Extreme pro- and anti-refugee groups often run parallel to one another, staying in their own lanes and echo chambers, but there are moderates and others who are trying to bring different assemblages into contact, to build bridges across the assemblages, such as the Narrative 4 story project (chapter 4), and to introduce new forms of commoning that are shaping community values in Fargo to be more hospitable and inclusive.

Commoning

In our research on the politics of taxes in Oregon, Sandra Morgen and I found that "incipient commoning" developed as a powerful, increasingly effective discourse to battle decades of antitax, antigovernment activism in Oregon (Morgen and Erickson 2017). We inserted the qualifier "incipient" before "commoning" to distinguish it from commoning practices that are typically created outside conventional political venues as "alternative systems outside of the market and state" (Bollier 2016, 3). Incipient commoning emerges in support for the "public" and of the "common good." It is often articulated in language about community, belonging, and collectivities that is more and other than the state. Attention to how "publics" conceive of themselves suggests that concepts akin to "the commons" circulate in the imaginaries and vocabularies of advocates resisting neoliberal policies, just as they are coopted by proponents of neoliberalism, like the Kilbourne Group (chapter 4), all of which can be seen around the globe. Struggles and defense of the commons, "from forests, seeds, and water to urban spaces and cyberspace, and the interconnections among them are increasingly visible and practicable" (Escobar 2018, 146; see also Bollier and Helfrich 2013).

Lutheran Social Services, Cass County Social Services, and a host of individual actors and institutions have contributed to incipient commoning in Fargo and shaped the meaning of citizenship to be more inclusive of New Americans. The state has been involved in these processes at all levels—from resettling refugees to Fargo in the first place (chapter 1), to providing social welfare (chapters 2 and 3), to facilitating the development of a more diverse civil society and challenging those who fight against resettlement (chapter 4). The role of state institutions should not be underestimated in providing more fertile ground for commoning practices to take shape in Fargo, in defense of refugee resettlement, a more diverse public sphere, and a broader, more inclusive approach to citizenship, including nonhuman species.

Anna Tsing extends conventional human-centered approaches to the commons to what she calls the "latent commons," which she explains are "ubiquitous," though we rarely notice them, and "undeveloped," though they "bubble with unrealized possibilities" (2015, 255). Tsing is clear that the latent commons are "not exclusive human enclaves" but rather include nonhuman species, even pests and diseases, which make for "divergent ecologies" and antagonisms. As such, the latent commons are not "good for everyone." Tsing continues: "Every instance of collaboration makes room for some and leaves out others." They "don't institutionalize well," because they are "catalyzed by infraction, infection, inattention—and poaching." Finally, Tsing believes that "the latent commons cannot redeem us," because humans are never fully in control (255). Tsing's research is both pragmatic and hopeful in its approach for explaining the variety of possibilities for life in a globalized capitalist world that at once brings humans and nonhuman species together in unexpected ways while also attempting to destroy them. A good example of both incipient commoning and the latent commons in Fargo is the Fargo World Garden Commons, or simply the Fargo Project.

The Fargo Project

I end this book by returning to the beginning and to the future: During the winter of 1996–1997, North Dakota experienced more than ten blizzards, the first in November and the last on April 5–6. Fargo recorded 117 total inches, about ten feet, of snow. Conditions did not get any easier when the weather warmed that spring. Rain, falling on top of lingering snow, swelled the Red River and caused the worst flooding Fargo had experienced in more than one hundred years, cresting at 39.72 feet above normal river level. In a sign of shifting meteorological patterns, this turned out to be only the first of three events that have upended the historical data used to determine the risk of flooding. The flood stage on the Red River is eighteen feet; the major flood stage is thirty feet; and the current floodplain map, as defined by FEMA, shows the land area that would be submerged if the river reached 39.3 feet above flood stage. In 2009, just a dozen years after the 1997 flood, Fargo experienced its most severe flood in history when the Red River crested at 40.84 feet. This happened despite the installation of twenty large neighborhood stormwater basins in 2000, part of a system of more than 350 miles of pipes throughout the city and twenty-one miles of permanent levees and floodwalls. Conditions such as fall precipitation, winter snowpack, the timing of spring thaws, spring storms, and streamflow in 2019 threatened to surpass this record, but the river crested at only thirty-five feet, despite a mid-April storm that dumped at least a foot of snow across the region. As the Sioux Water Protectors at Standing Rock have implored us to understand (Elbein 2017), water is life (in Sioux, *mni wičoni*). It can bring life and end it, create community and destroy it.

In 2010, the City of Fargo's planning director, Nicole Crutchfield, partnered with New York–based environmental artist Jackie Brookner to design a plan for transforming one of the city's twenty stormwater basins into something more than a drab-looking piece of barren land. Knowing that the basins are located in underserved neighborhoods with low or moderate-income residents, including Native American and New American populations, the designers wanted the project to be collaborative and beneficial to those who live in the neighborhood. With federal, state, and local funding, the Fargo Project was a pilot project to demonstrate how "holistic ecological restoration, socially engaged ecological art, and active community process can synergize to transform functioning stormwater infrastructure into vibrant and innovative green spaces for our urban community" (Brookner n.d.).[1]

The vision began with conversations between Brookner, local city leaders, and planning staff, but the final result was the product of an extensive, eight-year-long, public engagement process. Throughout the project, Crutchfield and Brookner guided teams of artists, city staff, community members, volunteers, technical experts, and minority group representatives through project visioning and implementation (NEA n.d.). They created relationships with city residents in order to understand what kind of commons people wanted and the research opportunities the site presented. Because the designers felt it was especially important to learn from the experiences of Native Americans in the region and to ground the project in the place where Native American values and ecological values intersect, their first major public event was a site visit and lecture by Lakota ecologist and ethnobotanist Linda Different Cloud.

Over several months, the ecological art team and volunteers engaged over four hundred people of all ages and backgrounds, culminating in a WeDesign workshop, which is an experiential approach to art and design. The project team visited nearby residences and businesses, went to churches and the mosque, and held participatory events with elementary, middle, and high school students. They met individually and in small groups with different New American groups and representatives from Native American nations, and they engaged with students and faculty from Fargo-Moorhead academic institutions. The WeDesign workshops used innovative, collaborative, participatory methods such as sandbox models, with props that residents could use to create different earthwork forms. These methods proved engaging for people of all ages and backgrounds, including those with limited English language skills. Organizers also created a "sketch and test" approach, which allowed for an "iterative, community-based design vision for the area to emerge—or, as Brookner called it, 'slow design'" (NEA n.d.).

The long-term goal of the Fargo Project was "to transform many of Fargo's stormwater detention basins into neighborhood amenities and to do this through a fully participatory community process." In so doing, "water quality, flood control, biodiversity, cultural diversity, and human health and well-being become the beneficiaries of recognizing and celebrating stormwater as a valuable resource" (Fargo Project n.d.). The Fargo Project highlights connections across urban and rural, and human and nonhuman landscapes, as well as across traditional political borders, rather than isolating the local from the global or the contemporary from the historical and geological. In a TEDxFargo Talk, Jackie Brookner (2012) said,

> We need to mainstream a different understanding of what being human can mean and our relationship to the larger context of life. . . . So perhaps water's multiple and fluid identity can help us open to the uncertainty and paradox of our own identities, that while we experience ourselves as individual wholes, we are really dependent parts of a magnificent interdependent universe. And the verbing of our existence . . .

is about *really* experiencing ourselves as part of this larger, ongoing process. Now this is not new knowledge, but we need to relearn it and bring it into our contemporary context—this ancient, ancient wisdom. I can think of no task more urgent for our survival as a species, because everything we do, any technology we come up with, is based on this foundation of who we think we are.

The designers of the Fargo Project approach the land from a perspective of deep ecology, which regards human life as just one of many equal components of a global ecosystem, and they work from a collaborative perspective that seeks to de-center traditional design models. With more than fifty stakeholders, there are bound to be disagreements about land use, ownership, and responsibility for taking care of the space, but Crutchfield said that they have tried to avoid such conflict by building diverse partnerships from the beginning and to learn through conversation. For example, Crutchfield said that many U.S.-born (white) people viewed the park as "active," a place to play sports. This is different from Brookner's approach, which encourages passive use of open, public spaces. The Commons is a place to bring these different approaches to public space into transformative conversations.

This design method allowed plans to be open, flexible, and adaptive to changing circumstances.[2] In an e-mail to me on February 27, 2019, Fargo-based artist Dwight Michelson shared one of his favorite memories from the project, which occurred when he led a nest-building activity. Participants were asked to "comb the site looking for natural items to make a nest. Then they wrote poetry or remembered songs from their homeland referring to home, nests, or place." One Southern Sudanese man began singing a song he had learned as a child that teaches children to take care of nature. As he sang, another Southern Sudanese man from a different region in the South recognized the song and began to sing along. They had not met before this day. Michelson writes, "I've never been so moved during the project." These commoning practices even brought Southern Sudanese together through song, nature, and art.

I pressed some of the participants and leaders of the Fargo Project to explain how conflict and different opinions were addressed, and one participant said that the project took so long that there were never any major conflicts. "Slow design" resulted in "slow conflict," which dissipated with time. The Fargo Project and the history of refugee resettlement to Fargo teach us that in order to achieve greater urban social justice, we need, as Ash Amin recommends, "to develop a sense of place that draws on disagreement, multiple geographies of attachment and plural political spaces and histories" (2007, 107). The commons do not emerge purely out of collaboration; they emerge out of diversity and disagreement (Tsing 2015).

FIGURE C.1. The Listening Garden in the center of the Commons.

Photo by author, 2019.

FIGURE C.2. The Fargo World Garden Commons.

Photo by author, 2019.

After several days of participatory planning based on community ideas and exercises such as the nest-building exercise above, organizers developed a schematic that would begin transforming the barren basin into a welcoming commons that would include plants, soil, and wildlife, as well as a sculptural landscape and wandering paths with the intention of reintroducing people to their cultural dependence on natural ecology (Fargo Project n.d.). It culminated in the Fargo Project. At the center of the Commons is a listening garden, which is loosely shaped as a human ear: "It is meant to be an intimate place where one can listen to the natural sounds of the Commons: the grasses moving in the wind, the insects, the birds, the water; and where people can also 'speak' back by making music with the slit drums and log marimba" (Fargo Project n.d.) (figure C.1). The Commons also includes an overlook, a deck at the top of the basin that is extended by "an outdoor room" for celebrations, and a wildflower research area (figure C.2).[3]

After Jackie Brookner passed away from cancer in 2015, local leaders managed the project as it moved into the construction phase. Reach Partners—a local company co-owned and managed by women that specializes in project management—resumed coordinating communication, event planning, and volunteer coordination among more than fifty stakeholders and partners. The Fargo Project was completed and held its grand opening, "Prairie for the People," in August 2018, though events have been held there since at least 2015, including New American Welcoming Week (see chapter 4). Some of these events were photographed by New American Ronald Albert, who came to the United States from South Sudan in 1998. Albert earned a bachelor's degree in Moorhead, works as a master controller, and started his own business, Amu Production, in 2015, where he is also a filmmaker, videographer, editor, and freelance photographer. Albert has photographed community events at the Fargo World Garden Commons, and his work was featured in a retrospective that traced the life work of Jackie Brookner at an exhibition in the Bronx in 2016 (Fargo Project n.d.).

Crutchfield told me by phone in February 2019 that one of the most eye-opening conversations she had had with New Americans was with a group of Bhutanese, who had told her they wanted a space to play music outside. When she pointed to the nearby playground at Rabanus Park and asked why they did not use that space, they responded, "We can use that?" Crutchfield was floored. She realized "there was a barrier there, an invisible barrier." This is an example of "white public space" (Page and Thomas 1994; see chapter 4), an infrastructure that is not necessarily built intentionally to exclude nonwhites but that nevertheless sends a message to nonwhites that they are not welcome. Crutchfield wanted to change this. I asked Crutchfield who would maintain the land for the Fargo Project, and she offered a quote by Jackie Brookner: "You don't maintain a baby.

You take care of a baby." In other words, care for the land, people, and nonhuman species is at the heart of this project. However, the city, the Fargo Park District, and other partners such as the public works department are in the process of creating an operations manual that establishes a common language for the care of the Commons. Caretakers will have to, for example, learn how to look after native plant species, which they have not been accustomed to doing in other public spaces. Once, for example, someone mistakenly mowed the space, inadvertently affecting the growth of the native species and research sites in the basin.

Team leaders created a list of twelve lessons learned and advice for how to make a project like this succeed. A key lesson, as shared in a published report, was "Design with, not for" (Asleson, Cunningham, and Ingram n.d., 30). Other lessons stressed the importance of vision leaders, artists, horizontal relationships, participatory methods, and activities that are integrated into existing programs, and that provide educational components to shape and influence community values. "This connection," the report states, "could replicate in the community" (35). It is too soon to know whether the Fargo Project is replicable, whether it will result in more, better commoning practices. The slow design methods used to create the Commons, Crutchfield told me in July 2019, have nevertheless shaped her approach to urban planning.

Even though Tsing cautions that the latent commons do not institutionalize well, I believe the Fargo Project can be considered a site for the latent commons. The project is relatively new and likely will exhibit some of the "infraction, infection, and inattention" that Tsing warns about (2015, 255). It would be surprising if it didn't. However, it has also proven to be a site for collaboration across institutional and disciplinary borders, including the state (or in this case, the city), thereby also demonstrating incipient commoning.

Traditional design is usually client or patron driven: "One or a few individuals determine the parameter, values, cultural image, and context of infrastructure design that may not align with how a community uses space, how they interact with their neighbors, streets or neighborhood. In traditional design, public participation is a box to check" (Fargo Project n.d.). Most of these spaces are grounded in "the normative white spatial imaginary" (Wilson 2018, 28; see also Escobar 2018). Traditional design visions, a Fargo Project collaborator told me in February 2019, represent an *ego*centric logic compared with the *eco*centric logic used by designers, partners, and supporters of the Fargo Project, including members of the Fargo Park District, who will also be programming the Block 9 civic plaza in downtown Fargo. Egocentric logic reflects neoliberal philosophies that are entangled with individuals, expert knowledge, markets, colonialism, and the economy, not community-centered approaches that allow space for human diversity, nonhuman species, and a range of world-making practices. The Fargo Project provides a stark contrast to the Block 9 (chapter 4) project in downtown Fargo, which was developed by corporations, designed by experts, driven by global capital, and, as a result, will likely be coded as white public space. However, as I explained above, commoning can occur in the most unexpected of places.

How cities deal with crises—the crisis of globalized capitalism and the inequality that it causes, as well as climate change, war, global migration, and diversity—reflects the culture, history, and people in those cities. Fargo faces dangers and opportunities related to geography, extreme weather, and vulnerability to flooding, outmigration, international migration into the city, and the influx of new forms of diversity, combined with a history of settler colonialism, white supremacy, Christianity, and capitalism. I have demonstrated in this book that people in Fargo have reacted to these challenges in ways that are at once unique to Fargo and indicative of larger urban patterns. As in other cities, in Fargo, economic development and neoliberal governance stress individualism, technology, business, and capital growth. These practices create a path to the future. As many analysts have shown, this path is fraught with economic inequality, racism, environmental degradation, (neo)colonialism, and a number of mechanisms that diminish one's chances for a share of the common good. People around the world, and in Fargo, have been creating new and different paths that are less well-known and less familiar but are nevertheless accessible. These paths stress a greater common good. They are tied to ecological sustainability, human and nonhuman diversity, and equity, and to a deeper history that can shape the future.

Notes

INTRODUCTION

1. Most names in this book are pseudonyms. I asked interlocutors if they wanted a pseudonym and if so, what name they would like me to use. Some told me that I could use their real name, but I gave them a pseudonym anyway to maintain privacy. I tried to choose pseudonyms that reflected each person's country of origin, language, age, and/or ethnicity, but some chose names that did not reflect their background. Most Southern Sudanese had Christian names, plus family names that reflected their lineage. There are public figures to whom I did not give a pseudonym because it is too difficult to ensure anonymity.

2. In the 1990s, advocates in Fargo began referring to refugees and immigrants as "New Americans" because it is a more inclusive term. Most (former) refugees prefer it to "refugee" because it makes them feel less victimized, more welcome, and agential. Refugees are also distinct from the high-skill migrants from China and India coming to Fargo to work in the software and engineering industries, who did not face the same kinds of public denouncement or criticisms that refugees did. In some respects, the term "New American" glosses over important differences in shaping access to resources and positions of power in the city; in other respects, it is a critical move toward inclusion that broadens the approach to citizenship beyond simple legal definitions. Thus, I use "refugees" when referring to discourse or practices that targeted people who came to Fargo as "refugees," a legal term, and "New Americans" when quoting someone directly, when the individual has gained U.S. legal citizenship, or when the broader term is applicable—for example, when it applies to all foreign-born migrants, not only refugees.

3. I write about some forms of violence that Bosnians and Southern Sudanese experienced as survivors of war and exile, but the wars in the former Yugoslavia (including Bosnia-Herzegovina) and Sudan/South Sudan, and the U.S. government's role in those conflicts, are not a focus of this book. Experiences with violence undoubtedly impact refugees, but violence did not always shape every aspect of life, and not all refugees experienced wartime violence, or the same kinds of violence. Violence warrants scholarly attention, but in prefacing violence and portraying refugees as victims of some of humanity's worse attributes, I fear that we fail to see multidimensional, longitudinal aspects of refugees' lives.

4. Fargo is technically situated on the Great Plains, but few people referred to themselves as "Plains people," though they did refer to themselves as Midwesterners, which is likely why anthropologist Faye Ginsburg, who wrote about the abortion debate in Fargo, also characterized Fargo as part of the "Midwest." In Fargo's promotional video, the narrator refers to Fargo as a city in the "Upper Midwest."

5. When referring to "Fargo," I usually mean the city of Fargo. Most of my data came from the city. However, cities do not exist in isolation from nearby communities or from each other. Thus, sometimes "Fargo" also encompasses West Fargo or Moorhead, which may also be referred to as "Fargo-Moorhead," "Fargo-West Fargo," "Fargo-West Fargo-Moorhead," "F-M," "the city," "the region," "urban area," and "metro area." I only address policies and practices in North Dakota, though some people lived, worked, and socialized across the border in Minnesota.

6. Janteloven are:

1. You shall not think that you are something.
2. You shall not think that you are as much as us.
3. You shall not think that you are wiser than us.
4. You shall not imagine that you are better than us.
5. You shall not think that you know more than us.
6. You shall not think that you are better than us.
7. You shall not think that you are good at anything.
8. You shall not laugh at us.
9. You shall not think that anyone cares about you.
10. You shall not think that you can teach us anything.

7. There is a scholarly tradition of capitalizing "Black" to emphasize its reference to a particular political and social identity. Black with a capital B refers to the people of the African diaspora, whereas "black" is simply a color (Lori L. Tharps, 2014, *New York Times* op-ed, cited in Stuesse 2016, 249–250n3).

8. By "the state" I mean "the liberal, representative, electoral, administrative, legislative, and judicial institutions and practices articulated within the confines of a liberal constitutional framework" (Cruikshank 1999, 4). It is a bundle of laws, policies, institutions, and people who carry out contested political, economic, and cultural mandates, and has many faces.

9. I interviewed other stakeholders in refugee resettlement: human resources managers; directors of the chamber of commerce, public health program, and the English-language-learning program; staff at nonprofit organizations that made refugees part of their mission; and city employees. I conducted formal interviews with sixty people, including New Americans, but most of my data emerged from participant observation. Local media provided data on phenomena that I did not witness firsthand, which helped to confirm patterns I was seeing in my participant observations. I followed stories about local refugee populations and the organizations that I was working with in local newspapers, and I watched broadcast news reports.

10. At the beginning, I met Bosnians and Southern Sudanese with help from connections in Sioux Falls and local institutions in Fargo. I met people at holiday gatherings, in grocery stores, in restaurants, and by chance. I attended multicultural events, birthday parties, church services, holiday celebrations, and social and political gatherings. I visited restaurants, stores, and homes. I spoke with Bosnians in Bosnian and English, or a combination of the two. I spoke with Southern Sudanese only in English, the lingua franca among many Southerners. Southern Sudanese usually spoke the language of their native ethnic group—for example, Dinka, Nuer, Kuku, or Acholi. Arabic is the lingua franca of Sudan, and many (but not all) of the Southern Sudanese I met with also spoke it, especially those who had attended school in Sudan or had lived in the North or in other Arabic-speaking countries. Still others learned Swahili. Some spoke Juba Arabic, a creole lingua franca common among those from the Equatoria region that combines Arabic, English, and local colloquialisms.

1. HISTORIES, ASSEMBLAGES, AND THE CITY

1. Not until the 1960s were Muslims recognized as a *national* ethnic group, like Serbs and Croats, and not only a *religious* group (Lockwood 1975, 27–28).

2. Albanians make up more than 90 percent of the population of Kosovo, which is referred to as "Kosova" in Albanian. Serbs, the minority population, refer to the region as "Kosovo." Those who wish to acknowledge the significance of both languages refer to it as "Kosovo/a" or "Kosov@."

3. Missionaries operated in South Sudan, refugee camps, and cities in neighboring countries. Due to their work, as well as that of other foreigners, the seeds of knowledge necessary to grow into a "worthy" citizen were planted before Sudanese refugees arrived in the United States. One Sudanese man told me that despite the insurmountable challenges that he and others faced as war orphans, there were "good things too"—for example, being introduced to Christianity. In addition to the spiritual role that it played in the lives of Southerners, it is important to understand the significance of the everyday help and guidance that missionaries provided to Sudanese refugees in the form of food, clothing, and education. Interactions with Christian missionaries influenced how Southern Sudanese entered into twenty-first-century citizenship practices in the United States.

4. For a review of Islamic fundamentalism and hegemony in northern Sudan, see Abusharaf 2002; Bernal 1997; Boddy 1995; Hale 1996; Hall and Ismail 1981.

5. Scholars have opted to replace the word "tribe," which has negative primordial connotations, with "ethnicity," which is malleable and can thus be applied almost universally. Anthropologists such as Jean and John Comaroff (1992) and Besteman (2016) have shown how ethnicities were historical creations, products of European colonialism vying for political and economic power in the postcolonial period. Dozens of distinct social groups in the region of South Sudan existed long before the British arrived in Africa and could be distinguished by language, spiritual beliefs and totems, and lineage. To call them "ethnicities" diminishes their precolonial, premodern history; these groups have changed over time in response to endogamous and exogamous pressures, but they are not simply "ethnic groups" like Muslims, Serbs, and Croats in Bosnia-Herzegovina.

6. See Jok and Hutchinson 1999 for a history of the conflicts within the SPLA/M.

7. In the 1970s, the United States resettled hundreds of thousands of Vietnamese, Laotian, and Cambodian refugees, as well as refugees from the former Soviet Union such as Ukrainians and Russians. Most of the refugees from Asia comprised upper and middle class families of fallen regimes in Southeast Asia who assisted the U.S. government in the Vietnam conflict. These groups became economically self-sufficient rather quickly. After receiving assistance to find homes and jobs, some supportive social services, and English language training, few of these refugees applied for public assistance (Wright 1981). By contrast, due to more pronounced cultural and class differences, lack of formal education in home countries, and fewer employable skills in the United States, later waves of Hmong, Cambodian, and Laotian refugees posed new challenges to resettlement and the public sector (Fadiman 1998; Ong 2003).

8. Tracing the role of U.S. government, military, and business dealings in *producing* refugees, that is, in contributing to the causes of violence that result in people needing to flee their homes and countries, is beyond the scope of this book. Anthropologists have written about these processes in different parts of the globe. For the role of the United States in producing Cambodian refugees and how Cambodian refugees fared in California, see Ong (2003). Besteman (2016) traces how Somali Bantu refugees came to the United States, including the role of the U.S. government and military in Somalia. Manz writes about genocide in Guatemala, including the role of the U.S. military in training some of the worst offenders of genocide, for which President Clinton gave an apology in 1999 (2004, 224). Nordstrom (2004) traces how extralegal shadow networks have fueled war and wreaked havoc upon people in Sri Lanka, Mozambique, Angola, the Democratic Republic of the Congo, South Africa, and Sierra Leone. Many other anthropologists have studied the effects of U.S. imperial policies and practices in the United States and abroad; see especially Gusterson and Besteman (2010) and Maskovsky and Susser (2009).

9. Refugee resettlement to the United States involves close cooperation between the Bureau of PRM in the State Department, and UNHCR, the International Committee of the

Red Cross, IOM, and the United Nations Relief and Works Agency for Palestine Refugees in the Near East. Roughly 90 percent of Bureau of PRM funds go to these organizations, which assist with arranging admission to the United States and overseas processing. The Department of Homeland Security and the Department of Justice assist with adjudication and security services.

10. Some refugees come through "priority categories" by (1) referral by UNHCR, an NGO, or by a U.S. embassy (Priority-1, or P-1), (2) as a group of special humanitarian concern identified by the United States (P-2), or (3) family reunification cases (P-3), which may include spouses, unmarried children under twenty-one, and parents of a person lawfully admitted to the United States as a refugee, asylee, or permanent residents. A relative in the United States must initiate a family reunification case by filing an Affidavit of Relationship with a resettlement agency. Procedures for applying to a P-2 category vary according to the particular group being defined (e.g., Russian Jews or Lost Boys from South Sudan).

11. The most active VOLAGS include the U.S. Conference of Catholic Bishops, Lutheran Immigration and Refugee Service International Rescue Committee, World Relief Corporation, Immigrant and Refugee Services of America, Hebrew Immigrant Aid Society, Church World Service, Episcopal Migration Ministry, Ethiopian Community Development Center, the International Catholic Migration Commission, and the State of Iowa's Bureau of Refugees Services (ORR 2006a).

12. This part of the act states, "No person in the United States shall, on the ground of race, color, or national origin, be excluded from participation in, be denied the benefits of, or be subjected to discrimination under any program or activity receiving Federal financial assistance." Executive Order 13166 (August 11, 2000) states that the above law also applies to persons with limited English proficiency or sensory/speaking impairments. In 1974, the Supreme Court ruled in favor of Chinese students who filed a class action, civil rights suit in which they argued they were not receiving necessary special help in school due to their inability to speak English, help they believed they were entitled to under Title VI because of its ban on educational discrimination on the basis of national origin. The case expanded the rights of limited-English-proficient students around the nation. Among other things, the law reflects the now widely accepted view that one's language is so closely intertwined with one's national origin that language-based discrimination is effectively a proxy for national-origin discrimination.

2. THE NGOization OF REFUGEE RESETTLEMENT

1. Neoliberalism as an economic philosophy became dominant in the 1970s. It is anchored in competitive market logic that calls for a downsizing of the state in favor of free market logic and individual initiative, which, it is assumed, will create a leaner and more efficient state (Ferguson and Gupta 2002; Harvey 2005). Processes of neoliberalism—which tie to privatization and globalization—aim to shrink the role of the federal government and shift state services to local governmental and nonstate actors. Neoliberal values that work to expand global capitalism include flexibility, self-sufficiency, entrepreneurialism, and individual responsibility. Neoliberal values include free market principles, private property rights, corporate stewardship, and productivity. They have become ideal qualities of "worthy" citizenship without regard to structural inequalities that limit, if not prevent, equal access to citizenship in any given location—inequalities such as in housing, education, healthcare, employment, or voting.

Scholars have demonstrated ill effects of neoliberalism, such as in how it disproportionately affects women, the poor, and people of color through an increased focus on economic self-sufficiency among groups of people who are overrepresented as social service recipients and as state employees in the human service sector (Fraser and Gordon 1994;

Goode and Maskovsky 2001; Kingfisher 2001 and 2002; Mink 1999; Morgen 2001; Ong 2003; Piven and Cloward 1993; Susser 1998). In the arena of human services, neoliberalism alters public-private partnerships by increasing the role of private sector organizations in carrying out, or compensating for, diminished state services (Jessop 1999; Morgen and Gonzales 2008; Morgen and Maskovsky 2003; Shields 2004). Another facet of neoliberalism has been the increased bureaucratization of the private sector, which neoliberals claim increases accountability in those sectors and decreases a reliance on the state.

2. Mimi Abramovitz and Sandra Morgen (2006) have shown that women and the very poor benefit *most* from social welfare because their incomes are so low that they are eligible for public assistance. Women and the poor, however, benefit *least* from the fiscal welfare system, which is "indirect, largely invisible, and not regarded as welfare"—for example, a regressive tax system that provides "enormous benefits to individuals and corporations—indirectly, through tax exemptions, deductions, and credits" (Abramovitz and Morgen 2006, 46–47; emphasis mine).

3. I borrow this idea from Lee (2016).

4. Authority: Secs. 103, 265 of the Immigration and Nationality Act, as amended by sec. 11, Public Law 97–166, 95 Stat. 1617 (8 USC. 1103, 1305).

5. In 2009, LSS opened a resettlement office in Bismarck that employed one full-time staff member, who resettled about thirty refugees per year. There is a LSS resettlement agency in Grand Forks that has one full-time and intermittent part-time staff, who serve thirty to forty refugees per year.

5. RESETTLED ORIENTALISMS

1. When referring to people from Bosnia-Herzegovina (BH), I use the broad term "Bosnian." When referring to someone who identifies as Gypsy, I use "Rom" (singular), "Roma" (plural), or "Romani" (adjective). I truncate "Bosnian Muslims" to "Muslims." Bosnian Roma often identified themselves as Muslim in terms of their religious beliefs, but I did not meet any Roma who practiced Islam—for example, praying five times a day—but some of them celebrated Bajram with other Bosnian Muslims. I use the term "Bosnians" when referring to ethnic Muslims and to Roma.

2. Some Bosnians in Fargo fought in the 1992–1995 war. Some lived in wartime BH and experienced violence, life in a concentration camp, compulsory military service, forced migration, or hunger. Others committed acts of violence. Still others, such as many of the Roma in Fargo, fled Bosnia before the violence began but experienced loss of family, friends, and a way of life. Experiences with war were an important part of Bosnians' lives—war and their refugee status are what facilitated their migration to Fargo—but war need not be the central component of every story about Bosnians. This chapter addresses Bosnians, including Roma, as actors and citizens in Fargo, not only as refugees.

3. These names are abbreviated versions of Mustafa or Muhamed; Sulejman; Husein, Husref, Hasan, or Hasib; and Fatima.

4. Roma negotiate their "gypsiness" (Silverman 1988). Even those who prefer to keep separate from gadje rely on them for economic and material support. Some Roma perpetuate common gadje stereotypes of them because it promotes their businesses, such as fortune-telling, and serves to conceal "real" Gypsy beliefs. Methods of passing as gadje change depending on context and individuals.

6. BEYOND BARE LIFE

1. I use quotation marks around this term because eventually the youth no longer felt lost and they grew into men. They continued to use the term to identify themselves and to distinguish themselves from other Sudanese.

2. In a lawsuit filed in U.S. District Court in Atlanta in February 2016, the Foundation for Lost Boys and Girls of Sudan and fifty-four former refugees are suing Alcon Entertainment, Ron Howard, and Imagine Entertainment, claiming that they gave interviews as the project was being developed and were promised that the foundation would receive compensation or co-ownership for their contributions to the film but did not receive any compensation after sharing their traumatic stories (Gardner 2016).

3. For Southern Sudanese, "the community" depended on the context in which it was used. Sometimes "the community" referred to Sudanese in the city of Fargo, or to the Southern Sudanese diaspora, or to ethnoregional/tribal identities in a particular location. It was a vacuous term and used often.

4. Equatoria is a region that is home to dozens of different ethnic groups, but they also have formed a sociopolitical group in South Sudan and the United States as a way to counteract the more dominant Dinka and Nuer, who make up more of the military and state in South Sudan.

5. For examples, see http://www.johndaufoundation.org, http://www.vadfoundation .org, http://www.lostboysfoundation.org, http://www.liliieducationproject.org, and https://www.lostboyscenter.org.

CONCLUSION

1. World Common Gardens, the pilot site for the Fargo Project, is underwritten by ArtPlace of America, the Kresge Foundation, the National Endowment for the Arts, North Dakota's Outdoor Heritage Fund, the Plains Art Museum, and the City of Fargo.

2. For an overview of this design project, see "The Fargo Project: WeDesign Community Workshop," YouTube, February 6, 2013, https://www.youtube.com/watch?v=-xos -YDa9Mk&feature=youtu.be.

3. For a virtual tour of the Fargo Project, see http://www.thefargoproject.com/2018/08 /03/basin-virtual-tour/.

Works Cited

Abramovitz, Mimi. 1996. *Regulating the Lives of Women: Social Welfare Policy from Colonial Times to the Present.* Boston: South End Press.

Abramovitz, Mimi. 1998. "Social Work and Social Reform: An Arena of Struggle." *Social Work* 43 (6): 512–527. https://doi.org/10.1093/sw/43.6.512.

Abramovitz, Mimi, and Sandra Morgen. 2006. *Taxes Are a Woman's Issue: Reframing the Debate.* New York: National Council for Research on Women.

Abu-Lughod, Lila. 2002. "Do Muslim Women Really Need Saving? Anthropological Reflections on Cultural Relativism and Its Others." *American Anthropologist* 104 (3): 783–790. https://doi.org/10.1525/aa.2002.104.3.783.

Abusharaf, Rogaia Mustafa. 2002. *Wanderings: Sudanese Migrants and Exiles in North America.* Ithaca, NY: Cornell University Press.

Abusharaf, Rogaia Mustafa. 2009. *Transforming Displaced Women in Sudan: Politics and the Body in a Squatter Settlement.* Chicago: University of Chicago Press.

Acker, Joan. 2000. "Revisiting Class: Thinking from Gender, Race, and Organizations." *Social Politics* 7 (2): 192–214. https://doi.org/10.1093/sp/7.2.192.

Acton, Thomas and Gary Mundy, eds. 1997. *Romani Culture and Gypsy Identity.* Hatfield: University of Hertfordshire Press.

Adelman, Madelaine. 2008. "The 'Culture' of the Global Anti-Gender Violence Social Movement." *American Anthropologist* 110 (4): 511–514. https://doi.org/10.1111/j.1548-1433.2008.00085_2.x.

Agamben, Giorgio. 1996. "Beyond Human Rights." In *Radical Thought in Italy: A Potential Politics,* edited by Paolo Virno and Michael Hardt, 159–164. Minneapolis: University of Minnesota Press.

Agamben, Giorgio. 1998. *Homo Sacer: Sovereign Power and Bare Life.* Stanford, CA: Stanford University Press, 1998.

Ali, Nada Mustafa. 2015. *Gender, Race, and Sudan's Exile Politics: Do We All Belong to This Country?* Lanham, MD: Lexington Books.

Amin, Ash. 2007. "Re-thinking the Urban Social." *City* 11 (1): 100–114.

Amin, Ash. 2012. *Land of Strangers.* Malden, MA: Polity Press.

Anderson, Benedict. 1983. *Imagined Communities.* London: Verso.

Anthias, Floya, and Nira Yuval-Davis, in association with Harriet Cain. 1992. *Racialized Boundaries: Race, Nation, Gender, Colour, and Class and the Anti-Racist Struggle.* New York: Routledge.

Appadurai, Arjun. 2001. *Modernity at Large.* Minneapolis: University of Minnesota Press.

Apte, Mahadev L. 1985. *Humor and Laughter: An Anthropological Approach.* Ithaca, NY: Cornell University Press.

Arendt, Hannah. 1958. *The Human Condition.* Chicago: Chicago University Press.

Arick, Bradford. 2016. "Health Risks of Resettlement Include Rising Rates of Tuberculosis Infection." *Valley News Live.* May. http://www.valleynewslive.com/home/headlines/Health-risks-of-resettlement-include-rising-rates-of-tuberculosis-infection-379725921.html.

Arson Case Briefs. 1996. "Kabob House Restaurant." interFIRE. October 23. Bureau of Alcohol, Tobacco, and Firearms. http://www.interfire.org/res_file/acb_kh.asp.

Asad, Talal, ed. 1973. Introduction to *Anthropology and the Colonial Encounter*, 9–19. London: Ithaca Press.

Asleson, Rachel, Anna Cunningham, and Mrill Ingram. n.d. "Integrating Artists and City Planning: The Fargo Project Lessons Learned." Accessed August 9, 2019. http://www.thefargoproject.com/wp-content/uploads/2017/08/IntegratingArtistsCityPlanningTheFargoProjectLessonsLearned.pdf.

Baker, Catherine. 2018. *Race and the Yugoslav Region: Postsocialist, Post-Conflict, Postcolonial?* Manchester: Manchester University Press.

Baker, Lee D. 2010. *Anthropology and the Racial Politics of Culture*. Durham, NC: Duke University Press.

Bakić-Hayden, Milica. 1995. "Nesting Orientalisms: The Case of the Former Yugoslavia." *Slavic Review* 54 (4): 917–932. https://doi.org/10.2307/2501399.

Bakić-Hayden, Milica, and Robert Hayden. 1992. "Orientalist Variations on the Theme 'Balkans': Symbolic Geography in Yugoslav Politics 1987–1990." *Slavic Review* 51: 1–15. https://doi.org/10.2307/2500258.

Baldwin, James. 1962. "A Letter to My Nephew." *Progressive*. January 1.

Balibar, Etienne. 2001. *Nous, citoyens d'Europe? Les fontières, l'État, le people*. Paris: La Découverte.

Barany, Zoltan. 2002. *The East European Gypsies: Regime Change, Marginality, and Ethnopolitics*. Cambridge: Cambridge University Press.

Bartnick, Kelly. 2011. Sudanese Beauty Queen Murdered. *Keloland Television*. September 28. http://www.keloland.com/news/article/other/sudanese-beauty-queen-murdered-.

Bascom, Johnathan. 1993. "'Internal Refugees': The Case of the Displaced in Khartoum." In *Geography and Refugees: Patterns and Processes of Change*, edited by Richard Black and Vaughan Robinson, 33–46. London: Belhaven Press.

Bascom, Johnathan. 1998. *Losing Place: Refugee Populations and Rural Transformations in East Africa*. New York: Berghahn Books.

Bell, David, and Mark Jayne. 2009. "Small Cities? Towards a Research Agenda." *International Journal of Urban and Regional Research* 33 (3): 683–699. https://doi.org/10.1111/j.1468-2427.2009.00886.x.

Bender, Thomas. 2010. "Postscript: Reassembling the City: Networks and Urban Imaginaries." In *Urban Assemblages: How Actor-Network Theory Changes Urban Studies*, edited by Ignacio Farías and Thomas Bender, 303–323. New York: Routledge.

Berg, Chris. 2016a. "Are Our Public Health Officials Being Open and Transparent?" *Valley News Live*, June 30. http://www.valleynewslive.com/content/misc/Are-our-public-health-officials-being-open-and-transparent-384771171.html.

Berg, Chris. 2016b. "BREAKING NEWS—First EVER Terror Attack by Resettled Refugee." *Valley News Live*, September 29. http://www.valleynewslive.com/content/misc/breakingnewsterrorrefugee-395350501.html.

Berg, Chris. 2017. "North Dakota Refugee Resettlement Bill Passes Committee Unanimously, but with a Twist." *Valley News Live,* February 3. http://www.valleynewslive.com/content/misc/North-Dakota-refugee-resettlement-bill-passes-committee-unanimously-but-with-a-twist-412747333.html.

Bernal, Victoria. 1997. "Islam, Transnational Culture, and Modernity in Rural Sudan." In *Gendered Encounters: Challenging Cultural Boundaries and Social Hierarchies in Africa*, edited by Maria Grosz-Ngaté and Omari H. Kokole, 131–151. New York: Routledge.

Bernal, Victoria. 2014. *Nation as Network: Diaspora, Cyberspace, and Citizenship*. Chicago: University of Chicago Press.

Bernal, Victoria, and Inderpal Grewal, eds. 2014. *Theorizing NGOs: States, Feminism, and Neoliberalism*. Durham, NC: Duke University Press.

Berry, Colleen, on behalf of Abdulaziz Moallin. 2015. "Support Juba Coffeeshop." December 8. https://www.gofundme.com/9ndxceb7.

Besteman, Catherine. 2016. *Making Refuge: Somali Bantu Refugees and Lewiston, Maine.* Durham, NC: Duke University Press.

Beswick, Stephanie. 2004. *Sudan's Blood Memory: The Legacy of War, Ethnicity, and Slavery in Early South Sudan.* Rochester, NY: University of Rochester Press.

Bex, Sean, and Stef Craps. 2016. "Humanitarianism, Testimony, and the White Savior Industrial Complex: *What Is the What* versus *Kony 2012*." *Cultural Critique* 92 (Winter): 32–56.

Bhabha, Homi. 1990. "DissemiNation: Time, Narrative, and the Margins of the Modern Nation." In *Nation and Narration*, edited by Homi Bhabha, 291–322. New York: Routledge.

Biolsi, Thomas. 1992. *Organizing the Lakota: The Political Economy of the New Deal on Pine Ridge and Rosebud Reservations.* Tucson: University of Arizona Press.

Biolsi, Thomas. 1995. "The Birth of the Reservation: Making the Modern Individual among the Lakota." *American Ethnologist* 22 (1): 28–53. https://doi.org/10.1525/ae.1995.22.1.02a00020.

Boddy, Janice. 1995. "Managing Tradition: 'Superstition' and the Making of National Identity among Sudanese Women Refugees." In *The Pursuit of Certainty: Religious and Cultural Formulations*, edited by Wendy James, 15–44. London: Routledge.

Bok, Francis. 2003. *Escape from Slavery: The True Story of My Ten Years in Captivity and My Journey to Freedom in America.* New York: St. Martin's Press.

Bollier, David. 2016. "Commoning as a Transformative Social Paradigm." *Next System Project*, April 28. https://thenextsystem.org/commoning-as-a-transformative-social-paradigm.

Bollier, David, and Silke Helfrich, eds. 2013. *The Wealth of the Commons: A World beyond Market and State.* Amherst, MA: Levliers Press.

Bonilla-Silva, Eduardo. 2014. *Racism without Racists: Color-Blind Racism and the Persistence of Racial Inequality in America.* 4th ed. Lanham, MD: Rowman and Littlefield.

Bošnjak, Branislava, and Thomas Acton. 2013. "Virginity and Early Marriage Customs in Relation to Children's Rights among Chergashe Roma from Bosnia and Serbia." *International Journal of Human Rights* 17 (5–6): 646–667. https://doi.org/10.1080/13642987.2013.831697.

Bowden, Charles. 2008. "The Emptied Prairie." *National Geographic.* January. http://ngm.nationalgeographic.com/2008/01/emptied-north-dakota/bowden-text.html.

Breidlid, Anders, Avelino Androga Said, and Astrid Kristine Breidlid. 2014. *A Concise History of South Sudan.* 2nd ed. Kampala, Uganda: Fountain Publishers.

Brenner, Neil. 2011. "What is critical urban theory?" In *Cities for People, Not for Profit: Critical Urban Theory and the Right to the City*, edited by N. Brenner, P. Marcuse and M. Mayer. New York and London: Routledge.

Brenner, Neil, David J. Madden, and David Wachsmuth. 2011. "Assemblage Urbanism and the Challenges of Critical Urban Theory." *City* 15 (2): 225–240. https://doi.org/10.1080/13604813.2011.568717.

Brenner, Neil, and Nik Theodore. 2002. "Cities and the Geographies of 'Actually Existing Neoliberalism.'" *Antipode* 34 (3): 349–379. https://doi.org/10.1111/1467-8330.00246.

Bringa, Tone. 1995. *Being Muslim the Bosnian Way: Identity and Community in a Central Bosnian Village.* Princeton, NJ: Princeton University Press.

Brodkin, Karen. 1988. *Caring by the Hour: Women, Work, and Organizing at Duke Medical Center.* Urbana, IL: University of Illinois Press.

Brodkin, Karen. 1998. *How Jews Became White Folks and What That Says about Race in America.* New Brunswick, NJ: Rutgers University Press.

Brodkin, Karen. 2000. "Global Capitalism: What's Race Got to Do with It?" *American Ethnologist* 27 (2): 237–256. https://doi.org/10.1525/ae.2000.27.2.237.

Brookner, Jackie. 2012. "The Fargo Project: Jackie Brookner at TEDxFargo." TEDx Talks. Filmed December 24 at TEDxFargo, Fargo, N.D. Accessed February 27, 2019. https://www.youtube.com/watch?v=yplULLsVYzc.

Brookner, Jackie. n.d. "Project Report" for the National Endowment for the Arts. Accessed February 15, 2019. https://www.arts.gov/exploring-our-town/sites/arts.gov.exploring-our-town/files/The%20Fargo%20Project%20low%20res.pdf.

Brooks, Ethel. 2012. "The Possibilities of Romani Feminism." *Signs: Journal of Women in Culture and Society* 38 (1): 1–11. https://doi.org/10.1086/665947.

Buck, Pem Davidson. 2012. "Whither Whiteness? Empire, State, and the Re-Ordering of Whiteness." *Transforming Anthropology* 20 (2): 105–117. https://doi.org/10.1111/j.1548-7466.2012.01155.x.

Buttigieg, Joseph A. 2005. "The Contemporary Discourse on Civil Society: A Gramscian Critique." *boundary 2* 32 (1): 33–52. https://doi.org/10.1215/01903659-32-1-33.

Çağlar, Ayse, and Nina Glick Schiller. 2018. *Migrants and City-Making: Dispossession, Displacement, and Urban Regeneration.* Durham, NC: Duke University Press.

Chaduvula, Raju. 2018. "North Dakota Sees Lowest Number of Resettled Refugees in Years." *Grand Forks Herald.* October 12. https://www.grandforksherald.com/news/4513097-north-dakota-sees-lowest-number-resettled-refugees-years.

Chari, Sharad and Katherine Verdery. 2009. "Thinking between the Posts: Postcolonialism, Postsocialism, and Ethnography after the Cold War." *Comparative Studies in Society and History* 51 (1): 6–34. https://doi: 10.1017/S0010417509000024.

Chase, Ken. 2018. "Cab Companies Dropping Refugees Off at Canadian Border in Deadly Weather." *Inforum.* January. http://www.inforum.com/news/4388587-cab-companies-dropping-refugees-canadian-border-deadly-weather.

City of Fargo. n.d. "Cultural Liaison Officer (CLO)." City of Fargo website. Accessed August 9, 2019. http://fargond.gov/city-government/departments/police/police-work/patrol-work/cultural-liaison-officer-clo.

Clarke, John. 2004. *Changing Welfare, Changing States: New Directions in Social Policy.* London: Sage.

Clarke, John, Kathleen Coll, Evelina Dagnino, and Catherine Neveu. 2014. *Disputing Citizenship.* Chicago: University of Chicago Press, 2014.

Clarke, John, and Janet Newman. 2012. "Brave New World? Anglo-American Challenges to Universalism." In *Welfare State, Universalism, and Diversity,* edited by Anneli Anttonen, Liisa Häikiö, and Kolbeinn Stefánsson, 148–175. Northampton, MA: Edward Elgar.

Coates, Ta-Nehisi. 2015. *Between the World and Me.* New York: Spiegel & Grau.

Cockburn, Cynthia. 1998. *The Space between Us: Negotiating Gender and National Identities in Conflict.* London: Zed Books.

Coen, Joel, and Ethan Coen, dirs. 1996. *Fargo.* PolyGram Filmed Entertainment.

Cohen, Lizabeth. 2003. *A Consumers' Republic: The Politics of Mass Consumption in Postwar America.* New York: Alfred A. Knopf.

Čolić-Peisker, Val, and Farida Tilbury. 2006. "Employment Niches for Recent Refugees: Segmented Labour Market in Twenty-first Century Australia." *Journal of Refugee Studies* 19 (2): 203–229. https://doi.org/10.1093/jrs/fej016.

Čolić-Peisker, Val, and Peter Waxman, eds. 2005. *Homeland Wanted: Interdisciplinary Perspectives of Refugee Resettlement in the West.* New York: Nova Science Publishers.

Collins, Jane. 2008. "The Specter of Slavery: Workfare and the Economic Citizenship of Poor Women." In *New Landscapes of Inequality: Neoliberalism and the Erosion of De-*

mocracy in America, edited by Jane Collins, Micaela di Leonardo, and Brett Williams, 131–151. Santa Fe, NM: School for Advanced Research Press.

Collins, Robert O. 1983. *Shadows in the Grass: Britain in the Southern Sudan, 1918–1956.* New Haven, CT: Yale University Press.

Collins, Robert O., and Francis M. Deng. 1984. *The British in the Sudan, 1898–1956.* London: Macmillan Press.

Comaroff, Jane, and John Comaroff. 1992. *Ethnography and the Historical Imagination.* Boulder, CO: Westview Press.

Connolly, James J. 2010. *After the Factory: Reinventing America's Industrial Small Cities.* Lanham, MD: Lexington Books.

Corbett, Sara. 2001. "The Lost Boys of Sudan: The Long, Long, Long Road to Fargo." *New York Times Magazine.* April 1. https://www.nytimes.com/2001/04/01/magazine/the-lost-boys-of-sudan-the-long-long-long-road-to-fargo.html.

Coughlan, Reed, and Judith Owens-Manley. 2005. "Surviving War, Starting Over: Adaptation of Bosnian Refugees in Upstate New York." In *Homeland Wanted: Interdisciplinary Perspectives of Refugee Resettlement in the West,* edited by Peter Waxman and Val Colic-Peisker, 127–145. New York: Nova Science Publishers.

Coughlan, Reed, and Judith Owens-Manley. 2006. *Bosnian Refugees in America: New Communities, New Cultures.* New York: Springer.

Cox, Wendell. 2014. "America's Densest Cities." *Huffington Post,* September 26. https://www.huffingtonpost.com/wendell-cox/americas-densest-cities_b_5888424.html.

Crenshaw, Kimberlé. 1989. "Demarginalizing the Intersection of Race and Sex: A Black Feminist Critique of Antidiscrimination Doctrine, Feminist Theory, and Antiracist Politics." *University of Chicago Legal Forum* 14: 538–554. https://chicagounbound.uchicago.edu/uclf/vol1989/iss1/8.

Crenshaw, Kimberlé. 1991. "Mapping the Margins: Intersectionality, Identity Politics, and Violence against Women of Color." *Stanford Law Review* 43 (6): 1241–1299. https://doi.org/10.2307/1229039.

Croegaert, Ana. 2011. "Who Has Time for Čejf: Postsocialist Migration and Slow Coffee in Neoliberal Chicago." *American Anthropologist* 113 (3): 463–477. https://doi.org/10.1111/j.1548-1433.2011.01354.x.

Crowe, David. 1995. *A History of the Gypsies of Eastern Europe and Russia.* London: Taurus.

Crowe, David. 2008. "The Roma in Post-Communist Eastern Europe: Questions of Ethnic Conflict and Ethnic Peace." *Nationalities Papers* 36 (3): 521–552. https://doi.org/10.1080/00905990802080752.

Cruikshank, Barbara. 1999. *The Will to Empower: Democratic Citizens and Other Subjects.* Ithaca, NY: Cornell University Press.

Daly, Mary W. 1991. *Imperial Sudan: The Anglo-Egyptian Condominium, 1934–1956.* Cambridge: Cambridge University Press.

Darling, Jonathan. 2013. "Asylum and the Post-Political: Domopolitics, Depoliticisation, and Acts of Citizenship." *Antipode* 46 (1): 72–91.

Davies, Christie. 1990. *Ethnic Humor around the World: A Comparative Analysis.* Bloomington, IN: Indiana University Press.

Davies, Christie. 2002. *The Mirth of Nations.* New Brunswick, NJ: Transaction Publishers.

Davies, Matthew. 2014. "Archaeology in South Sudan Past and Present: Gordon's Fort at Laboré and Other Sites of Interest." *Sudan and Nubia: The Sudan Archaeological Research Society* 18: 165–176. http://discovery.ucl.ac.uk/1524328/1/Davies%202014%20Arc%20in%20S.%20Sudan.pdf.

Davis, Dána-Ain. 2006. *Battered Black Women and Welfare Reform: Between a Rock and a Hard Place.* Albany: State University of New York Press.

Davis, Dána-Ain. 2007. "Narrating the Mute: Racializing and Racism in a Neoliberal Moment." *Souls* 9 (4): 346–360. https://doi.org/10.1080/10999940701703810.

De Angelis, Massimo, and Stavros Stavrides. 2010. "On the Commons: A Public Interview with Massimo De Angelis and Stavros Stavrides. *e-flux* 6 (17): 1–17. http://worker01 .eflux.com/pdf/article_8888150.pdf.

De Genova, Nicholas, and Ana Yolanda Ramos-Zayas. 2003. *Latino Crossings: Mexican, Puerto Ricans, and the Politics of Race and Citizenship*. London: Routledge.

De León, Jason. 2015. *The Land of Open Graves: Living and Dying on the Migrant Trail*. Oakland: University of California Press.

Deloria, Vine Jr.. 1969. *Custer Died for Your Sins: An Indian Manifesto*. Toronto: Macmillan.

Deluca, Laura. 2007. "It Takes Two Hands to Clap: Sudanese Refugee Women Contribute to Conflict Resolution in Sudan." *Anthropology News* 48 (6): 38–39. https://doi.org /10.1525/an.2007.48.6.38.

Deluca, Laura. 2008. "Sudanese Refugees and New Humanitarianism." *Anthropology News* 49 (5): 17–18. https://doi.org/10.1525/an.2008.49.5.17.

Deng, Francis Mading. 1978. *Africans of Two Worlds: The Dinka in Afro-Arab Sudan*. New Haven, CT: Yale University Press.

Deng, Francis Mading. 1995. *War of Visions: Conflict of Identities in the Sudan*. Washington, DC: Brookings Institution.

Dormegnie, Keiron Bone. 2016. "Communities to Receive Support for Welcoming New Americans." Welcoming America. March 29. Accessed December 17, 2019. https:// www.welcomingamerica.org/news/gateways-growth-challenge-grantees.

Drakulić, Slavenka. 1991. *How We Survived Communism and Even Laughed*. New York: HarperCollins.

Durington, Matthew. 2009. "Introduction: The Stakes of Whiteness Studies." *Transforming Anthropology* 17 (1): 2–3. https://doi.org/10.1111/j.1548-7466.2009.01035.x.

Edwards, Jane Kani. 2007. *Sudanese Women Refugees: Transformations and Future Imaginings*. New York. Palgrave Macmillan.

Eggers, Dave, with Valentino Deng. 2006. *What Is the What: The Autobiography of Valentino Achak Deng*. San Francisco: McSweeney's.

Ehrkamp, Patricia. 2011. "Internationalizing Urban Theory: Toward Collaboration." *Urban Geography* 32 (8): 1122–1128. https://doi.org/10.2747/0272-3638.32.8.1122.

Elbein, Saul. 2017. "The Youth Group That Launched a Movement at Standing Rock." *New York Times*. January 31. https://www.nytimes.com/2017/01/31/magazine/the-youth -group-that-launched-a-movement-at-standing-rock.html.

Emerging Prairie. 2019. "Diversity, Equity, and Inclusion Assessment Report Executive Summary." Accessed December 15, 2019. https://www.emergingprairie.com/wp-content/uploads/ExecutivesummaryDEI.pdf.

Emerson, Blair. 2017. "Senate Committee Votes against Bill to Study Refugees." *Bismarck Tribune*. March 24. http://bismarcktribune.com/news/local/govt-and-politics/senate -committee-votes-against-bill-to-study-refugees/article_2b6408ee-4f0e-52d3 -9a64-4b1397bd6f9e.html.

Emigh, Rebecca Jean, Eva Fodor, and Iván Szelényi. 2001. "The Racialization and Feminization of Poverty?" In *Poverty, Ethnicity, and Gender in Eastern Europe during the Market Transition*, edited by Rebecca Jean Emigh and Iván Szelényi, 1–32. Westport, CT: Praeger Publishers.

Engebrigtsen, Ada. 2007. *Exploring Gypsiness: Power, Exchange, and Interdependence in a Transylvanian Village*. New York: Berghahn.

Engebrigtsen, Ada. 2011. "Within or Outside? Perceptions of Self and Other among Rom Groups in Romania and Norway." *Romani Studies* 21 (2): 123–144. https://doi.org /10.3828/rs.2011.5.

Erickson, Jennifer. 2003. "Reflections on Fieldwork with Romani Women: Race, Class, and Feminism in Bosnia-Herzegovina." *Anthropology of East Europe Review* 21 (2): 113–117. https://scholarworks.iu.edu/journals/index.php/aeer/article/view/352.

Erickson, Jennifer. 2004. "Gendered Indifference: Romani Women in Bosnia-Herzegovina." MA thesis, University of Oregon.

Erickson, Jennifer. 2006. "Roma in Bosnia-Herzegovina: A Gendered Gaze at the Politics of Roma, (I)NGOs, and the State." *Identities: Journal for Politics, Gender, and Culture* 4 (8–9): 87–103.

Erickson, Jennifer. 2012. "Volunteering with Refugees: Neoliberalism, Hegemony, and (Senior) Citizenship." *Human Organization* 71 (2): 167–175. https://doi.org/10.17730/humo.71.2.152h5843163031pr.

Erickson, Jennifer. 2017a. "Intersectionality Theory and Bosnian Roma: Understanding Violence and Displacement." *Romani Studies* 27 (1): 1–28. https://doi.org/10.3828/rs.2017.1.

Erickson, Jennifer. 2017b. "Race-ing Fargo." *Cultural Anthropology*. August 5. https://culanth.org/fieldsights/race-ing-fargo.

Erickson, Jennifer, and Caroline Faria. 2011. "'We Want Empowerment for Our Women': Transnational Feminism, Neoliberal Citizenship, and the Gendering of Women's Political Subjectivity in South Sudan." *Signs: Journal of Women in Culture and Society* 36 (3): 627–652. https://doi.org/10.1086/657494.

Eriksmoen, Curt. 2008. "Woman Disguised as Man Had First White Child in N.D." *Bismarck Tribune*. June 28. http://bismarcktribune.com/news/opinion/eriksmoen-woman-disguised-as-man-had-first-white-child-in/article_93c839b1-2936-5c53-9b71-ac34d0ec742b.html.

Escobar, Arturo. 2018. *Designs for the Pluriverse: Radical Interdependence, Autonomy, and the Making of Worlds*. Durham, NC: Duke University Press.

European Roma Rights Center (ERRC). 2004. "The Non-constituents: Rights Deprivation of Roma in Post-genocide Bosnia and Herzegovina." *Country Report Series*, no. 13 (February).

European Roma Rights Center (ERRC). 2014. "Written Comments by the European Roma Rights Center, Concerning Italy." November. http://www.errc.org/cms/upload/file/italy-un-upr-submission-20-march-2014.pdf.

European Roma Rights Center (ERRC). 2015. "Written Comments by the European Roma Rights Center, Concerning France." July. http://www.errc.org/cms/upload/file/france-iccpr-5-june-2015.pdf.

European Roma Rights Center (ERRC). 2016. "Coercive and Cruel: Sterilisation and Its Consequences for Romani Women in the Czech Republic (1966–2016)." November 28. Accessed October 25, 2017. http://www.errc.org/article/coercive-and-cruel-sterilisation-and-its-consequences-for-romani-women-in-the-czech-republic-1966-2016/4536.

Evans, William, and Daniel Fitzgerald. 2017. "The Economic and Social Outcomes of Refugees in the United States: Evidence from the ACS." Cambridge, MA: National Bureau of Economic Research. http://www.nber.org/papers/w23498.

Fadiman, Anne. 1998. *The Spirit Catches You and You Fall Down: A Hmong Child, Her American Doctors, and the Collision of Two Cultures*. New York: Farrar, Straus & Giroux.

Fadl, Osman, and Ann M. Lesch. 2004. *Coping with Torture: Images from the Sudan*. Trenton, NJ: Red Sea Press.

Fargo-Moorhead-West Fargo. 2015. "Fargo: North of Normal Short Film." Vimeo. Accessed August 24, 2017. https://vimeo.com/119179906.

Fargo Project, The. n.d. "The Fargo Project World Garden Commons." Accessed March 1, 2019. https://www.thefargoproject.com/.

Fargo Public Schools. n.d. "English Learners." Accessed October 16, 2016. https://www
.fargo.k12.nd.us/Domain/109.

Faria, Caroline. 2009. "Imagining a New Sudan: The Diasporic Politics of Body and Nation." PhD diss., University of Washington.

Faria, Caroline. 2014. "'I Want My Children to Know Sudan': Narrating the Long-Distance
Intimacies of Diasporic Politics." *Annals of the Association of American Geographers*
104 (5): 1052–1057. https://doi.org/10.1080/00045608.2014.914835.

Farías, Ignacio, and Thomas Bender. 2010. *Urban Assemblages: How Actor-Network Theory Changes Urban Studies*. New York: Routledge.

Fennelly, Katherine. 2008. "Prejudice toward Immigrants in the Midwest." In *New Faces
in New Places*, edited by Douglas Massey, 151–178. New York: Russell Sage
Foundation.

Ferguson, James, and Anhil Gupta. 2002. "Spatializing States: Toward Ethnography of Neoliberal Governmentality." *American Anthropologist* 29 (4): 981–1002. https://doi
.org/10.1525/ae.2002.29.4.981.

Ferree, Paul, and Peter W. Smith. 2013. "Employment and Wage Changes in Oil-Producing
Counties in the Bakken Formation, 2007–2011." *Beyond the Numbers* 2 (11). https://
www.bls.gov/opub/btn/volume-2/employment-wages-bakken-shale-region.htm.

Ferris, Elizabeth. 1993. *Beyond Borders: Refugees, Migrants, and Human Rights in the Post-
Cold War Era*. Geneva: WCC Publications.

Finn, Janet, and Lyne Underwood. 2000. "The State, the Clock, and the Struggle: An Inquiry into the Discipline for Welfare Reform in Montana." *Social Text* 18 (1): 110–
134. https://doi.org/10.1215/01642472-18-1_62-109.

Flores, William V., and Rina Benmayor, eds. 1997. *Latino Cultural Citizenship: Claiming
Identity, Space, and Rights*. Boston: Beacon Press.

Florida, Richard. 2002. *The Rise of the Creative Class*. New York: Basic Books.

Florida, Richard. 2017. *The New Urban Crisis: How Our Cities Are Increasing Inequality,
Deepening Segregation, and Failing the Middle Class—and What We Can Do about
It*. New York: Basic Books.

Foner, Nancy. 2005. *In a New Land: A Comparative View of Immigration*. New York: New
York University Press.

Forman, Shepard, and Abby Stoddard. 2002. "International Assistance." In *The State of
Nonprofit America*, edited by Lester M. Salamon, 240–274. Washington, DC: Brookings Institution Press.

Forum of Fargo-Moorhead. 2001. "Valley to the World." December 9–11.

Forum of Fargo-Moorhead. 1995. "Fargo Fooled: Attack Faked." November 4.

Forum of Fargo-Moorhead. 2007. "New American Army." Accessed March 1, 2019. https://
research.newamericaneconomy.org/report/new-americans-in-the-fargo-moor
head-region/.

Foster, Sheila R., and Iaione, Christian. 2016. "The City as a Commons." *Yale Law and Policy Review* 34 (2). http://digitalcommons.law.yale.edu/ylpr/vol34/iss2/2.

Foucault, Michel, with Mauro Bertani and Alessandro Fontana, eds. 2003. *"Society Must
Be Defended": Lectures at the Collège de France, 1975-76*. New York: Picador.

Foucault, Michel, Graham Burchell, Colin Gordon, and Peter Miller. 1991. *The Foucault
Effect: Studies in Governmentality*. Chicago: University of Chicago Press.

Frankenberg, Ruth. 1993. *White Women, Race Matters: The Social Construction of Whiteness*. Minneapolis: University of Minnesota Press, 1993.

Frankenberg, Ruth. 1994. "Whiteness and Americanness: Examining Constructions of Race,
Culture, and Nation in White Women's Life Narratives." In *Race*, edited by Steven
Gregory and Roger Sanjek, 62–77. New Brunswick, NJ: Rutgers University Press.

Frankenberg, Ruth. 2001. "The Mirage of an Unmarked Whiteness." In *The Making and Unmaking of Whiteness*, edited by Birgit Brander Rasmussen, Eric Klinenberg, Irene J. Nexica, and Matt Wray, 72–96. Durham, NC: Duke University Press.

Franz, Barbara. 2005. *Uprooted and Unwanted: Bosnian Refugees in Austria and the United States*. College Station: Texas A&M University Press.

Fraser, Angus. 1995. *The Gypsies*. Oxford: Blackwell Publishers.

Fraser, Nancy. 1987. "Women, Welfare, and the Politics of Need Interpretation." *Hypatia* 2 (1): 103–121. https://doi.org/10.1111/j.1527-2001.1987.tb00855.x.

Fraser, Nancy. 1989. *Unruly Practices: Power, Discourse, and Gender in Contemporary Social Theory*. Minneapolis: University of Minnesota Press.

Fraser, Nancy, and Linda Gordon. 1994. "A Genealogy of 'Dependency': Tracing a Keyword of the U.S. Welfare State." *Signs: Journal of Women in Culture and Society* 19 (2): 309–336. https://doi.org/10.1086/494886.

Fujiwara, Lynn. 2008. *Mothers without Citizenship: Asian Immigrant Families and the Consequences of Welfare Reform*. Minneapolis: University of Minnesota Press.

Gardner, Eriq. 2016. "Judge Lets 54 Sudanese Refugees Pursue Copyright and Fraud Claims over Reese Witherspoon Film." *Hollywood Reporter*. March 24. https://www.hollywoodreporter.com/thr-esq/judge-lets-54-sudanese-refugees-878021.

Georgieva, Tsvetana. 1994. "Khora i bogove na Balkanite." *Balkanistic Forum*, no. 2, 33.

Gibson, Charles. 2008. "No Love for NoDak? The Folks of North Dakota Are on a Mission to Prove Their State Is Indeed Great." ABC News. January 18. http://abcnews.go.com/Video/playerIndex?id=4157223.

Gilbert, Andrew. 2006. "The Past in Parenthesis: (Non)post-socialism in Post-war Bosnia-Herzegovina." *Anthropology Today* 22 (4): 14–18. https://doi.org/10.1111/j.1467-8322.2006.00449.x.

Gilbert, Andrew, and Jasmin Mujanović. 2015. "Dayton at Twenty: Towards New Politics in Bosnia-Herzegovina. *Southeast European and Black Sea Studies* 15 (4): 605–610. https://doi.org/10.1080/14683857.2015.1130359.

Gilsenan, Michael. 1996. *Lords of the Lebanese Marches: Violence and Narrative in an Arab Society*. Berkeley: University of California Press.

Ginsburg, Faye. 1998. *Contested Lives: The Abortion Debate in an American Community*. Updated ed. Berkeley: University of California Press.

Glass-Moore, Adrian. 2015. "North Dakota Leads Nation in Refugee Resettlement per Capita." *Inforum*. October 4. http://www.inforum.com/news/3853303-north-dakota-leads-nation-refugee-resettlement-capita.

Glick Schiller, Nina, Linda Basch, and Cristina Szanton Blanc, eds. 1992. Introduction to *Towards a Transnational Perspective on Migration: Race, Class, Ethnicity, and Nationalism Reconsidered*. New York: New York Academy of Sciences.

Glick Schiller, Nina, and Ayse Çağlar. 2009. "Towards a Comparative Theory of Locality in Migration Studies: Migrant Incorporation and City Scale." *Journal of Ethnic and Migration Studies* 35 (2): 177–202. https://doi.org/10.1080/13691830802586179.

Glick Schiller, Nina, and Georges Eugene Fouron. 2001. *Georges Woke Up Laughing: Long Distance Nationalism and the Search for Home*. Durham, NC: Duke University Press.

Glick Schiller, Nina, and Garbi Schmidt. 2016. "Envisioning Place: Urban Sociabilities within Time, Space, and Multiscaler Power." *Identities: Global Studies in Culture and Power* 23 (1): 1–16. http://dx.doi.org/10.1080/1070289X.2015.1016524.

Goode, Judith. 2002. "From New Deal to Bad Deal: Racial and Political Implications of U.S. Welfare Reform." In *Western Welfare in Decline: Globalization and Women's Poverty*, edited by Catherine Kingfisher, 65–89. Philadelphia: University of Pennsylvania Press.

Goode, Judith, and Jeff Maskovsky. 2001. Introduction to *The New Poverty Studies: The Ethnography of Power, Politics, and Impoverished People in the United States*, edited by Judith Goode and Jeff Maskovsky, 1–36. New York: New York University Press.

Gordon, Linda. 1994. *Pitied but Not Entitled: Single Mothers and the History of Welfare, 1890–1935*. New York: Free Press.

Goździak, Elżbieta M., and Susan F. Martin, eds. 2005. *Beyond the Gateway: Immigrants in a Changing America*. Lanham, MD: Lexington Books.

Grabska, Katarzyna. 2010. "Lost Boys, Invisible Girls: Stories of Sudanese Marriages across Borders." *Gender, Place, and Culture: A Journal of Feminist Geography* 17 (4): 479–497. https://doi.org/10.1080/0966369X.2010.485839.

Greater Fargo Moorhead Economic Development Corporation (GFMEDC). 2015. "Regional Workforce Study: Greater Fargo/Moorhead Region." Presented by TIP Strategies, June. https://www.unitedwaycassclay.org/pdf/2015-06-1515_Fargo _EXECUTIVE_SUMMARY_FINAL.pdf.

Greenbaum, Susan D. 2015. *Blaming the Poor: The Long Shadow of the Moynihan Report on Cruel Images about Poverty*. New Brunswick, NJ: Rutgers University Press.

Griffin, John Howard. 1961. *Black Like Me*. New York: Houghton Mifflin Harcourt.

Guo, Jeff. 2015. "Where Refugees Go in America." *Washington Post*. September 11. https:// www.washingtonpost.com/news/wonk/wp/2015/09/11/where-refugees-go-in -america/?utm_term=.3fae4539933d.

Gusterson, Hugh, and Catherine Besteman, eds. 2010. *The Insecure American: How We Got Here and What We Should Do about It*. Berkeley: University of California Press.

Guy, Will. 2001. *Between Past and Future: The Roma of Central and Eastern Europe*. Hatfield: University of Hertfordshire Press.

Hagen, C. S. 2017a. "North Dakota's 100-Year War." *High Plains Reader*. February 9. https:// hpr1.com/index.php/feature/news/north-dakotas-100-year-war.

Hagen, C. S. 2017b. "White Supremacist's Church Burns in Nome." *High Plains Reader*. March 23. https://hpr1.com/index.php/feature/news/white-supremacists-church -burns-in-nome.

Hagen, C. S. 2017c. "Commission Study Shows Refugees Good for Fargo." *High Plains Reader*. April 13. https://hpr1.com/index.php/feature/news/commission-study -shows-refugees-good-for-fargo.

Hagen, C. S. 2017d. "White Power Seeking Limelight." *High Plains Reader*. April 27. https:// hpr1.com/index.php/feature/news/white-power-seeking-limelight.

Hagen, C. S. 2017e. "Showdown at City Commission Hall." *High Plains Reader*, May 8. https://hpr1.com/index.php/feature/news/showdown-at-city-commission-hall.

Hagen, C. S. 2017f. "Hate Crime Law Discussion Sparks Fierce Debate." *High Plains Reader*. August 1. http://hpr1.com/index.php/feature/news/hate-crime-law-discussion -sparks-fierce-debate/.

Hagen, C. S. 2017g. "White Supremacist Fliers Hit Fargo Streets." *High Plains Reader*. August 25. http://hpr1.com/index.php/feature/news/white-supremacist-fliers-hit -fargo-streets/.

Hagen, C. S. 2017h. "Local Feces Hate Crime Marks Sixth Racial Incident in 2017." *High Plains Reader*. September 19. http://hpr1.com/index.php/feature/news/local-feces -hate-crime-marks-sixth-racial-incident-in-2017/.

Hagen, C. S. 2017i. "Nation, City, Misleading Public on Refugee Costs." *High Plains Reader*. September 27. https://hpr1.com/index.php/feature/news/nation-city-misleading -public-on-refugee-costs.

Hagen, C. S., and Melissa Gonzalez. 2019. "North Dakota Has Created a Climate to Allow Hate Crimes to Exist." *High Plains Reader*. June 19. https://hpr1.com/index.php /feature/news/north-dakota-has-created-a-climate-to-allow-hate-crimes-to-exist.

Hale, Sondra. 1996. *Gender and Islam in Sudan*. Berkeley: University of California Press.

Haley, Alex. 1976. *Roots: The Saga of an American Family*. New York: Doubleday.

Halilovic, Hariz. 2013. *Places of Pain: Forced Displacement, Popular Memory and Trans-Local Identities in Bosnian War-Torn Communities*. New York: Berghahn Books.

Hall, Marjorie, and Bakhita Amin Ismail. 1981. *Sisters under the Sun: The Story of Sudanese Women*. New York: Longman.

Halpern, Joel M., and David A. Kideckel, eds. 2000. *Neighbors at War: Anthropological Perspectives on Yugoslav Ethnicity, Culture, and History*. University Park: Pennsylvania State University Press.

Hancock, Ian. 1988. *The Pariah Syndrome: An Account of Gypsy Slavery and Persecution*. Ann Arbor, MI: Karoma Publishers.

Hancock, Ian. 1999. "Symbolic Function of the Gypsy Myth." In *Race and Ideology: Language, Symbolism, and Popular Culture*, edited by Arthur K. Spears, 111–133. Detroit: Wayne State University Press.

Hancock, Ian. 2005. *We Are the Romani People = Ame sam e Rromane džene*. Hatfield: University of Hertfordshire Press.

Haney, Lynne. 2010. *Offending Women: Power, Punishment, and the Regulation of Desire*. Berkeley: University of California Press.

Hansen, Karen. 2013. *Encounter on the Great Plains: Scandinavian Settlers and the Dispossession of Dakota Indians, 1890–1930*. Oxford: Oxford University Press.

Haraway, Donna. 1991. *Simians, Cyborgs, and Women: The Reinvention of Nature*. New York: Routledge.

Hardin, Garrett. 1968. "The Tragedy of the Commons." *Science* 162 (3859): 1243–1248. https://www.jstor.org/stable/1724745

Harrell-Bond, Barbara. 1998. "The Experience of Refugees as Recipients of Aid." In *Refugees: Perspectives on the Experience of Forced Migration*, edited by Alastair Ager, 136–168. New York: Pinter.

Harrigan, Simon. 2004. "Relief and an Understanding of Local Knowledge: The Case of Southern Sudan." In *Culture and Public Action*, edited by Vijayendra Rao and Michael Walton, 307–327. Stanford, CA: Stanford University Press.

Harris, Anne. 2010. "I Ain't No Girl: Representation and Reconstruction of the 'Found Girls' of Sudan." *Race/Ethnicity: Multidisciplinary Global Contexts* 4 (1): 41–63. https://doi.org/10.2979/racethmulglocon.2010.4.1.41.

Harrison, Faye V. 1998. "Introduction: Expanding the Discourse on 'Race.'" *American Anthropologist* 100 (3): 607–715. https://doi.org/10.1525/aa.1998.100.3.609.

Hartigan, John Jr. 1999. *Racial Situations: Class Predicaments of Whiteness in Detroit*. Princeton, NJ: Princeton University Press.

Hartigan, John Jr. 2005. *Odd Tribes: Toward a Cultural Analysis of White People*. Durham, NC: Duke University Press.

Harvey, David. 2005. *A Brief History of Neoliberalism*. Oxford: Oxford University Press.

Harvey, David. 2006. *Spaces of Global Capitalism: A Theory of Uneven Geographical Development*. London: Verso.

Hayden, Robert M. 2000. "Muslims as 'Others' in Serbian and Croatian Politics." In *Neighbors at War: Anthropological Perspectives on Yugoslav Ethnicity, Culture, and History*, edited by Joel M. Halpern and David A. Kideckel, 116–124. University Park: Pennsylvania State University Press.

Hein, Jeremy. 1993. "Refugees, Immigrants, and the State." *Annual Review of Sociology* 19: 43–59. https://doi.org/10.1146/annurev.so.19.080193.000355.

Heinold, Randi Olsen. 2016. "A Welcome Display: Photo Project Tells Stories of People Who Have Made Fargo-Moorhead Home." *Forum of Fargo-Moorhead*. September 12.

Helms, Elissa. 2007. "'Politics Is a Whore': Women, Morality and Victimhood in Post-war Bosnia-Herzegovina." In *The New Bosnian Mosaic: Memories, Identities, and Moral Claims in a Post-war Society*, edited by Xavier Bougarel, Elissa Helms, and Ger Duijzings, 235–254. Aldershot, UK: Ashgate.

Helms, Elissa. 2008. "East and West Kiss: Gender, Orientalism, and Balkanism in Muslim-Majority Bosnia-Herzegovina." *Slavic Review* 67 (1): 88–119. https://doi.org/10.2307/27652770.

Helms, Elissa. 2013. *Innocence and Victimhood: Gender, Nation, and Women's Activism in Postwar Bosnia-Herzegovina*. Madison: University of Wisconsin Press.

Higgins, Andrew. 2018. "In Bosnia, Entrenched Ethnic Divisions Are a Warning to the World." *New York Times*. November 19. https://www.nytimes.com/2018/11/19/world/europe/mostar-bosnia-ethnic-divisions-nationalism.html.

Hodžić, Saida. 2014. "Feminist Bastards: Toward a Posthumanist Critique of NGOization." In *Theorizing NGOs: States, Feminisms, and Neoliberalism*, edited by Victoria Bernal and Inderpal Grewal, 221–247. Durham, NC: Duke University Press.

Holdman, Jessica. 2018. There Are More People Living in North Dakota Than Ever Before, Census Shows. *Bismarck Tribune*. December 19.

Holmes, Seth. 2013. *Fresh Fruit, Broken Bodies: Migrant Farmworkers in the United States*. Berkeley: University of California Press.

Holston, James. 2008. *Insurgent Citizenship: Disjunctions of Democracy and Modernity in Brazil*. Princeton: Princeton University Press.

Holtzman, Jon D. 2000a. "Dialing 911 in Nuer: Gender Transformations and Domestic Violence in a Midwestern Sudanese Refugee Community." In *Immigration Research for a New Century: Multidisciplinary Perspectives*, edited by Nancy Foner, Rubén G. Rumbaut, and Steven J. Gold, 390–408. New York: Russell Sage Foundation.

Holtzman, Jon D. 2000b. *Nuer Journeys, Nuer Lives: Sudanese Refugees in Minnesota*. Boston: Allyn and Bacon.

Hondagneu-Sotelo, Pierette. 2008. *God's Heart Has No Borders: How Religious Activists Are Working for Immigrant Rights*. Berkeley: University of California Press.

hooks, bell. 1995. *Killing Rage: Ending Racism*. New York: Henry Holt.

Höpken, Wolfgang. 1997. "History, Education, and Yugoslav (Dis-Integration)." In *State-Society Relations in Yugoslavia, 1945–1992*, edited by Melissa K. Bokovoy, Jill A. Irvine, and Carol S. Lilly, 79–104. New York: St. Martin's Press.

Howard, Ron, dir. 2015. *The Good Lie*. Alcon Entertainment. DVD.

Hromadžić, Azra. 2015. *Citizens of an Empty Nation: Youth and State-making in Postwar Bosnia-Herzegovina*. Philadelphia: University of Pennsylvania Press.

Huebner, Robin. 2019. "Doing the Work That's Not Always 'Popular,' Lutheran Social Services of North Dakota Marks 100 Years." *Inforum*, February 17. https://www.inforum.com/news/971824-ROBIN-HUEBNER-REPORTS-Doing-the-work-thats-not-always-popular-Lutheran-Social-Services-of-North-Dakota-marks-100-years.

Hurston, Zora Neale. 1935. *Mules and Men*. Philadelphia: J. B. Lippincott Co.

Hutchinson, Sharon. 1996. *Nuer Dilemmas: Coping with Money, War, and the State*. Berkeley: University of California Press.

Hutchinson, Sharon. 2001. "A Curse from God? Religious and Political Dimensions of the Post 1991 Rise of Ethnic Violence in South Sudan." *Journal of Modern African Studies* 39 (2): 307–331. https://doi.org/10.1017/S0022278X01003639.

Ilcan, Suzan, and Tanya Basok. 2004. "Community Government: Voluntary Agencies, Social Justice, and the Responsibilization of Citizens." *Citizenship Studies* 8 (2): 129–144. https://doi.org/10.1080/1362102042000214714.

Imamović, Damir. 2017. *Sevdah*. Zenica, Bosnia-Herzegovina: Vrijeme.

Ingersoll, Archie. 2017. "City Releases Report on Fargo Refugee Impact, Says Costs Can't Be Estimated." *Bismarck Tribune,* April 15. http://bismarcktribune.com/news/state -and-regional/city-releases-report-on-fargo-refugee-impact-says-costs-can/article _b5dc95d0-e443-5475-9742-8d8abece0c43.html.

Isin, Engin. 2002. *Being Political: Genealogies of Citizenship.* Minneapolis: University of Minnesota Press.

Isin, Engin. 2009. "Citizenship in Flux: The Figure of the Activist Citizen." *Subjectivity* 29: 367–388. https://doi.org/10.1057/sub.2009.25.

Jackson, Michael. 2002. *The Politics of Storytelling: Violence, Transgression, and Intersubjectivity.* Copenhagen: Museum Tusculanum Press, University of Copenhagen.

Jad, Islah. 2007. "The NGO-ization of Arab Women's Movements." In *Feminisms in Development: Contradictions, Contestation, and Challenges,* edited by Andrea Cornwall, Elizabeth Harrison, and Ann Whitehead, 177–190. London: Zed.

James, Wendy. 2007. *War and Survival on Sudan's Frontierlands: Voices from the Blue Nile.* Oxford: Oxford University Press.

Jansen, Stef. 2006. "The Privatisation of Home and Hope: Return, Reforms, and the Foreign Intervention in Bosnia-Herzegovina." *Dialectical Anthropology* 30 (3–4): 177–199. https://doi.org/10.1007/s10624-007-9005-x.

Jansen, Stef. 2007a. "Remembering with a Difference: Clashing Memories of Bosnian Conflict in Everyday Life." In *The New Bosnian Mosaic: Social Identities, Collective Memories, and Moral Claims in a Post-war Society,* edited by X. Bougarel, E. Helms, and G. Duijzings, 193–208. Aldershot, UK: Ashgate.

Jansen, Stef. 2007b. "Troubled Locations: Return, the Life Course, and Transformations of 'Home' in Bosnia-Herzegovina." *Focaal: Journal for European Anthropology* 49: 15–30. https://doi.org/10.3167/foc.2007.490103.

Jansen, Stef. 2008. "Misplaced Masculinities: Status Loss and the Location of Gendered Subjectivities amongst 'Non-transnational' Bosnian Refugees." *Anthropological Theory* 8 (2): 181–200. https://doi.org/10.1177/1463499608090790.

Jansen, Stef. 2014. "Rebooting Politics? Or towards a for the Dayton Meantime." In *Unbribable Bosnia and Herzegovina: The Fight for the Commons,* edited by Damir Arsenijević, 89–96. Baden: Nomos.

Jansen, Stef, Čarna Brković, and Vanja Čelebičić, eds. 2017. "Introduction: New Ethnographic Perspectives on Mature Dayton Bosnia and Herzegovina." In *Negotiating Social Relations in Bosnia and Herzegovina: Semiperipheral Entanglements,* 1–27. New York: Routledge.

Jensen, Robert. 2005. *The Heart of Whiteness: Confronting Race, Racism, and White Privilege.* San Francisco: City Lights.

Jessop, Bob. 1999. "The Changing Governance of Welfare: Recent Trends in Its Primary Functions, Scale, and Modes of Coordination." *Social Policy and Administration* 33 (4): 348–359. https://doi.org/10.1111/1467-9515.00157.

Johnson, Douglas H. 2003. *The Root Causes of Sudan's Civil Wars. The International African Institute.* Bloomington: Indiana University Press.

Johnson, Marit. 2016. "News Media Influence Perceptions of Refugee Resettlement." *Concordian,* April 21. http://theconcordian.org/2016/04/21/news-media-influence-perceptions-of-refugee-resettlement.

Johnson, Nicole. 2017. "Message for Community after Woman Says Man Told Her to Take Off Hijab." *Valley News Live,* May 20. http://www.valleynewslive.com/content/news /Message-for-community-after-woman-told-to-take-off-hijab-416675963.html.

Jok, Jok Madut. 1998. *Militarization, Gender, and Reproductive Health in South Sudan.* Ceredigion, UK: Edwin Mellen Press.

Jok, Jok Madut. 2001. *War and Slavery in Sudan*. Philadelphia: University of Pennsylvania Press.

Jok, Jok Madut, and Sharon Elaine Hutchinson. 1999. "Sudan's Prolonged Second Civil War and the Militarization of Nuer and Dinka Ethnic Identities." *African Studies Review* 42 (2): 125–145. https://doi.org/10.2307/525368.

Kalb, Don. 2017. "Afterword: After the Commons—Commoning!" *Focaal: Journal of Global and Historical Anthropology* 79: 67–73. https://doi.org/10.3167/fcl.2017.790106.

Karadawi, Ahmed. 1987. "The Problem of Urban Refugees in Sudan." In *Refugees: A Third World Dilemma*, edited by John R. Rogge, 115–129. Totowa, NJ: Rowman & Littlefield,.

Karadawi, Ahmed. 1999. *Refugee Policy in Sudan, 1967–1984*. New York: Berghahn Books.

Keillor, Garrison. 1997. "Wobegonics. A Prairie Home Companion." *National Public Radio*. Recorded April 19. http://prairiehome.publicradio.org/programs/19970419/97_0419WOBEGONICS.htm.

Kessler-Harris, Alice. 2003. "In Pursuit of Economic Citizenship." *Social Politics: International Studies in Gender, State, and Society* 10 (2): 157–175. https://doi.org/10.1093/sp/jxg008.

Khosravi, Shahram. 2010. *'Illegal Traveller': An Auto-ethnography of Borders*. New York: Palgrave Macmillan.

Kiel, Doug. 2014. "Untaming the Mild Frontier: In Search of New Midwestern Histories." *Middle West Review* 1 (1): 9–38. https://doi.org/10.1353/mwr.2014.0003.

Kingfisher, Catherine. 2001. "Producing Disunity: The Constraints and Incitements of Welfare Work." In *The New Poverty Studies: The Ethnography of Power, Politics, and Impoverished People in the United States*, edited by Judith Goode and Jeff Maskovsky, 236–272. New York: New York University Press.

Kingfisher, Catherine. 2002. *Western Welfare in Decline: Globalization and Women's Poverty*. Philadelphia: University of Pennsylvania Press.

Kingfisher, Catherine, and Jeff Maskovsky. 2008. "The Limits of Neoliberalism." *Critique of Anthropology* 28 (2): 115–126. https://doi.org/10.1177/0308275X08090544.

Korać, Maja. 2005. "The Role of Bridging Social Networks in Refugee Settlement: The Case of Exile Communities from the former Yugoslavia in Italy and the Netherlands." In *Homeland Wanted: Interdisciplinary Perspectives of Refugee Resettlement in the West*, edited by Peter Waxman and Val Colic-Peisker, 87–107. New York: Nova Science Publishers.

Koumpilova, Mila. 2008. "Critics Challenge the Reputation of Documentary's Focus: 'Lost Boy' under Fire." *The Forum of Fargo-Moorhead*, February 11.

Kretsedemas, Philip, and Ana Aparicio. 2004. Introduction to *Immigrants, Welfare Reform, and the Poverty of Policy*, edited by Philip Kretsedemas and Ana Aparicio, 1–12. Westport, CT: Praeger.

Krogstad, Jens Manuel. 2019. "Key Facts about Refugees to the U.S." Pew Research Center. October 7. https://www.pewresearch.org/fact-tank/2019/10/07/key-facts-about-refugees-to-the-u-s/.

Kurtović, Larisa. 2015. "'Who Sows Hunger, Reaps Rage': On Protest, Indignation, and Redistributive Justice in Post-Dayton Bosnia-Herzegovina." *Southeast European and Black Sea Studies* 15 (4): 639–659. https://doi.org/10.1080/14683857.2015.1126095.

La Flamme, Marcel. 2018. "Remaking the Pilot: Unmanned Aviation and the Transformation of Work in Postagrarian North Dakota." PhD diss., Rice University.

Lassiter, Luke Eric, Hurley Goodall, Elizabeth Campbell, and Michelle Natasya Johnson, eds. 2004. *The Other Side of Middletown: Exploring Muncie's African American Community*. New York: AltaMira Press.

Latham, Judith. 1999. "Roma of the Former Yugoslavia." *Nationalities Papers* 27 (2): 205–226. https://doi.org/10.1080/009059999109037.

Latour, Bruno. 2007. *Reassembling the Social: An Introduction to Actor-Network-Theory.* Oxford: Oxford University Press.

Lazar, Sian, ed. 2013. *The Anthropology of Citizenship.* Malden, MA: Wiley Blackwell.

Lee, Ken. 2000. "Orientalism and Gypsylorism." *Social Analysis* 44 (2): 129–156. http://www.jstor.org/stable/23166537.

Lee, Tina. 2016. *Catching a Case: Inequality and Fear in New York City's Child Welfare System.* New Brunswick, NJ: Rutgers University Press.

Lefebvre, Henri. 1968. *Le droit à la ville.* Paris: Anthopos.

Lemon, Alaina. 2000. *Between Two Fires: Gypsy Performance and Romani Memory from Pushkin to Postsocialism.* Durham, NC: Duke University Press.

Lewis, Desiree. 2011. "Representing African Sexualities." In *African Sexualities: A Reader,* edited by Sylvia Tamale, 199–216. Cape Town: Pambazuka Press.

Lewis, Oscar. 1966. "The Culture of Poverty." *Scientific American* 215 (4): 19–25. http://www.jstor.org/stable/24931078.

Lippert, Randy. 1998. "Rationalities and Refugee Resettlement." *Economy and Society* 27 (4): 380–406. https://doi.org/10.1080/03085149800000026.

Lippert, Randy. 1999. "Governing Refugees: The Relevance of Governmentality to Understanding the International Refugee Regime." *Alternatives: Global, Local, Political* 24 (3): 295–329. https://doi.org/10.1177/030437549902400302.

Lipsky, Michael. 1980. *Street-Level Bureaucracy: Dilemmas of the Individual in Public Services.* New York: Russell Sage.

Loescher, Gil, and John A. Scanlan. 1986. *Calculated Kindness: Refugees and America's Half-Open Door, 1945 to the Present.* New York: Free Press.

Loizos, Peter. 1981. *The Heart Grown Bitter: A Chronicle of Cypriot War Refugees.* Cambridge: Cambridge University Press.

Low, Setha. 2009. "Maintaining Whiteness: The Fear of Others and Niceness." *Transforming Anthropology* 17 (2): 79–92. https://doi.org/10.1111/j.1548-7466.2009.01047.x.

Lussenhop, Jessica. 2017. "Can a Life-Swap Exercise Stop a Community Tearing Itself in Two?" BBC, May 4. http://www.bbc.com/news/world-us-canada-39727185#.

Lutheran Social Services of North Dakota. n.d. "Refugee Resettlement in ND." Accessed January 18, 2019. https://www.legis.nd.gov/files/committees/652017/19_5061_03000appendixd.pdf.

Lutz, Catherine, and Jane Collins. 1993. *Reading National Geographic.* Chicago: University of Chicago Press.

Lyden, Grace. 2015. "Saturday Marks Tragic 20-year-Anniversary for Fargo's Bosnians." *Inforum,* July 10. http://www.inforum.com/news/3782979-saturday-marks-tragic-20-year-anniversary-for-Fargos-Bosnians.

Lynd, Robert, and Helen Lynd. 1929. *Middletown: A Study in Modern American Culture.* New York: Harcourt Brace Jovanovich.

Maček, Ivana. 2007. "'Imitation of Life': Negotiating Normality in Sarajevo under Siege." In *The New Bosnian Mosaic: Identities, Memories, and Moral Claims in a Post-war Society,* edited by Xavier Bougarel, Elissa Helms, and Gerlachlus Duijzings, 39–57. Aldershot, UK: Ashgate.

Maček, Ivana. 2009. *Sarajevo under Siege: Anthropology in Wartime.* Philadelphia: University of Pennsylvania Press.

Macklin, Audrey. 2004. "Like Oil and Water, with a Match: Militarized Commerce, Armed Conflict, and Human Security in Sudan." In *Sites of Violence: Gender and Conflict Zones,* edited by Wenona Giles and Jennifer Hyndman, 75–107. Berkeley: University of California Press.

Majumder, Maimuna. 2017. "Higher Rates of Hate Crimes Are Tied to Income Inequality." FiveThirtyEight. January 23. Accessed October 31, 2017. https://fivethirtyeight.com /features/higher-rates-of-hate-crimes-are-tied-to-income-inequality/.

Makeer, Joseph Akol. 2008. *From Africa to America: The Journey of a Lost Boy of Sudan.* Mustang, AL: Tate Publishing.

Malkki, Liisa H. 1995. *Purity and Exile: Violence, Memory, and National Cosmology among Hutu Refugees in Tanzania.* Chicago: University of Chicago Press.

Mamdani, Mahmood. 2002. "Good Muslim, Bad Muslim: A Political Perspective on Culture and Terrorism." *American Anthropologist* 104 (3): 766–775. https://doi.org/10 .1525/aa.2002.104.3.766.

Mamdani, Mahmood. 2018. "The Trouble with South Sudan's New Peace Deal." *New York Times.* September 24. Accessed February 27, 2019. https://www.nytimes.com/2018 /09/24/opinion/south-sudan-peace-agreement.html.

Manz, Beatrice. 2004. *Paradise in Ashes: A Guatemalan Journey of Courage, Terror, and Hope.* Berkeley: University of California Press.

Marshall, T. H. 1950. *Citizenship and Social Class.* Cambridge: Cambridge University Press.

Maskovsky, Jeff, and Ida Susser, eds. 2009. *Rethinking America: The Imperial Homeland in the 21st Century.* New York: Routledge.

Massey, Doreen. 2004. "Geographies of Responsibility." *Geografiska Annaler* 86 (1): 5–18. https://doi.org/10.1111/j.0435-3684.2004.00150.x.

Massey, Douglas, ed. 2008. *New Faces in New Places: The Changing Geography of American Immigration.* New York: Russell Sage Foundation.

Massey, Douglas S., and Nancy A. Denton. 1993. *American Apartheid: Segregation and the Making of the Underclass.* Cambridge, MA: Harvard University Press.

Matras, Yaron. 2004. "The Role of Language in Mystifying and Demystifying Gypsy Identity." In *The Role of the Romanies*, edited by Nicholas Saul and Susan Tebbutt, 53–78. Liverpool: Liverpool University Press.

Mayardit, Salva Kiir. 2007. "Salva Kiir Declares 16 May National Day in South Sudan." *Sudan Tribune.* May 18. Accessed May 1, 2010. http://www.sudantribune.com/spip .php?article21921.

McFeely, Mike. 2017. "McFeely: Chief Todd Hopes Community Takes Positive Lesson from Parking Lot Incident." *Inforum.* July 30. Accessed October 24, 2017. http://www .inforum.com/news/4305104-mcfeely-chief-todd-hopes-community-takes -positive-lesson-parking-lot-incident.

McIntosh, Peggy. 1988. *White Privilege and Male Privilege: A Personal Account of Coming to See Correspondences through Work in Women's Studies.* Wellesley, MA: Wellesley College, Center for Research on Women.

McKinnon, Sara L. 2008. "Unsettling Resettlement: Problematizing 'Lost Boys of Sudan' Resettlement and Identity." *Western Journal of Communication* 72 (4): 397–414. https://doi.org/10.1080/10570310802446056.

Medica Infoteka. 1999. *Živjeti s Nasiljem* [To Live without Violence]. Zenica, Bosnia-Herzegovina: Infoteka.

Medica Infoteka. 2001. *Nismo Naučile(i) Tako smo Živjele(i)* [How We Live(d)]. Zenica, Bosnia-Herzegovina: Infoteka.

Medicine, Beatrice. 2001. *Learning to Be an Anthropologist and Remaining "Native."* Champagne, IL: University of Illinois Press.

Mednick, Sam. 2018. "Oil-Rich South Sudan to Resume Production in War-Hit Region." *PBS News Hour.* August 30. https://www.pbs.org/newshour/world/oil-rich-south -sudan-to-resume-production-in-war-hit-region.

Memišević, Fadila. 1999. *Roma of Bosnia and Herzegovina: Documentation of the Bosnian Section of the Society for Threatened Peoples.* Sarajevo: Society for Threatened Peoples–Section for Bosnia and Herzegovina.

Mink, Gwendolyn. 1990. "The Lady and the Tramp: Gender, Race, and the Origins of the American Welfare State." In *Women, the State, and Welfare*, edited by Linda Gordon, 92–122. Madison: University of Wisconsin Press.

Mink, Gwendolyn. 1999. *Whose Welfare?* Ithaca, NY: Cornell University Press.

Montaigne, Michel Eyquem De. 1948. *Selections from the Essays of Michel Eyquem De Montaigne.* Translated by Donald M. Frame. Stanford, CA: Leland Stanford Junior University.

Moraga, Cherríe, and Gloria Anzaldúa, eds. 2002. *This Bridge Called My Back: Writings by Radical Women of Color.* Rev. ed. New York: Kitchen Table and Women of Color Press.

Morgen, Sandra. 2001. "Agency of Caseworkers: Negotiating Devolution, Privatization, and the Meaning of Self-Sufficiency." *American Anthropologist* 103 (3): 747–761. https://doi.org/10.1525/aa.2001.103.3.747.

Morgen, Sandra. 2002. *Into Our Own Hands: The Women's Health Movement in the United States, 1969–1990.* New Brunswick, NJ: Rutgers University Press.

Morgen, Sandra, Joan Acker, and Jill Michele Weigt. 2010. *Stretched Thin: Poor Families, Welfare Work, and Welfare Reform.* Ithaca, NY: Cornell University Press.

Morgen, Sandra, and Jennifer Erickson. 2017. "Incipient 'Commoning' in Defense of the Public? Competing Varieties of Fiscal Citizenship in Tax- and Spending-Related Direct Democracy." *Focaal: Journal of Global and Historical Anthropology* 79: 54–66. https://doi.org/10.3167/fcl.2017.790105.

Morgen, Sandra, and Lisa Gonzales. 2008. "The Neoliberal American Dream as Daydream: Counter-Hegemonic Perspectives on Welfare Restructuring in the United States." *Critique of Anthropology* 28 (2): 219–236. https://doi.org/10.1177/0308275X08090548.

Morgen, Sandra, and Jeff Maskovsky. 2003. "The Anthropology of Welfare 'Reform': New Perspectives on U.S. Urban Poverty in the Post-welfare Era." *Annual Review of Anthropology* 32: 315–338. https://doi.org/10.1146/annurev.anthro.32.061002.093431.

Moynihan, Daniel Patrick. 1965. "The Negro Family: The Case for National Action." Office of Policy Planning and Research. U.S. Department of Labor.

Mullings, Leith. 2001. "Households Headed by Women: The Politics of Class, Race, and Gender." In *The New Poverty Studies: The Ethnography of Power, Politics, and Impoverished People in the United States*, edited by Judith Goode and Jeff Maskovsky, 37–56. New York: New York University Press.

Mullings, Leith. 2005. "Interrogating Racism: Towards an Anti-racist Anthropology." *Annual Review of Anthropology* 34: 667–693. https://doi.org/10.1146/annurev.anthro.32.061002.093435.

Myland, Megan, and Jon Shenk, dirs. 2003. *The Lost Boys of Sudan.* Actual Films.

Nader, Laura. 1972. "Up the Anthropologist: Perspectives Gained from Studying Up." In *Reinventing Anthropology*, edited by Dell Hymes, 284–309. New York: Pantheon Books.

National Endowment for the Arts (NEA). n.d. "The Fargo Project." Accessed February 27, 2019. https://www.arts.gov/exploring-our-town/fargo-project.

New American Economy. 2016. "New Americans in the Fargo-Moorhead Region." October 20. Accessed March 1, 2019. https://research.newamericaneconomy.org/report/new-americans-in-the-fargo-moorhead-region/.

New American Economy. 2017. "From Struggle to Resilience: The Economic Impact of Refugees in America." June 19. Accessed October 24, 2017. http://www.newamericaneconomy.org/research/from-struggle-to-resilience-the-economic-impact-of-refugees-in-america/.

New York Times. 1995. "A Case of an Ethnic Attack Is Called a Hoax." November 4. Accessed April 2, 2010. http://www.nytimes.com/1995/11/04/us/a-case-of-an-ethnic-attack-is-called-a-hoax.html.

New York Times. 2017. "Rejected Report Shows Revenue Brought in by Refugees." September 19. Accessed October 24, 2017. https://www.nytimes.com/interactive/2017/09/19/us/politics/document-Refugee-Report.html?smid=tw-share&blm_aid=569361&_r=0.

Ngcobo, Gabi. 2017. "We Are All Postcolonial." Goethe Institute. Accessed February 27, 2019. https://www.goethe.de/en/kul/bku/20908725.html.

Nonini, Donald M. 2006. "Introduction: The Global Idea of 'The Commons.'" *Social Analysis: The International Journal of Social and Cultural Practice* 50 (3): 164–177. https://www.jstor.org/stable/23182116.

Nordstrom, Carolyn. 2004. *Shadows of War: Violence, Power, and International Profiteering in the Twenty-first Century*. Berkeley: University of California Press.

Norman, Jon. 2013. *Small Cities USA: Growth, Diversity, and Inequality*. New Brunswick, NJ: Rutgers University Press.

North Dakota Census Office. 2009. *Census Report*. North Dakota Department of Commerce. Accessed October 18, 2017. https://www.commerce.nd.gov/uploads/8/NDCensusNewsletter_August2014.pdf.

Office of Refugee Resettlement (ORR). 1982. "Report to the Congress: Refugee Resettlement Program." U.S. Department of Health and Human Services. January 31. Accessed September 18, 2019. https://www.acf.hhs.gov/orr/resource/archived-office-of-refugee-resettlement-annual-reports-to-congress.

Office of Refugee Resettlement (ORR). 1996. "Report to the Congress: Refugee Resettlement Program." U.S. Department of Health and Human Services. January 31. Accessed September 18, 2019. https://www.acf.hhs.gov/orr/resource/archived-office-of-refugee-resettlement-annual-reports-to-congress.

Office of Refugee Resettlement (ORR). 1999. "Report to the Congress: Making a Difference." U.S. Department of Health and Human Services. January 31. Accessed September 18, 2019. https://www.acf.hhs.gov/orr/resource/archived-office-of-refugee-resettlement-annual-reports-to-congress.

Office of Refugee Resettlement (ORR). 2006a. "National Voluntary Agencies." U.S. Department of Health and Human Services. Accessed February 2, 2006. http://www.acf.hhs.gov/programs/orr/partners/volunteer.htm.

Office of Refugee Resettlement (ORR). 2006b. "Report to the Congress." Table 4: Arrivals by State of Initial Resettlement 2002–2006. Department of State, Department of Homeland Security, Department of Health and Human Services. January 31. Accessed September 18, 2019. https://www.wrapsnet.org/resources/.

Office of Refugee Resettlement (ORR). 2009. "Report to the Congress." Table 4: Arrivals by State of Initial Resettlement 2007–2009. Department of State, Department of Homeland Security, Department of Health and Human Services. January 31. Accessed September 18, 2019. https://www.wrapsnet.org/resources/.

Office of Refugee Resettlement (ORR). 2015. "Wilson-Fish Program Guidelines." U.S. Department of Health and Human Services. Accessed October 18, 2017. https://www.acf.hhs.gov/orr/resource/wilson-fish-alternative-program-guidelines.

Office of Refugee Resettlement (ORR). 2016. "Preferred Communities." U.S. Department of Health and Human Services. January 8. Accessed October 18, 2017. http://www.acf.hhs.gov/programs/orr/programs/rph.

Office of Refugee Resettlement (ORR). 2018. "Reports to the Congress." Chart II-6: Summary of Refugee Arrivals by State for FY 2010–2018. Department of State, Department of Homeland Security, Department of Health and Human Services. January 31. 2010–2018. Accessed September 18, 2019. https://www.wrapsnet.org/resources/.

Okely, Judith. 1996. *Own or Other Culture.* London: Routledge.

Olsen, W. Scott. 2008. "Betrayed by a Love of My Life." Letter to the editor. *Forum of Fargo-Moorhead.* January 20.

Ong, Aihwa. 1996. "Cultural Citizenship as Subject-Making: Immigrants Negotiate Racial and Cultural Boundaries in the United States." *Current Anthropology* 37 (5): 737–762. https://doi.org/10.1086/204560.

Ong, Aihwa. 2003. *Buddha Is Hiding: Refugees, Citizenship, the New America.* Berkeley: University of California Press.

Ong, Aihwa. 2006. "Mutations in Citizenship." *Theory Culture Society* 23: 499–505. https://doi.org/10.1177/0263276406064831.

Ong, Aihwa, and Stephen J. Collier, eds. 2005. *Global Assemblages: Technology, Politics, and Ethics as Anthropological Problems.* Malden, MA: Blackwell Publishing.

Oprea, Alexandra. 2005. "Child Marriage a Cultural Problem, Educational Access a Race Issue? Deconstructing Uni-dimensional Understanding of Romani Oppression." *Roma Rights Journal.* July 21. http://www.errc.org/article/child-marriage-a-cultural-problem-educational-access-a-race-issue-deconstructing-uni-dimensional-understanding-of-romani-oppression/2295.

Ostrom, Elinor. 1990. *Governing the Commons: The Evolution of Institutions for Collective Action.* Cambridge: Cambridge University Press.

Ostler, Jeff. 2004. *The Plains Sioux and U.S. Colonialism from Lewis and Clark to Wounded Knee.* Cambridge: Cambridge University Press.

Ouradnik, Damon. n.d. "Stop Refugee Resettlement and Lutheran Social Services in North Dakota!" Change.org. Accessed April 12, 2016. https://www.change.org/p/cass-county-legislature-stop-lutheran-social-services-in-fargo.

Øverland, Orm. 2009. "Intruders on Native Ground: Troubling Silences and Memories of the Land-Taking in Norwegian Immigrant Letters." In *Transnational American Memories,* edited by Udo J. Hebel, 79–102. Berlin: Walter de Gruyter.

Page, Helán, and R. Brooke Thomas. 1994. "White Public Space and the Construction of White Privilege in U. S. Health Care: Fresh Concepts and a New Model of Analysis." *Medical Anthropology Quarterly* 8 (1): 109–116.

Pantera, Tom. 2005. "Living Like a Refugee: Photographer Chronicles Immigrants in Fargo-Moorhead." *Inforum.* March 20. Accessed October 18, 2017. http://www.inforum.com/news/2758357-living-refugee-photographer-chronicles-immigrants-fargo-moorhead.

Peake, Linda. 2016. "The Twenty-first Century Quest for Feminism and the Global Urban." *International Journal of Urban and Regional Research* 40 (1): 219–227. https://doi.org/10.1111/1468-2427.12276.

Peterson, Scott. 2001. *Me against My Brother: At War in Somalia, Sudan, and Rwanda.* London: Routledge.

Phillips, John. 2006. "Agencement/Assemblage." *Theory, Culture, and Society* 23 (2–3): 108–109. https://doi.org/10.1177%2F026327640602300219.

Phillips, Katherine Amy. 2004. "Intercultural Knowledge and Skills in Social Service Work with Refugees: Perspectives from Providers and Recipients of Service." PhD diss., University of North Dakota.

Piepkorn, Dave. 2016. Interview with Chris Berg. October 2. http://www.valleynewslive.com/content/misc/DeputyMayorPiepkornFargoBudget-395566611.html.

Pitya, Philip Legge. 1996. "History of Western Christian Evangelism in the Sudan: 1898–1964." PhD diss., Boston University.

Piven, Frances Fox. 1990. "Ideology and the State: Women, Power, and the Welfare State." In *Women, the State, and Welfare*, edited by Linda Gordon, 199–225. Madison: University of Wisconsin Press.

Piven, Frances Fox. 2001. "Welfare Reform and the Economic and Cultural Reconstruction of Low Wage Labor Markets." In *The New Poverty Studies: The Ethnography of Power, Politics, and Impoverished People in the United States*, edited by Judith Goode and Jeff Maskovsky, 135–151. New York: New York University Press.

Piven, Frances Fox, and Richard Cloward. 1993. *Regulating the Poor: The Functions of Public Welfare*. New York: Vintage Books.

Powell, Eve M. Troutt. 2003. *A Different Shade of Colonialism: Egypt, Great Britain, and the Mastery of the Sudan*. Berkeley: University of California Press.

Priyadharshini, Esther. 2003. "Coming Unstuck: Thinking Otherwise about 'Studying Up.'" *Anthropology and Education Quarterly* 34 (4): 420–437. https://doi.org/10.1525/aeq.2003.34.4.420.

Puar, Jasbir K. 2012. "'I Would Rather Be a Cyborg than a Goddess': Becoming Intersectional of Assemblage Theory." *PhiloSOPHIA: A Journal of Feminist Philosophy* 2 (1): 49–66. https://muse.jhu.edu/article/486621.

Quinn, Christopher Dillon, dir. 2007. *God Grew Tired of Us*. National Geographic.

Rabinow, Paul. 1989. *French Modern: Norms and Forms of the Social Environment*. Cambridge, MA: MIT Press.

Roberts, Dorothy. 1997. *Killing the Black Body*. New York: Pantheon Books.

Robinson, Jennifer. 2006. *Ordinary Cities: Between Modernity and Development*. New York: Routledge.

Rølvaag, Ole Edvart. 1927. *Giants in the Earth*. New York: Harper & Brothers.

Rosaldo, Renato. 1994. "Cultural Citizenship and Educational Democracy." *Cultural Anthropology* 9 (3): 402–411.

Rose, Nikolas. 1996. "Governing 'Advanced' Liberal Democracies." In *Foucault and Political Reason: Liberalism, Neo-Liberalism, and Rationalities of Government*, edited by A. Barry, T. Osborne, and N. Rose, 37–64. London: UCL Press.

Rothenberg, Paula S., ed. 2005. *White Privilege: Essential Readings on the Other Side of Racism*. New York: Worth Publishers.

Sacks, Karen Brodkin. 1989. "Toward a Unified Theory of Class, Race, and Gender." *American Ethnologist* 16: 534–550. https://doi.org/10.1525/ae.1989.16.3.02a00080.

Said, Edward. 1978. *Orientalism*. New York: Vintage Books.

Sandemose, Aksel. 1933. *En Flyktning Krysser Sitt Spor* [A Refugee Crosses His Tracks]. Oslo: Gyldendal.

Sassen, Saskia. 1991. *The Global City: New York, London, Tokyo*. Princeton, NJ: Princeton University Press.

Schmidt, Helmut. 2016. "Of the Languages F-M Students Speak at Home, Somali is Second to English." *Inforum*. May 2. Accessed October 24, 2017. http://www.inforum.com/news/4022491-dozens-languages-f-m-students-speak-home-somali-second-english.

Schott, Liz, Ladonna Pavetti, and Ife Floyd. 2015. "How States Use Federal and State Funds under the TANF Block Grant." Center on Budget and Policy Priorities. October 15. https://www.cbpp.org/research/family-income-support/how-states-use-federal-and-state-funds-under-the-tanf-block-grant.

Schuller, Mark. 2012. *Killing with Kindness: Haiti, International Aid, and NGOs*. New Brunswick, NJ: Rutgers University Press.

Scroggins, Deborah. 2002. *Emma's War: An Aid Worker, a Warlord, Radical Islam, and the Politics of Oil—A True Story of Love and Death in Sudan*. New York: Pantheon.

Shandy, Dianna. 2002. "Nuer Christians in America." *Journal of Refugee Studies* 15 (2): 213–221. https://doi.org/10.1093/jrs/15.2.213.

Shandy, Dianna. 2007. *Nuer-American Passages: Globalizing Sudanese Migration.* Gainesville: University Press of Florida.

Sharkey, Heather. 2003. *Living with Colonialism: Nationalism and Culture in the Anglo-Egyptian Sudan.* Berkeley: University of California Press.

Sharma, Aradhana. 2008. *Logics of Empowerment: Development, Gender, and Governance in Neoliberal India.* Minneapolis: University of Minnesota Press.

Sharma, Aradhana. 2014. "The State and Women's Empowerment in India Paradoxes and Politics." In *Theorizing NGOs: States, Feminisms, and Neoliberalism,* edited by Victoria Bernal and Inderpal Grewal, 93–114. Durham, NC: Duke University Press.

Sharma, Aradhana, and Akhil Gupta. 2006. "Introduction: Rethinking Theories of the State in an Age of Globalization." In *The Anthropology of the State: A Reader,* edited by Aradhaa Sharma and Akhil Gupta, 1–41. Malden, MA: Blackwell.

Shields, John. 2004. "No Safe Haven: Work, Welfare, and the Growth of Immigrant Exclusion." In *Immigrants, Welfare Reform, and the Poverty of Policy,* edited by Philip Kretsedemas and Ana Aparicio, 35–60. Westport, CT: Praeger.

Sikainga, Ahmad Alawad. 1996. *Slaves into Workers: Emancipation and Labor in Colonial Sudan.* Austin: University of Texas Press.

Silva, Mark. 2017. "North Dakota's Oil Boom Fuels Economic Growth." *U.S. News and World Report.* March 3. Accessed February 27, 2019. https://www.usnews.com/news/best-states/articles/2017-03-03/north-dakotas-oil-boom-fuels-economic-growth.

Silverman, Carol. 1988. "Negotiating Gypsiness: Strategy in Context." *Journal of American Folklore* 101 (401): 261–275. http://www.jstor.org/stable/540467.

Silverman, Carol. 2012. *Romani Routes: Cultural Politics and Balkan Music in Diaspora.* Oxford: Oxford University Press.

Simonse, Simon. 1992. *Kings of Disaster: Dualism, Centralism, and the Scapegoat King in Southeastern Sudan.* Leiden: Brill.

Smith, Neil. 2002. "New Globalism, New Urbanism: Gentrification as Global Urban Strategy." *Antipode* 34 (3): 427–450. https://doi.org/10.1111/1467-8330.00249.

Smith Tuhiwai, Linda. 1999. *Decolonizing Methodologies: Research and Indigenous Peoples.* London: Zed Books.

Sorabji, Cornelia. 2006. "Managing Memories in Post-war Sarajevo: Individuals, Bad Memories, and New Wars." *Journal of the Royal Anthropology Institute* 12: 1–18. https://doi.org/10.1111/j.1467-9655.2006.00278.x.

Staeheli, Lynn. 2003. "Cities and Citizenship." *Urban Geography* 24 (2): 97–102. https://doi.org/10.2747/0272-3638.24.2.97.

Stefansson, Anders. 2007. "Urban Exile: Locals, Newcomers, and the Cultural Transformation of Sarajevo." In *The New Bosnian Mosaic: Identities, Memories, and Moral Claims in a Post-war Society,* edited by Xavier Bougarel, Elissa Helms, and Gerlachlus Duijzings, 59–77. Aldershot, UK: Ashgate.

Stewart, Michael. 1997. *The Time of the Gypsies.* Boulder, CO: Westview Press.

Stewart, Michael, ed. 2012. *The Gypsy 'Menace': Populism and the New Anti-Gypsy Politics.* London: Hurst.

Stewart, Michael. 2013. "Roma and Gypsy 'Ethnicity' as a Subject of Anthropological Inquiry." *Annual Review of Anthropology* 42: 415–432. https://doi.org/10.1146/annurev-anthro-092010-153348.

Stoler, Ann Laura. 2002. *Carnal Knowledge and Imperial Power: Race and the Intimate in Colonial Rule.* Berkeley: University of California Press.

Stoller, Paul. 2013. "Anthropological Musings on Blogging Bliss." *Anthropology Now* 5 (3): 92–96. https://doi.org/10.1080/19428200.2013.11869143.

Stubbs, Paul. 1999. "Social Work and Civil Society in Bosnia-Herzegovina: Globalisation, Neo-feudalism, and the State." In *Social Work and the State International: Perspectives in Social Work*, edited by Bogdan Lesnik, 55–64. Brighton, UK: Pavilion.

Stuesse, Angela. 2016. *Scratching Out a Living: Latinos, Race, and Work in the Deep South*. Oakland: University of California Press.

Surk, Barbara. 2018. "In a Divided Bosnia, Segregated Schools Persist." *New York Times*. December 1. Accessed December 20, 2018. https://www.nytimes.com/2018/12/01/world/europe/bosnia-schools-segregated-ethnic.html.

Susser, Ida. 1986. "Political Activity among Working-Class Women in a U.S. City." *American Ethnologist* 13 (1): 108–117. https://doi.org/10.1525/ae.1986.13.1.02a00070.

Susser, Ida. 1998. "Inequality, Violence, and Gender Relations in a Global City: New York 1986–1996." *Identities* 5 (2): 219–248. https://doi.org/10.1080/1070289X.1998.9962616.

Susser, Ida. 2017. "Commoning in New York, Barcelona, and Paris: Notes and Observations from the Field." *Focaal—Journal of Global and Historical Anthropology* 79: 6–22.

Tefft, Pearce. 2017. "Letter: Family Denounces Tefft's Racist Rhetoric and Actions." *Inforum*. August 14. Accessed October 24, 2017. http://www.inforum.com/opinion/letters/4311880-letter-family-denounces-teffts-racist-rhetoric-and-actions.

Todorova, Maria. 1997. *Imagining the Balkans*. New York: Oxford University Press.

Tran, Tu-Uyen. 2016. "Fargo City Leader Wants to Know if Local Governments Pay Too Much for Refugee Resettlement." *Inforum*. September 26. Accessed October 24, 2017. http://www.inforum.com/news/4123786-fargo-city-leader-wants-know-if-local-governments-pay-too-much-refugee-resettlement.

Tran, Tu-Uyen, Kim Hyatt, and Helmut Schmidt. 2017. "'It Started with the Election': Tirade Gone Viral Thrusts Fargo into Nation's Culture Debate." *Inforum*. July 26. Accessed October 24, 2017. http://www.inforum.com/news/4303536-it-started-election-tirade-gone-viral-thrusts-fargo-nations-culture-debate.

Trouillot, Michel-Rolph. 1995. "The Power in the Story." In *Silencing the Past: Power and the Production of History*, 1–30. Boston: Beacon Press.

Tsing, Anna Lowenhaupt. 2015. *The Mushroom at the End of the World: On the Possibility of Life in Capitalist Ruins*. Princeton, NJ: Princeton University Press.

Turgeon, Lynn. 1990. "Discrimination against and Affirmative Action for Gypsies in Eastern Europe." In *The Political Economy of Ethnic Discrimination and Affirmative Action*, edited by Michael L. Wyzan, 114–128. New York: Praeger.

UN, Department of Economic and Social Affairs, Population Division. 2014. *World Urbanization Prospects: The 2014 Revision, Highlights*. Accessed October 24, 2017. https://esa.un.org/unpd/wup/publications/files/wup2014-highlights.Pdf.

UN High Commissioner for Refugees (UNHCR). 1967. "Convention and Protocol Related to the Status of Refugees." Accessed December 20, 2019. https://www.unhcr.org/en-us/protection/basic/3b66c2aa10/convention-protocol-relating-status-refugees.html.

UN High Commissioner for Refugees (UNHCR). n.d. "Figures at a Glance." Accessed March 17, 2018. http://www.unhcr.org/en-us/figures-at-a-glance.html.

UN High Commissioner for Refugees (UNHCR). n.d. "Figures at a Glance." Accessed January 9, 2020. https://www.unhcr.org/en-us/figures-at-a-glance.html.

U.S. Citizenship and Immigration Services (USCIS). 2004. "Refugee Arrivals into the United States by Region and Country of Chargeability: Fiscal Years 1990–2004." Accessed December 17, 2015. http://www.dhs.gov/publication/yearbook-immigration-statistics-2004-refugees-and-asylees.

U.S. Energy Information Administration. 2018. "North Dakota State Profile and Energy Estimates." February 15. Accessed February 27, 2019. https://www.eia.gov/state /analysis.php?sid=ND.

U.S. President. 2000. Executive Order 13166. "Improving Access to Services for Persons with Limited English Proficiency." *Code of Federal Regulations*, title 3.

Van de Port, Mattijs. 1998. *Gypsies, Wars, and Other Instances of the Wild: Civilization and Its Discontents in a Serbian Town*. Amsterdam: Amsterdam University Press.

Van der Veer, Peter. 2016. *The Value of Comparison*. Durham, NC: Duke University Press.

Vertovec, Steven. 2007. "Super-diversity and Its Implications." *Ethnic and Racial Studies* 30 (6): 1024–1054. https://doi.org/10.1080/01419870701599465.

Visweswaran, Kamala. 1997. "Histories of Feminist Ethnography." *Annual Review of Anthropology* 26: 591–621. https://doi.org/10.1146/annurev.anthro.26.1.591.

Vucetic, Srdjan. 2004. "Identity Is a Joking Matter: Intergroup Humor in Bosnia." *Spaces of Identity* 4 (1): 7–34. https://soi.journals.yorku.ca/index.php/soi/article/view/8011.

Walker, Ike. 2016. "Somali Activist Group Protests outside Valley News Live Studios." *Valley News Live*. May 22. http://www.valleynewslive.com/home/headlines/Protest -outside-Valley-News-Live-by-local-somali-refugee-group-380432781.html.

Walkowitz, Daniel J. 1999. *Working with Class: Social Workers and the Politics of Middle-Class*. Chapel Hill: University of North Carolina Press.

WalletHub. 2017. "2017's Most Diverse Cities in America." Accessed October 31, 2017. https://wallethub.com/edu/most-diverse-cities/12690/.

Ward, Jesmyn, ed. 2016. *The Fire This Time: A New Generation Speaks about Race*. New York: Scribner.

Watson, Peggy. 1997. "Civil Society and the Politics of Difference in Eastern Europe." In *Transitions, Environments, Translations: Feminism in International Politics*, edited by Joan W. Scott, Cora Kaplan, and Debra Keates, 21–29. New York: Routledge.

Weber, Max. 1958. *The Protestant Ethic and the Spirit of Capitalism*. New York: Scribner.

Wheeler, Andrew C. 2002. "From Mission to Church in an Islamizing State: The Case of Sudan." In *Christian Missionaries and the State in the Third World*, edited by Holger Bernt Hansen and Michael Twaddle, 284–297. Oxford: James Currey.

Williams, Brackette. 1989. "A Class Act: Anthropology and the Race to Nation across Ethnic Terrain." *Annual Review of Anthropology* 18: 401–444. http://www.jstor.org /stable/2155898.

Willis, Mary, and Janet Buck. 2007. "From Sudan to Nebraska: Dinka and Nuer Refugee Diet Dilemmas." *Journal of Nutrition Education and Behaviour* 39 (5): 273–280. https://doi.org/10.1016/j.jneb.2006.10.005.

Willis, William S. Jr. 1972. "Skeletons in the Anthropological Closet." In *Reinventing Anthropology*, edited by Dell Hymes, 121–153. New York: Pantheon Books.

Wilson, Barbara Brown. 2018. *Resilience for All: Striving for Equity through Community-Driven Design*. Washington, DC: Island Press.

Wolf, Eric. 1982. *Europe and the People without History*. Berkeley: University of California Press.

Woods, Phil, and Charles Landry. 2008. *The Intercultural City: Planning for Diversity Advantage*. New York: Taylor & Francis.

Woodward, Susan. 1995. *Balkan Tragedy: Chaos and Dissolution after the Cold War*. Washington, DC: Brookings Institution Press.

Wright, Robert G. 1981. "Voluntary Agencies and the Resettlement of Refugees." *Refugees Today* 15 (1–2): 157–174. https://doi.org/10.2307/2545334.

X, Malcolm, and Alex Haley. 1965. *The Autobiography of Malcolm X*. New York: Grove Press.

Younge, Gary. 2016. "How Trump Took Middle America." *Guardian*. November 16. https://www.theguardian.com/membership/2016/nov/16/how-trump-took-middletown-muncie-election.

Yuen, Laura. 2012. "Newcomers Say It's 'Nice,' but Not Warm." Minnesota Public Radio News. March 12. Accessed June 21, 2013. http://minnesota.publicradio.org/display/web/2012/03/ 12/outsiders1-is-minnesota-nice-to-newcomers.

Yuval-Davis, Nira. 2004. "Borders, Boundaries, and the Politics of Belonging." In *Ethnicity, Nationalism, and Minority Rights*, edited by Stephen May, Tariq Modood, and Judith Squires, 214–230. Cambridge: Cambridge University Press.

Žarkov, Dubravka. 2007. *The Body of War: Media, Ethnicity, and Gender in the Break-up of Yugoslavia*. Durham, NC: Duke University Press.

Zolberg, Aristide R., Astri Suhrke, and Sergio Aguagyo. 1989. *Escape from Violence: Conflict and the Refugee Crisis in the Developing World*. New York: Oxford University Press.

Index